SEEKING THE SIGNIFICANCE OF MUSIC EDUCATION

Essays and Reflections

Bennett Reimer

PUBLISHED IN PARTNERSHIP WITH

MENC: THE NATIONAL ASSOCIATION FOR MUSIC EDUCATION

ROWMAN & LITTLEFIELD EDUCATION

Lanham • New York • Toronto • Plymouth, UK

Published in partnership with
MENC: The National Association for Music Education

Published in the United States of America
by Rowman & Littlefield Education
A Division of Rowman & Littlefield Publishers, Inc.
A wholly owned subsidiary of The Rowman & Littlefield Publishing Group, Inc.
4501 Forbes Boulevard, Suite 200, Lanham, Maryland 20706
www.rowmaneducation.com

Estover Road
Plymouth PL6 7PY
United Kingdom

British Library Cataloguing in Publication Information Available

Library of Congress Cataloging-in-Publication Data

Reimer, Bennett.
  Seeking the significance of music education : essays and reflections / Bennett
Reimer.
      p. cm.
  "Published in partnership with MENC, The National Association for Music
Education."
  Summary: "Noted music educator Bennett Reimer has selected 24 of his previously
published articles from a variety of professional journals spanning the past 50 years.
During that time, he's tackled generating core values for the field of music education;
the core in larger societal and educational contexts; what to teach and how to teach
it effectively; how we need to educate our teachers; the role of research in our
profession; and how to improve our future status."—Provided by publisher.
  Includes bibliographical references.
  ISBN 978-1-60709-235-3 (cloth : alk. paper) — ISBN 978-1-60709-236-0 (pbk. : alk.
paper) — ISBN 978-1-60709-237-7 (electronic)
  1. Music—Instruction and study—Philosophy. I. MENC, the National Association
for Music Education (U.S.) II. Title.
  MT1.R44 2009
  780.71—dc22   2009002244

CONTENTS

A LETTER TO THE READER

Dear Reader,

Thank you for taking the time and making the effort to read (or perhaps browse through) this book. I am honored by your doing so.

Many people skip the prefaces of books, and I'm hoping to lure you with this letter. The book is a bit of a strange specimen, and a few explanatory words might help place it in perspective.

The two dozen essays it presents span half a century and address a variety of topics. In addition, I introduce each essay with a reflection about its context and significance.

In their professional dimension, the reflections and essays offer arguments, proposals, and critiques of long-standing issues of central importance to music education not only at the time they were written, but also in the present and no doubt long into the future. They are foundational matters requiring astute adaptation to changing conditions. Their significance is timeless; their challenges are endless.

In their personal dimension, my attempts to address these issues reflect my unfolding understandings as time has passed. This book is a kind of intellectual memoir of a life spent grappling with intractable questions relating to music education. Doing so has an effect on one's life, both in savoring the challenges and occasionally feeling that some measure of progress with them has been achieved, yet in knowing full well that definitive resolutions are likely never to be reached. Some feelings of success are experienced along the way, tempered always with humility at their transience—a dichotomy, I feel certain, experienced in one way or another by all who attempt to live a thoughtful life. A sense of that lifelong adventure is given in these selections and in my musings about them.

The 24 essays, drawn from around 150 I've had published, were chosen in a state of intellectual and emotional anguish. Every piece I write represents a birth—a mental offspring. Which children must be left behind? Will they haunt my unconscious, pleading to be saved from disappearance? How can I betray their hopes to live another day? Alas, my publisher is firm (and sane): "Cut it down, Bennett. We're not in the encyclopedia business!" On the cutting-room floor lies a large pile of regrets.

The essays are presented as they were printed, regularized into book format. I've made a few strictly editorial changes but no substantive alterations have been made, despite my yearning to do so. They are as they were, warts and all. And I have added a question to you, dear reader, at the end of the final chapter.

In retrospect, I recognize that my life's work has consisted largely of a lover's quarrel with the profession of music education. I have been and remain still in love with it and still insisting that it fulfill a destiny it has not yet achieved. From start to present I've never been entirely satisfied with what we do, how we do it, and why we do it, as this book makes very clear. Yet I've never lost my conviction that music education (along with the other art education fields) deserves to be an essential component of schooling for all students if their lives are to be as fulfilling as they possibly can be.

That, in my view, is the goal of a meaningful life. That we have succeeded in providing musical and thereby personal fulfillment to so many wins my deepest admiration. How we can better do so remains our ongoing quest.

Sincerely yours,
Bennett Reimer

I

OUR VALUES AS A SCHOOL SUBJECT

GENERATING CORE VALUES

Every subject worthy of study, including music, embodies a diversity of values, all deserving our attention. Some of the values seem so important as to warrant our deepest devotion. One task of a philosophy of music education is to illuminate what those might be, so that in pursuing them, our effects on our students can be as beneficial as music is capable of making them. There is no official list, of course. Different eras, communities, and individual interests each view the values of music through its particular lens.

The essays in this section represent some of my efforts over the years to identify values at the most important end of the continuum. All music educators benefit from making such attempts so that their work can be as significant as possible. It is unlikely that our choices will be identical, nor need they be. Perhaps my labors will help those seeking clarity to identify what matters most among our professional contributions.

❶

WHAT MUSIC CANNOT DO

It's 1958. I'm all of twenty-six years old, working on my doctorate in music education at the University of Illinois and so thrilled with the heady ideas I'm encountering about music and music education that I can hardly contain myself. I am convinced that music is a precious dimension of the human condition—something so special, so valuable, that educating others in music will be my life's work. Persuasive reasons for that belief have entered my consciousness through my extensive readings in philosophy of music and the arts. To my dismay, many concepts that I had once thought to be compelling are crumbling to ashes. A new world of scholarship is leading me to understandings that are affecting me profoundly, their power so much more deeply grounded as to make me ashamed of my previous naiveté.

Typically for me, I want to proclaim my newfound insights to all who might listen. After two of my articles are published in the *Music Educators Journal (MEJ)* and two in *The Instrumentalist*, all dealing with performance, I am beginning to believe that my thoughts are worth sharing. "I'm going to deal with a larger issue," I vow to myself. "Music education needs to take a hard look at how it goes about justifying its existence. We can't go on relying on trivia." The combination of youthful bravado, the brashness of my Brooklyn street-corner upbringing, and my love of

writing inspires me to get to work. Not for me the modesty of recognizing my novice status in matters philosophical and educational. Within a
month I finish "What Music CANNOT Do" and, with high hopes, mail
it off to *MEJ*.

I get more than I expected. *MEJ* Editorial Board reviews are impas-
sioned, both pro and con: "I have to agree, whether I want to or not."
"Personally, I oppose giving space to negative thinking." "At least one
can admire a music educator sane enough to look at his profession without rose-colored glasses." "I am in complete agreement." "I just can't buy
this." "Some things that need saying."

The article is published. I taste the sweetness of controversy—a delight for a young activist ready to take on the world.

It will be decades before I am able to bring the positions I so confi-
dently declare in my youth to more thoughtful fruition. The positions
themselves, deepened, broadened, and refined over time as they greatly
needed to be, remain as valid for me now as they were then. Nevertheless, the profession's advocacy efforts in promoting music education
largely remain as disappointing as those I first denounced.

How little some things change. Our growing philosophical and professional sophistication allows us to articulate ever more deeply reasoned
rationales, yet the same marginal values remain dominant, counterproductive at best, embarrassing at worst. I will in time significantly
moderate the stance taken here, but I will persist in pursuing the goal of
expressing the significance of music education as authentically as the art
of music deserves.

And it will be my fate to continue to roil the profession's waters, happily.

(It should be explained that in the article, the comment under 3. *Musical activity leads to democratic social relationships*, refers to the societal
tensions at a time when the rising tide of the civil rights movement was
clearly drowning old assumptions, to the dismay of many. Can music
education really resolve such deeply problematical issues, something no
one seems to know how to do?)

The following essay was originally published in the *Music Educators Journal* 46, no. 1 (September–October 1959). Used by permission.

No one likes a spoilsport. But I'm going to risk it. Someone has to. The
cheers, the hurrahs, the slapping of backs, all for the cause of music, have
reached deafening proportions. Amid the chorus of "yeas" I should like to
register a small but emphatic "nay!"

The literature on music education has traditionally included a generous amount of self-justification. This is understandable in a field which constantly feels the hot breath of public opinion on its back. Since this opinion is from a public only dimly aware of the "finer things in life" which "good" music is somehow supposed to bring—a public prone to asking embarrassing questions and to staying away in droves from concerts and recitals which attempt to force-feed bits of this "good" music to it—the practice of self-justification is more than understandable. And so, in an effort to sell music education no claim made in behalf of music was considered too small for literary attention. Now, with its foundation alarmingly shaken by the [Sputnik] satellite scare, the music education literature of self-justification has risen to a new low. One finds, along with flashes of brilliance and occasional lapses into lucidity, a disconcerting preoccupation with the power of music to heal most if not all of the world's ills.

I should like to examine some of the more common claims made for music and the teaching of it, to determine the degree of validity they possess. I do so in the light of my experience as a music student, a music teacher, and a professional performer, and as one who has embraced the field of music education as his life's work.

I. THE MAKING OF MUSIC LEADS TO SOUND, HEALTHY BODIES

Stated in various ways, this assertion has been a mainstay for music teachers anxious to prove their worth. One can imagine the reaction of a physical education teacher when thus apprised of this power of music—his raised eyebrows would bear eloquent witness to his disbelief, especially since he has probably been badgered for years to let music students out of physical education classes, a practice equally as common to colleges as to high schools. He would wonder, and rightfully so, what *his* job was supposed to be, and it would strike him as odd that the hours spent in the confines of a practice room were equally beneficial to muscle tone as to musical tone. If he were a reflective sort, he might ponder about the great musicians of western culture, and he would discover that for each ruddy Bach there was a sick Beethoven, for every healthy Haydn, a dissipated Wagner. Try as he might, he would not discover any logical or empirical grounds for the belief that the study of music is any more or less beneficial to physical health than the study of history, chemistry, or home economics. And he would wonder mightily at the music teacher's concern for physique in the first place, since he always thought that music had its own, unique, indispensable contribution to make. We wonder with him.

2. THE MAKING OF MUSIC PROMOTES INTERNATIONAL UNDERSTANDING

Implicitly or explicitly, this claim is based on the well-worn concept of music as the "Universal Language," with all the beliefs that accrue to it. The efforts of Susanne Langer, George Santayana, John Dewey, and practically every existentialist writer and artist, as well as hosts of twentieth-century semanticists, symbolists, and psychologists, seem to be of little avail in breaking down this popular misconception. Benedetto Croce's *Aesthetic as Science of Expression and Linguistic* has had its effect. Music educators who perpetuate the "Universal Language" concept compound the error by confusing the public and by placing themselves in an untenable position when regarded by the increasing number of people acquainted with modern aesthetic thought.

Since hundreds of books have been written on the subject (the names mentioned above are basic to the field) it must suffice here to point out that music lacks precisely the main quality of language, i.e., consummated symbols—dictionary meanings. To call it a language is to stretch that word to the point where it approaches meaninglessness. The confusion stems primarily from the loose employment of the word "communication." Since music "communicates" it is immediately assumed to be a language. This confusion is admirably dispelled in Langer's *Philosophy in a New Key* and in Meyer's *Emotion and Meaning in Music*, to mention but two books in a rapidly growing literature.

As to the "universality" of music, a moment's reflection makes it clear that the concept is specious. There is no need to point out the gulf in understanding between Occidental and Oriental music, or the difficulty in relating to music written longer than three hundred years ago. It is enough to take cognizance of the complete lack of understanding of serious music by myriads of jazz enthusiasts, the equal incomprehension of jazz by countless classical music lovers, or the bewilderment occasioned by modern music to a goodly portion of both of these classes. Indeed, music's greatest contribution seems to be in serving a particular culture in a particular period of its history, and all too few people are capable of savoring the cultures of foreign lands or different periods in history through an understanding of their arts.

In the light of these facts, it is most difficult to set much store in music's power to promote international understanding. It is doubtless true that any activity which acquaints us with the life of foreign peoples tends to help us understand those peoples. This holds for music, food, dress, or manners. And it is also true that at a high enough level, the arts are eminently sensitive guides to an understanding of a foreign culture's deepest motivations. Yet the purpose of music education is not to develop comparative sociologists. Again we wonder—does not music have its own unique, indispensable contribution to make?

3. MUSICAL ACTIVITY LEADS TO DEMOCRATIC SOCIAL RELATIONSHIPS

This paper is being written in the Commonwealth of Virginia, December 1958. I assume that the place and the date make further comment entirely unnecessary.

4. MUSIC AFFORDS TRANQUILITY AND PEACE TO THE MIND

This assumption often includes such values as entertainment, relaxation, and even, on occasion, morality. A logical deduction from the above would lead one to the conclusion that the greater the musician, the more tranquil, peaceful, and moral would he be. Yet it is widely understood that the more sensitive the artist, the less likely is he to be at peace with himself and the world. Prodded by insights deeper than the ordinary, fired with the never-ceasing desire to create anew, he stands in direct opposition to the placid and self-satisfied minions who have succeeded in settling once and for all every human problem of moment, either by themselves or by totally accepting a package deal which does it for them. As for morality, we have only to call to mind the legions of stories connected with the great in art and music to hastily reassess our opinion of music's efficacy in this field. In truth, if we are primarily concerned with promoting tranquility and morality as generally understood, we should do better to abandon immediately any attempts at imparting more than the most superficial knowledge of art.

In the fields of relaxation and entertainment, it must be acknowledged that music education has been phenomenally successful. Even so keen an observer of the American scene as *Life* magazine has acknowledged this success, summing up for the nation the real achievement of music education by covering its special U.S. Entertainment issue of December 1958, with a picture, in 38 glorious colors, of 1,076 high school trombonists expressing themselves through a rendition of "Seventy-six Trombones." Anyone who pointed out that cherishing art for its entertainment value is like appraising the value of a six-dollar Porterhouse steak for its power to soothe a black eye, or that any real experience with music, as a composer, performer, or listener, is invariably exhausting as well as rejuvenating, or that when music succeeds in relaxing one, a warm bath would have been even more successful, is really practicing spoil-sportism with a vengeance. So I shall refrain from doing so. I shall only ask again, is there no unique contribution which music is capable of making?

5. THE STUDY OF MUSIC IMPROVES SOCIAL COMPETENCIES

The old slogan, "Be the Life of the Party with Music" has fallen into disrepute of late, being too flagrantly common for sensitive ears. It has been replaced by more subtle phrases, usually couched in the most acceptable educational jargon. We find now that the study of music gives a sense of achievement, that it affords opportunity for participation with the group, that it develops the individual's self-sufficiency, that it promotes cooperation, that it engenders a healthy sense of competition. It is interesting to replace the word "music" in the above sentence with "basketball," or "modern warfare," or "science" or "after dinner speaking." Each works equally as well as the other. Indeed, one could be the "life of the party" by making a sort of game out of this process. But no matter how many fields of study were named, music included, it would finally be admitted that in developing social skills, Dale Carnegie did it better. Again we are led to reiterate, cannot music make some contribution of its own?

The list of fatuous claims made for music in the name of music education may be continued indefinitely. But there is no need to do so. The principles which apply to the claims stated above apply to all such claims. They are:

1. Music education places itself in an extremely tenuous position when it justifies itself by pointing out its service to qualities that other fields can serve as well if not much better. Such justification is not only unnecessary, it is debilitating.

2. Any claim made for music must be made in the light of a thorough understanding of the latest philosophical and aesthetic thought. It is both a disservice to our students and a source of embarrassment to the profession to perpetuate concepts which have fallen by the wayside.

3. Justification for teaching music must be based on music—not teaching. Many of the claims cited above hold true in that good teaching will actually lead to the results implied in the claims. This is true of good teaching of practically anything. But while we may convince all and sundry that we are good teachers by claiming that we are, we do nothing by this device to strengthen the conviction that *music* must be taught.

4. Any great discipline must, to be worthy of survival, make a unique contribution to a society and its members. That is the main point. And the fact that music is not only capable of doing so, but that its contribution is one of the most vital of all, makes our preoccupation with its lesser values a species of moral crime. It is for this reason that it is of the utmost importance that any self-justification for music education be rid of the appurtenances which obscure and weaken its real import.

And what is its import? I should like to quote from a few writers who have spent their lives in a search for truths far deeper than those surface ones which occupy too much of our thoughts; writers deeply concerned with what is called "The Good Life," and in what way art is essential to it.

Says Susanne Langer:

the emotive content of the work (of art) is something much deeper than any intellectual experience, more essential, pre-rational and vital, something of the life rhythms we share with all growing, hungering, moving, and fearing creatures: the ultimate realities themselves, the central facts of our brief, sentient existence.[1]

John Dewey, in a passage notable in his writings for its emotional eloquence, says, in speaking of that exquisite intelligibility and clarity we have in the presence of an object experienced with aesthetic intensity:

We are, as it were, introduced into a world beyond this world of ordinary experience. We are carried out beyond ourselves to find ourselves. We are citizens of this vast world beyond ourselves, and any intense realization of its presence with us and in us brings a peculiarly satisfying sense of unity in itself and with ourselves.[2]

Says Carl Jung:

> The secret of artistic creation and of the effectiveness of art is to be found in a return to the state of *participation mystique*—*to* that level of experience at which it is man who lives, and not the individual, and at which the weal or woe of the single human being does not count, but only human existence. This is why every great work of art is objective and impersonal, but none the less profoundly moves us each and all.[3]

These statements point to the fact that the function of art is to symbolize for man the very deepest and most profound elements in his experience. The only way a human being can apprehend and taste of what he calls "reality" is through such symbolization. Art uses symbols to construct a cosmos in order to give the life of man a setting and a meaning. It is with the depth of each individual's personal experience with which art is concerned, and not, as is so commonly thought in art education, the horizontal relationships between person and person.

It is only this function as an art that justifies the teaching of music in our public schools. In an age of the "other directed" or the "organization man," an age which Paul Tillich characterizes as being plagued with "meaninglessness," music offers a glimpse of richness, understanding, and fulfillment. It is vitally important for every person to have the opportunity to probe the potential richness which simply being human affords. It is our job, as music educators, to provide this opportunity.

Lest it be thought that the above statements are just another bid for keeping the music teacher complacent and assuring him of his value, I must hastily point out that the implications of this view lead to far-reaching alterations in the common run of school music teaching. To draw these implications fully would require a good-sized book, but a few may be hinted at.

In the field of teacher education, it can be seen that a music student who graduates without an acquaintance with the field of aesthetics is like a medical doctor who completes his training with no knowledge of the blood stream. Aesthetics is the blood stream of art education, but I know of no college that requires even one course in this field for the bachelor's degree in music education. In the actual teaching of music, the old question of the use of top-quality music which might be too difficult for school groups to perform professionally, versus the use of low-grade material with which the group may dazzle with its virtuosity all within hearing, seems to find an answer here. The problems of how much to stress performance, how much extra-musical activity should be included, how the general music class should be handled, who should be included in the instrumental music program—all these and many more take their direction and sustenance from a knowledge of what music *can* do. For, once realizing what music as an art is capable of meaning to everyone who comes into contact with it, one is forever spoiled for concern with those things it cannot do or only does poorly.

The greatest minds of our age offer us justification unbounded. With the availability of such nourishing tidbits of "good mete and redde wyn" as are quoted above, it is incomprehensible that music education should prefer to subsist on whipped cream. For too many in our field, an immediate and radical change in diet is most sorely needed.

NOTES

1. Susanne K. Langer, *Philosophy in a New Key* (New York: New American Library, 1953), 211.

2. John Dewey, *Art as Experience* (New York: Minton, Balch, and Company, 1934), 195.

3. Carl G. Jung, "Psychology and Literature," in Brewster Ghiselin, *The Creative Process* (New York: New American Library, 1955), 223.

2

ESSENTIAL AND NONESSENTIAL CHARACTERISTICS OF AESTHETIC EDUCATION

A phrase can become a signal of a person's identity. That happens to me with "aesthetic education." The term is in its infancy when I am introduced to it in the mid-1950s, as I begin my serious study of the philosophy of music. It will serve as a powerful organizer for my growing understandings. As its meanings expand and deepen for me and for many others across the field of the arts in education, the idea of aesthetic education becomes so influential as to make it a catchphrase for the entire field's aspirations.

My many writings about music education as aesthetic education, particularly the initial version of my book *A Philosophy of Music Education*, lead to my being strongly identified with the term. In one sense, that's fine with me. In another, the identification associates me with a view that eventually deteriorates for some into a narrow, rigid conception of what aesthetic education means. I become increasingly uncomfortable with this situation.

This article emphasizes the open nature of aesthetic education while also identifying some of the characteristics that give it an identity. This is a necessary task if music education is to be grounded in a convincing belief system while also being receptive to change. It is not unusual for a term to become, over time and with common usage, a restrictive end rather than a dynamic means. I ponder, here, the extent to which this has become the case with aesthetic education, and whether it might be wise to just let the term go.

I am not ready to do so at the time I write this piece. It will not be until over a dozen years later, in the third massively reconstructed version of what has become *A Philosophy of Music Education: Advancing the Vision* (2003), that my use of the term dwindles to the point of almost disappearing. Yet its basic values, adapted to expanded understandings of the nature of music and of teaching music, remain for me and for many others a compelling source of ideals for the enterprise of music education.

The following essay was originally published in *The Journal of Aesthetic Education* 25, no. 3. Copyright © 1991 by the Board of Trustees of the University of Illinois. Used with permission of the University of Illinois Press. Reprinted in Estelle R. Jorgensen, ed., *Philosopher, Teacher, Musician: Perspectives on Music Education* (Urbana: University of Illinois Press, 1993). Used with permission of the University of Illinois Press.

I have chosen to discuss the concept of aesthetic education for two reasons. First, it has been, with little question, the most visible, most widely acknowledged philosophical orientation in music education for some three decades. That is why, no doubt, Michael Mark was recently led to suggest that we are now living in the period of Aesthetic Education, which began around 1960.1 While that judgment can be and has been disputed,2 it is significant that it could have been made at all and even more significant, and interesting, that it is the only period among the five he proposes that is based on a philosophical position. None of the others even remotely relates to a particular philosophy as its basis, nor do any of the nine periods previously suggested by Edward Bailey Birge in his History of Public School Music in the United States.3

We seem to be getting some message from this, but the message is far from clear. On the one hand, music educators devoted to philosophical scholarship should rejoice that philosophy—*any* philosophy—has exerted such influence that it seems at all feasible to name a period of our profession's history after it.

On the other hand, being involved with philosophy, we are likely to have a great mixture of responses to such an occurrence. That is partly, no doubt, because philosophers tend to have a great mixture of responses to everything, simplicity being anathema to their characters. But there are, I think, good and substantial reasons for having a great many perplexed thoughts about this unprecedented elevation in music education of a particular philosophical orientation to the status of a historical era. So the second reason I have chosen this topic relates to my conviction that it would be fruitful for us as a community of scholars to pay attention to some of these perplexing thoughts about aesthetic education and that, in fact, it would be fruitful for music education as a whole if we were to achieve better understandings about them. My discussion will make abundantly clear how ambitious this agenda actually is.

In this article I want to explore some of the important features of this concept. I must make it clear at the outset that not only is this task not easy, it is also to some very real extent incapable of being accomplished authoritatively. This stems from the fact that there exists no accepted, definitive definition or explanation or even interpretation of what aesthetic education actually is. There is no holy writ we can consult or no constitution to which we can refer.

Philosophers should not be discomfited by that fact because few philosophical positions which have achieved the status of having had a name attached to them have had clear, incontrovertible "first sources." But the irony of our situation as people who do philosophy of music education is that our profession—music education as a whole, that is—is characterized, to a remarkable and some would say pathological degree, by the propensity to reify anything with a name attached to it. This tendency is not limited to nonphilosophers in music education who, perhaps, should not be expected to know better. It extends, I am afraid, to the philosophical community, in which aesthetic education is sometimes viewed as a set of dogmas incapable of being breached and doctrines incapable of being changed.[4]

I want to argue that there are no such dogmas or doctrines, although I will suggest my own candidates for what, in my opinion, are typical characteristics of aesthetic education. I will propose that aesthetic education is not a body of immutable laws but instead provides some guidelines for a process that, by its very nature, must be both ongoing and open-ended.

Fourteen years ago, at one of the Aspen conferences sponsored by the Central Midwestern Regional Educational Laboratory as part of its Aesthetic Education Program, one of the influential early thinkers about aesthetic education, Harry Broudy, addressed the general topic I am addressing now. He began by saying, "No consensus on the meaning or the usage of the term 'aesthetic education' being discernible, what follows refers pretty much to my own concept of it."[5] I am in the position now of echoing those words precisely. Broudy then listed five generalizations about aesthetic education frequently made by various groups that have shown an interest in the concept. These remain pertinent today, so I will use them to structure my discussion.

First, many believe that all children should be educated about the broad family including all the arts, and that it is possible to structure a curriculum to provide such an education.

Second, there is a shared hope that the arts will achieve a more solid position in the schools than they have been able to in the past, even to the extent of being a required rather than an elective subject.

Third, there seems to be a widespread belief that an aesthetic education is possible and desirable for all students in schools and need not be limited to those with special artistic talent.

Fourth, there is continuing debate and disagreement among aesthetic education advocates on the degree to which "extra-aesthetic" values—moral, political, economic, social, and so forth—should be attended to as part of arts study. This lack of agreement extends to the use of aesthetic learnings to facilitate learnings in other subjects.

Fifth, the least agreement is to be found about the aesthetic and educational theories by which aesthetic education could be explicated and justified.

I will comment about each of these five generalizations about or descriptions of or characteristics of aesthetic education, with somewhat more concentration on the fifth, which is the most complex and troublesome and which is also most germane to the interests represented in this special issue. But any discussion of aesthetic education must range more broadly than within aesthetic theory alone, because the ramifications of the concept of aesthetic education are very broad, covering most if not all aspects of educational theory, educational practice, and philosophy of education. In fact, a major point I will try to make is that aesthetic issues as such—that is, issues associated with the field of professional aesthetics—while they are essential to any viable concept of aesthetic education, are not sufficient for an understanding of its nature and are not the sole determinants of what it might be or might become.

Item one, having to do with teaching all the arts rather than just one or a few, has generated a whole literature of its own, so my treatment of it here will have to be very selective. I want to make a point about each of three levels of this issue—the political level, the curriculum level, and the philosophical level.

At the political level, we should remind ourselves that aesthetic education in one of its dimensions began as a political movement; that is, as an attempt to win for the arts the support, money, school program time, staffing, and prestige that its advocates dearly desired but had had a notable lack of success achieving in American education. In unity, perhaps, there might be political strength. So in the middle 1960s, when the term "aesthetic education" had begun to enter the lexicon of educators in the arts, the term was appropriated by a major initiative to build a comprehensive arts program—the CEMREL Aesthetic Education Program. That program, given its multi-art focus, and given that it then was, while not the only game in town, certainly the major one, and given the political clout wielded by a well-funded program in which major figures from all of the art education fields participated, cemented in the minds of many the view that "aesthetic education" automatically means "arts education."

I have never held that view, despite my having been the official music education participant in the initial, definitional stage of the Aesthetic Education Program leading to the publication of its *Guidelines for Aesthetic Education*,[6] and despite my involvement since that time in a host of arts education endeavors at both the theoretical and practical levels. I have certainly been an advocate of comprehensive arts programs, partly, of course, for political reasons in that I tend to believe that each of the arts would be more secure in education under the aegis of a comprehensive program than is possible when each stands entirely alone.

My point here is that such a position is a political position, not a theoretical one. There are, of course, theoretical *implications* of this position, which have for many years fascinated me because I find them so challenging and so enlightening. But it has been my view that music education in and of itself as a professional entity can be conceived as aesthetic education, as can each art in and of itself. It is debatable whether music education and the other art education fields *should* cooperate politically, but no position in that debate depends on the prior assumption that, in order to be aesthetic education, the arts must be conceived as a unified political body.

The second level of item one concerning the issue of arts education is an extension of the first to include more than the political dimension. The curriculum, as I conceive it, includes the broadest possible range of all the issues impinging on the nature of education and how it can be provided, and the nature of various subjects within education and how they can be provided. The question here is, can a *bona fide* curriculum, fulfilling all the multiple demands of both theoretical and practical curriculum issues, be achieved by a single art? Or are such demands so inclusive that no single art could reasonably or possibly fulfill them all, so that at this level of the aesthetic education endeavor more than one art or, perhaps, all the arts, would be required to be treated together rather than individually?

I have taken the position that music, by itself, can fulfill all dimensions requiring to be addressed in a total curriculum and be, by itself, an instance of aesthetic education. It is certainly possible to build a comprehensive curriculum for all the arts, but the decision to do so and the attempt to do so are not, in my view, in any way required in order for aesthetic education to be achieved.

But what about the philosophical level of the issue beyond the political and the educational? Is there anywhere within the philosophy of art or aesthetic theory a set of principles or a persuasive argument which would cause us to believe that music would be misrepresented, or falsely understood, or deprived of essential characteristics, if it were not studied as part of the larger field including the other arts?

This is a very difficult and complex question, because it raises the issue, so heavily debated for so long in history, of the nature of the interrelations among the arts. As I understand that historical debate, it seems to take place across a continuum of arguments. At one end of the continuum is the view that the arts are essentially unitary, the various arts being different only in insignificant features. At the other end of the continuum is the position that the arts are essentially autonomous, any similarities being quite inconsequential. And, of course, between these extremes are arguments at every point along the way.

The continuum in theorizing about this point is reflected in the continuum of positions adopted by educators in the arts. At one end have been those who assume that to teach art one must capitalize the word, treat it as homogeneous, and demonstrate that any seeming differences among the arts are essentially trivial. At the other end (usually ulcerated by their irritation with the position I have just described) are those who regard any fraternization among the arts as being tantamount to artistic depravity, in that each art can only be destroyed in its veracity (not to mention its virginity) by consorting in any way with any of the others.

I hope I will not disappoint by not providing the correct theory, finally, as to whether and how and to what degree the arts are interrelated. But I need not disappoint as to articulating where I stand on the education continuum, because I only need to reiterate what that stance has been from the beginning of my involvements with arts programs and continues to be to this day.

If one envisions the continuum of positions as a yardstick, with the "arts as unitary" view on the right and the "arts as independent" view on the left, I am positioned about an inch and a half to two inches from the left end of the stick. I am persuaded that the essential value and meaning of each art must be attained within the domain of value and meaning that particular art exemplifies. As I put it in *A Philosophy of Music Education*, for arts programs to be effective, *"the distinctive ways that each art operates must become progressively clearer. . . .* Glossing over the uniquenesses, diluting them by forced combinations, dulling them by constant equating of one with another, making them more obscure by ignoring the peculiar, particular flavor of each, can only weaken aesthetic sensitivity and limit the capacity to share aesthetic insights in the wide variety of ways they are available."[7]

Nevertheless, I have allowed myself that inch and a half or two, because I also believe that similarities among the arts exist and that those very similarities provide a powerful opportunity to explore below their surfaces to the level at which each art manifests them distinctively. That opportunity to appreciate fully the maxim I have long followed—that the arts are not redundant—is presented only when more than one art is being examined, one of them serving as the foil to understand better the particularities of the other. So my advocacy for comprehensive arts programs includes, in addition to my beliefs in their political efficacy and their curriculum feasibility, the theoretical conviction that the arts as a totality constitute a meaning domain sufficiently different from others to be counted as a genus, and in which the nature of the domain derives from the accumulative contributions of each of its exemplifications.

My conclusion from this aspect of the issue is that it is certainly not necessary for music education as aesthetic education to be pursued within a structure including other arts. However, doing so would not be counter-indicated by theory, and there may be good practical reasons for doing so. The essential point is that a cooperative arts program should never, in any way, threaten the integrity of any of the arts it includes.

The second of Broudy's five generalizations about aesthetic education raises the issue of whether it is essential to the nature of aesthetic education in any single art that the philosophy be used as the primary advocacy basis for helping that art achieve a more solid position within the education establishment. Many music educators, when first encountering the ideas connected to aesthetic education, seemed to have thought so and came to regard aesthetic education as a means for demonstrating, in a more solid, more defensible, more thoughtful way than previously, that music education was a necessary subject in schools.

Now here I must make an important distinction. It is between philosophy and what it attempts to do, and advocacy and what it attempts to do. The distinction is subtle because a philosophical position can be used for advocacy purposes; that is, purposes intended to persuade others to give more support to a particular endeavor than they are likely to do otherwise. But the fact that it can be used to do so does not mean that it is required to do so or even that it be conceived that it would ever be used to do so.

A professional philosophy—that is, a coherent position about the nature and purpose of a professional field providing a set of principles on which actions can be based—serves a function that is essentially "intramural." It forms and shapes the belief system and value system of a field so that the field can be guided in its actions and in its growth in coherent ways and in ways founded on its most distinctive aspects rather than on its superficial aspects.

The function of advocacy, on the other hand, is essentially "extramural." It exists to achieve a particular purpose with a variety of constituencies with which a field must interact. That purpose—winning support—can often be served most effectively by arguments *ad hoc* and *ad hominem*. The danger with such arguments, of course, is that they can be made with no connection to an underlying belief system which provides a sufficient level of restraint and veracity to keep those arguments from becoming fallacious. When that occurs, the unintended effect is to weaken or demean the field in either the short or long run. So a philosophy, while capable of providing direct advocacy arguments, must be used for that purpose circumspectly; that is, when it is felt that it will be more effective than other possible arguments or when it can provide a useful dimension to other arguments. In short, a philosophy is necessary but not sufficient for effective advocacy.

But there is a different sense of "advocacy" for which a professional philosophy is essential and should be sufficient. That sense has to do with a profession's self-understanding of its inherent character and its fundamental reason for being. In this sense, the word "philosophy" means not just "the critical study of the basic principles and concepts of a particular branch of knowledge," but also "a system of principles for guidance in practical affairs." (Both definitions are given under "philosophy" in the *Random House Dictionary*.) This distinction, I would suggest, is profound, and to treat it with the seriousness it deserves would require, at the very least, a separate essay of the sort being published here. So I must limit myself to a few observations.

Music education existed in the United States from the days of the early colonists until around 1960 with little cohesion at the level of an explicit set of philosophical principles guiding its actions. Aesthetic education was the first movement to attempt to articulate a substantial and coherent set of such principles, to demonstrate their efficacy for practice, to speak to and to be determined by the implicit intuitions about music and music education long held by the field, and at the same time to attempt to satisfy the requirements of critical, analytical philosophy. That it attempted—and attempts— so much accounts for its strength in having provided a working philosophy for so many practitioners of music education as to have won a place for itself as a plausible symbol for a period of the profession's history.

But that very breadth, which has made it so influential throughout the profession, also has its price in requiring that continual clarification and correction take place in its underlying premises at the level of analytical scholarship. The creative tension here is to keep in dynamic balance the need for a viable philosophy—one that is applicable to the broadest possible range of activities and programs in music education—with the equally pressing need for it to be valid at the level of the most exquisite analytical-critical refinements in its infinite details.

It may be impossible to achieve complete success at both ends of this rather long continuum, especially in that each end tends to require specialists who focus on the particular tasks each end entails—robust application at one, meticulous scholarship at the other. In all such continua the tendency is for each end to lose sight of the other and to go its separate way.

Avoiding that professional disaster requires that some people specialize in keeping the ends connected. Having so specialized for most of my career, having experienced the pleasures and rewards of doing so but also the abiding frustrations in attempting to do so because of the inevitable inadequacies in being as expert at both ends as one would like to be, I am in little need of instruction as to the difficulties entailed in building an intellectually valid philosophy that is also professionally useful across the entire spectrum of applications to the teaching and learning of music.

It is an essential characteristic of aesthetic education, I think, that it attempts to fulfill both needs. One may dispute any and all philosophical principles and educational applications proposed in its name, but it is my sense of its essential character that aesthetic education is founded on the premise that sound scholarship and sound practice depend on each other in mutually supportive, necessary ways, and I think that is a major reason aesthetic education has had such an important impact in the history of music education.

Item three in Broudy's list of generalizations frequently made about aesthetic education is that, whatever it is, it is applicable to all children in schools and not just the small percentage at the tail of the curve who demonstrate unusually high competencies in the arts. Now this generalization, I have always believed, is the easiest to which to give assent as an essential characteristic of aesthetic education, although there has been a conviction on the part of some that aesthetic education implies an elitist view of both art and education—a view I have spent a fair amount of energy disputing. I would propose that aesthetic education should clearly be conceived to apply to all students no matter their level of interest or talent in the arts. Ironically, the tough issues here have to do with curricular applications. If aesthetic education is conceived to be for all students, what are the essential learnings with which all should be provided?

In music education this question immediately translates into the issue of performance versus appreciation or, if you prefer, expression versus impression. Our history in regard to this issue as to which of the two is essential has been to offer both, but in what I would roughly estimate would be a 90-10 split overall in favor of performance. We have had very few people arguing for a reversal of that ratio, except, perhaps, in regard to high school humanities courses and appreciation-type courses. But we have had many who would be comfortable with more like a 99-1 split in favor of performance and who, in fact, practice methodologies based on pretty much that kind of split. The interesting question is, where on that scale should aesthetic education be conceived to be?

Characteristically, aesthetic education has taken a comprehensive stance to the curriculum dimension of this issue. A useful music curriculum, in this view, is one that includes all possible ways people interact with music—listening, performing, improvising, composing. It also includes all the ways people think about and know about music—its history, its social contexts, how to criticize it in relevant ways, its many functions, the many issues related to how we can best understand its nature, and so forth.

But it is not just in being comprehensive that an aesthetic education curriculum achieves its purpose—it is also in promoting an interaction with music of a characteristic sort, and that interaction can be achieved in any and all aspects of a total program. A performing group concentrating on performance as such can be, and should be in my opinion, an instance of aesthetic education because it is or should be providing an engagement with and an experience of—one kind of experience of—music itself. How that experience can best be provided in a performing group is a valid, important question, but if it is being provided at all, it is, to that extent, an instance of aesthetic education as I conceive it. Exactly the same can be said for a course devoted entirely to listening—say, at the high school or college level.

So the essential characteristic of aesthetic education in relation to this particular issue is not that there always must be one particular balance among the many ways people can be engaged with music, although inclusiveness or comprehensiveness should be a feature of the total program. What seems to me to be essential to aesthetic education is that any engagement at all with music must include—and, it is to be hoped, emphasized above all else—a quality of interaction that we as professionals would recognize as being inherently "musical." What is that quality of interaction? I will attempt to answer that question in my discussion of item four.

Broudy's item four, you will remember, has to do with the degree to which aesthetic education should be linked with extra-aesthetic—moral, political, economic, religious, civic—values. It also extends to the question of whether aesthetic materials could be used to facilitate the teaching of other subjects.

Now these may seem to be rather simple matters, to be disposed of summarily. In actuality, they raise some of the thorniest, most intractable problems in the entire field of aesthetics, to which whole literatures have been devoted and about which there exists a tremendous diversity of opinion. Again, I am forced to tackle an infinitely complex problem—whether various modes of knowing or experiencing exist, whether the aesthetic is such a mode and why, and if so, whether it relates in any way to others—as but one item among several others in my discussion. I will offer some thoughts about this matter and use those thoughts as a segue to item five, because they launch me directly into issues of aesthetic theory proper.

It is possible to view music as having no connection whatsoever with "extramusical" matters. Such matters would be conceived as anything other than sounds organized to be intrinsically meaningful or significant or compelling in that they form a perceptible or potentially perceptible self-determined and self-contained structure of interrelations. Such a view, dismissing anything but interactive sonorous events as being musically meaningful, has been called "absolutism" in the aesthetic literature, and as with all such "isms," proponents for it may be found as supporting more or less pure versions of it.

I personally have spent a great deal of intellectual and psychic energy attempting to alter my seemingly natural propensity to be an almost pure absolutist. I have been influenced to make some small degree of modification by the opposing view, generally called "referentialism," which tends to downplay or dismiss musical form (in the sense I am using the term) as being the essential determinant of aesthetic meaning or significance and concentrates, more or less exclusively, on associative or representational content in works of art as being the essential factor in how they achieve meaning.

But I have been much more heavily influenced to soften my absolutistic bent by the rather persuasive set of arguments one confronts when dealing with thinkers whose home discipline has not been music; that is, people trained in the other arts. They tend, if I may be so bold as to generalize, to be much more suspicious of what they construe as "formalism" than those in music, more easily seduced by referentialism, but usually quite convinced that neither can account as fully as is necessary for the range of meanings the arts can mediate.

I have, therefore, succeeded in budging myself about an inch and a half to two from the end of this particular yardstick. I would argue that so-called extra-artistic matters can indeed be and often are important determinants of the aesthetic meaning available from works of art, but that in every case a necessary transformation in their nature must take place in order for that meaning to qualify as being aesthetic. That transformation—and I mean the word in its literal sense as a change in form "across" or "beyond"—is caused by and is a function of that quality or set of conditions which characterizes art and sets it apart as a genuine meaning domain.

That quality, I am convinced, is indeed its capacity to create intrinsically meaningful structures and to transform anything else it chooses to incorporate, such as conventional symbols, political statements, moral exhortations, stories and icons, and whatever else, by setting such material as one dimension of—often an important dimension of—its intrinsic structure. The transformation of meaning through formed interrelationships occurs particularly and necessarily with emotions, I would argue. Emotional states or moods, like any other incorporated materials, can influence aesthetic expressiveness, but such expressiveness always transmutes, through the structures into which it is cast, any representation of an emotion as it might exist in experiences outside art.

The "beyondness" or "transcendence" achieved by intrinsically meaningful form is, I think, the essential characteristic of the aesthetic. This transcendence is achieved in all arts of all cultures at all times in history. Each culture achieves it in ways characteristic of that culture, ranging from Western concert halls to Balinese group ritual dances to African drum ensembles. Whatever the social context, art shapes and molds individual and communal experience into meaningful forms sharable by those participating in that culture.

That realization, that art is not the property of any one particular culture such as that of Western Europe, opened music education in the 1960s to all the musics represented by our polycultural society. The long-held, entrenched idea that the music studied in schools should be "school music" began to be replaced by a far more liberal attitude toward what is musical. While a good deal of conservatism still remains in music education about this matter, aesthetic education, I think, has gone a long way toward helping music education become more comprehensive in what music it includes as well as more comprehensive in the ways it engages students with music.

It would follow that an essential characteristic of aesthetic education is its attempt to enhance people's ability to gain the meanings available from culturally embedded expressive forms. Everything in our world can be regarded as potentially yielding such meanings; that is, regarded as and responded to as an instance of meaningful form (which is another way to say "to be aesthetically experienced"). Art is the activity of creating objects and events and processes that yield such meanings, and therefore art adds the crucial dimension of human engagement in the processes of generating, capturing, and sharing the cognitions available from this mode of representation.

So aesthetic education is likely to deal primarily, although not necessarily exclusively, with works of art. It is important to understand that the word "work" in "work of art" functions as both noun and verb. In some cultural settings a "work" is generally understood to be the product of an artistic endeavor. In other settings it is more likely to be conceived as a process engaged in by people during the act of creating an expressive form ("forming"). Both meanings are equally valid, I believe, and both are included in my concept of "work of art."

Engagements with works that emphasize their meaning as art—their ability to yield meanings from their structures of interrelated sounds and to transform words, images, ideas, emotions, and any other socially shared human values by incorporating them as meaningful aspects of musical structure—may be understood to be aesthetic education. We would recognize engagements of the sort I have described as being "musical," I feel reasonably sure, no matter what the particular kind or type of music is in question, ranging from music completely lacking in material other than form through the most non-form-laden examples one might choose.

So long as a structure of sounds both incorporates and to any degree envelops additional content it can be conceived as musical and responded to as such. There is no "correct" or "desirable" standard, as far as I know, for what the ratio of form to content should be, some genres or types or styles of music around the world having high form-to-content proportions and others low.

In the Western classical music tradition, of course, composers throughout history have chosen to incorporate a great variety of materials but have been careful to remind us that their music must be considered to be more than any such incorporated content. A recent striking example is given by the composer John Corigliano, whose Symphony No. 1 was premiered by the Chicago Symphony Orchestra in March 1990. The piece reflects Corigliano's anger, despair, and sense of impotence in having lost so many friends to AIDS. The symphony is "a cry 'Of Rage and Remembrance' [the subtitle of the first movement] for those I have lost and for those I'm still losing," says Corigliano. But the composer insists he does not wish for the piece to be known as an "AIDS symphony."

> That is why I assigned the subtitle "Of Rage and Remembrance" only to the first movement. I want it to be known as a symphony because it is a major work of art and should be heard that way. I want the human part of it to be part of the subtext, but I don't want it to be the only thing with which people identify this piece. I wanted this to be an abstract work, because I think that abstract music can touch the deepest and most basic emotions.[8]

In his review of the performance in the *New York Times* (March 18, 1990), John Rockwell said:

> There are all kinds of reasons why the current Chicago Symphony subscription concerts at Orchestra Hall are significant. But the most compelling is that they mark the arrival of a major new orchestral score, one that addresses a terrible crisis of our time and also manages to make impressive sense on abstract esthetic terms. . . . Music is the most abstract art, and its application to topical issues can sometimes seem forced, a too-easy purchase on the emotions. This symphony sounds almost overwrought at times in its emotional extremism. Yet it is also full of an esthetic coherence that could convince even one utterly ignorant of its inspiration. Knowing that inspiration only lends it a greater poignance.

Corigliano and Rockwell are struggling here to articulate the principle I have tried to articulate and that so many aestheticians have also tried to articulate—that art transcends referential content through its form and that that transcendence yields meanings "deeper and more basic" than the meanings of the content it incorporates, meanings specifically and characteristically "aesthetic." So I am attempting here to argue that there is an identifying set of characteristics, or conditions, or symptoms, or values, or ways to experience, or ways to exercise percipience, or to be phenomenally aware (and on and on depending on whom you are reading) that particularly pertain to the aesthetic domain; that works of art from any place and of any sort—classical, popular, or whatever—are determined in their nature as art (or, as some would suggest, as "art enough") by such characteristics as they are understood to exist among members of a cultural community cognizant of them; that music is one instance of "works of art"; and that

attempts to provide tuition about how to interact in relevant ways with musical phenomena can be construed as aesthetic education. Moral, political,
religious, and any other cultural values can indeed be implicated in such
tuition in the way I have explained, and often *must* be, or a particular piece
of music or musical process could not be understood appropriately.[9]

It is difficult for me to imagine how such tuition would facilitate the
teaching of other subjects, except, of course, as an excellent way to help
students understand such things as that other subjects go about creating
meaning in other ways, that there are interesting and often puzzling overlaps among those ways, that cognition can be understood to be multifaceted
with aesthetic cognition as one of the several genuine, intersecting facets,
and so on. That would indeed be fruitful, I would feel, as educational
material, so long as that which is most characteristic about the aesthetic
domain, or any domain, is not misrepresented or forced to serve functions
not characteristic of it.

These considerations and recommendations bring me smack up against
the final item in Broudy's list—the lack of agreement about the aesthetic
and educational theories on which a concept of aesthetic education might
be built. What I have just proposed about the essential characteristic of
what is musical and the way people engage themselves with music "musically" and therefore what would count as musically educative under a
consequent notion of aesthetic education, all represent a particular point of
view founded on a particular segment from aesthetic theory, translated into
recommendations for educational practice equally founded on a particular
view of educational theory.

I would go so far as to say that any coherent position taken by anyone
on the issue in question would be equally founded on some one or other
theoretical base.

"Eclecticism," for example, is not just a random assortment of bits and
pieces from any and all philosophical positions, but requires a painstaking
selection and coordination and reconciliation of aspects of several views,
forging a position of its own from diverse sources. If it does not do that,
but is simply a smatter from any and all *bona fide* philosophies, it is mindless and therefore useless, degenerating into a kind of free-form pluralism.
Philosophical pluralism states a truism—that there are many contending
philosophies—and is incapacitated by that truth. Any viable philosophy of
music education must take into account the fact of cultural-artistic pluralism, attempt to make some sort of sense of it by explaining its nature, and
attempt to suggest how education might most reasonably contend with it.
A philosophy might explain why musical heterogeneity should be ignored,

or celebrated, or undermined, or strengthened, or whatever that particular philosophy led one to do about it. It would be a strange philosophy indeed that simply did not take it into account. It is not a philosophy, but an abdication of the philosophical imperative, I believe, to take no theoretical position about the nature of musical diversity so that one can act coherently according to that position, but simply to maintain that no position is possible because of the fact of that diversity.

Not only is that a philosophical evasion, it is an educational one as well. A philosophy, I think, is obligated to carve out a position—not to avoid taking one—and that position, by virtue of its being a position, must be positioned somewhere along the spectrum of all possible theoretical bases.

That spectrum has itself widened exponentially in recent years. In 1970, in the first edition of my *A Philosophy of Music Education*, I commented, with no small measure of frustration, that in the face of the diversity of views in aesthetics "one is tempted to throw up one's hands in despair, turn one's back on the entire field of aesthetics, and proclaim that in aesthetic education one might as well do whatever strikes one's fancy, since there probably exists plenty of justification for whatever this happens to be."[10]

Twenty years later that comment almost sounds optimistic. An increasingly tightening inward spiral of critical analysis has taken place, not only of every aesthetic issue but of the notion that the concept "aesthetic issue" is itself viable. This has been accompanied by an increasingly loosening outward spiral in which the field of aesthetics, by concentrating on an examination of its own products rather than of the objects and events it had previously presumed to explain (and therefore having become meta-aesthetics or, one is tempted to say, megalo-aesthetics in its narcissistic self-absorption), has so gnawed at its own carcass as to have led some to suggest that it is time we abandon the beast as being moribund.[11]

I often feel (in fact, it is getting to the point where I usually feel) that this is a blessed suggestion. Unfortunately, I'm afraid it can't be followed. The great color-field artist Barnett Newman no doubt had a point when he quipped, "Aesthetics for artists is like ornithology for the birds." But I think music educators with a philosophical bent are stuck with having to think carefully about such things as music and its nature, and I would generally call the careful articulation of such thought "aesthetics." The question becomes, is it possible to avoid being sucked so strongly into the exploding and imploding forces of contemporary Western theoretical-formal-analytical aesthetics as to be rendered sterile as functioning music educators by them, while at the same time continuing to seek enlightenment and even guidance from the field of aesthetics so that we can do more intelligently what we think it is important to do?

The form of my question indicates my suggested answer. It is that we as music educators have no alternative but to do aesthetics ourselves and also to seek guidance from professionals in aesthetics proper.

But it is also that we who seek in aesthetics must know where to look. Much of aesthetics has, in fact, little if anything to do with what music educators must attempt to deal with in order to create a viable professional philosophy, and that is because much of aesthetics is simply not interested in the issues we need to address.

I would not go so far as to say we should be oblivious of the larger field of aesthetics within which we must conduct our goal-directed searches, because we do need to be aware of the struggles going on even at the borders of that discipline (and that, of course, is where the bloodiest battles always take place). We may not want to go so far as Francis Sparshott did, in the preface to his monumental *The Theory of the Arts*, when he said, "My concern is to develop a coherent line of thought, and little of what other people have written proves to be of actual use when one's own direction has become specific."[12] But we can certainly sympathize with the feeling that our own agenda should guide our scholarship.

That agenda, I want to suggest, requires us to focus on the needs of our field—music education or, if one chooses, music education as aesthetic education—as providing us with our obligatory issues, about which aesthetics can then, perhaps, give us some guidance. Harry Broudy said this very well, I think, in the chapter I have used to structure this essay:

It is especially difficult to make the connection between aesthetic education and the kind of writing that is concerned primarily with the discourse about aesthetics, "meta-aesthetics." The logical properties of aesthetic judgments and definitions are not themselves aesthetic objects. This is not to say that speaking precisely is not important to aesthetic education. On the contrary, if one is to distinguish aesthetic experience from other kinds, if one is to defend one attitude toward the aesthetic object rather than another, then discussions of definitions and criteria for usage cannot be avoided. But, whereas in formal aesthetics this can go on as an end in itself without engaging in concrete transactions with particular aesthetic objects, this cannot be the case in aesthetic education. Accordingly, aesthetic theory has to be given educational relevance, a task that is not quite the same as generating either aesthetic or educational theory.[13]

This argument has been updated recently to reflect the tangled situation in professional aesthetics over the past decade or so to which I referred above. In a 1987 article in the *Journal of Aesthetics and Art Criticism* entitled "The Liveliness of Aesthetics," Marx W. Wartofsky presents a point of view in consonance with Broudy's and with what I am attempting to propose.

He begins by saying that his essay is not "in" aesthetics but is "about" aesthetics. If it were "in" aesthetics, he says, it would be about such matters as "art (artworks, the artworld, art talk, art biz, artists, etc.) or about criticism or the theory of art, or the experience (reception, evaluation, appreciation) of art; or if not about art, then about the aesthetic, or aesthetic concepts like Form, Beauty, Style, Taste; or if none of these, then about representation in art, or depiction, or semblance, or about expression, and more and more." I quote this sentence to make the point that despite a decade or more of some attempts to either discredit or dismiss such matters, they remain, with little question, the enduring foundation for the great majority of scholarly efforts in aesthetics.

Wartofsky discusses the variety of claims in recent analytical aesthetics, the fashions and styles of discourse they adopt, and the distance they have generated between their concerns and the basic issues relating to how and why we value art, leading, he says, to the derivativeness and dreariness of this segment of aesthetics. What is the antidote? To pay attention, Wartofsky asserts, to art.

> Art, in its career, its changes, its corruptions and failures as well as in its successes and epiphanies, is a naturally vital source of problems and insights in aesthetics. . . . The fact is that, analytic or not, the liveliest range of books in aesthetics, as well as essays, symposia, etc. has been stimulated by an immediate relation with and competence in the arts, and a close knowledge of their present state and of their history. . . . the arts constantly provide one with something to say—to understand them, to make them accessible to others, to engage the practitioners and performers in reflection on their *metiers*, to submit one's own work to their criticism, and that of one's colleagues. Enough and more to do in full aesthetic autonomy. The liveliness of aesthetics lies, I think, in such intercourse with the arts.[14]

I want to propose that the liveliness of music education philosophy lies in its relevance to problems and issues of learning and teaching the art of music in valid ways; that is, in ways that scholarship can help us validate. More than ever before, and certainly more than twenty years ago when I first expressed the thought in the first edition of *A Philosophy of Music*

Education, the formation of a useful and tenable philosophy of music education "must start with an acquaintance with the field of music education: its problems, its needs, its history, its present status. Aesthetics must be used by music educators to serve their own purposes. Otherwise they are likely to lose themselves in the history and problems of aesthetics, never to emerge with a workable philosophy."[15] I added to this thought in the second edition of *A Philosophy* the sentence "Aesthetics must never be the master of music education—it must be its servant."[16]

Music education, I am proposing, must be regarded to be a "music educationworld." The world it represents and creates is just as real and as valid and as stipulative of what can go on in it as is the "artworld" with which it intersects and with which it engages in a great variety of influences and counterinfluences. I would assert, therefore, that an essential characteristic of aesthetic education is that it attempts to address the philosophical issues of the world or culture of music education by seeking helpful, relevant, and intellectually defensible resolutions from whatever sources it can, including, necessarily and importantly, the field of professional aesthetics.

That endeavor requires, first, that the fundamental philosophical problems arising within music education be articulated clearly and, second, that solutions be sought that are relevant not only to the nature of those problems but also to the nature of music education as a social-cultural institution.

Both conditions require a philosophy amenable to and dependent on change as an essential characteristic, because it is a given that the philosophical problems considered to be fundamental to music education will change over time, the availability of viable solutions to them will also continually change, and the social-cultural nature of music education will also continue to change. It must be an essential characteristic of aesthetic education as a professional philosophy, then, that it not consist of one particular set of problems or issues, resolved in one particular fashion, relevant to one particular institutional Zeitgeist as it exists at any one particular period in history.

This principle applies as well to the maintenance of a recognizable political-cultural entity such as a nation. The United States, for example, has existed as a characteristic entity despite enormous changes over time in its philosophical self-understandings, the available resources for addressing its self-definitional issues, and the social-cultural contexts within which the issues must be addressed. Longevity and identity are both essential for the viability of a cultural institution, and both can be achieved only if mechanisms for change are built into the institution's guiding principles.

Aesthetic education, as I understand it, is an attempt to articulate a philosophical orientation that can be both temporally pertinent and progressively developmental.

The philosophical agenda for music education, under this view, remains constant while its contents evolve. The agenda is to articulate what the most pressing issues are, to attempt to resolve them in light of the most useful and persuasive available scholarship, and to use the resolutions as the basis for applications to the teaching and learning of music as it is embedded in the existing overall culture as well as within the existing culture of the field of music education.

Debate within the music education philosophical community can then take place in a context of both theoretical and practical significance. What are the central philosophical issues now facing us? That question will always provide music education philosophers plenty to deal with. What are the most viable and defensible solutions to those issues? Again, a question allowing a great deal of room for healthy argument. How can suggested solutions be translated into helpful practices in educational settings, and how do those translations reflect back on and validate or invalidate the solutions? Another fruitful domain for scholarly efforts.

What has been missing in the history of music education has not only been an active, ongoing philosophical community, but also a structure within which such a community could flourish as an integral part of the larger music education endeavor. Perhaps we are now ready to begin establishing such a community and a cooperative structure within which individuals, while retaining their intellectual independence, can also contribute to shared goals.

What might such shared philosophical goals be at this point in history? It would be impossible to articulate any unless there existed for the person doing so a sense of what music education now consists of as a profession and a philosophical orientation that would be pertinent to that sense. Given my image of what music education has become as an institution, and my philosophical orientation based on several essential characteristics of what I term "aesthetic education," I would like to focus briefly on just two important philosophical goals (among many others that might be mentioned) now very much needing to be better achieved.

The first has to do with our understanding of the relation between music and feeling. This is not only because this relation continues to be as much of an enigma for contemporary aestheticians as it has been throughout history, but because any philosophy of music education neglecting or disclaiming this dimension of musical experience will not speak to a major if not the major personal and professional value of music to music educators. Largely because aesthetic education in its earliest formulations took the nature of musical feeling to be one of its most important topics, this philosophy seemed relevant to the profession at large. That situation has not changed, in my view, nor is it likely to, so a viable philosophy of music education needs to continue to clarify this issue so that educational practices can more validly and effectively reflect our better understandings.

That will not be a simple task, as history has shown us. One of the important early contributions of aesthetic education was to clarify that music did not function as emotional expression; that is, as a translation into sound of a composer's or performer's present affective state.

The key to unlocking this new set of ideas was provided at that time in history by Susanne K. Langer, who was a pioneer in formulating a different basis for understanding feeling in music than the prevalent "expression of emotion" theories and therefore helped us turn attention inward, to musical form and the experience of it rather than outward, to emotions music was ostensibly referring to by means of sounds as conventional symbols.

As Francis Sparshott explains,

> According to her theory, it is just because the artist's (and other people's) repertory of "knowledge" of the possibilities of feeling is not available as knowledge but exists as a sort of empathetic capacity, that art is necessary to symbolize the modes of sentience. The conundrums that her critics pose for her, that we cannot know that art does this unless we can already recognize the symbolized modes of sentience, so that the symbolization is unnecessary, is readily solved: all that we know is that the work of art before us gives form to *some* form of sentience; *what* form that is we can say only by describing the work.[17]

Such a description, Langer would have added, must be of the musical form (or "forming") as such—the "work"—rather than of affective states of being, which are incapable of being mediated by language.

Her insistence on this point had the further effect of turning attention in music teaching to sounds as such and to the experience of those sounds as being affectively dependent on their form and therefore incapable of being more fully experienced except by more and more refined perceptual awareness of their intrinsically musical form (including, of course, whatever other social-cultural materials were implicated as determining components of that form).

Langer's seminal yet partial contribution did not still the outpouring of debates on this issue (I hardly need say), and we continue to read, in a great many books and journal articles on the matter, still more tortured attempts to explain why and how and wherein a sad piece of music achieves its sadness. This is important work, no doubt, but I want to call attention to what I think is even more important—the increasing recognition that affect, or feeling, is not just a concomitant of musical experience but is an active ingredient in the intelligence with which such experience is mediated.

I refer here to Nelson Goodman's claim that to experience a work of music aesthetically is a cognitive achievement in which "the emotions function cognitively: in organizing a world, felt contrasts and kinships, both subtle and salient, are no less important than those seen or inferred."[18] Further, one cannot discern the musical properties of formed sounds without an engagement of feeling. "Emotional numbness," says Goodman, "disables here as definitely if not as completely as . . . deafness."[19]

Roger Scruton puts it this way: "To understand musical meaning, therefore, is to understand how the cultivated ear can discern, in what it hears, the occasions for sympathy. I do not know *how* this happens; but *that* it happens is one of the given facts of musical culture."[20] It is certainly, I would add, one of the essential facts of music education culture, and it would seem to me, therefore, an essential characteristic of a professional music education philosophy such as aesthetic education aspires to be that it continue to attempt to clarify for the larger profession how feeling is implicated in musical experience as insights about that implication continue to deepen.

These considerations lead me directly to the second philosophical issue to which I think we must pay particular attention as part of our professional agenda—the issue of musical cognition. Musical knowing, as both Goodman and Scruton imply, seems to be intimately connected with the phenomenon of musical feeling, the former being incomprehensible without the guidance and formative powers and phenomenological pervasiveness of the latter.

It may very well be the case, and I would argue that it certainly is the case, that musical meaning or knowing depends on or dependently implicates feeling. Mikel Dufrenne's explanation seems to me apt. "Simply described," he says, "feeling reveals an interiority."

> It introduces us to another dimension of the given. It is not only a state or mode of being of the subject, it is a mode of being of the subject which corresponds to a mode of being in the object. . . . Aesthetic experience will show us that feeling . . . is an immediacy which has undergone mediation. . . . Furthermore, such feeling, in which perception is realized, is not emotion. It is

knowledge. . . . This feeling has a noetic [cognitive, mindful, reasoning] function. It reveals a world. . . . Feeling . . . is a capacity of receptivity, a sensibility to a certain world, and an aptitude for perceiving that world.[21]

Dufrenne is focusing here on "knowing of"—one of what I conceive to be two essential and interconnected modes of knowing in music. The second mode of knowing essential to musical experience is, I think, "knowing how," which is the engagement of the self in creating music whether by composing or performing or improvising. "Knowing how" entails feeling, of course, and depends on "knowing of" as the *sine qua non*, but adds the dimensions of active imagination and employment of the competent body—in itself, I would argue, as would many others, a realm of experience with cognitive resonance.

I would also argue, but cannot take the time to do so here, that listening entails a particular kind of "knowing how" also to be conceived as creative, in the sense David Best proposes when he says that the term creative "applies equally to the creator and spectator, for it requires imagination to understand a work of imagination."[22] We particularly need to learn much more than we know at present about the "knowing how" entailed in composing, which has been largely neglected in music education but over the next several decades may become as important in our programs as performance has been.

In addition to the two essential aspects of musical cognition—"knowing of" and "knowing how"—two supplementary modes exist—"knowing about" (or "knowing that") and "knowing why." The former deals with verbal and symbolic conceptual knowledge about music as a phenomenon; the latter with the same kind of knowledge but about the cultural-historical belief systems in which music as a social institution exists. The philosophical agenda in regard to musical cognition is to clarify what each dimension consists of so that each may be taught more carefully as both an entity and as one aspect of the larger whole to which it contributes.

Especially complex is the precise nature of the interface between the exteriority of "knowing about" and "why," on the one hand, and the interiority of "knowing of" and "how," on the other, in that, while a great deal of empirical evidence exists that the former does indeed influence the latter, we know too little about how, precisely, that occurs and therefore cannot arrange our education strategies as intelligently as we need to. I am aware, when I suggest that we explore that interface more intensively, that it raises profound and difficult issues relating to the nature of the human mind and the nature of consciousness itself. That those issues are, in fact, issues so deeply important to the field of music education attests to the centrality of our field in the larger domain of cognitive scholarship. It is time we both recognize and proclaim that centrality.

Given the assumptions I have made about several essential and non-essential characteristics of aesthetic education, the question arises as to whether it is important or helpful to retain the term "aesthetic education" at all. Of course, none of us owns the term, and people will or will not use it as they wish. But what should we desire about it? Obviously some will want very much to continue to use it while others have long since said good riddance to it.

I confess to a good deal of ambivalence in this matter. On the one hand, one grows accustomed to a much-used phrase as to a comfortable pair of old shoes, its tears and scuffs and loose threads and worn spots being perceived not so much as imperfections but as signs of its adaptability to the rough-and-tumble to which it has been subjected and the durability of a wise initial investment.

On the other hand, one is tempted by some of the snappy new styles. Conceived this way, one vacillates.

Conceived differently, however, and in a more rigorous intellectual manner, aesthetic education can be taken to symbolize a process rather than an entity. In that sense I suspect it might serve a useful or even essential function, reminding us as scholars and practitioners to keep our eye on what matters and helping us define what it is that matters. For me, the most essential value of aesthetic education is not its name but its agenda. It is as a reminder and symbol of that agenda that the term "aesthetic education" may continue to prove useful.

NOTES

1. Michael L. Mark, "A New Look at Historical Periods in American Music Education," *Council for Research in Music Education*, Bulletin 99 (Winter 1989). The previous periods Mark identifies are (1) The Colonial Period (1620), (2) Public School Music (1800), (3) Curricular Development (1864), and (4) The Expansion of Musical Performance (1920).

2. J. Terry Gates, "*Fermez la porte?*: On Michael L. Mark's 'A New Look at Historical Periods in American Music Education,'" *Council for Research in Music Education*, Bulletin 103 (Winter 1990).

3. Edward Bailey Birge, *History of Public School Music in the United States* (Washington, D.C.: Music Educators National Conference, 1928). The periods Birge proposes are (1) The Development of the Singing School, (2) The Magna

Charta of Music Education in America, (3) 1838–1861—The Period of Pioneering, (4) The Beginnings of Method—(1861–1885), (5) Concentrating on Music Reading—(1885–1905), (6) The Turn of the Century, (7) The Twentieth Century, (8) Music Teachers' Associations—The Conference Movement, (9) Recent Trends and Developments in Music Education.

4. For a clear example of such a view, see David J. Elliott, "Structure and Feeling in Jazz: Rethinking Philosophical Foundations," *Council for Research in Music Education*, Bulletin 95 (Winter 1987).

5. Harry S. Broudy, "Some Reactions to a Concept of Aesthetic Education," *Arts and Aesthetics: An Agenda for the Future*, First Yearbook on Research in Arts and Aesthetic Education, ed. Stanley S. Madeja (St. Louis: CEMREL, Inc., 1977).

6. Manuel Barkan, Laura H. Chapman, and Evan J. Kern, eds., *Guidelines: Curriculum Development for Aesthetic Education* (St. Louis: CEMREL, Inc., 1977).

7. Bennett Reimer, *A Philosophy of Music Education*, 2d ed. rev. (Englewood Cliffs, N.J.: Prentice Hall, 1989), 230.

8. John von Rhein, "Absent Friends," *Chicago Tribune*, March 11, 1990.

9. An excellent example of how music is influenced by, absorbs, and transcends a theatrical story is given in Roger Scruton, "Analytical Philosophy and the Meaning of Music," *Journal of Aesthetics and Art Criticism* 46 (Special Issue on Analytical Aesthetics, 1987): 175. For a careful explanation of how conceptual information is made to yield aesthetic cognition, see Kenneth Dorter, "Conceptual Truth and Aesthetic Truth," *Journal of Aesthetics and Art Criticism* 48, no. 1 (Winter 1990).

10. Reimer, *Philosophy*, 1st ed., 12. Not succumbing to that temptation, I added, "The question is, can one accept this condition and at the same time develop a point of view which helps one's efforts to be as consistent, as effective, as useful for one's purposes as intelligence and modesty allow? There is really no alternative but to answer yes."

11. Francis Sparshott suggests an alternative to the notion of music as art in *What is Music?*, ed. Philip Alperson (New York: Haven Publications, n.d.).

12. Francis Sparshott, *The Theory of the Arts* (Princeton, N.J.: Princeton University Press, 1982), viii.

13. Broudy, "Some Reactions," 254, 255.

14. Max W. Wartofsky, "The Liveliness of Aesthetics," *Journal of Aesthetics and Art Criticism* 46 (Special Issue on Analytical Aesthetics, 1987).

15. Reimer, *Philosophy*, 1st ed., 13.

16. Reimer, *Philosophy*, 2d ed., 15.

17. Sparshott, *Theory of the Arts*, 321.

18. Nelson Goodman, *Of Mind and Other Matters* (Cambridge, Mass.: Harvard University Press, 1984), 147.

19. Nelson Goodman, *Languages of Art*, 2d ed. rev. (Indianapolis: Hackett, 1976), 248.

20. Scruton, "Analytical Philosophy," 174.

21. Mikel Dufrenne, *The Phenomenology of Aesthetic Experience* (Evanston, Ill.: Northwestern University Press, 1973), 376–79.

22. David Best, *Feeling and Reason in the Arts* (London: George Allen and Unwin, 1985), 76.

3

THE EXPERIENCE OF PROFUNDITY IN MUSIC

What's at the bottom of people's love for music, expressed in all periods of history and all over the world? There are many reasons for the appeal of music and the values it confers. Underneath all of them, I believe, is the power of music to move us—to touch us at the core of our being by engaging our feelings, whether slightly or greatly.

I am fascinated by the "greatly" possibility. Just how deeply into feeling can music take us? And how does it take us there? These are questions all music educators would like to have answered to better help their students achieve not only the many transitory pleasures music affords but also the deeply self-actualizing experiences it is capable of providing.

As an undergraduate it occurs to me that music seems to have the ability to take us to depths commonly associated with religious experiences. Are there similarities between those two recognized sources of deep-rooted undergoings? I immerse myself in studies of contemporary religious views on the nature of spiritual experience. John Dewey's book *A Common Faith* (1934) opens me to new ways of conceiving "the religious in experience." The same is true later for the writings of the theologian Paul Tillich, which prove to be equally if not even more mind-opening. Both of these writers, and the works of many others I explore, take me closer to my need for a clearer understanding of human beings' deepest levels of experience.

I propose to Charles Leonhard, my doctoral advisor, that I do my dissertation on the relation of aesthetic experience and religious experience as conceived by such scholars. He thinks I must be nuts. "You're supposed to do a dissertation on music education," he says, incredulously. "What in the world is in your head?"

I persevere over several months, arguing that a philosophical basis for music education of real importance lurks somewhere in this topic, and I hope to be the one to bring it to light. He gradually softens, wanting me to develop my philosophical chops even though the topic seems to him far outside the traditional boundaries of music education scholarship. Finally he gives in.

The result is my 1963 dissertation *The Common Dimensions of Aesthetic and Religious Experience* (the first philosophical dissertation in music education, as far as I can tell), and my abiding interest, religion aside, in musical feeling and its depth potentials.

The article following casts the issue in terms of the profundity of experience that music so commonly affords, experience that can be described as genuinely spiritual if not religious. At the present time when music education philosophers are emphasizing political and moral aspects of the responsibilities of music educators—a valuable direction—I continue to hope that the dimension of music's gifts of spirit will not be as neglected as they have become among many intellectuals in our profession. Too much of great value awaits our further understandings of the depth dimensions of music, both for ourselves as professionals devoted to enhancing the musical experiences of our students and for the spiritual health of our culture and our world.

The following essay was originally published in *The Journal of Aesthetic Education* 29, no. 4 (Winter 1995). Copyright © 1995 by the Board of Trustees of the University of Illinois. Used with permission of the University of Illinois Press.

INTRODUCTION

If any generalization can be made about music (and I believe many can be made) surely the one articulated by Francis Sparshott would qualify as defining one of music's essential characteristics: "that it is more nearly true of music than it is of anything else that it offers an alternative reality and an alternative way of being."[1]

A compendium of claims that have been made for the power of music to alter the reality of human experience and to alter humans' way of being, as Sparshott believes it can, would fill several very large volumes, as would descriptions of instances in which music has done just that. Such volumes would include material from sociology, ethnography, anthropology, psychology, philosophy in most of its branches including of course aesthetics, history, religion, linguistics, musicology, psychoanalysis, cognitive science as it has recently emerged, physiology, and no doubt numerous other fields from which insights could be gained.

There is good reason for this remarkable breadth of thought relevant to the unusual power of music to transform human experience. This power reaches to the very roots of the human condition, that humans are conscious of their individual and collective existence in a world both including them and transcending them, on which they are dependent for life and meaning and to which they contribute life and meaning. Music is, in a certain sense, only one of a multitude of demonstrations of the subject-object interplay that characterizes human reality.

But in another sense, music is a remarkably vivid and concentrated instance of the self-within-the-world human condition. Perhaps more fully than any other endeavor, music manifests selfness for the sheer sake of the human need to demonstrate selfness, and it does this with materials, sounds, that exist entirely and are employed sheerly for the sake of self-manifestation—self as instance of the universal human condition, as instance of the culturally determined human condition, as instance of the individuality of each human's condition.

REPORTS OF PROFOUND EXPERIENCES OF MUSIC

Such reflections, grandiloquent as they may seem, pale compared with what people have actually reported music has done to them. We have most of our evidence about musical profundity from verbal reports of musical experiences. Such reports are almost entirely about the subjective dimension of the subject-object polarity of musical experience. In recent years we have had some attempts to focus on the objective dimension, the qualities of music itself that are causative of profound experiences. I will address that dimension after characterizing how people have described such experiences. To review such descriptions in any exhaustive way would be quite impossible in a single essay, of course, given the breadth, complexity, and magnitude of the data. But a brief overview will, I think, yield some useful insights.

We must keep in mind, when examining verbal reports of musical experiences, that we are thrown, by necessity, into the realm of metaphor, imagery, euphemism, figurative language of various sorts, because those are the only modes of language in which inner experience can be expressed. The "truth" of such language is a truth appropriate to its subject, which by its nature requires representation by oblique suggestion rather than by objective exactitude.[2]

The classical work of the twentieth century on that level of human experience to which the word "profound" applies was carried on by Abraham Maslow. Maslow was interested in the fact that experiences traditionally associated with ecstatic religion or mysticism were in fact commonly reported in association with a wide variety of stimuli or situations having little or nothing to do with religious settings, such as "experiences of the aesthetic, of the creative, of love, of sex, of insight, etc."[3] He coined the term "peak experiences" for such occurrences, which he described as "moments of highest happiness and fulfillment."[4]

The effects of such experiences, according to Maslow, are sometimes "so profound and so great as to remind us of the profound religious conversions which forever changed the person."[5] When not at that deep level, they can nevertheless be positive in a variety of ways. One feels more like a real person, more responsible, active, self-determined, loving, and accepting, able to feel gratitude that such fulfillment is indeed possible. "What had been called the 'unitive consciousness' is often given in peak experiences, i.e., a sense of the sacred glimpsed *in* and *through* the particular instance of the momentary, the secular, the worldly."[6] Maslow's data are clear that the effects of profound experiences, including profound experiences of music, are long-lasting on those that have them. They can change such persons' sense of themselves and of their place in the world positively and pervasively.[7]

The effects of peak experiences of music were probed by Robert Panzarella in a study of "The Phenomenology of Aesthetic Peak Experiences."[8] Panzarella collected and analyzed written and aural descriptions of visual art and music peak experiences from 103 persons (52 for visual art and 51 for music) in an attempt to refine Maslow's insights. He found that the responses fell into four major categories: "renewal ecstasy," "motor-sensory ecstasy," "withdrawal ecstasy," and "fusion-emotional ecstasy."[9]

In renewal ecstasy, the person reports a new vision of the world, a world seen as better, more beautiful than it seemed before, even though it continues to contain all the tragic, imperfect aspects it always had. A deep, profoundly moving experience of music can somehow yield an altered perception of the world, in which the paradox of simultaneous good and evil is not seen as something to be overcome but as something to be accepted.

Interestingly, some people reporting this experience were motivated to produce music but these were only people who already were able to do so with some degree of competence. "There was no instance," Panzarella reports "of an experience which converted a non-performer to [becoming] a performer."[10] He adds that "it may be true, too, that the impulse to be creative is inherently antithetic to the continuation of ecstatic enjoyment and terminates ecstasy in order to initiate creative probing and testing."[11]

I want to suggest that creative work in music, composing, performing, improvising, can indeed include profound or ecstatic dimensions of experience but that an additional concept may have to be added to explain this. I will treat this issue further on.

In "motor-sensory" ecstasy people report a variety of bodily responses such as faster or slower heartbeat or breathing, shivers, chills, tinglings, sweating, a feeling of being "high" or of "floating." These experiences "are rarely described as satisfying, fulfilling, renewing, or the like,"[12] nor do they seem to produce more than temporary effects. Far more people report such experiences with music than with visual art (35 percent against 19 percent), which is something we have long assumed given so many reports over history of music's power to affect people physically as well as emotionally.

The withdrawal ecstasy involves a "loss of contact with both the physical and social environment. A perceptual narrowing occurs; attention is riveted to the aesthetic stimulus."[13] In the fusion-emotional ecstasy, that attention takes on an intensely affective character, as the person feels emotionally connected or fused with the music. For example, "The only way I can describe it is as being one with the music and not only with the music but with the people, concert hall, etc. It was as if it were inside me. I can't remember any feeling but a sort of crazy joy."[14]

Panzarella identified three temporal stages in aesthetic peak experiences: onset, climax, and post-climactic. In stage one aesthetic judgments and analyses trigger the response, along with disruptions of perceptual set, like surprise and amazement. A sense of loss of self begins and lasts into the second stage. Here, at the climax, there was often a sense of intense motor response or loss of motor sensations: "I felt as though I could bear it no more, almost that I would leap from the balcony," or, "I became aware of a feeling of elevation, as though my mind were not part of my body but floating above it, in complete freedom. The music seemed to be a force that could be felt moving through my body. My thoughts were very free floating, although the sounds and vibrations of the music held my attention. I was

completely free."[15] In the third stage, emotional responses and transforma-
tions tended to cluster.

Panzarella offers some interesting conclusions from his study, although
all must be taken as extremely tentative. While the most often cited triggers
for musical peak experiences were so-called masterworks (Bach, Mozart,
etc.) reflecting the musical preferences of his subjects, the range of triggers
was quite broad, including popular music, folk songs, and rock 'n' roll. The
structural characteristics of the music were sometimes but not often discussed. Similarly for the performance-skill aspect of the experience. "Apart
from operas, no music was experienced as a vehicle of communication for
ideas or emotions. . . . In opera experiences the emotion felt in response
to performance qualities sometimes utterly contradicted the emotion the
music was attempting to convey."

Strikingly, the number of cognitive-perceptual responses in music reports was virtually equaled by the number of bodily sensations. "Music,"
Panzarella suggests, "is a more physical experience than most aesthetic
theories take into account."[16] I find that a compelling observation, not only
from the listener's viewpoint but particularly from the performer's viewpoint, which I will discuss later.

One other study of musical peak experiences will add to this overview of
what people have reported when profoundly affected by music. Alf Gabrielsson and Siv Lindström of Sweden pursued the concept of "strong" experiences of music by gathering verbal descriptions from some eight hundred
persons using both questionnaires and aural reports about "the strongest
(most intense) experience of music that they ever had."[17]

Gabrielsson and Lindström suggest that, while each strong experience of
music is unique, seven features seem to appear quite regularly. The first,
"General Characteristics," are responses characterizing the experience as
a whole: "unique," "exceptional," "fantastic," "incredible," and so on, including claims that the experience is difficult or impossible to describe in
words. The second feature relates to physical responses: shivers, stillness,
goose flesh, weeping, gliding in space, and so on. The "Perception" feature
includes auditory, visual, and tactile phenomena, but the researchers point
out (echoing Panzarella) that "on the whole . . . most people do not talk very
much about musical details in describing their SEM" (strong experience of
music).[18]

The "Cognition" feature includes changes of one's attitude in which concentration on the music overwhelms other awarenesses. Surprisingly, they
say that "a music-analytic attitude, common among musicians, is abandoned
in favor of an 'open,' receptive attitude."[19] In another place, Gabrielsson

says, "There were surprisingly few references to the musical structure and little use of music terms in the descriptions, even among the musicians."[20] In addition, there is a merging with the music, an altered experience of one's body in time and space, the arousal of various associations and images including internally heard, imagined music, and a sense of perfection—that the experience is at the height of what can be achieved by humans.

In the "Emotion" feature there is a range from positive feelings (pleasure, enjoyment, love, peace, euphoria, ecstasy, the most common being a sense of happiness) to negative ones (grief, anxiety, anger, horror, panic), although there were relatively few of these. In the "transcendental" feature there are reports that the experience transcends ordinary life and reality, taking on a religious or spiritual dimension.

In the "Personal Development" category, a sense is gained of new insights, new possibilities, of a mental and physical purification and of a sense of being "healed." In a related paper, Gabrielsson and Lindström focus on this therapeutic dimension, giving a great many reports of how people experience it. They conclude that strong experiences of music do indeed have therapeutic implications. "Our SEM project convincingly demonstrates the power of music to affect individuals and groups in ways that few other means are capable of doing."[21]

Limitations of the Verbal Reports

All the above material—only the tip of an iceberg of similar material—focuses on the capacity of people to experience music and other aesthetic stimuli at a level well characterized by the term "profound." Clearly there is a universal dimension to this capacity: it seems to be ubiquitous in human experience. But two very important factors are left unexamined by such material.

The first has to do with the musical-cultural contexts in which profound experiences occur. In practically all cases reported, such experiences took place within a well-defined community of musical expectations. The music to which people responded at levels of deep engagement was music with which they were familiar, not necessarily with the particular piece or performance (although that was the case quite often) but at the level of cultural identification. It occasionally was reported that a profound experience took place with music of a genre not usually enjoyed by a person—classical music with a rock enthusiast and a jazz enthusiast, for example. But I have come across no description of a profound musical experience with music of a culture quite foreign to the person experiencing it.

This is not to say that it is impossible, only that it seems to be rare or nonexistent in the literature. We very much need to know with more certainty whether profound musical experiences take place largely or exclusively within the context of the culture of which the person is a member. At the moment it seems safe to say that it is far more likely. That likelihood has important implications for music education if, as I will propose in my conclusions, music education should do all it can to encourage profound musical experiences to take place.

The second factor not explained by and seldom mentioned in verbal reports of deep responses to music is that of the particular qualities of the music that were implicated in causing or triggering the response. We are left by such reports with little guidance or insight about specific musical characteristics that operate to cause the reported responses.[22] It is easy to assume that, given a particular musical belief system, that is, an identification with a particular cultural manifestation of music, any music at all within that system could trigger such a response: all depends on the psychological/emotional readiness and susceptibility of the respondent.

That is an attractive hypothesis, but I believe it goes too far. Certainly the person's immediate subjective state must be an important causative factor in allowing a strong experience of music to occur. After all, such experiences do not occur infallibly with all musical experiences any person has with very similar or even identical music. The subjective side of the subject-object duality must have major determining effects on whether a profound experience will take place on any particular occasion.

But we cannot write off the qualities of the music itself or even the qualities of the performance of it as another determining factor. John Blacking provides a useful insight about this in a story he relates of being involved as a performer in a Venda ritual. He points out that a particular Venda possession dance does not send every Venda into a trance, as it is intended to do. "They send only the members of the cult, and then only when they are dancing at their own homes, with which the spirits of the ancestors who possess them are familiar. The effectiveness of the music," Blacking says, in a confirmation of my point, "depends on the context in which it is both performed and heard."[23] He goes on to say, however:

> But ultimately it depends on the music, as I found out once when I was playing one of the drums. Dancers take turns coming out into the "arena," and at first there were no complaints about my efforts. Very soon, however, a senior lady began dancing, and she was expected to go into a trance because the music was being played for her cult group. However, after a few minutes she

stopped and insisted that another drummer should replace me! She claimed that I was ruining the effect of the music by "hurrying" the tempo—just enough, I suppose, to inhibit the onset of trance.[24]

Clearly, the qualities being perceived in the music and its performance must play a decisive or at least an important role if one's experience of the music is to be deep enough to warrant the term "profound," no matter whether one is a Venda tribesperson or a North American. It is facile, even narcissistic, to assume that musical quality is of concern only to those privileged to live in the West but is of little or no concern to those in so-called primitive cultures for whom cultural or religious beliefs are entirely responsible for what transpires in various rituals in which music plays a part.

This point is made even more clearly than Blacking made it by Denis Dutton, in an article criticizing Arthur Danto's neglect of the factor of aesthetic sensitivity in tribal people's discernment of quality in various manifestations of their art. "Most primitive artworks," Dutton reminds us, "capture attention not only because of the ideas they embody, but because they are made to look striking, shocking, beautiful, grotesque, etc." We cannot "deny the crucial and determining role of discriminating perception (as opposed to conception) in understanding primitive art . . . it is a matter of gaining cultural knowledge in order to see aesthetic qualities which have intentionally been placed in the objects to be seen."[25]

MUSICAL QUALITIES CAUSATIVE OF PROFOUND EXPERIENCES

It seems reasonable to include, as one essential factor in profound experiences of music, qualities of the music itself in addition to the self-induced, subjective responses of the people experiencing the music, no matter the particular cultural context in which the experience takes place. Is it possible, then, to identify with some precision just what those musical qualities need to be if they are to cause profound experiences to occur?

Peter Kivy makes an interesting if ultimately futile attempt to do just this in regard to that music in which he is interested, the genre of music most capable of being separated from external meanings, contexts, representations, and so forth. In pure Western instrumental music, or "music alone," as he calls it, we have the clearest instance of a music that can be construed as "a quasi-syntactical structure of sound understandable solely in musical terms and having no semantic or representational content, no meaning, making reference to nothing beyond itself."[26] Unlike the usual position of musical purism, Kivy makes clear that his version of it includes the possibility that such music "does present or embody the garden-variety emotions as part of its aesthetic fabric, at least on some occasions."[27]

How can such music be regarded, Kivy asks, as being profound, as it frequently is? It cannot be profound by virtue of being about a profound subject matter as some literature is because it is about nothing at all. And it cannot be profound because it is expressive of the more profound, serious, darker, more weighty emotions, which would seem to be a reasonable explanation, because "there seems absolutely no reason for believing that a structure with serious expressive properties is any more profound than a structure with frivolous or happy ones." Further, since "music expressive of serious emotions is not about them, that it is expressive of them is no grounds at all for ascribing profundity to it."[28]

Perhaps, Kivy suggests, we can ascribe a certain meaning to pure music in the sense that it is "about" the very possibilities of musical sounds themselves, and that a composition is a discovery of possibilities of musical sounds and hence can be construed to be "about" music itself. Therefore, musical craftsmanship, when it is at its highest levels, elicits the judgment "profound" because it is about the furthest reaches of musical possibilities. Works of consummate craftsmanship are candidates for being called profound because they have a profound subject matter—music itself—and they present that subject matter in an "artistically supreme and exemplary way."[29]

Unfortunately, Kivy goes on to explain, this careful argument cannot be sustained. The problem with it is its claim that music itself is a subject worthy of the term profound. There seems to be no rational justification for such a claim, says Kivy, as there does seem to be of other subjects such as those with which literature often deals. "For even if the [musical] works we describe as profound have a subject matter, and that is debatable, the only subject matter they can plausibly be thought to have, namely, musical sound itself, does not bear, at least on the face of it, any obvious mark of profundity, as do such subject matters as freedom of the will or the problem of evil, love and marriage or crime and punishment, and so forth: the subjects of 'profound' literary works."[30] We can go on saying that some works are profound but we cannot rationally justify our doing so. We are reduced, says Kivy, to the only thing we can possibly say when asked to justify why we think a particular work is profound: "Play it again, Sam."[31] We are thrown right back to subjectivity.

Kivy's views on the issue of profundity and related matters have generated something of a cottage industry of debate and extension, any full treatment of which would be impossible in this context. In my own view Kivy's assumption that music must be "about" something profound in order to qualify as itself being profound is extremely questionable. He is on the right track, I believe, to say that "pure" music (if there really is such a thing) is "about" music, in the sense that it yields meanings available only from music and that are "musical" in essence. I would go further to say that any music, whether or not some subject matter is explicit or implicit in connection to it (I include the "garden variety emotions" as subject matter)[32] has musical meaning as its essential subject matter above and beyond whatever other subject matter it happens to entail.

To produce musical meanings, I would argue, is the fundamental reason for music's existence, and it is such meanings that in fact seem to cause profound experiences for many if not most people who have such experiences. Kivy says that he takes the word profundity, "when applied to music, as having the same implications as it would have when applied to literature or philosophy. In other words, I have taken it seriously."[33] I believe he has, instead, taken it inappropriately. It may be difficult or impossible to describe specifically any particular musical characteristics that are regularly causative of profound experiences, but that such experiences are caused by music *qua* music is evident.

Several attempts have been made to probe further than Kivy did into the power of music to induce profound experiences. David A. White suggests that musical characteristics such as unity, whole and part, identity and difference, are, despite Kivy's skepticism, worthy of being considered "essential elements in the articulation of profundity precisely because these concepts are necessary to any account that purports to describe reality."[34] While music, White argues, is not intended to be metaphysics, the qualities of music shared by the qualities of human reality allow musical experience to serve as a kind of "simulacrum of reality."[35]

The problem, says White, is to find a way to relate our experience of the expressive content of the music as being distinctively aesthetic, to the fabric of our nonmusical, nonaesthetic existence. That, of course, is a problem that has challenged musical aesthetics throughout history, and I suspect it always will until the unlikely time when human consciousness itself can be thoroughly explained. Nevertheless, White proposes a parallelism between certain musical features and the metaphysical features of our experience of reality itself.

Alan Goldman tackles the issue head on by raising the key question: "How can mere sequences of sounds, detached from all practical affairs and daily concerns, be of such importance?"[36] Notice that this question separates "pure" music from music experienced in contexts that are themselves conducive to profound or at least important experiences, exactly as Kivy and White attempt to do. The point here is that profound experiences can easily be attributed to factors other than the music itself when such other factors are dominant or even present, such as music experienced in the context of religious or other culturally significant rituals or ceremonies. In some reports of profound experiences of music the setting could well explain the experience that transpired. Music was perhaps not the key factor in the experience, only contributing another dimension to the experience or serving as an accompaniment to the experience.

Yet in many other reported experiences it was clearly the music itself that caused the profound response, even to the point where faulty performance got in the way of such response. So it is helpful to use as a mechanism for understanding how music itself might be experienced profoundly that particular genre of music least associated with auxiliary contexts that may confuse the issue—the genre of Western instrumental concert music. This is not to argue that even that genre can be completely dissociated from social-cultural contexts that influence the experience we have of it. Nothing in our experience can be so completely dissociated. It is only a matter of degree.

Goldman's tack on the issue of musical profundity is to ascribe it to music's power to present us with "an alternative world, in which we can be actively, but not practically, engaged."[37] We are engaged in such a world not by virtue of any reference to ordinary emotions or events outside the musical context itself but in response to the "broader structures of musical works, structures possessed only by them, as these uniquely unite form as cognitively grasped and affectively felt."[38] Reference, Goldman argues, including as reference the world of ordinary emotions, "has value in music not because of what it reveals about that world (as this can be of utmost value in literature), but because of the way that it adds to or completes the world of the music."[39]

That musical world, in which we can become fully immersed, both satisfies and challenges our capacities to think and feel. We experience this as an "alternative reality and an alternative way of being," to use Sparshott's formulation, because the world that music creates is one "completely created by the human spirit."[40] In it, says Goldman, we meet and share the minds of the composer, performer(s), and audience. This meeting of minds and feelings, because it is within the context of the music, "appears to take place . . .

in a wholly different, ideal world . . . constituted by the common musical experience."[41] While literature and (representational) painting also present us with worlds experienced through the eyes and minds of their creators, those worlds are opaque, being filled with materials related directly to our normal lives, while in music, in that it "is forever disappearing as it appears," we experience directly the creative force that caused its being. "Thus, music is not only another world. It is a world that can be completely satisfying and fully revealing of the creative powers of other minds. Its peculiar value lies in the purity of its revelation of the human spirit."[42]

It would seem reasonable to extrapolate from Goldman's analysis the implication that powerful revelations of the human spirit would indeed be interpreted quite naturally by people as being connected to the divine, the spiritual, the therapeutic, the deepest meanings of which humans are capable; in a word, to profundity. One need not limit oneself to the genre of "music alone" in the Western tradition as the sole example to which we can ascribe these characteristics. Any music would seem capable of being revelatory of the creative powers of the human mind as connected to cultural values, beliefs, and occasions, and therefore be regarded with the awe so often experienced in connection with music.

I do not believe it is possible to describe particular musical features that would always be implicated in profound experiences because that would require a split in the subject-object duality not capable of being made. However ritualized and regularized the musical formulae might be for calling forth transcendent experiences, as they are, for only one example, in particular Venda practices, the contribution of the believing, willing subject is essential if such an experience is to take place. But we cannot go so far as to negate the factor of the music itself as the causative stimulus, including features of the music that, it is evident, have the power to be perceived as reflecting profound forces experienced as such. It is likely that such features are culture-specific and perhaps even type-specific.[43] What we can say with confidence is that most if not all cultures produce music capable of being experienced as profound by initiates.

A DEFINITION OF THE EXPERIENCE OF PROFUNDITY IN MUSIC

At this point and in light of the ideas expressed above I am emboldened to offer a summative description, or definition, of the experience of profundity in music. It is, quite simply, *being moved deeply in response to music*.

This seems relatively uncomplicated, but it harbors within it a host of issues capable of extensive if not infinite analysis. At this point I can provide only enough of such analysis to demonstrate the fruitfulness of the definition (or description) and then to draw some implications for practices in various aspects of music education.

The simplest part of the definition is the last—"in response to music." But this is not, it turns out, entirely simple. I mean by it that we can attribute to music itself all of, or most of, or at least some of, the profound experience attained. The experience may come from any musical engagement—listening, composing, performing, improvising, conducting, and so forth—and in any setting in which music is being experienced, from the only relative "purity" of the concert hall to music as part of a cultural ritual to which it contributes only one part. (I would point out again that context must always be a factor in musical experience or no musical meaning could exist.)

While it may be difficult or perhaps impossible to eliminate from the experience a variety of factors that can cause it other than the sounds themselves, including the person's subjective complex of feelings brought as predispositions before the sounds actually occur, it is nevertheless reasonable to attribute to the musical sounds a significant portion—even the determining portion—of the profundity experienced. The evidence, after all, is overwhelming that this actually occurs. So "in response to music" assumes that music is at least strongly implicated in if not entirely causative of the profound experience being undergone.

The other three terms of the definition—being, moved, and deeply—are each infinitely complex. "Being," in the simplest sense, refers to an engagement of the self as a sentient organism with sounds understood to be musical. But in saying this we are immediately thrown into the complexities and perplexities of the primary ontological issue at the core of metaphysics—the possibility and nature of being as such. My intent in this regard must be very modest; to clarify, to some small extent, that possibility of human experience we call "musical" by explaining some recent thinking about it.

The term "moved" raises the issue of experienced subjectivity, the human capacity to feel and to be aware of that which is being felt as being meaningful; that is, as being significant and self-determining. I hardly need mention the breadth and depth of the complexities surrounding the issue of the relation of music to feeling. They are well known to anyone who has attempted to think about the nature of musical experience. Again, my purpose here is extremely circumscribed: to reflect briefly about the role of feeling as a *sine qua non* of profound musical engagements.

The term "deeply" is also rife with complexities, being based in the long tradition of belief that human meanings exist not on a single plane but on a spectrum, ranging from the trivial to the quintessential. This belief is intimately related to the ontological issue, as is the notion of feeling. Both the "moved" and the "deeply" terms of the definition are ultimately rooted in a concept of being—of particularly "human" being—which in turn is determined to a large extent by the possibility of feeling deeply. So the terms of my definition overlap in their meanings, their implications, and their complexities. I am afraid that any definition less complex would not do justice to the intricacies this topic entails. Again, my program in regard to the "deeply" component is modest in the present context: to explore briefly the idea that music can, indeed, be a powerful factor in taking human experience beyond the plane of the ordinary.

Explanations of the Definition

A particular helpful analysis of musical being, musical feeling, and musical depth is provided by Kenneth Dorter in his explanation of the differences between conceptual truth and aesthetic truth.[44] Dorter points out that "there are at least four levels of experience at which art seems to express a certain kind of truth: those of (1) our emotions, (2) cultural values, (3) sensory experiences, and (4) the elusive *significance* of our experience."[45] It is this fourth level of truth that particularly concerns us here, in that it includes the others and raises the issue of profundity.

At this level a dimension of human undergoing outside the range of the experience itself appears—a dimension of *meaning* unperceived in the stimulus itself yet at the same time experienced in light of that stimulus. The most common way this occurs is through religion. Religion has characteristically aligned itself with art because of the power of art "to represent significance in sensuous objects," as both Kant and Heidegger maintained in their arguments that art deals with meanings of a nonconceptual sort.[46]

Such meanings are always metaphoric. They are embodied in the particular expressive conditions of the particular musical materials being employed. But they point beyond themselves to a sense of significance, the significance of our experience as valuable in and of itself because it is also metaphoric of the very foundation of what is real in human experience, that our being is one of consciousness of being. By deploying its materials "in such a way as to prevent our taking them literally" music focuses our thoughts "beyond definite concepts to an indefinite significance" encompassing our feelings, our consciousness of feeling, the shared life of feeling among human beings, and a sense of the nature of "the experienced world itself, something that is not accessible to conceptual understanding."[47]

Dorter's explanation of the metaphoric relation between the expressive materials of sound and the significance of our experienced world is compatible with Goldman's notion of "an alternative world" in which music engages us and with White's suggestion that musical features are parallel with features of our experience of reality itself. These views, I believe, are far more productive of insights into the nature of musical profundity than Kivy's attempts to locate it in a profound subject matter "about which" music needs to be.

Another view compatible with Dorter's, Goldman's, and White's is offered by the phenomenologist Mikel Dufrenne. Aesthetic perception, Dufrenne points out, examines an object with thoroughness by means of feeling and discovers in the object an internal world existing in the realm of feeling. This world

> can bear witness to the real, not by propounding what [the real] is in positive fact but by presenting its countenance to us. Thus we can now see what the proper function of art is. By allowing us to perceive an exemplary object whose whole reality consists in being sensuous, art invites us and trains us to read expression and to discover the atmosphere which is revealed only to feeling. Art makes us undergo the absolute experience of the affective.[48]

In doing so, art "orients and refines our perception of reality," while reality "becomes aestheticized at the same time it is humanized." Art "gives us keys" to what is real, or at least to the affective aspects of what is real. Through aesthetic experiences "something human is revealed in the real, a certain quality by which things are consubstantial with man, not because they can be known, but because they offer to the man capable of contemplating them a familiar face in which he can recognize himself without having himself composed the being of this face."

Art, then, is that phenomenon "without which things would be only what they are." The aesthetic object, in presenting the affective possibilities of human experience, "does justice to and thus authenticates the human dimension of the real. The artist is the chosen locus where the real attains to consciousness in terms of what is more secret and yet most visible in it—its humanity."[49]

The art and artists Dufrenne is discussing need not be construed to be of any particular sort or limited to any particular culture. Nor need the capacity to experience the arts profoundly be construed as being possessed only by adults, let alone only by highly trained or artistically sophisticated adults. I understand Dufrenne to be describing what any human beings, in any culture, are capable of experiencing through engagements with the arts whether as perceivers or producers of them. All human beings seem to be, by nature of being human, able to experience in music the defining characteristics of profundity conceived as "being moved deeply."

The "being" of profound experiences of music blurs the distinction of subject and object.[50] Subjective meaning, feeling, and knowing take on an extended reality by merging with significant, imaginative instances of musical creation.

The feeling in profound experiences of music is not the result of interpretation or conceptualization or representation: "It appears to be something found or recognized"[51] in the qualities of the music with which one is engaged. Our self is "moved" affectively from where it was to a new position by the confrontation with such qualities.

That new position is, metaphorically, "deep," implying something not able to be seen when one is positioned at the surface. "*Profundity*, in the metaphorical use of *depth*, is of something that is hidden from view."[52] When that which is hidden is suddenly seen—suddenly experienced—our foundations are shaken. We are seized, physically, emotionally, and mentally by meanings resonant with a sense of that which is most real to us—our consciousness of our selves as being in and of the world. In such moments the wholeness of the self is experienced.

As Katherine Lee explains in her article "Transcendence as an Aesthetic Concept," aesthetic encounters achieve transcendence "when there is a perceived wholeness in which the scattered details of the object or event fall immediately into order and coherence and resonate with the individual's understandings and feelings. It is a moment of great magnitude because of the transformative insights it affords the individual."[53]

All this occurs frequently and powerfully with music, to a degree so remarkable as to suggest that our susceptibility to profundity in music may be the very paradigm of the human capacity for significant experience.

MUSICAL CREATION AND PROFUNDITY

Such susceptibilities exist in any kind of musical response. But creating music—composing, performing, improvising—adds a necessary ingredient not present in listening: the ingredient of critical self-reflection and concomitant decision making required when acting as a musician. Panzarella found that this ingredient can negatively affect the ecstatic experience of music. This needs to be taken into account in attempts to understand the profundity experienced by musicians when acting as musicians.

An aspect of experience that can help explain how musicians overcome the possibly detrimental effects of critical consciousness is what Mihalyi Csikszentmihalyi has termed "flow." As is now well known, the flow experience occurs when a person's level of skill is matched by the challenges presented to it, in a context of focused attention, in which the activity itself is its own reward:

> At the core, the flow model states that the perception of high challenges (or action opportunities) and high skills can lead people to a state of consciousness (flow) in which high levels of control, concentration, unselfconsciousness, and a strong sense of involvement are experienced. This "negentropic" state of consciousness contrasts with an "entropic," confused, or random state of consciousness. Persons in flow are deeply concentrated and feel a merging of action and awareness, their attention is centered on a limited stimulus field, and they may experience a "loss of ego" and feel in control of their actions and the environment. A further crucial component of the flow experience is its autotelic nature. In other words, the person in flow does not strive for goals or rewards beyond the activity at hand. The activity provides its own intrinsic rewards.[54]

Composing and performing, clearly, offer remarkably potent opportunities for the experience of flow to occur in connection with musical experience being undergone intimately and absorbedly. The flow experience occurs in listening as well, obviously,[55] but the added dimension of the necessary exercise of craftsmanship gives composing and performing a particularly rich set of opportunities for it to occur.

In addition, the involvement of the body in performance focuses and strengthens the intimacy of one's contact with the sounds being experienced, further encouraging the possibility that one will "be moved deeply."[56] There are hazards here, of course, in that the technical demands of performing can become the focus, leaving the musical experience enervated rather than strengthened. As Csikszentmihalyi points out, "When children are taught music, the usual problem often arises: too much emphasis is placed on how they perform, and too little on what they experience."[57]

This problem is overcome in effective performance instruction, of course, in which musical experience, through and by the exercise of creative, sensitive craftsmanship, is the goal. This can occur in solo performance, of course, and it can occur in ensemble performance as well, in which case the group effort to create musical experience communally adds still another dimension to the potential profundity of the experience. Evidence of the depths to which ensemble performance can take one is provided in a poignant and sometimes amusing way by members of an Ohio high school band who were asked to write about what they felt when performing a recent concert. Here are some of the responses:

> Climaxes, shivers. I can feel my heart flowing into my instrument and can see the notes floating into the air, up and out into the world.
> Goose bumps, shivers, felt great, exciting.
> Totally awesome! Really moved and very touched.
> Unity, oneness, family.
> I could imagine a flowing intermixing spirit fly around our band like *Raiders of the Lost Ark*, except the spirit was good, and together, and musical.
> The confidence and force of the band was (such) that being in the midst of all this glorious music that at times it almost brings tears to your eyes.
> When I play well, I can feel the music coming out of my heart, it isn't from my fingers or tongue.[58]

Surely such remarks are illustrative of the occurrence of musical experiences at the level of the profound or at least approaching that level. Surely teachers of music in the schools, whether general music teachers, performance teachers, newly emerging composition teachers, hope that profound musical experiences will occur as a consequence of their efforts, if not always or even often then at least occasionally. We might even go so far as to say that the achievement of such experiences—of being moved deeply in response to music—is the ultimate goal of instruction in music, encompassing yet transcending all the other goals toward which a good music program aims.

What can now be said about what we need to know and what we need to do to optimize the possibilities that such experiences will indeed occur as a result of our work?

ENCOURAGING PROFOUND EXPERIENCES OF MUSIC

Three essential factors are implicated in profound experiences of music understood as experiences of being moved deeply in response to music. The first is the individual who has the experience. The second is the context in which the experience takes place. The third is the musical stimulus for the experience. The three must interrelate, in ways we know much too little about, if a deep musical experience is to occur.

We know too little about it because we have not examined sufficiently, with the seriousness and carefulness it deserves, the issue of how music education practices might affect, directly and significantly, the depth of musical experience we hope our students will attain. I believe that, ultimately, music means so much to us because it has moved us deeply, and I believe our zeal for music education stems, ultimately, from our desire to help others be so moved. It is high time we included as a primary goal of our scholarly research activities the attempt to learn as much about this most important of all issues as we have in attempting to learn about a host of matters infinitely less important. Of course everything we learn about music and music education helps us in some way. To learn more about what concerns us ultimately about our field would help us profoundly.

It should go without saying that continuing work in philosophy of music education will be needed to help us further clarify the nature of musically profound experiences so we can be more secure about what it is we are trying to influence.

But in addition to the need to lay a great deal of philosophical groundwork we also need to extend that work through many and diverse empirical studies. In the matter of individuals who experience music we need to know much more than we do about the content of their reported profound experiences at different ages, in different musical/cultural contexts, under a variety of impinging conditions, and about how these interrelate with their musical backgrounds, their personality types, their level of acquaintance with the triggering music, and so forth, so that our background of descriptive data can begin to be sifted for useful correlations.

Luckily we now have available to us research procedures able to help us investigate higher-order experiences rather than only lower-order responses, and we are increasingly admitting such qualitative procedures into our repertoire of what is conceived as respectable research. Whether we are ready to regard as respectable research the quest to understand ultimate values rather than scattered minutiae is an open question. I am hopeful that if we encourage research scholarship dealing with higher or highest musical responses we can produce far more knowledge of use to us, and of meaning for us, than we have by our overwhelming concentration on lower or lowest musical responses. Certainly our research literature would become more interesting.

I want to suggest several lines of scholarship and action that, at this point, would seem fruitful for encouraging profound experiences to occur as a result of music education practices.

First, I believe we should recognize that such experiences can and do occur often—perhaps *most* often—from listening. I suspect this happens because most people can be more fully engaged in music of high levels of affective magnitude, conducive to deep experiences, from listening than they are likely to be from other kinds of musical involvements. Whatever a person's capacity for fullness and challenge in musical experience, music capable of providing maximal levels of those qualities can be encountered quite readily through listening. Profound experiences of music are most likely to occur when they approach the boundaries of musical fullness—perceptually and emotionally—capable of being internalized by an individual. It is simply more likely for more people to encounter that interface between their own capacities to be engaged with musical repleteness, and music of a variety of sorts fully satisfying that capacity, from listening than can be expected from the far less frequent, far more specialized activities of performing and composing.

I believe, therefore, that we are likely to provide more people with more musically deep and satisfying experiences of music from listening engagements than from anything else we can do. To the extent there is merit in that supposition it will be important for us to learn as much as we can about how to engage students of all ages in deeply satisfying listening encounters, a research agenda that is daunting but capable of yielding very high rewards.

It is likely that profound experiences through listening will occur both when people are alone and in the company of others, in degrees and ways about which we need to know much more than we do. Our social orientation in schooling very naturally provides more group experiences than solitary experiences. While the sharing of musical experience, and the sharing of reports of feelings of profundity among those involved, is among the most precious gifts of music, we should not neglect or minimize the fact that solitary experiences of music can also have their particular benefits and deep-reaching qualities. The celebrated fiction, poetry, and essay writer May Sarton is said to have remarked that music is much too important to be experienced with others. We need not entirely agree in order to appreciate her insight. We would do well, I think, to provide opportunities for "alone time with music" during school and to encourage our students to provide it for themselves outside of school.

But whatever the opportunities to experience music deeply when listening, the experiences available from performing, composing, and improvising must continue to play essential roles in our attempts to encourage fulfilling experiences of music, both in general education settings and in specialized elective settings. Here we must add to the full engagement of the individual with the depths of significance of the music he or she is creating (and I most emphatically include performance as "creating" music) the factor of that compatibility of challenge with competency called "flow." We must be far more conscious, in our musical creating activities, and far more in control of the need to reach for the edge at which technical capacities and musical richness merge with the experiencing self in moments of deepest meaning. We know that this can happen at every level of competence if the musical repleteness aspect—the level of musical meaning sufficiently abundant to challenge and sufficiently accessible to be "taken within"—is sufficiently provided.

This means that, as in listening, we must take great care to avoid so concentrating on details that the wholeness of the experience is weakened rather than strengthened. In all our activities we need to keep an optimal balance between parts and wholes, the wholes—the completeness of musical experience—and the parts—the exploration of the significant details out of which the whole emerges—reinforcing each other in the service of deeper perception and deeper reaction.

And it is also far more likely that fulfilling experiences of music will occur when students are in an atmosphere where they are secure, unthreatened by the potential of failure or negative appraisal, and able to give themselves fully to the power of the music they are creating or listening to, unfettered by anxieties about being judged by others.[59]

The wholeness of music is, no doubt, more likely to be experienced with music whose language is native than foreign. Here we need to avoid two extremes. On the one hand we can so emphasize the familiar music of a particular culture, reveling in its accessibility of moving, significant experiences, as to neglect our obligation to broaden the scope from which deeply satisfying musical experiences can be gained.

On the other hand we can be so "other" oriented, so devoted to exploring uncharted territory, as to neglect the need everyone has to be at home in a secure world in which one's soul finds fulfillment. "Soul music" is music that often touches our soul; that is, satisfies our deepest musical needs. Everyone deserves to have such a music, or musics, from which such deep pleasure can be regularly gained.

To keep in balance all the factors relating to individuals, contexts, and music that are implicated in musical profundity, in educational settings optimizing their interrelations so as to encourage all students to be moved deeply by music, is as complex and as sensitive a task as any in all of education. That is because music is capable of serving humans at the very depths of what can be experienced. At such depths "an alternative reality and an alternative way of being" are achieved, in which wholeness of meaning is attained in a world full of division and alienation. We may not be able to guarantee that experiences of musical profundity will take place because of what we do as music educators—that music will exert its profound powers to "make whole," to "heal," as a direct result of our efforts.

But we can try, by working to understand better what musical profundity consists of and learning how we can best invite it to be experienced by those whose musical education is entrusted to us. Those things *are* doable. They deserve, perhaps more than anything else in music education, our best professional efforts.

NOTES

1. Francis Sparshott, "Aesthetics of Music: Limits and Grounds," in *What Is Music?* ed. Philip Alperson (New York: Haven, 1987), 89.

2. See the discussion of this point in Abraham H. Maslow, *Religions, Values, and Peak-Experiences* (Columbus: Ohio State University Press, 1964), 84–90. For an excellent explanation of the ineffability of musical experience, see Diana Raffman, *Language, Music, and Mind* (Cambridge, Mass.: MIT Press, 1993). An interesting (and problematic) attempt to gather data about musical peak experiences, using a dial device by which listeners registered the intensity of their "aesthetic experience" while listening to recordings, is reported in Clifford K. Madsen, Ruth V. Brittin, and Deborah A. Capperella-Sheldon, "An Empirical Method for Measuring the Aesthetic Experience to Music," *Journal of Research in Music Education* 41, no. 1 (Spring 1993): 57–69. Several of the findings of that study coincide with the verbal reports given below.

3. Maslow, *Religions, Values*, xi.

4. Abraham H. Maslow, *Toward a Psychology of Being* (Princeton, N.J.: Van Nostrand, 1962), 69.

5. Ibid., 66.

6. Ibid., 68.

7. Ibid., 74–82.

8. Robert Panzarella, "The Phenomenology of Aesthetic Peak Experiences," *Journal of Humanistic Psychology* 20, no. 1 (Winter 1980): 69–85.

9. Ibid., 74–78.

10. Ibid., 75.

11. Ibid.

12. Ibid., 76.

13. Ibid.

14. Ibid., 77.

15. Ibid., 79.

16. Ibid., 83.

17. Alf Gabrielsson and Siv Lindström, "On Strong Experiences of Music" (manuscript for *Musikpsychologie,* Jahrbuch der Deutschen Gesellschaft für Musikpsychologie).

18. Ibid., 15.

19. Ibid., 16.

20. Alf Gabrielsson, "Intense Emotional Experiences of Music," *Proceedings of the First International Conference on Music Perception and Cognition* (Kyoto, Japan, 1989), 375.

21. Alf Gabrielsson and Siv Lindström, "May Strong Experiences of Music Have Therapeutic Implications?" (manuscript of a paper presented at the Conferences on Psychophysiology and Psychopathology of the Sense of Music, Munich, September 28–30, 1992), 7–8.

22. For some hints as to particular musical characteristics to which listeners respond intensely, see Madsen, Brittin, Capperella-Sheldon (note 3, above). For an example of a study attempting to locate particular musical events that cause peak emotional experiences, see John A. Sloboda, "Music Structure and Emotional Response: Some Empirical Findings," *Psychology of Music* 19 (1991): 110–20. Sloboda's data suggest support for Leonard B. Meyer's theory that musical tendencies and inhibitions are strongly implicated in causing emotional responses.

23. John Blacking, *How Musical Is Man?* (Seattle: University of Washington Press, 1973), 44.

24. Ibid., 44–45.

25. Denis Dutton, "Tribal Art and Artifact," *Journal of Aesthetics and Art Criticism* 51, no. 1 (Winter 1993): 20.

26. Peter Kivy, *Music Alone: Philosophical Reflections on the Purely Musical Experience* (Ithaca, N.Y.: Cornell University Press, 1990), 202.

27. Ibid.

28. Ibid., 205.

29. Ibid., 215.

30. Ibid., 217.

31. Ibid., 218.

32. For further discussion of this point see Bennett Reimer, "What Knowledge Is of Most Worth in the Arts?" in *The Arts, Education, and Aesthetic Knowing,* ed. Bennett Reimer and Ralph A. Smith (Chicago: University of Chicago Press, 1992), 35–39.

33. Kivy, *Music Alone,* 218.

34. David A. White, "Toward a Theory of Profundity in Music," *Journal of Aesthetics and Art Criticism* 50, no. 1 (Winter 1992): 32.

35. Ibid., 33.

36. Alan Goldman, "The Value of Music," *Journal of Aesthetics and Art Criticism* 50, no. 1 (Winter 1992): 35.

37. Ibid., 39.

38. Ibid., 37.

39. Ibid., 42.

40. Ibid., 43.

41. Ibid.

42. Ibid.

43. Compare the discussion of this point in Lewis Rowell, *Thinking about Music* (Amherst: University of Massachusetts Press, 1983), 163–64.

44. Kenneth Dorter, "Conceptual Truth and Aesthetic Truth," *Journal of Aesthetics and Art Criticism* 48, no. 1 (Winter 1990): 37–51.

45. Ibid., 37. Emphasis in original.

46. Ibid., 40. Compare to the comment by Arturo B. Fallico, that art "carries . . . an element of seriousness which can only be called *religious* in the profoundest sense of the term. For, just so long as the creations of art are a reality, all our realities remain tinged with a veil of insubstantiality and provisionality, as if awaiting final approval. Art keeps alive our sense of the omnipotent; it feeds the soul with its profoundest intimations of the divine—of the memory, that is, of Being itself." Arturo B. Fallico, *Art and Existentialism* (Englewood Cliffs, N.J.: Prentice-Hall, 1962), 73–74.

47. Ibid., 38–49.

48. Mikel Dufrenne, *The Phenomenology of Aesthetic Experience* (Evanston, Ill.: Northwestern University Press, 1973), 542.

49. Ibid., 453–60.

50. Jean Gabbert Harrell, *Profundity: A Universal Value* (University Park: Pennsylvania State University Press, 1992), 19.

51. Ibid., 21.

52. Ibid., 20.

53. Katherine Lee, "Transcendence as an Aesthetic Concept: Implications for Curriculum," *Journal of Aesthetic Education* 27, no. 1 (Spring 1993): 77.

54. Mihalyi Csikszentmihalyi and Ulrich Schiefele, "Arts Education, Human Development, and the Quality of Experience," in *The Arts, Education, and Aesthetic Knowing*, ed. Reimer and Smith, 181.

55. Mihalyi Csikszentmihalyi, *Flow: The Psychology of Optimal Experience* (New York: Harper and Row, 1990), 110. Here the author takes the position that listening in both live and recorded settings can equally provide flow experiences: "But to argue that live music is innately more enjoyable than recorded music would be just as invalid as arguing the opposite."

56. For a more detailed discussion of the physical dimension of performing experience, see Bennett Reimer, "Is Musical Performance Worth Saving?" *Arts Education Policy Review* 95, no. 3 (January/February 1994): 2–13.

57. Csikszentmihalyi, *Flow*, 112.

58. Personal correspondence from John Kratus to the author.

59. Compare the discussion of this point in John A. Sloboda, "Empirical Studies of Emotional Response to Music," in *Cognitive Bases of Musical Communication*, ed. Mari Jones and Susan Holleran (Washington, D.C.: American Psychological Association, 1991), 39.

4

SHOULD THERE BE A UNIVERSAL PHILOSOPHY OF MUSIC EDUCATION?

A footnote literally changes my mind, affecting my insights in a brand-new way.

Shortly after writing the previous article, in a source I cannot remember, I note a citation of the anthropologist Robert Plant Armstrong, someone I've never heard of but who sounds interesting. I dig up his out-of-print books and give them a look.

I'm enthralled. Armstrong accomplishes something that many other thinkers have intuited but have never been able to pin down as convincingly— where and how we can find the quintessential characteristics of human mental capacity at both the universal and cultural levels. With clarity and specific examples he explains how works of art give us tangible evidence of what he calls "the living forms of consciousness itself," universally present in all people, expressed differentially in each culture. In a grand conception based on the careful observations characteristic of anthropologists, Armstrong offers understandings of the necessity of the arts that I have spent much of my life seeking.

Immediately I want to share these revelations with the worldwide community of music educators. I have approval for a proposed paper at the upcoming conference of the International Society for Music Education in Amsterdam in 1996 on whether it is possible or desirable to have a universal philosophy of music education. Armed with newly acquired comprehensions, I recast my topic at a deeper level. Lucky break.

Universality requires, for me, inclusiveness and comprehensiveness, a vision large enough to encompass seemingly or actually incompatible beliefs and values. Is it possible to achieve a universal stance on the nature and values of music education when we also insist on cultural authenticity, valuing as much as we do the "multi" in multicultural music education?

Our cherished individualities are amenable to commonality when we adopt an inclusive rather than exclusive posture. Armstrong's vision explains how that can be achieved and how the arts are the strongest possible evidence that a level of human universality exists. (A more detailed discussion of his work is presented in my *A Philosophy of Music Education: Advancing the Vision*, 2003). With his insights as a basis, music education might, with difficult but fascinating efforts, attain a shared worldwide vision while also honoring the individuality of each culture's accomplishments.

If music and the arts demonstrate this possibility, can we exploit it in all of or at least more of the issues that divide our world so dangerously?

The following essay was originally published in the *International Journal of Music Education* 29, no. 1 (1997). Used by permission.

ABSTRACT

The four themes of the conference focus on the universal dimension of music, claiming that music speaks universally to all generations, times, cultures, and nations. If that is the case it should also be the case that a universal philosophy of music education—a coherent system of beliefs about the nature and value of music and its role in education and in life, applicable to all generations, times, cultures, and nations—should exist or can exist or does exist. However, no such universal philosophy has been articulated and has been recognized by the world's music educators to be universally acceptable. In fact, many would claim that a universally persuasive philosophy is unlikely if not undesirable. Lacking such a philosophy, claims for the universality of music have no firm foundation. Yet the intuition that there is, indeed, a universal dimension of music and of music education remains persuasive or at least attractive. Is it possible to identify universally accepted values of music and the teaching and learning of music? Would it be useful for the international community of music educators if attempts were made to do so? This paper will argue that it would be extremely useful to make such an attempt, and will suggest some of the strategies by which the attempt might prove fruitful.

INTRODUCTION: THE UNIVERSAL/PARTICULAR PARADOX

The idea that music is a "universal language" is widespread, particularly among the general populace but also to some degree among professionals in music education. For example, the theme of the 1996 Conference of the International Society for Music Education in Amsterdam (July 21–27), claimed, as if axiomatic, that music is a universal language for all generations, times, cultures, and nations.

Such a claim must give us pause. First, it raises the issue of whether and in what sense and under what theory music may be construed to be a language at all. This issue is so contentious in the literature of music philosophy and psychology as to warrant separate and lengthy treatment. I choose to ignore this issue in the present discussion, however, preferring to focus on the universal dimension of the universal language idea. I will take the language aspect of the idea to be largely rhetorical rather than substantive, indicating simply that music "speaks to" all people—that music is applicable to, has relevance for, and is an important component of the lives of people of all generations, times, cultures, and nations. In that rather casual sense it would seem quite acceptable.

The argument for universality, however, cannot easily be made. It raises questions which, particularly at this time in history, call for our most serious attempts to provide answers more satisfactory than have so far been generated. The tenor of our times, philosophically and politically, seems much more to be focused on differences among peoples of various generations, times, cultures, and nations than on similarities, to the point where, in philosophy, many would be offended by any claim for universality, taking such a claim to be a threat to the individuality—the authenticity—of each generation, time, culture, and nation.

In political terms this cherishing of exclusiveness over inclusiveness had led to fierce, bloody conflicts between people of different religions, nationalities, cultures, and even generations. Each of these conflicts, so sadly common in the world in which we live and throughout human history, testifies to the ferocious power of the human psyche's need to be a member of a group different from other groups. The preservation of the differences is often seen to be worth fighting for, killing for, and dying for.

In that music is among the deepest expressions of the human psyche, would it not seem likely that protection of one's own music from that of conflicting others would be as strong a drive as exists in so many other manifestations of people's need to preserve their authenticity? Surely the claim that music is universal in the sense of all-encompassing within a single perspective can be regarded as empty or even disrespectful of human diversity. Surely an argument can be made that it is what divides people, musically as well as in so many other ways, that determines how we think, what we believe, what we cherish, and how we act.

According to this line of reasoning any attempt to forge a universal philosophy of music education will be and should be enormously difficult if not impossible. On what basis should we assume that we can articulate a music education philosophy—an explanation of the nature and value of music and of the teaching and learning of music—so all-embracing as to subsume within it the multitudinous and often contradictory if not conflicting beliefs and practices of cultural groups all around the world? And even if it was possible to do so, would we not, by attempting the task, diminish the very differences among musical belief-and-practice systems which each system exists to preserve and protect?

So it may not only be impossible or at least very improbable that we can articulate a universal philosophy of music education, it may also be undesirable or even harmful to attempt to do so.

I find such arguments to be quite persuasive. But I do not believe they are persuasive enough to cause me and others devoted to such issues to simply abandon the challenges they present and to retreat to less difficult ones also needing our attention. I believe the music education profession would benefit in important ways from attempts to articulate the issues related to a universal philosophy of music education, to go as far as we are able toward proposing resolutions of those issues, and to formulating positions that, while perhaps falling short of a single, completely acceptable, worldwide philosophy—a *gesamtphilosophie* if you will—would nevertheless help us portray what such a philosophy might look like. I suggest that doing those things would not only be philosophically interesting and educative, but would also be a healthy counterbalance to the view that human beings are definable largely in terms of what separates them rather than what unifies them.

I have no quarrel with the conviction that human beings are, in certain important respects, like particular other human beings; that is, that our group identifications play a large role in defining who we are. All music educators, all over the world, are members of particular nations/cultures.

This gives us an important and precious dimension of our identities. We want very much to learn more about each other's identities, which is a major reason the international community of music educators gathers together every two years, but without any sense that we either will be led to change our own identity to that of another, or that creating a "melting pot" identity—an amalgam of all our group identities—is the purpose of such meetings or of the many other international involvements in which many music educators participate. We want to influence one another by sharing our ideas and practices and musics, but with no desire, I take it, to lose any of the distinctive characteristics each of our cultures gives us.

The counterbalance to this focus on our different cultures is that all of us, at the same time that we are members of a particular culture, are, universally, music educators, and therefore a group separate from and different from others in the world. Our identification as music educators cuts across our national citizenship, unifying us in a common cause, common interests, common problems, and common beliefs. That is also why we cooperate in a variety of endeavors and meet every two years, to celebrate our universality as a subculture, our shared characteristics transcending our cultural differences. Our international music education community is in many respects a real community, influential in who we are and how we act, just as is the particular national community in which we live.

So the universal dimension of our identification as music educators coexists paradoxically but comfortably with our separateness. That is why I believe it is worthwhile to focus our attention on the philosophical aspects of our universal identity. We can, I believe, respect our particularities of cultural identifications, and at the same time attempt to clarify that which we hold in common as music educators. A universal philosophy of music education, then, would consist of a statement of beliefs and values shared by, or at least potentially able to be shared by, many or most if not all music educators from all parts of the world.

In the following discussion I will focus, in turn, on three dimensions of the task of articulating a universal philosophy of music education. First, I will suggest that there is a level of values, not very far below the surface, at which it would not be terribly difficult for widespread agreement to be reached among the world community of music educators. I will mention several such values for illustration.

Second, I will argue that while we can start the journey toward universality with such values, they do not take us very far, and we will have to face more difficult and contentious issues if we are to make significant progress toward a universal philosophy. I will discuss several influential positions on what the most consequential values of music and music education might be, and I will suggest that none of them separately can be adequate for a universal philosophy.

Third, I will argue that our most difficult philosophical task will be to reconcile the seemingly disparate views these positions represent (along with disparities among positions I will not deal with here) in a gestalt which both includes all of them and transcends all of them. I will explain the point of view of a recent cultural anthropologist whose thinking, I believe, takes us quite far toward the formulation of such a gestalt, and I will argue that his success leads us to be optimistic that a convincing universal philosophy of music education might be possible to attain.

SOME VALUES HELD IN COMMON

Several values related to the music education enterprise seem to be embraced to a large extent across the spectrum of different generations, times, cultures, and nations. These values reflect a largely universal belief that music is or can be a positive force in people's lives, and that education can influence the quality of people's musical experiences in positive directions. While some cultural belief systems impose restrictions on which musics are acceptable (Tahir, 1996), and some provide little if any formal instruction in music in school settings, most if not all cultures, in all periods of history, have regarded music and the learning of music to be at least a desirable aspect of culture and often a deeply important aspect of culture. While a universal philosophy of music education will have to take account of some possible exceptions or reservations, it will be able to assume that as a whole music and music education are and have been valued sufficiently to be supported in various ways and at various levels across the world's cultures.

An outgrowth of the positive value music usually holds is the widespread belief that, ideally if not actually, some level of education about music should be accessible to all young people, in order for them to be able to participate in relevant ways in a culture's musical life. The level of support a culture is able to provide has of course varied and continues to vary greatly depending on a host of impinging factors, but it may generally if not entirely be accepted that universal access by the young to an effective musical education is a desideratum for most if not all cultures.

Increasingly, the value of comprehensiveness in music education may be claimed to be universally or at least widely recognized. This refers both to the variety of musics included in education and to the variety of involvements with those musics. Of course more internationally minded cultures are likely to want to include a greater diversity of music to be experienced than more insular cultures, but given the modern world's high level of interconnectedness it is reasonably safe to assume that the inclusion of musics from a range of cultures outside each particular culture, and representations of a range of musics from within each particular culture, is likely to be regarded as a positive value in most places around the world.

In the matter of the comprehensiveness of ways to be involved with music, cultures are likely to value the inclusion of as many as possible of the important ways music is manifested in them, and even to include involvements not native to their culture in order to expand people's experiences beyond their own particular cultural practices.

In cultures in which a great many musical involvements are indigenous, widely accessible, and valued, such as composing, performing, improvising, and listening, and a great variety of involvements related to them are equally accessible and valued, such as judging music, learning about various cultural contexts of music, addressing various aesthetic issues relating to music, viewing music as part of the larger family of arts and as related in various ways to subjects outside the arts, and so forth, comprehensiveness in the broadest sense becomes a goal of music education. In cultures less inclusive musically or educationally, more modest aspirations for comprehensiveness may suffice, although I believe that the wider conception is becoming more and more the benchmark around the world.

Other values at this level of common agreement might include a universal expectation that music education be supported in reasonable ways by every culture's education system; that music study for all children should represent thoughtful attempts to systematize learnings over time rather than to consist only of sporadic and unorganized activities; that obligations exist to offer children who have unusually high musical potentials the opportunity to discover and develop those potentials as fully as possible, but that educational opportunities to be involved with music should not be limited to only those who seem to have such potentials.

THE DEEPER PHILOSOPHICAL ISSUES

Values such as the above, in that they seem to be widely held across generations, times, cultures, and nations, can be a starting point for efforts to formulate a universal philosophy of music education. But while they are important they are also insufficient. By themselves they do not raise the deeper philosophical questions requiring to be asked and answered by any persuasive philosophical argument.

Such questions center around the assumption, mentioned briefly at the beginning of the previous discussion of values held in common, that music is widely regarded to be a positive dimension of human experience. Why, exactly, is music positive for people or essential for people? What is it about music that has caused it to be ubiquitous in all of human history and in all cultures? What are the values of music so important for the healthy actualization of human potentials that those values have often allied music with the spiritual dimension of human experience? While music at one end of its continuum of contributions to human welfare has been understood to provide light-hearted and momentary entertainment of modest conse- quence, it has also been understood at the other end of the continuum to offer the deepest, most profound satisfactions and meanings available to *homo sapiens*. How can such a diversity of contribution be accounted for, and how can music's potential for fulfilling the most deep-seated needs for significance in human life be actualized in education?

These questions take us to the heart of the philosophical enterprise, where philosophy is conceived as the attempt to understand and provide principles for how humans can lead more fulfilling lives. For us as educa- tors, that conception of the philosophical challenge needs to be paramount. That challenge, of course, is the most difficult in all of philosophy.

While I have in other places attempted to take a particular position on questions such as these (Reimer, 1989, 1992, 1995), my purpose here is more inclusive. I will discuss four influential positions that have been articulated about music's most important values and where such values reside. A universal philosophy of music education, I want to suggest, will have to take account of these four positions in some considered way and will have to reconcile them as mutually supportive components of an inclusive philosophy. I do not insist that the four positions I will discuss are the only possible ones that can be taken; only that they need to be included in any examination of major options that attempt to explain the most significant values of music and music education.

(a) Formalism

The first of the four positions is one which emphasizes the products of musical creativity, usually called musical works or pieces, as being the key component in understanding what music is and does, why it should be val- ued, and what about music is most important in education.

In this position the domain of music is characterized first and foremost by its tangible examples—those events created by people intending to create them (such people being called musicians) and being sharable by others (generally called consumers, audiences, percipients, responders, and so forth). Such people approach works of music as potential bearers of the kind of experience often called "aesthetic experience." The purpose of being a musician is to create works of music. Anyone who creates a work of music—a formed sonorous event in which its content of meaningful, interconnected occurrences is a major reason for its being—is, by virtue of engaging in musical creativity, at that moment of engagement "being a musician." A child creating a melody on a set of bells, guided in the process by decisions about which sounds seem to be musically compelling, is 'being a musician' (in this case a composer or improviser), and the melody, however simple, limited, or naïve, is nevertheless a genuine instance of music. A great composer creating an elaborate piece is doing essentially the same thing, but at a very different level of expertise.

"Music," then, is not the quality of the activity or product, but the kind of thing being done, the making of particular kinds of events different from all other events because they exist to do the particular thing music does—to create, with sounds, significant or intrinsically meaningful forms, embodying sets of interrelations capable of yielding musical responses by those able to be engaged appropriately with them.

Because of its focus on artistically formed materials as the *sine qua non* of music (and of all the arts) this position has usually been called "formalism." In its narrow sense, as a term used to identify a particular philosophical movement among several influential thinkers in the West at the end of the nineteenth and beginning of the twentieth centuries, formalism was a position which separated or isolated works of art from all other human endeavors. These formalists insisted that the experience of art was essentially unconnected to all other life experiences. They argued that form in and of itself was the bearer of artistic and aesthetic value and should not be polluted by concerns other than excellence of form. The great works of art—construed to be the exemplars of artistic form in Western culture—were unlikely, they felt, to be sharable in aesthetically meaningful ways by those not inherently or through concentrated education able to immerse themselves in the aesthetic meanings contained in artistically formed materials.

Such beliefs have continued to exert influence to this day in the Western world and much of the rest of the world, and continue to affect many music education practices. Focusing on the "great works of music" (the counterpart to the "great books") as the appropriate examples for study, cultivating the musical talents of those with special gifts as being the main purpose of music education, elevating the taste of the masses to be able to better appreciate the exemplars of music as an additional obligation of music education, improving the level of a culture by supporting its "classical" or "serious" music as opposed to its "popular" or "transient" music; all these are remnants of formalistic beliefs as they were articulated by several influential thinkers a century or so ago (Bell, 1914; Fry, 1924; Hanslick, 1891).

As with most other positions in philosophical aesthetics, formalism may be understood to exist in degree, or on a continuum. At one end of the continuum the focus on formed products can be so narrow as to exclude many important dimensions of music not entirely attributable to the form of musical works. At the other end of the continuum formed sounds continue to be understood to be an essential component of music, but additional dimensions, such as represented by the three other positions I will explain, are also seen to be important in establishing the nature of music as a way of bringing a particular kind of meaning into being through intrinsically significant forms musically created. Construed in this broader way, formalism, I will argue, will be a necessary ingredient in a universal philosophy of music education.

(b) Praxialism

In contrast to formalism, which emphasizes products as the major distinguishing characteristic of that realm of human endeavor called music, and the intrinsically compelling form of those products as their major feature qualifying them to be regarded as musical, "praxialism" emphasizes the process—the doing, the acting, the creating involved in music—as being the essence of music. The products of the process are decidedly secondary. Products are outcomes of the doing: attention should be paid to pieces of music not as having an identity in their own right, capable of yielding meanings separate from the acts and circumstances of their coming into being, but as necessarily and essentially connected with those acts and having meaning only insofar as those acts themselves determine their meanings. Indeed, one responds to music as something being done, not to the product of that doing. Music should primarily be construed as a verb—"musicing" if you will. To "music" is to do a certain kind of thing—to make sounds that a particular culture, through its accumulation of musical doings, construes to be what musicing properly consists of.

Just as formalism exists in degree, ranging from the fundamentalist, or orthodox, or dogmatic version all the way to construals quite open, inclusive, and broad-ranging, praxialism also exists along that spectrum from the conservative to the liberal.

Recently a very clear example of fundamentalist praxialism has been articulated by Elliott (1995), arguing that "what music is, at root, is a human activity," "a particular form of action." "Fundamentally, music is something people do" (pp. 14, 39). Music should not be conceived as being a product, according to this position. Even a well-recognized, revered instance of music such as Beethoven's *Eroica* Symphony must not be regarded as having an authentic individuality, a "beingness" in and of itself, but instead can only be understood as an outgrowth of what Beethoven did, and the doing, not the outcome, is what is important. "What we are presented with [in the *Eroica*] is the outcome of a particular kind of intentional human activity" (p. 39). This is the case, Elliott argues, with any and all so-called musical products. All are to be seen and understood and valued as process manifestations. The process is paramount. The manifestation is adjunctive.

Because of this overwhelming focus on process, and depreciation of the product of the process, Elliott's extreme version of praxialism focuses overwhelmingly on performance as the major goal, purpose, and value of music and music education. To appreciate music one must be a performer. To understand music one must be a performer. To value music appropriately one must be a performer. And to learn music, the single, essential, required thing one must do is to learn to perform.

Music education, then, consists, at all levels, and in all situations, of instruction in performance. For Elliott, no distinction exists among various aspects of a music program such as general music or various electives because all instruction in music is always the same—learning music equals learning to perform music, performance being the correct way to encounter music in all its dimensions (Elliott, 1995).

While music education all over the world has always included performing as one important or even essential way to be involved with and to learn about music, and while some cultures, such as that of the USA, have historically given major emphasis to performance, few if any other music educators, even in the USA, have taken the extreme position about it argued by Elliott. It is difficult to conceive a music education program in any generation, time, culture, or nation which did not include instruction in performance as one important component. But it is also difficult to conceive any music education program that is so massively devoted to performance as the be-all and end-all of what should be learned about music as to neglect or even denigrate the need to encounter music and to learn about music in ways other than performing.

The fact is, in many cultures around the world most people do not perform as the major way they enjoy music in their lives, or even as a secondary way, and this is fast becoming more and more the reality in most cultures around the world. As music educators who have themselves largely been involved with music as performers of it we may regret that others do not share our perspective on the importance of performance. But we cannot be so narcissistic as to insist that our particular priority for how music can be enjoyed must determine the musical choices all people should make.

Especially at this point in history, when more and more music educators around the world are recognizing and beginning to cope with the narrowness of what school music programs have consisted of, and are opening up opportunities for students to be engaged in the rich diversity of musical involvements and learnings becoming more and more accessible around the world, we can no longer assume that so long as our students are singing and playing we are doing all we can do to provide an effective music education. The newly adopted national standards for musical education in the USA are one example of an important movement toward comprehensiveness in the music curriculum. While those standards were conceived in the context of that particular culture, there seems to be, around the world, a growing recognition that we have served students poorly by being so narrowly focused on performing.

Certainly we can agree universally that performance remains a crucially important dimension of musical experience and of musical education. We can appreciate, universally, the challenges and gratifications of performance as a deeply cognitive act, in which, as I have argued, humans are afforded one of their relatively few ways to be intelligent (Reimer, 1994). We can honor and celebrate the role of process in music as an essential aspect of what music is, because no musical products can exist without the processes that create them. However, no processes in music can be separated from the products—the musical results of the processes—which always determine the nature and quality of the processes being employed.

Formalism, when understood as calling attention to the products created by musical processes and how those products can be experienced, and praxialism, when understood as calling attention to the processes by which musical products come into being and are shared, are not, except in their extremist versions, incompatible. Indeed, music cannot exist without products and processes as completely interdependent.

Music education, I would argue, will have to incorporate a balanced, mutually supportive amalgam of principles from both formalism and praxialism if it is to be authentic to the nature of music as it has existed in all generations, times, cultures, and nations, and if it is to serve the musical needs of all students in the world today and in the future. Music education will not be able to accomplish this under fundamentalist, or extreme versions of formalism or praxialism, as exemplified by turn-of-the-century writers about the former and by David Elliott recently about the latter. But if we are able to look beyond the severe and debilitating restrictions those exaggerated positions proposed we will be able to exploit to useful ends the insights about products and processes, and the balance of the two, embedded in reasonable construals of both formalism and praxialism.

(c) *Referentialism*

Under the heading "referentialism" I mean to include a variety of positions about the essential nature and value of music and of music education different from those focusing on either music as product or as process. While there is a good deal of diversity among these positions they share the conviction that, fundamentally or primarily, the values of music are gained less from conceiving music as significant form or significant action than from conceiving it as a powerful instrumentality for achieving values to which music can lead us. Such values, while resulting from involvements with music as product or process, are not focused on either the products or processes as the locus of those values. The consequent, or derivative values of musical engagements are what count in determining whether those musical engagements are valuable or desirable.

Two general types of referentialism can be identified. The first tends to focus on the content of experience people have when engaged with a piece of music either as a listener or as a composer, and sometimes as a performer. The referentialist listener attends to the sounds being heard (the product) and to the sounds as they are made (the process) with the assumption that those sounds contain a message or messages not unlike those communicated by the sounds of language. Musical sounds, like words, refer. They point outside of themselves to meanings, images, ideas, emotions, descriptions of places, things, people, events, and so forth.

All music, in this view, is essentially programmatic. Music with words is obviously so. The words transmit the music's meanings and the sounds through which the words are enunciated reinforce those meanings. Music without words functions in the same way, except that more imagination has to be exerted to locate and identify the meanings, especially if the composer has not assisted in that task by indicating, as in a title or in program notes, what the music is referring to.

So, because music without words does not always refer clearly or directly, the listener must "interpret" its meaning by seeking a variety of clues, inside the music, in the kinds of gestures it is presenting, and/or outside the music, as in the circumstances surrounding the music's origination or its connection with cultural events and so forth. Whether the meanings of music are designated by its words, or by its stipulated or interpreted programs, or by its association with cultural events or artifacts or practices, referentialism proposes that musical experience be conceived, at least largely if not entirely, as the recognition of such meanings and their incorporation as an essential ingredient in one's experience.

Music, then, is to be regarded as a particular way in which "communication" occurs, the language model of communication being the paradigm. Composers have messages to communicate. They choose sounds which will encode those messages to make them receivable. Performers transmit those messages by means of their skills of expressing them. Listeners decode the messages to the extent they are skilled in the ways music requires one to grasp the messages being communicated. Music is good, or valuable, to the extent the communicated messages are culturally regarded to be good, valuable, and effectively communicated.

The second general type of referentialism is usually less connected to that term in the literature of philosophy of music, but conveniently can be included under it. In this view music is a useful instrumentality for the achievement of a great many aims stemming from musical involvements but leading out from them to nonmusical consequences. Such consequences have typically been claimed to be, for example, the attainment of discipline, or of heightened social skills, or better ability to succeed in nonmusical school subjects, or increased critical thinking skills, and a plethora of additional outcomes musical involvements are believed by some to foster.

Often the nonmusical results of musical experiences claimed by this version of referentialism are quite general, such as "self-growth," "enjoyment," "self-esteem," and "optimal experience" (what Mihalyi Csikszentmihalyi termed "flow") (Elliott, 1995, pp. 109–136). The broad nature of such outcomes sets them further along the continuum of the auxiliary benefits from musical involvement than the previous, more specific values.

Referentialism, whatever its type, has two troublesome consequences for music education. First, in looking outward from musical experience in seeking to locate its value, referentialism ignores or denigrates the philosophical attempt to explain how music has values inherent within it; values peculiar to and obtainable only from musical engagements.

Second, the referentialist point of view leads inevitably to the logical conclusion that the values of music are just as readily available from a great many involvements having nothing to do with music as they are from music. The combination of seeking outward rather than inward for benefits of music, with the inevitable result that any benefits identified will also be achievable without music, puts music, and therefore music education, on shaky ground as to justifications for supporting it and as to decisions about what and how to teach about it. Certainly, every subject important to include in schooling will have consequences additional to those intimately connected to the ways of thinking, experiencing, and knowing inherent within that subject. Certainly, we can universally hope that positive consequences, such as, for example, self-growth, enjoyment, self-esteem, and optimal experience will occur in students' lives from the study of every subject in which they are engaged, and therefore will add, serendipitously, to the particular values of studying those subjects.

This applies to music just as well (when the claimed values actually do occur as a result of musical involvements, at any rate). So we can certainly include auxiliary values as a dimension of a universal philosophy of music education if we are careful not to neglect to focus on the unique products and processes which give music its essential reason for being.

Music's communicative function (I am using this term, remember, in the special sense in which it is analogous to language) does indeed play a role, often an important role, in the musics of many if not all cultures and times, so it will have to be accounted for in an acceptable universal philosophy, and music's instrumental utility can certainly be included appropriately. As with formalism and praxialism, referentialism by itself is insufficient as the sole basis for a convincing philosophy of music education. All three will have to contribute to such a philosophy.

(d) *Contextualism*

The final position I will discuss here, "contextualism," is less distinct than the other three even though those three obviously overlap a good deal. Contextualism is intertwined with each of the other three. Musical products and their intrinsically expressive or significant forms, on which formalism focuses, always exist in the context of particular cultures and times, so are contextualized by necessity. Musical processes as the practices of music-making employed in particular times and places are also, by necessity, situated in the beliefs, traditions, and values of those times and places: they are always contextual. And the referential context of music, whether in words or programmatic suggestions, as well as the auxiliary values claimed for musical involvements, are equally as located within time and place as the other two dimensions of music.

In addition, music always entails a product of some sort no matter how purposeful or casual; always entails a process of some sort no matter how studied or haphazard; can always be construed to refer or to yield concomitant values; and all those dimensions of music must exist within the context of particular systems of belief just as every other human endeavor must. These four positions, then, should be seen as four interconnected dimensions of a complex phenomenon dependent on all four in various configurations.

What makes each of them a "position" *is the particular dimension it emphasizes in explaining music.* Each of the emphases, as I have suggested, can be exclusive, in so magnifying that dimension as to obscure or even deny the existence of the others, or it can be inclusive, in which the dimension on which it focuses is seen to be particularly important but also dependent on or augmented by the others.

In the contextualist view, the sociocultural functions of music are the focus of attention. What matters most about music is its status as a means of cultural/social engagement. Music is, first and foremost, a playing out of, or manifestation of, or aural portrayal of, the psychological, emotional, political, and social forces of the human context in which it exists. As such, it is the function music plays in cultural participation that most explains its nature and its value.

Viewing music as bearing certain cultural traditions and values, as transmitting those traditions and values, as inculcating them, commenting on them, sometimes calling them into question or even opposing them; that is, viewing music as an instrumentality for engagement with the traditions and values of a particular culture is what is emphasized in the contextualist point of view. Music must be issues-oriented, value-centered, sociologically and politically involved in the culture's ongoing life.

At one extreme of the contextualist belief system the very existence of the aesthetic domain, and of the arts as an identifiable phenomenon, are severely called into question:

> Some theorists in the late twentieth century have denied that the aesthetic and the "fine arts" can legitimately be separated out and understood as separate, autonomous human phenomena; they argue instead that these conceptual categories themselves manifest and reinforce certain kinds of cultural attitudes

and power relationships. These theorists urge that aesthetics can and should be eliminated as a separate field of study, and that "the aesthetic" should not be conceived as a special kind of value. They favor instead a critique of the roles that images (not only painting, but film, photography, and advertising), sounds, narrative, and three-dimensional constructions, have in expressing and shaping human attitudes and experiences. (Feagin, 1996, p. 11)

Related to this position is the institutional theory of art, which argues that art has no identifiable, intrinsically recognizable qualities, but instead becomes art by virtue of being conferred that status by the institutions that constitute the art world. Music, then, is whatever a culture's institutional policy-makers decide to call music (Danto, 1964; Dickie, 1974).

Attempts to deconstruct the concept of music as being a recognizable phenomenon among other phenomena that are not music; that is, attempts to so contextualize music that music no longer exists as something with any identifiable qualities, are interesting, provocative, and no doubt convincing to some degree. But that degree need not be so excessive as to negate the equally interesting, provocative, and convincing positions espoused by formalism, praxialism, and referentialism when each of them is understood inclusively rather than dogmatically. We can recognize the essentiality of context in our construals of what music is and does while at the same time recognizing that what music is and does has to do with something identifiably musical. Here is the way Roger Scruton attempts to recognize both the contextual and the musical dimensions of musical functioning, each playing its roles in the human capacity for musical understanding:

What is the aim of art? The first thing to say is that every work of art aims to secure a certain response from its audience. This response is not to the "information contained" in the work, but to the work itself. To put it slightly differently: the work of art is designed as the object of a certain response and is therefore composed on the assumption that the response in question is possible, that it lies within the available human repertoire. Responses depend upon prevailing psychological and social conditions. And if a response is to be significant to the person who feels it, it must bear some relation to his life as a whole: it must be part not only of his enjoyment, but also of his *concern*. Musical communication is possible only because certain sounds are heard as music—are heard, in other words, as exhibiting a certain "intentional order," the order of rhythm, melody and harmony. This order is not a material property of the physical world. It resides in the perceptual experience of those who hear with understanding. Unless such people exist, or can be brought into existence, the act of composition is incoherent. (Scruton, 1986, p. 353)

Our task in regards to contextualism, I suggest, as with each of the other positions, is to recognize and honor its insights while avoiding doctrinaire extremes to which it can take us.

TOWARD A UNIVERSAL PHILOSOPHY

How can we incorporate the insights of the four points of view I have described in a universal philosophy of music education which includes the particular position each view calls us to acknowledge and also transcends the particularities of each of them? It is highly unlikely, in my opinion, for a philosophy of music education to be developed that is sufficiently broad and deep to warrant a claim to universality if these four positions are not given all due consideration as components of such a philosophy. Reconciling these four positions, along with others I have not attempted to discuss here, will no doubt be difficult, especially in the face of extreme versions of each. I continue to believe that the attempt is worth making, if only to clarify for all music educators all over the world what it is we hold in common at the level of our deepest values and fundamental beliefs.

As a step in this direction I want to call attention to the thinking of the cultural anthropologist (he called himself a "humanistic" anthropologist) Robert Plant Armstrong (1970, 1971, 1975, 1981) whose books explore a variety of the world's cultures, with emphasis on the art of those cultures. Armstrong (1975) deals with Yoruba culture and the roles the arts play in it. The book is intended to present a paradigm case for the roles the arts play in all cultures in all times and places.

Armstrong's (1975) humanistic stance differs from traditional anthropological work in its focus on the varieties and qualities of human experience as these shed light on the nature and value of such experience. Rather than simply describing the various structures of a culture, as if those structures themselves explain a culture, Armstrong attempts to get beneath the structures and patterns endemic to a culture, to the level at which the condition and experience of being human in that culture can be glimpsed. "Humanistic anthropology recognizes the culturally obscure, nonverbal, aconceptual nature of much of human experience and so seeks 'evidence' different from that of traditional anthropology" (pp. 2, 3). So humanistic anthropology is an "inner" rather than "outer" anthropology, seeking to reveal and understand the lived, experienced meanings of people in a culture.

Since the inner can only be made manifest in the outer, the humanistic anthropologist regards a culture's manifested patterns of activity as containing a significance beyond, or below, any description of it, at the level of the very beingness, or phenomenality, the culture provides for its members. At this level we reach a universal condition of all cultures—that all derive from a common imperative which is aconceptual and existential. Armstrong's (1975) work is devoted to the exploration of this "progenerative imperative in the universe of experience, lying determinedly, if enigmatically, at the root of all phenomena of culture, giving to them an identity and order" (p. 8). Such explorations, Armstrong suggests, are powerfully accomplished through the study of a culture's arts.

The field devoted to the study of the arts is aesthetics. For the anthropologist, Armstrong argues, aesthetics "is best defined as the *theory or study of form incarnating feeling*" (p. 11). But since the word "feeling" is often construed in its restricted, romantic sense as referring to specific emotions such as joy, sadness, and so forth, the word "affect," he proposes, is probably more apt.

> Indeed a work may be created not to incarnate a feeling [emotion] at all, but rather an unaccountable and basic fact of one's awareness, about which one feels significantly. Thus, as we shall see, it is possible to incarnate in the affecting presence [the work of art] . . . the very primal stuff of the universe as it is presumed by a particular people to be. (Armstrong, 1975, p. 11)

The affecting presence—an artwork—is not grasped when the work is conceived merely as an object, or as a function, or as a symbol which communicates. These are all facets of the affecting presence but they do not account for the profundity of what artworks accomplish:

> The affecting presence is at least a direct presentation of the feelingful dimension of experience. It proceeds at its root not through mediation, as a symbol does—though it may do this as well—but through what we may only call *immediation*. The affecting presence is directly and presently what it is, and precisely is in those physical-significant terms in which it is presented for our witnessing. My use of this term "witnessing" rather than "viewing" or "seeing" or "hearing" or "perceiving" is intended to suggest not only that the confrontation between man and work is an *act* but also that it is an act of consequence to which the role of witness is of critical importance. What we behold in the affecting presence is less of the world of object than a phenomenon of the personal world of man—not a utensil but an act ever in the process of enacting itself—an instance of incarnated experience. . . . The study of the affecting presence is the study of man in those terms which finally are his definitive ones, that is to say those that comprise the elements of the process of living-as-a-man. His presented experience in the affecting presence brings us his

living forms, *the living forms of his consciousness.* Though affecting works may have ascribed, referential functions which may serve to make symbols or signs of some of them, nonetheless what they are in and of themselves are presentations of being. Indeed insofar as a particular work embodies the cultural form—that least common denominator of particularity which uniquely establishes one culture—it is a presentation of the basic and irreducible being of the culture. Great works, it goes without saying, greatly incarnate these vitalities. (Armstrong, 1975, pp. 19, 20)

The "vitalities" of consciousness itself are charged with feeling, in that they are the foundational determinants of all that humans can experience. Artworks present to the world certain feeling-charged experiences and beliefs through culturally derived restraints and schemata that the materials of the arts provide, so that affect and values can be managed, given form, made palpable in the affecting presence of a work of art.

Each culture gives its own stamp—its own set of qualities of inner experience—to the artworks produced within it, so each culture embodies (incarnates) in its arts the patterns of affect shared within that culture. What is universal about the affecting presence, about music, for example, is not a universal affect: each culture's affective quality of life experience is its own. What is universal is music's power to incarnate its culture's affective consciousness—to universally serve as a powerful means for processes to be activated which capture within them, in the forms they produce, the outward manifestations of the aconceptual, experienced meanings at the root of the human condition as each culture experiences that condition.

Music, universally, is sonic form incarnating affect. Music, culturally, is the particularity of the affect incarnated by a culture's musical processes as they create its musical products.

Armstrong provides in this particular book a series of detailed, penetrating analyses of several Yoruba artworks. In these analyses his attention ranges over the formal structures of the works, the dynamic interactions of their elements, the artists' skills and insights and affective sensitivities in the processes of creating these expressive forms, and the cultural references incorporated as meaningful dimensions of the works but transformed into deeper meanings by the ways they are made to embody meaning rather than only to refer to meaning. These intimately interactive forces of product, process, and subject (or reference), are activated in the context of the implicit cultural consciousness within which the artist works and for which the artist provides tangible presences for all to experience:

> The universality of affecting works suggests that consciousness is character-ized at least in part by a need to electrify the external world with the dynamics of its own vitality, humanizing it [the external world] after its own image. Thus does man make the world! . . . It is a human imperative that consciousness be imposed upon the world: it is a cultural imperative that in a *particular* group of people *particular* patterns of knowing and feeling prevail. . . . In the affecting presence we witness consciousness itself laid bare and existent. . . . The affecting presence incarnates consciousness itself, in its own terms, and it arrests flux, fixes the mutable, renders physical the metaphysical. . . . The af-fecting presence . . . *celebrates* consciousness. (Armstrong, 1975, pp. 79–90)

It is impossible in the context of this paper, unfortunately, to explain, in the detail it deserves, Armstrong's insights into what he calls the "most basic *human* need"—the need to create presences, artworks, which incarnate the dynamics of consciousness to be shared in experience with others in one's culture. The implications of his thinking are profound for music education, I believe.

They point us in a direction in which musical products, considered as affecting presences, can be understood to arise out of the consciousness each culture exists to foster, are created through the culturally sanctioned processes relevant to the forming of "consciousness-instilled immedia" (p. 81) and in which the culture's experiences and values are referred to and transformed into sharable embodiments. The dimensions of form, practice, reference, and context are seen through his vision to be inseparable compo-nents of music, in what music is, what it does, and how it serves the deepest of human needs.

Music education, it can be argued under this conception, celebrates and perpetuates the most fundamental quality of the human condition—that humans are conscious of themselves among other similar selves, are capable of experiencing the qualities of that consciousness, are capable of creat-ing presences which make that human condition sensible (available to our senses) and therefore sharable. The tasks of a universal philosophy of music education are to build on these insights, to further reconcile what only seem to be irreconcilable viewpoints, to honor the distinctiveness of each of the world's cultures and musics, and to continue to clarify that which is univer-sal about both culture and music.

These tasks, I believe, can indeed be accomplished convincingly and use-fully. To the degree we are successful in doing so our worldwide profession can become more unified while retaining its precious diversity. And our music education practices, by incorporating balanced attention to musical products, processes, references, and contexts, can best represent to all students the power of music to provide fulfillments at the deepest levels of human need.

REFERENCES

Armstrong, R. P. (1970). *Forms and processes of African sculpture*. Austin: University of Texas African and Afro-American Research Institute.

Armstrong, R. P. (1971). *The affecting presence: an essay in humanistic anthropology*. Urbana: University of Illinois Press.

Armstrong, R. P. (1975). *Wellspring: on the myth and source of culture*. Berkeley: University of California Press.

Armstrong, R. P. (1981). *The power of presence: consciousness, myth, and affecting presence*. Philadelphia: University of Pennsylvania Press.

Bell, C. (1914). *Art*. New York: Putnam.

Danto, A. (1964). The artworld. *Journal of Philosophy*, 571–584

Dickie, G. (1974). *Art and the aesthetic*. Ithaca, NY: Cornell University Press.

Elliott, D. J. (1995). *Music matters*. New York: Oxford University Press.

Feagin, S. L. (1996). "Aesthetics." In Robert Audi (Ed.), *The Cambridge dictionary of philosophy*. Cambridge: Cambridge University Press.

Fry, R. (1924). *The artist and psycho-analysis*. Hogarth Essays London: Hogarth.

Hanslick, E. (1891). *The beautiful in music*. London: Novello.

Reimer, B. (1970, 1989). *A philosophy of music education*. Englewood Cliffs, NJ: Prentice Hall.

Reimer, B. (1992). "What knowledge is of most worth in the arts?" In Bennett Reimer and Ralph A. Smith (Eds.), *The arts, education, and aesthetic knowing*. Chicago: University of Chicago Press.

Reimer, B. (1994). Is musical performance worth saving? *Arts Education Policy Review, 95*(3), January/February, 10–12.

Reimer, B. (1995). The experience of profundity in music. *The Journal of Aesthetic Education, 29*(4), Winter.

Scruton, R. (1986). "Musical understanding and musical culture." In Philip Alperson (Ed.), *What is music?* New York: Haven.

Tahir, R. (1996). Musical experience from an Islamic perspective: implications for music education in Malaysia. Ph.D. dissertation, Northwestern University.

5

ONCE MORE WITH FEELING: RECONCILING DISCREPANT ACCOUNTS OF MUSICAL AFFECT

"**[D]**espite so much attention to [musical affect, or feeling] over the centuries, we have not yet reached a definitive resolution and perhaps never will."

In this quote from the following article, I recognize the indeterminacy of the issue of musical feeling despite its having been tackled by so many important thinkers over the centuries, by so many musicians in pursuit of it and listeners sharing it in every imaginable musical context, and by so many music educators striving to bring it into being in their students.

No wonder I am drawn to the issue over and over again, each time getting a bit closer to and wiser about the nature of this phenomenon while not expecting to ever entirely solve its puzzles. Those who teach music want to help their students get as much of its essential gift as they possibly can. The clearer we are about what there is to get and how to get it, the better we can assist in its acquisition.

In this address to an International Symposium on Philosophy of Music Education, I suggest a potentially useful reconciliation between two well-known, long-standing, and foundational aspects of musical affect, the "inherent" (how musical sounds themselves capture and display feeling) and the "delineated" (how musical sounds portray or refer to beliefs, situations, and events that are then the bases for what is felt). I argue that these two seemingly incompatible positions can be reconciled, and that doing so allows us to be better teachers. We can then more effectively (and affectively) influence the musical feelings our students undergo in their creation of musical experiences, whether in the role of musicians or of participant-consumers of the offerings of musicians.

I also challenge the assembled music education scholars/philosophers to rethink whom the philosophy of music education is for. "Doing philosophy" is as important for all our students, no matter their age, as it is for us professionals. It is impossible to become more musical without being thoughtful about what music is all about: its values, its approaches to experience, its pleasures and fulfillments. Until we philosophers pay serious attention to infusing all musical learning with "knowing why" human beings treasure music, we will have left our students bereft of an essential foundation for musical experience. A new level of practical relevancy for students of music and their teachers appears for those who, like philosophers, specialize in thinking carefully and deeply.

The following essay was originally published by Indiana University Press in the *Philosophy of Music Education Review* 12, no. 1 (Spring 2004). Used by permission.

When I was sixteen, a junior in high school in Brooklyn, I auditioned for the All-City High School Band of New York and was placed as first chair clarinet. At the first rehearsal, a piece we played (I don't remember what it was except that it was new to me) had a long, melodic clarinet solo, with accompaniment. When I finished playing it the director stopped the band and said "Very nice, first clarinet. Let's do it again, this time with more feeling." Then he said "Letter C," (or whatever) and we started again.

I could not have known, then, that I was to spend much of my life in pursuit of some sort of clarification of what transpired in that episode, as in this paper, where I deal once more with feeling. I had no idea that his apparently simple instruction to me raised issues so complex that many of humankind's most important thinkers had struggled with them in search of a resolution, as I, infinitely more modestly, was also to do. I was unaware that philosophical blood, sweat, and tears had been spilled through the centuries in various contentions as to the relation, if any, of musical feeling to feeling outside musical experience. I knew nothing of metaphor, of effability and ineffability, of embodiment and designation, of issues of authenticity of feeling, and semantic density, significant form, semiotics, the relation of feeling to emotion, to gender, to meaning, and on and on with seemingly endless and intractable debates centered on how and why and when music is related to feeling.

Being unencumbered with any of this (how one longs, sometimes, to return to one's philosophical Garden of Eden) and having to play that solo again immediately, I did what my novice performer's instincts told me to do—the only thing I knew how to do. I placed more emphasis on what the notes of that melody seemed to want to do, where they seemed to want to go and how they got there. Feeling their melodic tendencies more concentratedly and making them more apparent by the way I sounded them, I felt in myself a deeper sense of union—of the music as part of my undergoing—than I had the first time.

When I finished, the director stopped the band again, looked at me for several seconds, and said "Lovely, first clarinet. Very musical. Let's go on."

I would not have been able at the time that event occurred to describe, as I just did, what I did and how I felt. I did not have the conceptual apparatus to do so, although I did have, luckily for me, enough intuitive musicianship to have survived that test. My description or perhaps interpretation of how I reacted and how I experienced it can only reflect who I am now, with the cognitive structure allowing me to understand what happened as I reflect about it. Nevertheless I believe that several important matters relating to musical feeling can be clarified in relation to how I now interpret what I experienced as a youth in that band.

I am aware now that I did what I did in ignorance of the fact that I was not the first to have played that solo. If I had known about and studied previous performances by a variety of clarinetists I would have, without doubt, been influenced by their solutions to the challenge of expressive interpretation it presented. Especially if I had been guided by a sensitive teacher, I would have reflected those influences in my own sounding. Perhaps I would have imitated what seemed to me the most musical rendition. If I had done so, I am now aware, that would have been regarded, in my culture at any rate, as a sign of my novice status, a more mature stage of musicianship requiring that I both reflect the history of previous interpretations, that is, of performance practice, and also contribute to the evolution of that practice by what I added to it.

Consider now the assumptions about musical feeling embedded in what I have articulated so far. Musical feeling is contained within or is a function of the way the notes in a melody suggest, because of established expectations for how that particular melodic system functions as a culturally determined artifact, the ways they can properly interact within that system. To play "musically," which essentially means to play "with appropriate feeling," requires that one be aware, whether overtly or covertly, of the rules and regulations culturally established, to reflect them in one's sounding and, in Western and other cultures, to add one's own imaginative expressions to those considered exemplary.

Musical feeling, then, resides in how performers, guided by the sounds imagined by the composers they are interpreting, actualize the interactive sound-implications a musical system affords. Feeling is undergone by the person or persons doing the sounding and is also undergone or potentially undergone by those who hear what has been sounded, who when feeling what the melodic events have been caused to do can judge the result as being, say, "very musical." That means suffused with feeling as a function of tones sounded in a particular way.

And while I have used melodic interactions as my example the assumptions can be applied validly to any and all interactive dimensions such as rhythm, timbre, texture, dynamics, and so on, in any and all musical systems. And the melody in question (or the rhythm or whatever) need not be composed, of course. It can just as well be improvised. The performance practice would then be of the accepted ways improvisation is accomplished in the culture in which that particular instance of it resides and the history of improvisations with that particular instance. The basic assumption remains intact, that feeling is contained and expressed in sounds configured within some musical system and that the way the sounds are disposed in relation to each other within that system is the way they will be felt.

This assumption resides comfortably within a view of musical affect variously described as embodiment, or intra-musical expressiveness, or intrinsicality, immanence, presentational form, significant form, innateness, incarnation, indwelling, interiority, and so forth. All these terms, and others that various thinkers have used, express the belief—and the practice of that belief—exemplified in what I did with that clarinet solo to "play it with more feeling" and by the band director's response to what I did. So common is that belief system and the practice of it in Western and other cultural contexts that I am certain that all who have been performers within these cultural contexts have experienced what I experienced in the episode I related or, at the very least, understand precisely what occurred in that episode.

We understand what occurred because we share—we are saturated with—a culturally determined construct of how music works or, more accurately, one important way music works. That way has been so influential in Western history and elsewhere around the world as to have been one mainstay of philosophical reflection about music since such reflection began. While I was ignorant of that body of thought at age sixteen I had nevertheless breathed it in from the musical experience I had amassed as a budding performer within the classical tradition and within the jazz tradition. Both those traditions (the classical more dominant) led me to play out my culture's presumptions as I did. In that sense I was a testament to the success of my musical education (at least as a performer).

I want now to explore the substantive alternative belief system to that of inherence (if I may summarize the position I just described by that term). This is the construct called by Lucy Green and others "delineation." I hope this will clarify to some degree how complex the issue of musical affect is and why, despite so much attention to it over the centuries, we have not yet reached a definitive resolution and perhaps never will.

I was confronted with a delineation belief system in a dramatic and amusing way during my three-month study in China of the Chinese system of music education. In Chengdu, the capital city of Sichuan province (known to Chinese food enthusiasts for its fiery seasonings), I was treated to a private recital at the Chengdu Conservatory of Music by the faculty Traditional Chinese Music Ensemble. The first piece they played was what I would describe as an energetic, extremely active, and quite loud selection played on an assortment of traditional instruments. I admired the energy of their performance and the clearly virtuosic level of their playing.

When they finished, the apparent leader of the group (they play with no conductor) approached me and asked, in quite good English, "So what do you think that piece was about?"

If he had only known what a snake pit he had stepped into! I was completely thrown by his question. I had not assumed for a moment that what I was listening to was "about" anything. Clearly he and the others had not only assumed it was, they knew exactly what it was about, that is, something the sounds were describing or delineating, and expected that their performance would have made that something crystal clear to me. And if it didn't there was something very wrong either with me as a listener or with them as performers.

I wanted to please them, being more concerned about the social interaction with them than with matters of aesthetics, but for the life of me I could not conjure up any image or occurrence that would have anything vaguely to do with the musical affect I had undergone as I had listened. "Well," I said lamely, "it seemed to me to be about very active musical events with a great deal of inner energy and melodic and rhythmic complexity, coming to a climax shortly before the piece ended." He looked at me with incomprehension, as I knew he would. What he thought, I am sure, was either that I was a musical idiot or that their performance had utterly missed the mark. So he said, tactfully, "We'll play it again."

He spoke to the ensemble briefly and they repeated the piece, this time even louder and more frantically. I sat there in a cold sweat, desperately trying to think of a gracious way out of the dilemma this confrontation of two belief systems was causing. The best I could do was to say, when they finished, "Well, it sure is an exciting situation there." "But you still don't know what is going on?" I shook my head. "It's about a battle in a swamp," he said, incredulous that their performance could have been any clearer that that was what the music was describing. I suspect that he told the musicians, after the first performance, something like "Let's do it again, this time with more feeling—of a battle going on in a swamp." And the musicians were likely to have put themselves into the mood of conflict, feeling in themselves the forces of conflict and then more clearly projecting those feelings onto or into the music. I'm sure he thought, after their second performance, "Ah, very battle-like. Very swamp-like. He can't possibly not get it this time."

They played a few more pieces, but I sensed they were dispirited and they asked me no further questions. My effusive thanks and expressions of admiration when they had finished did not make up, I'm afraid, for their disappointment, either in me or themselves, for the failure to communicate.

What the Chinese musicians were attempting to do was to establish a clearly illustrative mood, not only as an abstraction—a "battle" mood—but specifically as the battle occurred in a swamp. All over the world, including in Western classical music, the view is shared by many that feeling in music is a function of delineation—the capturing in sounds of an emotion, mood, situation, or message delineated by those sounds and made apparent to others by the clarity of the delineation. Yes, Western music does have an entire literature with names such as *Symphony in D*, or *Quartet in Bb*, but there is also an important literature with names such as the *Eroica Symphony*, the *Pathetique Sonata, Danse Macabre*, and on and on, each designating a particular emotional content, parallel to the battle, that the music conjures up to be felt in experience. There is also, to go further, an equally important literature comparable to the swamp aspect—the specificity of imagery beyond mood or emotion: "La Mer," "The Blue Danube Waltz" "The March to the Gallows," "The Night on Bald Mountain," and so forth. These Western literatures reflect the belief, alive and well and flourishing, that music delineates, and thereby makes available for sharing, moods or emotions and also places and events and natural occurrences such as the seasons and cultural issues of a variety of sorts and so on, and the feelings associated with them.

But in Chinese musical practice as I witnessed it in countless observations of lessons, classes, demonstrations, and performances, a great deal of attention was paid to inherent characteristics of expressiveness having nothing whatsoever to do with delineation. Major effort was expended in pursuit of the exquisite refinement and subtle gradations of tonal relationships and rhythmic nuances, and so forth, that any of us would immediately recognize to be the quest for inherent musicality. So in China as in the West inherence and delineation are both alive and well, in practice at any rate.

Both those belief systems are cultural constructions, as all human beliefs are. Both capture a truth of sufficient persuasiveness to add useful meanings to the musical lives of those influenced by the beliefs. Because both inherence and delineation seem to have succeeded in apprehending a truth-seeming set of constructs, they have survived for a very long time and remain viable to this day.

For some people one position constitutes the whole truth and nothing but the truth, the other ipso facto being false. For some others, especially now under the influence of postmodernism (although its history stretches far back before that term existed) one is taken to be true but as one truth among others with valid claims to truth. (In postmodernist thinking, the rejection of essentialisms does not forbid a person from regarding a particular position as being true and acting accordingly, as the postmodern theorist Stanley Fish has pointed out. It only warns that one should avoid the belief that any truth is universal, thereby forbidding other, contending truths from existing.) For still other people both inherence and delineation are viable and interchangeable aspects of musical experience, to be called upon as different musics, different social situations, and different psychological/emotional/aesthetic needs or desires dictate, in kind of a "mix-and-match" position.

Underlying this assortment of responses is the assumption that there are, indeed, substantive, distinguishing differences between the two positions. So still another view about them is that there are no such differences, that both coexist in musical affect and musical experience, that underneath they are indistinguishable from one another. What seems to be inherent in "the conventional interrelationships of musical materials," as Green characterizes inherence, also at the same time "metaphorically sketches, or delineates, a plethora of contextualizing, symbolic factors," as she characterizes delineation.[1]

Much past and present philosophical debate about musical affect, musical meaning, and musical practice has to do, I believe, with the question of

how we are to understand inherence and delineation and their interrelationships (if any). The question also underlies much of our uncertainty, perhaps
confusion is a better word, about how properly to teach these fundamental
aspects of music. Until around the middle of the twentieth century both
positions tended to coexist in music education with little concern about or
awareness of their potentially conflicted—even corrosive—disaccordances.
With the advent of serious philosophical scholarship in music education as
we now conceive that to be, and crucially with the rise of postmodernism,
that naiveté could no longer be sustained. We have been thrown out of our
innocence, quite rudely as it has turned out, into a maelstrom of conten-
tion about how we can understand the implications of inner and outer or
whether such terms any longer make any sense in regard to musical experience and therefore to music education.

The position that inherence and delineation are distinct and irreconcilable and therefore that one is forced to choose between them on the assumption that truth is unitary seems to me unfortunate in its excessiveness.
Too much is lost in our ability to both explain and enjoy musics that seem to
exemplify one or the other condition authentically. A further disadvantage
of this one-sided view is that it is too simple, even a bit lazy. It avoids the
hard work of probing beneath the surface to discover if and how the two
might be related.

The position that both views are correct and can readily be called upon
as the basis for musical experience whenever one or the other is operative
is attractive in its inclusiveness. But it also seems to me to stop short of considering the more challenging and interesting issue of whether in fact they
are so distinct that a pluralistic position will suffice. Pluralism, I usually feel,
settles too soon for the obvious: that there are many different defensible
positions in our lives. Of course there are. But is that all there is to say? And
is that the best or only guide to how we should act? Underneath the surface
of what seems to be a plurality of convincing views is where the action is, I
would argue, both philosophically and operationally.

The mirror opposite of pluralism, that is, philosophical unitarianism in
which the two positions are seen as identical, avoids making distinctions even
when they seem to be required, as they do, I believe, in this case. That too
misses the action and therefore the possibility of deeper understanding.

That leaves us (or at least me) in the very uncomfortable position of believing that there are authentic distinctions between inherence and delineation and also believing that there are fruitful interrelations between them.
Preliminary to an attempt to resolve this dilemma it should be mentioned
that I, and I would suspect most if not all of us, assume that all music por-

trays or enacts or delineates the cultural assumptions under which it is conceived, whether to support, expand, critique, or undermine them. To put it in another way, inherent in each music is a culturally supplied assumptive base upon which it is founded.

I do not question that conviction. However, I will limit myself here to the distinction between inherence and delineation as exemplified by the performances of the clarinet solo and the swamp battle piece. And I include as delineation, in addition to musics intending to portray a mood, or emotion, or event, or locality, and so forth, those intending to make a social/political statement, whether about feminism, racism, sexual orientation, ethics, or any other such issue that music regularly addresses.

The complex problem of reconciling inherent and delineated characteristics is raised in a powerful way in Tia DeNora's sophisticated book, *Music in Everyday Life*.[2] She points out the extreme danger of attributing delineated meanings in "presumably abstract" contexts. She quotes the following passage from Susan McClary's book, *Feminine Endings: Music, Gender, and Sexuality*:

> The point of recapitulation in the first movement of Beethoven's Ninth Symphony unleashes one of the most horrifyingly violent episodes in the history of music. . . . The entire first key area in the recapitulation is pockmarked with explosions. It is the consequent juxtaposition of desire and unspeakable violence in the moment that creates its unparalleled fusion of murderous rage and yet a kind of pleasure in its fulfillment of formal demands.[3]

DeNora comments on this passage as follows:

> This reading is attenuated because it is not anchored in anything beyond the analyst's identification of connotations. Identifying abstractions such as "the feminine" or "the masculine," "violence" or sadistic "pleasure" (or for that matter any type of non-musical content) and perceiving these things "in" the music has no grounds outside of what the analyst says. It is therefore indistinguishable from simple assertion, from an "I'm telling you, it's there" form of analysis. . . . This strategy, which consists of a kind of linguistic legerdemain, helps to frame the reader's perception of her analytical object, so that the qualities perceived in the music itself can in fact be ones that have been attributed to it. This is what Agatha Christie's Miss Marple meant when she uttered the phrase, "they do it with mirrors."[4]

Here we are confronted with several questions that seem to me to be at the core of the issue. Are delineations necessarily *attributed* to the sounds of what DeNora calls "the music itself"? Are perceptions of mood, story,

feminist or racist or other delineations of the sounds heard, merely imposi-
tions by the commentator on sounds meaningful entirely on the basis of
their inherent interrelations?

Perhaps that is so, but many musical delineations seem so obvious (albeit
within cultural norms) as to strain credulity to deny them. Nevertheless
one can easily, even habitually, respond to music with seemingly evident
delineative content, whether in performing it or listening to it, with no
knowledge of or attention to or interest in its delineative aspects, the music
experienced entirely for inherence.

On the other hand, is the notion of inherent meaning undermined by the
fact of its being itself, necessarily, a cultural construction, not a God-given
absolute, and thereby susceptible to other such constructions such as delineative possibilities? Perhaps that is so, but we must also remember that, as
Shepherd and Wicke argue in their book, *Music and Cultural Theory*,

> No aspect of music is capable of being understood independently of the wider
> gamut of social and cultural processes . . . yet, *because* of this, it is possible that
> there are *aspects* of social and cultural processes which are revealed *uniquely*
> through their musical articulation. . . . There are aspects of affect and meaning
> *in culture* that can only be accessed through an understanding of the specific
> qualities of the signifying practices of music as a cultural form: that is, its
> sounds.[5] (Emphases in original)

We are back, here, to "the music itself" as the source of inherent meanings, available only from its sounds with no imposition of delineative content. Such meanings are as important in understanding a culture as understanding its cultural context is for understanding its music.

I do not deceive myself that these conundrums are entirely resolvable, as
the contentious history of musical aesthetics demonstrates. But I am willing
to suggest a possible accommodation that seems to me, while perhaps not
entirely solving the puzzles, to be a reasonable basis for both preserving
the validity of both inherence and delineation while also unifying them in
musical practice so that one position does not deny or exclude the other. I
will introduce my suggestion through several questions.

When I played that clarinet solo, would the choices I made about the
tonal tendencies the melody suggested have been influenced if I was reminded by the conductor of the calm, peaceful nature of the music in the
section in which the solo appeared? Or if the section was riotously boister-
ous, would being reminded of that have influenced me to make somewhat
different or significantly different decisions? In both these cases would such
delineations of mood quality have allowed me also to be deeply immersed

in the tonal tendencies the melody embodied? Or would such instructions by the director have impeded my ability to feel and sound those inherent tendencies? What if the director had said, "Let's do it again, this time with a smoother, more legato flow," or, "With more rhythmic energy." Would those instructions have influenced me in different ways than the delineative ones? Which of those scenarios, including the one that actually occurred, would have led to a "better" performance?

When the Chinese ensemble played its swamp battle piece for the first time were they ignoring or insensitive to the melodic/rhythmic/dynamic dimensions of the sounds in their inherent interrelations in the system of which that piece was an instance? In their second performance, intended to help their apparently ignorant guest "get the point," did they necessarily de-emphasize inherence in favor of delineations they hoped would be more apparent? If they did, would that have made that performance, as compared with the first, better or worse?

I want to propose that it is indeed possible to be appropriately influenced by delineations while also being guided by—being musically bound within—inherent sound-relations in whatever system is being employed. In such cases, I believe, delineations become music. That is, an idea or story or mood or message—whatever—is transformed into being music. The specifics of sound-interactions, as a culturally supplied system makes them available, can be influenced by—are to some extent determined by—delineations. But delineations become transfigured by immersing them within inherently meaningful sounds. If that were not so, if inherence had no role in musical affect, all affect being entirely dependent on delineations, it would be difficult to explain why music exists at all.

The affective experiences music offers, I submit, are necessarily functions of what sounds are made to do that add inherent meanings to any and all delineations, or to put it differently, that transmute delineations into musical inherence while also including the delineations as a dimension of that inherence. That transmutation is what is called "musical," and people who accomplish it are called "musicians." I believe Francis Sparshott may have gone too far in his treatment of this matter when he says, in his introductory chapter to the book, *What is Music*,

> The most approved uses of the [delineative] devices are those in which what is recognized and relished as referential is at the same time experienced as musical—that is, in which we feel that what we hear would be formally justified even if nothing were being referred to. . . . The characteristic musical delight in all such devices, for composers as much as for audiences, lies in the way

music is being made of them: the exact way in which, having been what they were, they have now become completely music.[6] (Emphasis in original)

If "completely music" means "devoid of delineation," as Sparshott seems to be saying, then for me his position would be too exclusive of delineation in its influence on and, therefore, its presence within inherence. For me, "completely music" can and often does include delineation in that it affects what inherence makes of it.

However, if delineation so outweighs inherence in any particular performance (or composition for that matter) that little or no transmutation into inherence has occurred we are likely to regard the result as lacking in musicality. I believe that is the case in every culture's music, at least of which I am aware, because every culture seems to recognize the transformative power of musical inherence and to cherish it and those who create it; that is, musicians.

So my answers to the questions I raised are that, while I could have indeed been influenced by my director's delineative suggestions, I would hope that they would not have diminished or eliminated my attention to inherent sound-gestures in that melody. If they did, my sounding would have been in danger of becoming a parody of music.

Would it have been safer, then, for the director to have made his suggestions in terms of, say, rhythm or articulation, as in the examples I gave, so as to avoid the possibility of a too extreme response in the direction of delineation? Remember, he was dealing with young and relatively inexperienced musicians who may not have been sufficiently sophisticated musically to have struck the needed balance. Or did he have an obligation to me and to the band to help us become more aware of the need for that balance by explicitly presenting us with the issue, leading us to recognize that delineative contents of a variety of types do indeed exist in music and that musicians must learn how to both include and transform them?

In the case of the Chinese ensemble, their first performance was influenced not only by their belief that music necessarily delineates but also by their being performers whose musicianship, reflecting their status as among the best in China, was as superbly what those in the West are likely to call "deeply musical" as those of, say, The Chicago Symphony Orchestra or the Dave Brubeck Quartet. In their zeal to make me get the delineated point, their second performance, I am certain, did distort their musicianship. I believe they felt embarrassed by that, a bit diminished by it, and that their subsequent dejection was caused at least in part by what they felt was their having played with less inherence than they should have.

My answers reflect my beliefs about the need for a particular kind of balance in the inherent and delineative dimensions of music. What about the view that argues for the opposite balance, that inherent characteristics serve as a means to enhance, intensify, and raise to higher levels of consciousness a variety of delineations that music exists to make apparent? Here we are thrown into the difficult but also extremely interesting issues of intentions, proclivities, interests, and purposes of people in their engagements with and beliefs about music. Conceived as a continuum, we would have at one end the formalist so pure in thralldom to inherence as to make Eduard Hanslick look like a social activist. At the other end, carrying a placard, would be the ideologue so devoted to a cause as to make Karl Marx look like an elitist. At these ends, the issue of balance is academic, pure inherence or pure delineation being music's goal and purpose. Proponents of each extreme would answer my questions radically differently from each other and from the way I answered them.

As is usually the case, it is the complex middle that poses the provocative dilemmas. I believe that, in addition to being more challenging philosophically than the extremes, the more holistic middle, embracing both dimensions of music's power and reconciling them as I have attempted to do or as others might do differently, gets us closer to a satisfactory resolution of the complex issues involved. "Closer" is probably as much as we can hope for in a realm where absolute truth is no doubt an illusion.

The position one takes about the workings of inherence and delineation in musical feeling will inevitably affect how one conceives the obligations of music education in regard to feeling. My position about the proper interrelation of the two has many practical consequences for teaching, as does every other view people might take. Fundamental to my view is that in engagements with music in the many musical roles cultures make available and for all students no matter their age or level of achievement, musical teaching should include attention to delineative aspects but not be content with them alone, separated from what inherence creatively does with them.

Sometimes, of course, one or the other will be emphasized for particular purposes and interests as, on the one hand, an exploration of different systems of tonality as they exist in a variety of world musics or, on the other hand, how music has been used around the world to both support and critique societal constructions of gender. Such concentrations on one or the other serve useful purposes as instruction proceeds. I would caution, however, that the general spirit in teaching best serves musical experience when instruction about details of inherence are constantly embedded in contexts related to feeling in actual music, and when explorations of de-lineations are placed in contexts in which they are understood to influence feeling while also necessarily being merged with inherent meanings. Both cautions amount to the same thing: avoid causing musical learnings of any sort to be artificial by separating them from actual experiences of music. In such experiences, I believe, the music will quite naturally include both dimensions in the balance I believe is characteristic of it.

One more point about the obligation of music education. The issues I have raised here and many others equally implicated in our attempts to understand music should be, I would argue, essential contents in any music education curriculum intended to influence the level of people's musical intelligences. Dealing with such issues, which I have termed "knowing why," has profound effects on the quality and veracity of the musical experiences people undergo. Our almost total neglect in music education of the "whys" of music—the beliefs, values, and controversies in which music is necessarily embedded—produces an unreflective, even ignorant populace about matters central to any convincing conception of what it means to be musically educated. To infuse music education for students at every age and in every musical involvement with appropriate philosophical challenges remains a largely unaddressed requirement for the success of our profession.

It is not enough to address philosophy only among those who practice it professionally. Until our concerns pervade all dimensions of music education, *including what students are taught in school music programs*, philosophy will be regarded as being largely irrelevant to the realities of teaching and learning music, as it tends to be regarded now by many if not most music teachers. Philosophy will continue to be viewed as something for those people, slightly odd, who enjoy debating, endlessly, matters interesting to them alone, as far removed from what students in schools need to learn about music as the man in the moon.

When and where and how do we who are devoted to philosophy turn our attention to the issue of involving all students in the very same matters to which we are devoted, in ways that share with them the challenges and the pleasures of doing music philosophy? When and where and how do we plan together to infuse our interests, so basic to being musically educated, into the realities of school music programs? Until we address these questions we will continue to talk to each other, comfortably and luxuriously, with little effect on what happens in schools. If we have any purposes in addition to continuing to meet the intellectual needs of our small philosophical community, this one, I submit, should be at the top of the list.

NOTES

1. Lucy Green, *Music, Gender, Education* (Cambridge: Cambridge University Press, 1997), 6–7.

2. Tia DeNora, *Music in Everyday Life* (Cambridge: Cambridge University Press, 2000).

3. Susan McClary, *Feminine Endings: Music, Gender, and Sexuality* (Minneapolis: University of Minnesota Press, 1991), 128. Quoted in DeNora, *Music in Everyday Life*, 29.

4. DeNora, *Music in Everyday Life*, 29–30.

5. John Shepherd and Peter Wicke, *Music and Cultural Theory* (Maldan, MA: Blackwell, 1997), 33–34. Quoted in Bennett Reimer, *A Philosophy of Music Education: Advancing the Vision*, 3rd ed. (Upper Saddle River, NJ: Prentice Hall, 2003), 169.

6. Francis Sparshott, "Aesthetics of Music—Limits and Grounds," in *What Is Music?* ed. Philip Alperson (New York: Haven, 1987), 66–67.

IB

CORE VALUES IN LARGER CONTEXTS

As the twentieth century draws to a close, music education begins to open. In the face of our profession's long history of insularity, new and pressing issues are acknowledged. We now recognize to a greater degree the many musics in the world, including those represented in multimusical cultures such as the United States and others. Civil rights; women's rights; our responsibilities to social justice, music, and morality; music as related to learnings in other subjects, all enter our consciousness to heightened degrees. Our core values expand in new and challenging directions, enriching them with a refreshing awareness of the many cultural realities in which we do our work and offer our gifts.

All this engages me in learning from and contributing to the new debates and challenges. These are exciting times for music education and for me in my growth as a philosopher. The essays in this section portray my attempts to incorporate new concerns into what I regard as abiding responsibilities of music education.

6

SELFNESS AND OTHERNESS IN EXPERIENCING MUSIC OF FOREIGN CULTURES

Ours and theirs—this distinction is pervasive in our lives and identities, and in our music as well. Each of us has a kind of music, or several, that in significant ways identifies us as a member of a musical community—"our" community. We might be a member of many, but we can't be a member of all of them across time or throughout the world. There are simply too many that remain "theirs," foreign to our experience, our understanding, and our selfhood.

Is this okay? Should we openly accept that people crave membership in particular groups, small and large, that provide a precious sense of belonging different from those of others? Or is this just being narrow-minded?

I am fascinated with questions such as these, especially as regards music education. Where do our professional obligations lie in regard to the musics we value enough to teach, especially in a country like the United States and so many others around the world that encompass a wide variety of musics, inevitably including "theirs"? We are urged constantly to be musically multicultural, and it would be politically incorrect, to say the least, to reject that posture. But is it really possible, really desirable, to aim for complete multimusicality for ourselves and all our students? And if not complete, how much is enough?

On and on go the questions, among the most complex and certainly among the most interesting our field must cope with. So I try to cope, and each try takes me farther into the intricacies of the topic. Underneath the many conundrums, I conclude, is one that underlies all of them—the core issue of *self* and *other-than-self*. We need both if we are to be whole. Too much of one or the other imbalances us seriously, even to the point of mental illness.

How does that translate into useful guidance for our work as professionals in fostering musical wholeness? Is there some way to have the cake of selfness and frost it with otherness? This article addresses the matter, seeking a balanced position as to how we can cherish what is "ours" while also benefiting from "theirs." Not by diluting the power and necessity of either, an ever-present danger if we are not careful, but by incorporating both into our enriched selfness. Doing so enhances the core values we claim for music rather than diminishing them. And, best of all, it is indeed doable. (I've also used the opening story in this essay as a riff in my *A Philosophy of Music Education: Advancing the Vision* [2003], in my treatment of the broad issue of music as a contextually situated phenomenon. In this chapter my focus is on the personal situatedness of our experience as related to that of others. Clearly my visit to China had a profound effect on me, deepening in a dramatic way my "knowing within" my personal identification as a self, and my capacity to internalize a very "other" identification as a welcome new aspect of my self.)

The following essay was originally published in *The Quarterly Journal of Music Teaching and Learning* 2, no. 3 (Fall 1991). Used by permission.

On an early summer day in 1986 I sat in the gymnasium-like rehearsal room at the Liaoning Province Opera School in Shenyang, a large city in northern China in the region traditionally called Manchuria. The advanced opera students were going through several scenes from a traditional Beijing (Peking) opera, and I was completely absorbed in the music and the acrobatic displays. I had been in China three months, studying the music education system of that country from preschool through conservatory levels.[1] During that time I had heard Chinese opera often, in performances, rehearsals, practice rooms, and studios. Conservatory teachers and students had demonstrated the particular kind of singing style it employs and had even made several attempts (futile, it turned out) to get me to sing that way.

Toward the end of the rehearsal a young woman dressed in Western-style sweats and sneakers came out to perform a scene: if she were walking across an American campus she would be indistinguishable from the many Chinese college students in our country. As the orchestra at the side of the room started up she began to sing, solo and with other singers, all of them acting in the typical stylized way these operas are performed. I was riveted by her performance. Everything in me, as a musician, an educator, a writer on musical experience, a newly sensitized listener to (if not performer of) this music, told me that I was witnessing something extraordinary—a quality and intensity of music making I had seldom encountered in a lifetime of musical involvements. I sat transfixed.

When it was over I turned to the old man sitting next to me, the director of the school, who is one of China's experts on this musical genre. "Tell me about that young woman," I said. "Ah," he replied. "She is a most remarkable person. She is already very famous throughout China. She is going to be among the very best opera singers in China's history. Such a person comes along only a few times in any century."

So I was right. I exulted.

I have pondered that incident many times since it occurred, trying to understand what it implied about the nature of musical experience as being both intensely personal and intensely social and contextual. In one sense, I owned the experience I had. All that makes me who I am, not only as an individual but as a product of the Western culture in which I have been steeped, came into play as I experienced that performance. The meaning of what I experienced could only be meaningful as a function of the complex meaning systems—musical, cultural, personal, professional—that define my particular selfness. As all who have traveled to the far corners of the world have discovered, sometimes to our dismay, we inevitably take ourselves along on the journeys.

But in another sense the music I heard defined my experience. That music, including the dramatic setting in which it functions, is itself a meaning system, its sonorous gestures embodying a culturally laden complex of implicit connotations, a rich amalgam of socially shared subjectivities, and a historically embedded set of significations. I had been given an extraordinary opportunity to be inducted into the musical and social contexts of Chinese opera, but that certainly did not make me Chinese: nothing could. Will not the fact that this music is a product of a culture other than my own always be a determinant of my experience of it? To what extent, then, can my experience of it be congruent with that of a native Chinese?

Such questions have been thrust upon us with increasing force in recent years as we struggle to include in music education the many musics comprising the multimusical culture of America, in which practically all musics of the world have gathered in sometimes uneasy cohabitation. We need not travel abroad to encounter foreign music: it surrounds us. Even within the culture of the West there are so many diverse styles and types of music that few can be familiar with (feel "in family" with) all of them; some are bound to be "foreign."

We have been importuned for at least twenty-five years since the Tanglewood Symposium, and recently with mounting fervor, to become more multimusical, to the point of questioning whether the heritage of Western concert music deserves any privileged or significant place in the literature we teach.[2] So the questions beg for attention as to whether or to what degree it is possible for people from different cultures to share the same or even similar meanings from various musics, whether we deceive ourselves to think that efforts to be "multicultural" can be more than windowdressing, whether we as individuals or the profession as a whole can cope with the many philosophical, sociological, political, psychological, musical, and educational conundrums entangled within this deeply complex issue.

Certainly all these questions cannot be addressed in a single article. I intend, however, to touch upon some of the issues needing ongoing, focused attention if we are to achieve more than a superficial understanding of the many complexities entailed in cross-cultural musical experience.

The complexities are raised by the existence of two seemingly opposed positions. One position is that our selfness is largely limited to the culturally familiar, and that, concomitantly, all otherness is dominantly other. While perhaps we can share some small measure of other cultures insofar as they are related to our indigenous one, the circle of meaning in which we are capable of operating is severely circumscribed. Furthermore, in order to achieve the depths of meaning of which we are capable we need a set of limits on the breadths of meanings we incorporate, to avoid the kind of facile dilettantism that dabbles in a little of this and a little of that with only superficial understanding.

This position is widespread in American culture at all levels. People, it is often said, are at home in the world only within the shelter of a highly defined culture. They may venture out into the world of other cultures during the day and evening, but at night, when the psyche requires homecoming, the cloak of immediate cultural family is what provides it. In truth, cultural sharing in America does seem to be largely an activity of daylight and the evening hours. When it is time to go home, a retreat to the safety of social uniformity often occurs, both physically in where people live and psychologically in how they live. We have, perhaps, more instances of fully integrated families and neighborhoods than many if not most countries, but even in cities, where such integration is most likely, cultural enclaves seem to be the rule.

There is a positive and a negative side to the reality of cultural homogeneity. On the positive side is the comfort and strength one receives from having a defined base from which to encounter and understand the larger world. That base, derived first from the home in which one was reared and later from the interrelated system of similar homes defining a subculture, provides a sense of self so powerful as to warrant the term "soul." Soul food, soul rites and rituals, soul music, is that which lies at the root of our identities, nourishing us at the wellsprings of our selfness. We are who we are in large degree because of the home we claim in a bewildering world, and that home is a culturally defined one. Music is a powerful agent in forging such a definition.

The negative side to cultural individuality is separatism, or what is often called particularism. In that view community is defined according to the separate history and present condition of each particular social group, the separateness being a function of the oppressive forces that have marked the group as being different. Self identity then relies on the safety one's cultural enclave provides from threatening forces outside it, that safety requiring the protection of the enclave by strict adherence to its tenets and its cultural practices. The soulfulness of being a member of a cultural family becomes imbued with a pressing political purpose, inevitably affecting the psychology of membership in the direction of segmentation from the larger society.

We are now witnessing the resultant conflicts of particularism in education, in the presence of ideological extremism based on cultural divisions.[3] This is perhaps inevitable given the realities of racial and ethnic tensions in American history.

But another aspect of that reality is the existence of an ideal beneath the politics—an ideal of a shared American culture that is by nature also multicultural, in which people's spiritual identification with a subculture is defined by that spirit rather than by their need for protection. Clearly we have not achieved that ideal. That accounts for much of the complexity in the task of creating a music education program that honors and reaps the benefits of both the selfness of cultural identification and the otherness of cultural diversity.

The second position often encountered about the issues of our multimusical American culture focuses on otherness as an aspect of selfness. It stresses the universality of musical experience, claiming that all cultural musics are manifestations of a single human need for the meanings music uniquely provides. Otherness, this position claims, is primarily stylistic, and can be managed by exposure to a variety of musical styles along with background information about how each music works within its cultural setting. Selfness, while no doubt influenced by particularly familiar musics, can be expanded to include one's sharing of all the other musics one encounters in whatever attempts one makes to encounter them. Music education should be one of the major influences on the catholicity of young people's tastes, helping introduce them to the many musical styles they might otherwise not have the opportunity to incorporate into their personal repertoires of experience.

As in the position stressing selfness and cultural identification, the second position, stressing an open sharing of musics other than one's own and an identification with all the musics available in the larger culture, also has both positive and negative sides.

The positive side is the reality that music is a panhuman phenomenon, existing always and everywhere to serve particular human needs. Those needs, it may be argued, stem from the possession by all human beings of a common nature. The playing out of that shared nature, however, takes many diverse forms. That fact, unfortunately, has led some people to assume that the diversity of cultural behaviors, customs, beliefs, styles of thinking, and so forth, demonstrates that there is no common human nature. It has also led to the claim that each human being is entirely able to choose what he or she will become, free from any defining essence in a shared human nature. Such positions render futile any attempt to find universally existent human characteristics underlying an activity such as music, and each culture's music would have to be regarded as being *sui generis*.

As Mortimer Adler explains in a recent book on such issues, we can concede the role of culture in determining the patterns of human behavior. "Since there are no instinctively determined patterns of human behavior, as there are in social insects and other lower animals; since all human behavior is learned behavior, which is not the case in other animals—it follows that the way human beings have learned to use their minds determines how they behave. Their different styles of behavior reflect acquired differences in mentality—in the ways their minds have been shaped by experience and by nurture."[4]

But such concessions, he claims, do not in any sense contradict the other aspect of human reality—that there exists "a specific human nature and a common human mind shared by all persons regardless of the subset of human population to which they belong and regardless of their idiosyncratic individuality."[5] There is a level of the human condition that is both transcultural and transpersonal. Unlike other species, in which many if not all patterns of behavior are predetermined by actual innate endowment, behaviors of humans are based on innate endowment of *potentialities*. All human communities and cultures share the same desires and needs, the same potentialities of sensibility and memory and imagination and intellect, even though these shared characteristics are nurtured differently under different social conditions.

> What the cultural anthropologists are describing when they report diverse patterns of human behavior in different subsets of the human population are all nurtural differences. These nurtural differences exist as acquired behavioral habits or dispositions. Underlying diverse habits are the same natural powers or potentialities. Nurtural differences should never be interpreted either as natural differences or as a basis for denying the existence of a common nature. All the forms of racism and sexism with which we are acquainted have been prejudices bred by the error of attributing to nature what are only the products of nurture.[6]

Music, I would suggest, is a paradigm case of the validity of Adler's position. The diversity of musics of various cultures reflects nurtural differences in the human being's innate propensity to create meaning systems by using sounds purposively deployed. The variety of deployments is vast: the potential to so deploy sounds is inherent in the human creature. And the belief that purposively formed musical sounds are humanly meaningful is ubiquitous. As Robert Walker asserts in his book about culturally diverse musical belief systems,

> What can be confidently asserted is that all cultures tend to believe that their respective musical practices reflect their respective value systems as both symbols and as more than symbols. They regard musical sound as intrinsically possessing certain powers that pertain to the most important things in life—whether to a notion of scientifically defined perfectness or to the source of ultimate power and creation itself emanating from a spirit world. . . . The place of music in the belief systems of all cultures suggests that music itself must be, to some degree, systemically organized, just as the society to which the music contributes such a powerful force is systemically organized.[7]

The view stressing the universality of music (not the universality of any particular musical belief system or particular cultural practice but the universality of the human potential to find music individually and culturally meaningful) provides a basis for communion both within and across cultural boundaries. The otherness of foreign music is precisely why we need to

attend to it in an attempt to integrate what we can of it into our own experience. If it were not other, there would be no issue to discuss.

But that otherness consists of particular playings out of the universally
shared trait of musicality, and we can explore those particularities with
some measure of musical and educational coherence. We can assume, as
a working hypothesis, that all musics will involve the powers of the human
mind to structure sounds, to be able to perceive those structures, and to
find them subjectively compelling as individually experienced and as a
socially shared experience. Music always engages the human imagination,
the human capacity for skilled control of the body to produce sounds sensitively, the ability to remember sounds both within particular musical events
and across the many events comprising a style. To make musical sounds, all
cultures use both the voice and a variety of invented instruments to extend
what the voice can do. All cultures recognize both continuity and diversity
in musical performances and products, ranging across a continuum stressing
continuity (Japanese, Chinese) to stressing change (some African societies,
North American Plains Indians).[8] It may even be the case, as suggested by
the work of recent music theorists, that many intramusical processes—the
particular uses of pitch, attack, duration, intensity, timbre, to form groupings, metrical structures, hierarchies of events, and so forth—operate in
some way in all musics.[9]

Even in terms of belief systems about music and the arts there are often
striking similarities among some cultures that would otherwise seem, on
the surface, to have little in common. The separatist tendency to bifurcate
the world, assuming that there is ours and then all the rest which must be
entirely other, misrepresents by its lack of subtlety the reality that cultural
differences are often differences in degree rather than necessarily in kind.
It is simply too facile to think that Western art consists of one thing and
that all other art is entirely another; this grossly misrepresents a far more
complex set of interrelations.

Let me cite as an example the art of the Yoruba people (now some 18
million) in southwestern Nigeria, who represent an ancient culture divided
into city states much like those of ancient Greece. A recent exhibition of
masterworks of Yoruba art spanning nine centuries, displayed at the Art
Institute of Chicago (February 10 to April 1, 1990), presented the following explanatory note displayed at the entrance to the gallery (copied in its
entirety):

> The Yoruba have developed a vocabulary of aesthetic criticism for discussing
> works worthy to be called art. The Yoruba have the concept of "oju-inu"—the

inner eye—the insight—of the artist, and the artist's discernment or under-standing of the subject portrayed. The term "aju-una" refers to the design con-sciousness of the artist, to the originality of the composition. "Ifarabale" de-notes the artist's reason, self-control, and composure, reflected in the mastery of the instruments with which the sculptor, blacksmith, potter, beadworker, or weaver works. Viewing a work, knowledgeable members of the community will comment on its sensitivity and perceptiveness ("imoju-mora") and on its enduring qualities ("tito").

Surely Yoruba art has its authentic being in its own vision of the human condition. But just as surely that vision has a good deal in common with that held in the Western world. Access to the experience of Yoruba art would be aided by an understanding of its similarities with Western art as well as its differences from it.

This may be the case, to some lesser or greater extent, with every cul-ture's art, even if at the opposite end of the continuum where similarities are not apparent. Fundamentally, all art springs from the same source in the common human condition of sentience—of being conscious of one's self in a world of others and of being capable of exploring the shared expe-rience of being a self among others through humanly created, perceptible forms. The positive aspect of the position focusing on the universality of art is that it provides a basis for believing that sharing of foreign musics is at least possible.

What, then, is the negative aspect of this position? The image of a con-tinuum on which some musics are quite similar to others and some are very dissimilar, raises the issue of degree. To what *degree* is it possible to hope to share the distinctive characteristics of the culturally different musics existing on a continuum of similarity and dissimilarity from one's own? The negative aspect of the universalist viewpoint is its tendency to gloss over the real and important differentia that constitute the uniqueness of each culture's music, and that precisely such uniqueness constitutes the essential character of each music.

We should want to preserve rather than dilute the differences in each music because every difference is a lens through which we are provided a glimpse of the human condition that only that particular music can pro-vide. Each such glimpse is precious. No matter where on the continuum, the differences themselves are essential for each music to be experienced for what it genuinely is, as differentiated from others anywhere else on the continuum. So a focus on the distinctive characteristics through which a culture's music manifests itself, as much as on any similarities, would seem to be required if we are to confront the authenticity of that music.

That, of course, exacerbates the distinction between self and other. To the degree that one focuses on distinctiveness one is confronted with more and more otherness. To the degree that one focuses on universals, one approaches the self but with less of a genuine confrontation with the being of the other. We are thrown against the fundamental dilemma inherent in being selves among others.

But are we prone, perhaps, to overestimate differences among musics, making the dilemma seem more vexing than it really is? Can we not project our own system of musical thinking on another and assume that it will overlap a little or a lot, as the argument for universality suggests is possible? Can proper and determined effort take us a long way toward being able to share more otherness than we might fear we cannot, especially if we make the effort in a willing and open spirit?

Probably not easily and not entirely. While Walker recognizes underlying unities among culturally diverse musics, as mentioned previously, he also makes the argument that differences are fundamental and real, and that music is a particularly difficult phenomenon to grasp when one is not a member of its culture:

> The situation of the outsider trying to understand unknown musical sounds and behavior is similar to that experienced by anthropologists when they seek to investigate some unknown culture. Music poses problems in this regard because its sonic structural and symbolic systems obey different laws from those of language, or those of visual art, making it a most difficult form of communication to understand from the outside. . . . Unlike the sounds of language or the shapes of visual art, the sounds of music relate only to music. . . . The general problem in music thus hinges on the difficulties experienced by the outsider attempting to decode communications that are known by the insider—someone who has grown up with the musical code. More specifically, the problem in music concerns decoding and understanding the significance of the particular choices of sound made by each musical culture, which tend to be very different from each other. . . . [I]t is in such choices that cultural belief systems are reflected. One understands the choices in terms of the belief system, not the other way round, and in such understanding lies the key to the musical and cultural significance of musical sound.[10]

Although much about Walker's position deserves a closer examination than he provides, certainly it is a given that much more is involved in musical understanding than can be gained at the level of sheer sonic analysis. One can reasonably claim, as he does, that the search for universals has been fixated at the level of formalistic dissection.[11] But that does not in any way negate the role of those "particular choices of sound" that make each culture's music sound the way it does as systematically organized, as Walker demonstrates by his own recognition of important shared qualities among all musics including, essentially, qualities of form.

It would seem to be necessary, in order to appreciate the cultural distinctiveness of a particular musical practice, to investigate both its cultural context and its musical existence as sounds organized in particular ways. The interaction of the two is where the deepest insights can be found about both distinctiveness and commonality, I would argue. Every music will manifest both its distinctness to its culture and its universality as music in that interaction between its general cultural contexts and its particular musical features and their organization.

Neglecting either factor, or their interactions, is likely to yield a skewed and incomplete picture of the reality of any music. A "social studies" approach to studying music will not be sufficient. Neither will sonic analysis.

This view is expressed precisely by Marcia M. Eaton, who, after a careful examination of several issues relating to both context and criticism, offers the following summary (presented in terms of the visual arts but intended by her to apply to all the arts):

1. In discussions of art, information about context (history of production) draws the viewer's attention to certain intrinsic features of things.
2. The features to which attention is thus drawn are considered worthy of attention in some aesthetic tradition(s).
3. Aesthetic traditions are those which identify intrinsic features that yield delight upon perception and reflection.
4. Objects whose intrinsic features repay sustained perception and reflection are aesthetically valuable.[12]

Yet, useful as this may be in drawing attention to the need to balance an experience of music by including both an awareness of its cultural context and of its musical individuality, the act of awareness itself must be understood to be contextually embedded. That is, one cannot simply add contextual information to a piece being experienced as if it was contextless. The experience itself—the perceptual awareness of what is being heard—is itself a function of what Jerrold Levinson calls "appropriate construal" within a musical-cultural context of meanings.[13]

The embeddedness of music in cultural habituations applies to Western music as well as to any others. For example, to correctly or relevantly construe Bruckner's Fourth Symphony, Levinson argues, a "comprehending listener" would have to hear the music as tonal, as symphonic, as Romantic, as roughly in sonata form, as specifically Brucknerian, as a series of connected events including responses to tensions and releases and expectations and fulfillments, as an act of performance, as being gestural and emotional, and as having wider resonances (mythic, nature loving).[14]

Listeners outside the culture of this music, unable to incorporate such construals in their experience of it, could not be said to "understand" it. One's understanding need not be at the level of verbalizations: musical understanding is essentially nonconceptual in the sense of not having to be verbally mediated.[15] Understanding is tacit and intuitive, resting fundamentally on a history of aural absorption. We need to be able, to some degree, to internalize musical events (Eaton's "intrinsic features") as events occurring within a tradition. While all music is musical, all music is also culturally conditioned and must be construed as such if it is to be understood.

We find ourselves confronting what seem to be several overlapping yet divergent forces. Selfness is real. We cannot simply shed the culturally derived beingness of our selves whenever we might choose to. Nor should we want to—it is, after all, what defines us as individuals and provides us with an identity. We can savor that identity without building separatist walls around it to isolate it in order to keep other selves safely out.

Those other selves are also part of our lived world. We know that all other cultures share the universal human condition and all manifest that condition in the phenomenon we call music. That phenomenon is identifiable as such despite its diverse manifestations: it is comprised of many features common to all cultures. But the diversities are precisely what provide each music with its particular selfness. In the distinctiveness of each culture's music lies both its authentic being and, inevitably, its otherness for those not members of that culture.

The seeming impasse created by the coexistence of selfness and otherness can be addressed in a meaningful way by a notion found useful in the philosophy of both natural and social science—the notion of incommensurability.

In his book exploring the dilemmas caused by both objectivism and relativism, the philosopher Richard J. Bernstein traces the development of ideas that have altered our understanding of the nature of rationality in scientific inquiry, leading us to recognize that rationality is historically situated, serves practical ends that are humanly defined, and involves choices and judgments.[16] In social science as well, hermeneutics, the practice of interpretation, plays a defining role. Both in natural and physical science we are faced with the necessity to understand orientations and practices different from our own. How is it possible to do so?

In the natural sciences, thinkers such as Thomas S. Kuhn and Imre Feyerabend have raised the issue of different paradigms—competing schools of thought about how to construe the world and how science should be conducted. It would seem impossible for any dialogue between proponents of different paradigms to take place or for any genuine understanding of each different paradigm to exist, given the fundamentally different premises of each. Bernstein traces the complex (and often convoluted) issues entailed, and concludes that "rival paradigm theories are logically *incompatible* (and, therefore, really in conflict with each other); *incommensurable* (and, therefore, they cannot always be measured against each other point by point); and *comparable* (capable of being compared with each other in multiple ways without requiring the assumption that there is or must always be a common, fixed grid by which we measure progress)."[17]

This position from the natural sciences can apply as well to the fields of sociology and anthropology. As Feyerabend explains in an example of trying to understand the art of a long dead culture such as that of ancient Greece, we are not reduced, by virtue of the archaic Greek style and world view being incommensurable with those that have replaced it, to being able to only dumbly contemplate it with no hope of understanding it. We can indeed gain valid insights about ancient Greek art by the skillful application of comparisons and contrasts, and in order to accomplish this we must both preserve the selfness of us who are making the judgments, and the otherness of what we are attempting to understand. "The basic presupposition here is that we can understand what is distinctive about this incommensurable style and form of life—and we do not do this by jumping out of our own skins (and language) and transforming ourselves, by some sort of mystical intuition or empathy, into archaic Greeks. Rather, the analysis proceeds by a careful attention to detail—to the various 'building blocks'—working back and forth in order to appreciate and highlight similarities with and differences from other styles and forms of life."[18]

Accomplishing this requires that we avoid two extremes. One is to assume that differences are so complete that we can only stand in mute ignorance before an example of art from a past or different culture. The other extreme is to facilely project our own beliefs and attitudes onto the foreign art. In between, if we apply patience, insight, imagination, and attention to detail, we can develop understandings that are, at the least, defensible if not incontrovertible.

Further, the very act of doing so not only leads us to reasonably valid interpretations of foreign art but also helps us become, through our attempts to understand their distinctiveness, more sensitive to and critically aware of our own particular biases and presuppositions.

Here also there are two extremes to avoid—the romantic fantasy that what is foreign is also necessarily superior, and the reverse, which is that our own position is the truly correct one:

> For at their best, Kuhn and Feyerabend show us that we can understand the ways in which there are incommensurable paradigms, forms of life, and traditions, and that we can understand what is distinctive about them without imposing beliefs, categories, and classifications that are so well entrenched in our own language games that we fail to appreciate their limited perspective. Furthermore, in and through the process of subtle, multiple comparison and contrast, we not only come to understand the alien phenomenon that we are studying but better come to understand ourselves. This openness of understanding and communication goes beyond disputes about the development of the natural sciences; it is fundamental to all understanding.[19]

The fundamental requirement for understanding is to take into account what exists outside ourselves. This seems to me the major factor in the need for all people to encounter and to try to understand musics both from their own culture and from those with which they are less familiar. Encountering any music honestly, openly, and sympathetically requires an act of expansion of the self, because every musical experience presents one with something outside one's self needing to be assimilated.

This applies as well, I would argue, to the creation of music through composing, performing, or improvising, in that to do so authentically one must go beyond one's present self, through sounds being encountered, to a self not yet known but discovered through the decisions one is led to make by the act of creation. Even when a performance is of a ritual music fully ingrained, the performance requires an adjustment of the self at that moment to the needs of the musical practice—an adjustment of one's self to demands from outside the self. And when listening to music composed and/or performed by other people one is confronted with what is "fundamental to all understanding," the bending of who one is to the demands of something exterior to oneself.

The same process is in operation in all human relationships. In each act of relationship our selves are confronted with and must sympathetically adapt to the reality of an other. Music manifests powerfully this fundamental reality of human consciousness—that we exist in a world of meanings we experience alone in our own skins while also being capable of recognizing and being influenced by the coexperience of those with whom we share the world. The expansion within us of that coexisting world is thus an expansion of our selves.

Every act of musical experience expands our inner world. The experience of foreign musics does so dramatically, in forcing us to push beyond the circle of assumptions more easily accommodated within a familiar system to a circle incommensurable with the familiar yet understandable through sympathetic effort. In studying the musics of others—especially foreign others—we come to a deeper understanding both of our selves as individuals and our selves as relative to other systems of being we can experience meaningfully.

As I listened to the rehearsal of traditional Chinese opera in Manchuria I was aware of the growth I had undergone over the three months since I had arrived there and had first been introduced to this operatic tradition. My initial experiences were so saturated with my Western heritage and its tacit presumptions about appropriate vocal tone color, instrument timbres, melodic variety, harmonic interest, and so on, including acting style being appropriately based on a realistic model, that it was difficult for me to even begin to respond empathically. It was only with growing insights about and awareness of its cultural functions and history, its connectedness with language and myth and social values, and its intramusical and dramatic techniques, that it began to be accessible to me through the barriers of my own very different musical and cultural belief system.

I wanted to be open to its otherness, but at first I found myself resistant to yielding something of my selfness. As I managed to yield, I found myself becoming more and more intrigued by the very differences—contextual and musical—I had at first found so difficult to assimilate within my own experience. I discovered that I did not have to give up who I am, and that in fact I could not do so, but that I could be something I never was before in adapting myself to a way of experiencing quite new to me.

My selfness was not abandoned: it was expanded. The foundation of my self remained what it had become, and I did not then and do not now deceive myself that I was listening as a native. But I was listening as a different foreigner—one who had become able, I think, to internalize some measure of the authenticity of this very other genre into my own broadened subjectivity.

I was also aware of the many changes taking place in Chinese opera, and in all Chinese traditional musics, as a result of recent unprecedented influences from the West. So powerful are Western cultural and artistic incursions into Chinese life that many there feel that the old ways may soon be lost or so altered as to become essentially different from what they were. In the nine conservatories in China, the Traditional Chinese Music departments are overshadowed in support and prestige by the Western Music departments; and throughout popular Chinese culture, especially in the more up-to-date cities, Western influences are ubiquitous and powerful. Fewer young people want to attend Chinese opera, and everyone professionally engaged in it fears that it is fast becoming an anomaly.

So changes are being made. The orchestra I listened to that afternoon had several electronically amplified instruments ("To appeal to young people"), performances are bypassing some of the less dramatically active sections, more excerpts of the "popular" segments are being presented, and so forth. So what I heard in China was very much a genre in process of significant change, ironically in response to and in the direction of the belief system I represented and that I was trying, with some measure of success, to adapt to theirs.

This phenomenon of growing Western cultural hegemony is, of course, occurring throughout the world. Within our United States boundaries there seems to be a continuum of effects as foreign musics and Western musics come into contact with one another. At one end of the continuum the overwhelming availability of Western musics can so erode the viability of some foreign musics as to cause them to become progressively weaker as a cultural force and eventually to be abandoned. This possibility adds special poignancy to our task of helping to preserve the variety of musics immigrants have brought and continue to bring with them.

At the other end of the continuum has been a heightened sense of urgency during recent years about that preservation effort, and an increasing acceptance of ethnic self-identification as being a healthy posture for Americans to take. There are many points along the continuum, adding greatly to the complexities of the issues we face as music educators.

My personal experiences of the benefits to my self in encountering foreign musics, and my growing understanding of the theoretical bases for how and to what degree such encounters are possible for everyone, lead me to hope that members of the music education profession will continue to address these issues wholeheartedly and thoughtfully, both in theory and in practice.

NOTES

1. My work in China was part of a research exchange program sponsored by the Rockefeller Brothers Fund and administered by Harvard Project Zero and the

Center for U.S.-China Arts Exchange at Columbia University. For a report of the entire program, see *The Journal of Aesthetic Education* 23, no. 1 (Spring 1989), which includes my "Music Education in China: An Overview and Some Issues."

2. A clear example of this view is given by Austin B. Caswell, "How We Got into Canonicity and What It Has Done to Us," *The Journal of Aesthetic Education* 25, no. 4 (1991). A summary of Caswell's paper, and a response to it by Michael L. Mark, is presented in the *Philosophy of Music Education Newsletter* 3, no. 1 (November 1990).

3. For a trenchant discussion of this situation, see Diane Ravitch, "Multiculturalism Yes, Particularism No," *The Chronicle of Higher Education*, October 24, 1990.

4. Mortimer J. Adler, *Intellect: Mind Over Matter* (New York: Macmillan, 1990), 136.

5. Adler, *Intellect*, 136–137.

6. Adler, *Intellect*, 138.

7. Robert Walker, *Musical Beliefs* (New York: Teachers College Press, 1990), 195.

8. Bruno Nettl, "Music of Other Cultures," in Bennett Reimer and Edward G. Evans, *The Experience of Music* (Englewood Cliffs, NJ: Prentice-Hall, 1972), 387.

9. This is particularly suggested by Fred Lerdahl and Jay Jackendoff, *A Generative Theory of Tonal Music* (Cambridge: MIT Press, 1983).

10. Walker, *Musical Beliefs*, 12–13.

11. Walker, *Musical Beliefs*, 4.

12. Marcia M. Eaton, "Context, Criticism, and Art Education: Putting Meaning into the Life of Sisyphus," *The Journal of Aesthetic Education* 24, no. 1 (Spring 1990): 105.

13. Jerrold Levinson, "Musical Literacy," *The Journal of Aesthetic Education* 24, no. 1 (Spring 1990): 25.

14. Levinson, "Musical Literacy," 19–20.

15. Levinson, "Musical Literacy," 24.

16. Richard J. Bernstein, *Beyond Objectivism and Relativism: Science, Hermeneutics, and Praxis* (Philadelphia: University of Pennsylvania Press, 1983).

17. Bernstein, *Beyond Objectivism and Relativism*, 86.

18. Quoted in Bernstein, *Beyond Objectivism and Relativism*, 90. An interesting discussion of the implications and limitations of the notion of incommensurability for educational research is offered by Steven I. Miller and Marcel Fredericks, "Postpositivistic Assumptions and Education Research: Another View," *Educational Researcher* 20, no. 4 (May 1941).

19. Bernstein, *Beyond Objectivism and Relativism*, 91–92.

7

GENDER, FEMINISM, AND AESTHETIC EDUCATION: DISCOURSES OF INCLUSION AND EMPOWERMENT

"We have experienced some significant erosion in our philosophical/ emotional bonds as a nation as we have lost some of our naiveté about our story."

This sentence from the following essay applies as well when "nation" is replaced by "profession." The social upheavals the United States has experienced, starting with the 1960s and continuing to this day, make this country a better place, I believe, but not without some costs to its previously more tranquil yet largely undeserved self-concept. Achieving a more clear-eyed vision of our society is not always pleasant. That applies as well to our profession, especially when taking a hard look at weaknesses as well as strengths.

One major advance toward social justice is the feminist movement, addressing, often understandably with anger and resentment, the inequities women have suffered in our culture and, of course, in world cultures throughout history. Feminist activism and literature burgeon during these decades, eventually reaching the domain of music education. I am stunned when I read an article in *Philosophy of Music Education Review* attributing "Exclusion and Oppression" of women to the aesthetic education movement. "What?" I shake my head in disbelief. "Aesthetic education, calling attention to the uniqueness of musical meanings as accessible to all, is . . . what?"

CHAPTER 7

The response that follows expresses my views on an issue that means a great deal to me in my personal life but has not been addressed in my professional philosophy (along with dozens if not hundreds of other pressing social issues our world confronts) because it has not occurred to me as being an appropriate responsibility. I am offended by the article's attribution of injustice toward women to aesthetic education and to me as its spokesperson. I try, in my response, to rise above my dismay and to clarify what our posture might be in an area so complex and variable as to confound even its most ardent and deeply thoughtful advocates. Doing so affords me a timely and healthful opportunity to advance music education, and myself, toward an expanded vision of what our obligations are in addition to what we have customarily conceived to be our responsibilities.

The following essay was originally published by Indiana University Press in the *Philosophy of Music Education Review* 3, no. 2 (Fall 1995). Used by permission.

The second half of the twentieth century brought several social revolutions of far-reaching consequence. The civil rights movement, the feminist movement, and the gay and lesbian movement, among others, forced reassessments of long-held, seldom-questioned attitudes and assumptions. Consciousness of inequities, injustices, prejudices, and suppression of individuals and of groups, whether by overt design or by the inertia of custom, was raised to new levels by the pioneering and often self-endangering work of a variety of leaders/activists. Our culture became politicized in new and challenging ways as balances of power began to shift because of heightened awareness that all was not well for a great many people, now able to articulate why and to make the case, through persuasion or forceful action, that change was necessary.

Adding to the volatility and probably the effectiveness of these social upheavals was a changing attitude toward history. History has often been a self-serving exercise, emphasizing the value agenda of those telling the story and downplaying unwelcome or embarrassing contradictions. In the United States as elsewhere history has tended to be celebratory, creating myths that served cultural purposes rather than probing for unsavory realities underneath the surface. But with the myth-shattering events of the Vietnam War and Watergate an attitude of skepticism and distrust has grown about how we tell our story, whose story gets told, and whose purposes get served by historical accounts. We are much more critical now about our history as a nation and about the previously unexamined portrayals that have given us a largely positive picture of our national identity. We are more prone to be doubtful—to assume that there are bugs under our flagstones—and to be ready to face the consequences of recognizing our faults along with our virtues.

Those consequences can be dangerous, by pushing our attitudes to extremes of mutual suspicion if not paranoia, and weakening our communality as a result. We have experienced some significant erosion in our psychological/emotional bonds as a nation as we have lost some of our naiveté about our story. We have become more defensive of the particular values with which we happen to identify and more combative in our relations with those holding other values—certainly more litigious in those relations. As many social observers have pointed out, we have become a more uneasy society.

That is, inevitably, the shadow side of the gains that have accrued from our more realistic, more critical self-image. The status of traditionally oppressed groups has in fact changed because of the power struggles of our times, in the direction of more equality if not yet the level of equality many are likely to find satisfactory. The struggle for equal rights, equal opportunities, equal respect and dignity must and will continue until that (unlikely) time when human societies have learned to perfect themselves. In the interim, we must find ways to work cooperatively toward the correction of inequities and the creation of a more healthy (healed, whole) social order.

Within the larger struggle toward equality in American life the confluence of feminism with music education has occurred only very recently, at least at the obviously visible level. Two journals have devoted an entire issue to feminist perspectives on music education—*The Quarterly Journal of Music Teaching and Learning* (Winter 1993/Spring 1994) and the *Philosophy of Music Education Review* (Fall 1994)—reflecting a growing awareness that here, tucked away from the more noticeable areas in which feminist efforts have concentrated (business, politics, religion, reproductive rights, and so forth) is another area that can be analyzed from the perspective of feminist concerns.

Also, it has taken some time for a cadre of feminist music education scholars to have emerged. After all, music education has not had a long tradition of social-conscious analytical work, just as it has not had a long tradition of philosophical scholarship. It takes time for the perspectives and skills of specialized thinking to emerge in fields historically devoted to other matters.

So now the struggle has been joined, and it is likely that, as in every other area where the quest for consciousness about the need for equity has taken place, music education will have lost its innocence in this regard and will have entered the complex and problematic arena of value conflict and value clarification now being experienced in practically every corner of our culture.

Several dimensions of the feminist perspective are not predominantly philosophical, focusing largely on matters of equal access to opportunity, neglect or denigration of women's contributions, unequal pay for equal work, and a host of other issues that while inevitably including value components are primarily concerned with socially imposed inequalities crying for redress.

For example, Judith Delzell explores how gender role stereotyping has influenced access to band teaching positions, including choice of instrument as a determining factor in later opportunities.[1] Molly Weaver reports on gender distinctions in faculty ranks and salaries at Big Ten universities.[2] Laree Trollinger reports on research studies dealing with sex/gender differences in musical abilities as well as factors of personality, preferences, gender association, attitudes, anxieties, and so forth.[3] Vicki Eaklor deals with the history of music education as being saturated with gender assumptions held by the society in which it arose, inevitably affecting both male and female music educators and the roles they could play.[4]

Such work is invaluable in giving a clearer picture of the pervasive influence of gender-related beliefs in forming our profession's self-concept and shaping its actions. Philosophical issues lurk just below the surface of all this scholarship (and sometimes are brought directly to the surface) because this work is rife with issues of value and principle. It would be impossible in a single article to begin to probe the underlying questions raised by all this work. They deserve extensive treatment and I hope they will be given serious attention as philosophically inclined music educators begin to deal with them.

Other dimensions of the feminist perspective are more specifically philosophical in the sense that their focus is directly on the beliefs, values, assumptions, principles, and systems of reasons by which our profession has conducted its work. Such scholarship scrutinizes gender-determined beliefs to ascertain whether they are valid. Here we are thrown directly into the arena of feminist philosophy, and into the many complex issues it raises. Again, no one article could hope to do more than examine a very selective sample of such issues, given their enormous breadth and depth (not to mention the now extensive and continually growing literature of feminist philosophy).

I will, therefore, focus my discussion on one particular article, from the *Philosophy of Music Education Review*, which will allow me to raise several questions and probe for some tentative directions for answers very much needing our reflection if feminist scholarship is to be of maximum benefit to the profession; that is, if it is to help all of us better understand what we believe and do and how to improve what we believe and do.

Julia Koza's article "Aesthetic Music Education Revisited: Discourses of Exclusion and Oppression,"[5] gives me a particularly fertile field for exploring some basic feminist issues in that it deals almost entirely with my own work (limited, unfortunately, to the book *A Philosophy of Music Education*,[6] which, while central to my thinking, only partially represents it). Naturally I am interested in Koza's treatment of this book, but I am interested far more in learning as much as I can about the mechanisms at work in shaping my thinking and, by extension, the thinking of all—males and females—who attempt to do philosophical work in music education. Have assumptions related to gender affected my beliefs in exclusionary and oppressive ways, as Koza's title claims they have?

If the answer to this question is "yes," I and many others who share my beliefs need to know this and ponder the implications. If the answer is "no," that too needs to be considered as to why such a claim would be mistakenly made. Whatever answer emerges we would all be well served by our greater clarity about the issues being raised in the feminist literature and what our obligations may be in light of them. As will be seen in what follows, what will emerge from my analyses are far more questions than answers, questions begging for clearer and more persuasive answers than have so far been generated. The raising of useful questions is itself of great benefit to philosophy of course, being the fodder for continuing philosophical reflection. I believe the questions that will be raised by the following exercise will indeed prove nourishing for more useful scholarly efforts in this particular arena than have so far been made.

The first question, or set of issues, is preliminary to the details of Koza's analysis. It is the general question of whether a political agenda should or should not be the major criterion for judging, understanding, or evaluating what are conceived by those involved in them as being nonpolitical endeavors. Koza, like all feminists and like all others who approach their work with a political agenda (be it race, religion, class, or ideology) as their point and purpose, see and interpret the world through their particular lens. That is precisely their mission. For example, in an article about choral methods texts Koza says, after reviewing many of them, that "As a feminist, I was troubled by topics and issues these texts did not address, by the omissions that came to light when I asked 'Who is not at the table and what is not

being discussed here?' It was quite clear, for example, that almost no attention had been given to diversity issues."[7]

I am sure Koza is correct in that description. I am just as sure that almost
no attention (or no attention) had been paid in this particular literature to
economic inequality issues, fetal rights issues, ageism issues, immigrant mi-
gration issues, balance of trade issues, Jewish persecution issues, and a host
of other pressing, very real, very troubling matters plaguing our world, and
that, therefore, this literature on choral methods is vulnerable to the very
same criticism from each of those perspectives (and countless others).

Further, Koza can apply her particular point of view to any aspect of
music education (or anything else she chooses) to see if her perspective
has been addressed in the manner she would choose to have it addressed.
Feminist analyses of Orff, Kodály, Suzuki, Dalcroze, Manhattanville, CMP,
Gordon, *ad infinitum*, can just as well be made, not only from Koza's particular viewpoint but from a great many others including feminist perspectives quite different from Koza's across a wide range from very conservative
to extremely radical.

So there are important consequences when one adopts the Marxist dictum that "everything is political" as Koza does, making it the linchpin of her
work. The entire world becomes a playing out of a single interest, which is
how the politics of power has affected women. When any other interests
are being pursued in absence of her particular one, the neglect of hers cannot be seen as benign or neutral—it can only be seen as destructive. Since
my book does not directly address issues of gender politics it must, for
Koza, be intentionally and overtly negative in its implications for women.
She says, "To suggest, for example," (as I do by not addressing it) "that the
cultural politics of power should be of less importance than other matters
is to trivialize one of the main means by which we can understand women's
marginalized place in musical realms and can work to end the oppression
of women in our own field."[8]

Imagine how frustrating such a criticism must be to me or anyone else
who happens to be pursuing other agendas. I would find it just as frustrating to be criticized for not regarding a great many other valid, even crucial
social issues to be "of less importance than other matters" such as the ones
I happen to work with, and to then be held accountable for trivializing all
I have not addressed.

We could say to Koza, for example, that her neglect of drug abuse problems in American life suggests that they are "of less importance than other
matters (and) is to trivialize one of the main means (etc., etc.)." "Wait a
minute," she is likely to say. "I did not imply that drug abuse is trivial. I just

have not happened to focus on it in my work." Well, by not making it (and a few thousand other issues) the focus of her work she can only be judged, by her own criterion, as producing maleficent consequences for it and all the others she has so unconscionably neglected.

This is a tough knot to try to untie. I would greatly appreciate, from Koza and anyone else doing social-political critiques, some guidance as to how and when we can gain good insights about ways to clarify and improve music education without paralyzing our efforts by forcing them to be prioritized according to all the pressing, seemingly equally valid social issues surrounding our work. I do not believe it is helpful for Koza, or anyone else, to define our agenda according to, in her case, Cornel West's call for philosophies that are "overtly politicized," and that move "toward the historicized and politicized wilderness" to which West directs us[9] without explaining the priorities by which she judges me (and would judge everyone else in music education, because none has done so) to be villainous for not adopting West's, and her, particular orientation.

Is it possible to do philosophy, in our case philosophy of music education, in such a way that it is applicable to a broad range of people and issues in our culture while not having to be "overtly politicized" and therefore being required to address all political agendas? I do not question the importance of gender inequality as an issue of major importance, now and in all of history and throughout the world. And I do not question its relevance to the work we do in our particular corner of our culture: we are not exempt from *any* of our culture's ills. Is it possible, however, to deal with issues of music education focused directly on music and education rather than on all of the societal issues that will always surround music education?

It would be helpful, I think, to reflect about how to best make use of Sam Hope's distinction between power *in* art, which focuses on the characteristic ways that music makes its contributions to all our lives, and power *from* art, which "involves the multiple world of action and response where matters of art are the primary catalyst. In U.S. society, power *from* art is regularly considered in financial and political terms."[10] The consequences of politicizing the world of the arts have been severe, according to Hope:

Most K–12 arts educators and professors of the arts in higher education have worked with devotion to a democratic ideal that seeks to bring "the best" to everyone, whether in performance, exhibition, or in the context of study. . . . The democratic best-for-all ideal has been damaged temporarily because matters of political power have become omnipresent and overriding. In such a paradigm, art is not to be considered on aesthetic grounds—on the artist's ability to use powers *in* art—but rather on the extent to which certain kinds of power can be drawn *from* art. . . . Need it be said that a power-*from*-art context is not as grounded in the democratic ideal as the power-*in*-art context? The first is often focused on using art for propaganda, the second, on developing individual capacity to produce, contemplate, study, and decide on individual terms.[11]

I understand that Koza would find such ideas extremely distasteful, but I also feel it would benefit all of us to discuss, with as much mutual respect as we can muster, the difficult issues we face because of the politicization of the field of the arts in education. Despite Koza's insistence that politics (in her case the feminist agenda) be the primary if not exclusive focus of music education, such politicization would not, I suggest, be an unmixed blessing, as Hope makes clear.

In addition to finding my book wanting because it is guilty of the most important sin of omission (not being focused on her agenda), Koza faults it for several sins of commission. The first of these is that it attempts to speak of universally shared characteristics of music, of people, and of education. I am guilty, she says, of taking a "traditionalist" posture in arguing that there is a "universally shared human nature . . . which creates a common human experience [in which] sentience and subjectivity" are salient features.

I further claim, she correctly points out, "that experiencing the arts is an effective way for people to understand their shared nature," that the arts "give people opportunities to know about 'the common sentient condition of humans,'" and that music "has a universal appeal, which is to the heart and mind." Further evidence of my "traditionalist" assumptions are my beliefs that "sounds have inherent meaning and that music has intrinsically expressive properties," and that good art "transcends its time of creation and is relevant to human experience in general." When experiencing and studying music from cultures other than our own, I suggest, we should include specific cultural references but also understand it at levels that transcend particulars and allow others to share its musical power. "It is, after all, as *music* that we treasure this or that piece, and it is, after all, for *musical experience* that we aim," she aptly quotes me as asserting. In addition, I claim "that insights into human subjectivity lie in the artistic qualities of works of art," so that art educators "should help people experience the insights found in these works."[12]

Koza likes none of these ideas. To discredit them (along with many more related to them) she gives them all a bad name—"traditionalist." Who, after all, could support "traditionalism," with all the awful connotations such a word brings to mind? That her own posture is a playing out of an ancient tradition—political criticism—goes unnoticed. Also unnoticed is the fact that the issues I address are at the center of ongoing scholarship in philosophy in general, in aesthetics in particular, in ethnomusicology, and in the burgeoning field of cognitive sciences. Scholars in each of these fields are energizing mightily on issues of the shared nature of human cognition, the nature of feeling and its role in what we know and experience, the representations of mind and feeling the arts make available, the transcultural underpinnings of mental and emotional functioning, the implications of increasing availability of musics from a great diversity of cultures on the musical practices and beliefs of particular cultures, and on and on—all complex, recalcitrant problems far from easy resolutions.

Yes, these issues have a long history. No, they are far from being dead; they are alive and well and continuing to perplex, challenge, and invigorate the work in a variety of scholarly communities. I suspect that this is because of their centrality in our ongoing quest to understand more of what makes humans tick. They are, therefore, likely to be with us for a very long time.

But why does Koza find such ideas so repugnant? There are two reasons for her reaction. First, she argues that there are no characteristics or concepts universally applicable to people, music, or education. "'Humanity,' 'art,' and 'education' are historically specific and ever-changing cultural constructs integrally connected to power relations," she asserts.[13]

This assertion, of course, is, precisely, a universal. What Koza is saying is that it is universally the case that (1) people, art, and education are always limited to constructs existing at particular times in history, (2) that these constructs always keep changing, and (3) that they are always related to power. So it is not that universally applicable constructs do not exist (she proclaims these as being universal givens, not recognizing that she has claimed a universal) but that she prefers her own to the ones I employ. That of course is a horse of a different color.

The fact of this matter about universals is that my own view of them encompasses hers (save for item 3, which has not been a factor in my thinking). In her enumeration of constructs I use she quotes the following: "human beings are both universally alike and culturally different."[14] I continue to believe that this is precisely the case. I also add to this belief a third dimension, yielding a tri-partite paradox: that humans are, in several important respects, (a) like all other humans, (b) like some other humans, and (c) like no other humans.

This concept has guided my thinking about music, music education, and a great many related areas for a long period of time. I have found it to give much-needed insight about several of our most vexing conundrums in philosophy, curriculum, research, and so on. The fact that this insight stems from a paradox is, for me, particularly compelling in that I tend to view the human condition as rife with paradoxes, accounting for its maddening uncertainties and contradictions but also for its most deeply satisfying complexities.

More particularly, this construct helps me understand that music does indeed have important characteristics universally applicable at all times and in all cultures.[15] At the very same time, each period of history and each particular culture plays out these characteristics in ways both individual to each and influenced by others, accounting for the striking diversity of musical practice that has always existed in the world. But at still another level, each person engages in music uniquely, for each person is individual and, in a paradoxical sense, incomparable.

The neglect of any of these three dimensions of human reality yields a partial, faulty picture of the complexity of the human condition, of history, of music and the arts, of education, and yes, of social issues such as feminism. I will return to that last application of the construct in my discussion of how we might do better at dealing with the deeper issues of gender inequality than Koza and many others so far writing about it as it applies to music education have been able to do. At the moment, the point needs to be established that "universals" help us identify important constants in human experience (as Koza herself employs them), that these shared characteristics are always manifested in particular contexts and under particular circumstances, and that each human being experiences and manifests these characteristics in an individual way.

Given this multidimensionality of the human condition it would be anomalous for someone to believe that his/her beliefs could be construed to be universal and not historically located and personal. Koza, for example, says that "one shortcoming of aesthetic education stems from Reimer's failure to acknowledge that his own views are situated and partial."[16]

If true, this would seem to be a clear violation of the principle that guides my thinking. Why then does Koza not quote my discussion of the necessary situatedness and partiality of my position, especially in that she quotes other material from the same section in which that discussion appears? "It would be presumptuous in the extreme," I write in chapter 1, page 2, of the book in question,

> To imply that any philosophy, the present one included, can be taken to be a statement "for all time." Music education, as everything else, changes with

time. . . . As one studies the changes in concepts about music education in history it becomes impossible to entertain the notion that any single philosophy can be more than transient. This state of affairs keeps would be philosophers humble (a most salutary condition), but it does not relieve them of the obligation to articulate the underlying beliefs of the time in which they live. Above and beyond the effect of time and the changes time brings is the matter of the variability of beliefs at any one time in history. . . . A philosophy, then, must be conceived as being "of a time," and must also give recognition to the fact that it can only provide a point of departure for practitioners of that time. . . . [T]he little word "A" in the title of this book indicates that the philosophy to be offered is a *particular* philosophy (it is not, to be very explicit, offered as *the* philosophy of music education . . .).[17]

The second reason Koza does not like the universal dimension of philosophical discourse is a political one: universals are capable of being abused in ways that are harmful to women. She gives a long explication of ways this can happen: the definitions selected as universals could be wielded by those in power to exclude women (and men of color); the universals chosen can have devastating material effects on those excluded; biology-as-destiny constructs have wreaked havoc on women's lives and aspirations; ideas of "natural," "inherent," "intrinsic" characteristics can be made to seem commonsensical and then be used to help fuel oppression; universals and consensus can silence dissent and obliterate diversity; if differences are suppressed, alternate perspectives of marginalized groups can be silenced; and on and on with a veritable panoply of horrors.

But what has any of this to do with the actualities of my discussions of music education? I feel tarred, by Koza, with the same brush with which she identifies all the awful things from which women have suffered and can be made to suffer. I have no doubt that women have suffered these things by the abuse of ideas—not just "universalist" ideas but also "contextualist" ideas. These can be and have been perverted to validate sexist views by pointing out how widespread sexism is in diverse cultures so that it can be taken to be therefore, *ipso facto*, acceptable.

Koza leaps unconscionably from the level of specificities about music and the teaching and learning of music with which I deal to the level of gross generalities about how women have fared poorly in this world, implying direct connections that (of course) do not exist and that could not possibly exist except by truly monumental distortions and misapplications by anti-female music education zealots. I cannot imagine who Koza has in mind from the field of music education. Has there been anyone, male or female, who has proposed or even hinted at such destructive ideas as those of which she seems to be so fearful? If I suspected that she believed such ideas to be objectives of my positions about music education I would be both appalled and offended. I prefer not to suspect that however; only to assume that her own zeal carries her away and causes her to be defensive to an unfortunate degree.

I would remind Koza that several important ideals—universals—inherent in American democracy have championed women's and minority's rights and have been beacons to those around the world who reside in countries that do not hold such ideals: human rights, equality of opportunity, freedom of belief, the dignity of individuals, equal treatment before the law, and on and on with all the good impulses representing that which is best about our particular culture. That we have not achieved these ideals is patent: that the ideals deserve our continued fealty is also patent. These are "universals" by which we should strive to live. Koza should be careful not to dismiss the many positive beliefs our culture holds sacred and universal by arguing that since they can be perverted they should be regarded as evil. No one gains by this including feminists and those who support their cause.

The next set of issues Koza addresses as an instance of how my views are destructive to females has to do with "inside/outside dichotomies." I claim, she says correctly, that some things are art and some things are not. I further claim that we should not lump the different arts together, but instead should honor their distinctiveness in teaching them and experiencing them.

These claims are oppressive and exclusionary to women, Koza then asserts, because—predictably—they can be and have been used in such a way as to oppress and exclude women. "For example, when museums display swords, suits of armor, and bludgeons but not quilts or lacework . . . such decisions both reveal and reinforce gendered power relations." (Of course, when the reverse happens to be the case the same result would occur. She does not mention that.) Relegating women's creations to the "not-art category" raises, for feminists, the issue of "the political motivations for promulgating discourses that are, by definition, exclusionary."[18]

So, as before, Koza proposes that we should find reprehensible, because it can possibly be abused, an idea so unremarkable in our culture—that not everything is art—that to discard it would be both pointless and impossible for us. No matter: it is "exclusionary" so it must go.

Is Koza really suggesting this, as she seems to be? Is she suggesting that if everything were to be regarded as art, so that no distinctions could be made between art and anything else, women would then be protected from exclusionary practices? Koza points out that in Bali, "art and life are viewed as one and the same,"[19] (thus, apparently, completely invalidating western constructs of art). But this cliché throws little light on the actualities of Balinese arts, which are defined in that culture not as identical with everything else in Balinese life (not, for example, feeding animals, being sick, quarreling, doing business, making love, educating children, doing the laundry) but as a particular endeavor with particular characteristics serving particular purposes. I Gusti Putu Raka, director of the Art Centre in Dempasar and an official of the Ministry of Culture, says:

> I consider everything, whether static or dynamic, to be art which distinguishes itself by good design and which is able to touch the hearts of men by expressing greatness, sublimity or sensitivity. In other words, for me art is those things that reveal a relationship between man and God. Seen from another perspective, art is the mirror of religious thought.[20]

There is a high level of specialization in Balinese arts:

> In Bali one does not simply make music; one plays the flute, the drum or the ten-key metallophone . . . one does not simply dance, one dances *baris* or *legong*, and here a further distinction is made between the various roles and types. In other words, specialization is very far-reaching in these fields of Balinese art, too.[21]

Further, artistic criteria of goodness are well known and widely applied. While many if not most people get involved in doing art, given the pervasiveness of religious rituals in life and the close connection between art and religion (although there are types and genres that "can only be seen as an expression of the pure pleasure taken in decoration"),[22] not everyone, and not every artistic activity, is regarded as equally successful. I Gusti Gede Raka, an elderly man who is a patron of the arts and an accomplished artist, says (quite beautifully and accurately, I think) "art is thought expressed by the hands. The essentials are form and life." "Here in Bali," he goes on to explain,

> many people produce a bit of art in the *gotong royong* (the system of mutual assistance through work in groups). For example, everyone who knows the shapes and measurements of cremation coffins is obliged to take part in the preparations for a cremation. With all the decorations and ornaments that we have to make, everyone has some artistic practice. But only a few have the gift of searching for what is essential (*cari inti*). There are not so many good artists.[23]

There is a further issue about which Koza seems unaware relating to this culture (which, as it turns out, shares a great deal with our own and others):

> Until very recently the only place for women in Balinese musical life was either as a singer—in the temple or as a character actress in a dramatic performance—or as a performer in the informal *oncangoncangan*, a kind of music made from the interlocking sounds of bamboo poles striking the ground during rice husking. Women's roles in traditional artistic life were generally restricted to dancing, weaving and the making of offerings. Men monopolized the plastic arts of painting and carving, shared the dance stage with women, and played gamelan. . . . During the past decade there have been some changes.[24]

"Exclusion and oppression," it would seem, even in paradise.

I want to suggest that Koza's treatment of the "inside-outside" issue stretches the borderlines of credibility. She asserts, for example, that I believe people who work with their minds are more valuable than people who work with their hands—completely, if not absurdly, misconstruing my explanations of what artists do and how they do it. She declares that I use "highly masculinist" terms to describe what artists do—that they confront resisting material and shape their decisions in a struggle to create an expressive result. This is offensive, says Koza, because women are excluded from such "male turf" in that they have been socialized "that it is not ladylike to fight." "In short, although he seems to believe that women can be artists," (I am deeply grateful for this acquittal, however begrudging) "Reimer associates artists with stereotypically masculine activities and characteristics. Artists, he infers, think and act as white middle-class men typically are socialized to think and act; apparently, women must become like men in order to be artists."[25]

But why does Koza accept what is, to me, the outrageously simplistic stereotype that the struggle artists must go through to create is an inherently male endeavor? I find that idea, which had never occurred to me until Koza articulated it, to be indefensible. Is the hard work required to compose and perform a gender-determined trait, let alone a "white" and "middle-class" trait? If that is true, and therefore excludes women from composing and performing (because they have been socialized that it is unladylike to work hard) what would Koza's remedy be? To suggest that the making of art does *not* require the struggle of creation, so that women, who are apparently incapable of struggling, could then be included in the arts?

Similar (to me) absurdities are abundant in all this material, in both misrepresenting my views and misapplying their implications. I believe, Koza points out, that references in art (stories in program music, for example) are transformed by what artists do with them to achieve meanings transcending the references themselves. These meanings, I have explained, reside in the expressive conditions artists create, and can be shared by those who interact with them. Such interactions always have a creative dimension because the meanings are not fixed, immutable entities, but sets of possibilities requiring an investment of the self in causing meaning to occur. "The point being made here," I explain in my book, "is that all musical experience is self-created whether or not a person is composing or performing."[26]

> The perceiver of the work, upon experiencing its expressive qualities . . . both *shares* the artist's subjectivity captured in the work's expressive qualities and *explores* new possibilities of feeling opened to him by the work's exploratory nature . . . the creator is one person and the perceiver another. Each will respond differently to the expressive qualities created or perceived in the work by virtue of their different lives.[27]

But Koza, unaware of or unwilling to acknowledge my position, opposes it to "those who argue . . . that meanings are constructed and that meaning making is an interactive process," (as if I had to be informed of this) and then, predictably, twists the issue to make it seem to have negative implications for women: "for the most part, women have been excluded from the circles where judgments are passed on what constitute legitimate meanings."[28]

Again, we must ask Koza for guidance as to what she suggests needs to be done about this confused state of affairs, because no guidance is given. Are we to believe that composers do *not* make compositional decisions about how to treat programmatic material? Would that aid the feminist cause? Should males confer with women about what meanings males should regard as "legitimate" when responding to music, so that they do not exclude women's judgments? Which women? What judgments would women make, as women, about what should be found legitimate in engagements with music? Would such judgments be relevant for males, or must we assume that, since women have been excluded from "circles where judgments are passed," there could only be male *or* female responses, and never the twain shall meet?

I trust that my analysis to this point of several of the issues Koza raises gives enough of a sense of her *modus operandi* that I need not continue with detailed explanations of all the rest of her material: doing so would make for a very long paper indeed and would be too tedious both for me to write and readers to read. Those who read Koza's material, and are acquainted with my own, will be readily able to assess whether her treatments of my ideas are persuasive or not. A few important issues not yet addressed need to be attended to, however, so that I can better reflect about needed feminist scholarship.

Koza cites a great many stereotypes about males and females in her attempt to demonstrate that I devalue the female dimension of the stereotype in favor of the male dimension. In her adoption of these binaries she raises two troubling issues. The first is, do I really argue the superiority of the "male" side of the dichotomy? The second is, should I, or anyone, accept the stereotyped dichotomy as having validity in the first place?

For example, she accuses me of favoring the mind over the body in musical experience. This, in itself, she argues, is misguided. Also (since there is always a political point to be made) privileging the mind over the body damages females because the mind has traditionally been regarded as male and the body female.

In my explanations of musical experience and the role feeling always plays in it I emphasize that the sensuous dimension—the "body-feel" of music—is a constant in all musical experience no matter how cerebral some such experience may be, because there is no way to separate what the body feels from what the organized, expressive sounds are doing. I suggest that musical experience has three dimensions: the sensuous, the perceptual, and the creative. "All three dimensions are present in all musical experiences: they are listed in order only because that is the only way language is capable of dealing with things, consecutively rather than simultaneously. Musical experience includes all three simultaneously in various mixtures."[29]

Compare this sentence by Koza: "To suggest that each successive dimension builds onto the previous one is to construct a hierarchy, and Reimer quite clearly considers more to be better—the musical experience, according to his definition, contains all three dimensions."[30] How disheartening this portrayal by Koza is. First she misrepresents by 180 degrees what I said—that these three dimensions are precisely *not* a hierarchy, and then suggests that what I *do* say—that all three dimensions are present in musical experience—is somehow suspect or misguided or harmful.

In my discussion of the sensuosity of musical experience (music "felt tactilely"[31]) I point out that the sensuous sometimes so dominates that the second and third dimensions are obliterated, rendering the experience partial. But, of course, the perceptual dimension can so dominate that the experience is also partial in that body-feeling—the somatized undergoing of musical sounds—is no longer present, the experience having become "the coldly clinical ear training which characterizes the technical-critical response."[32]

The point is that sensuosity, or sound as experienced in the body, and perceptivity, which "includes, in addition to the ever-present sensuous dimension, (1) discernment to some degree of the constituent elements of music—melody, rhythm, harmony, and so on, and (2) reaction to the expressiveness of the perceived musical interrelations"[33] are inseparable and integral to musical experience. Therefore, "no matter what type of music is being used, no matter what the age of the students, no matter what the activity—singing, playing, composing, listening, and so on—musical learning will include some attention to the sensuous level of aesthetic responsiveness."[34]

I regret very much that Koza reads my ideas as separating what I tried very hard to explain cannot be separated. The inseparability of the rational-emotional, the objective-subjective, the mind-body in musical experience has been an absolutely bed-rock concept on which my understanding (and, I had hoped, my explanations) of musical experience have been founded. I have been impressed and encouraged by recent scholarship that adds further depth to the understandings that mind and feeling are more unitary than traditionally held.[35]

The many binaries Koza employs, and her unquestioning attribution of masculinity and femininity to each of their opposed terms, are, I suggest, seriously misrepresentative of the complexity and androgyny of maleness and femaleness. I simply cannot accept the vacuous way she employs these stereotypes—that "mind" is male and "body" female,[36] that "active" is male and "passive" female,[37] that "objectivity" is male but "subjectivity" female,[38] that "rationality" is male and "emotionality" female,[39] that music itself is "feminine,"[40] and so on. Her adoption of these stereotypes is supposed to serve her political purpose of showing that masculine traits have dominated feminine ones, and that my (alleged) preference for the male qualities marks me as anti-female.

But in using the stereotypes for this purpose she perpetuates their harmful premises—premises I reject out of hand. This same point is made by Deborah Knight in her (largely positive) review of a recently published collection of feminist essays:

> Some of the papers here endorse a view of the woman artist that strikes me as entirely of a piece with the very sorts of essentialist oppositions that feminists want to overcome. Many of the authors here characterize the (male) artist as the active manipulator of raw material or content, as one who imposes shape/

form/structure, and thus as one who is understood to stand in a God-like relationship to the art he produces. This is of course a characterization of what
some of these writers refer to as a masculinist or patriarchal aesthetic. But to
counter this conception of the artist with a view which extols the woman artist
as an essentially passive conduit by means of which women's actual experiences
come into artistic representation; to counter this masculinist view of the artist
with one which holds that women artists are little more than documenters,
or detached observers, or mirrors of some extra-literary or extra-artistic set
of experiences, seems to do little more than to come back with the familiar
binarisms that feminist theory ought to have moved beyond. Stephen Heath
noted nearly twenty years ago the problem of feminist theory reverting to the
same old binarisms, the same old images (male as active, female as passive;
male as maker, female as conduit; male as producer of meaning, female as
transmitter of a pre-given meaning). This is of course the risk one runs when
one relies on binary opposition as an argumentative strategy. So if I may offer
a methodological criticism, it is that there is an overemphasis on the logic and
rhetoric of binarisms in some of these papers. It is time to move beyond the
enumeration of binary pairs toward a more complex and contextual analysis of
the situatedness of women's artistic practices.[41]

I believe feminists such as Koza need very much to take Knight's criticism
to heart, because little advance can be made in feminist theorizing when
words are taken by them to be bogeymen (an apt term in this context).

The word "objective," for example, sets off alarm bells for Koza. She is
so offended by the supposed masculinity of the word—its bogeyman function in being "an imaginary evil character"—that she responds to the word
as evil rather than to the way the word is used. I use the word "objective"
to refer to the conditions of musical sound in which expressiveness—feeling—resides. What we need to do, I point out (probably excessively), is
to get our students in closer touch with the conditions of feeling residing
in musical sounds, so those embodied feelings can be experienced sensu-
ously, perceptually, and creatively, whether through listening, performing,
composing, or improvising. Feeling cannot occur if a person does not invest
emotional energy when engaged with musical sounds. The musical sounds
themselves, however, influence what is felt. If they do not—if they are not
heard and internalized—the person may be "experiencing to the accompaniment of music," but is not "experiencing music."

At the ends of chapters 3, 4, 5, and 6 [of A *Philosophy of Music Education*], I suggest four ways we can help musical sounds more powerfully engage our students' subjective experiences of them, by (1) using the broadest
possible spectrum of expressive music, (2) allowing the full power of the

music to be experienced by avoiding an overly technical, overly detailed, overly piecemeal approach in which the wholeness of the music is obscured, (3) focusing on what is teachable in music—its expressive sounds and what those sounds are doing musically—rather than on telling people what they must or should feel. The music can be trusted to be felt. We as teachers should not determine what our students feel—that is the prerogative of each student who has been helped to get closer to the music, especially since the subtleties of musical feeling cannot be specified by language.

However, "while the affective response to the elements of music is indeed ineffable, the elements which can arouse response are not. They are the teacher's stock in trade, constituting the basic materials for teaching and learning at every level and in every activity."[42] Finally, I suggest that the language we use to call attention to what is going on in the music should not interfere with each student's creative, personal response, by specifying what the student is "supposed to" feel.

> Words must be chosen carefully for their power to call attention to the events in music which present the conditions for feeling. But words should never stipulate what that feeling should be. Only one thing can properly cause feelingful responses to music: the sounds of the music themselves. Words which attempt to influence feeling inevitably intrude themselves between the music and the perceiver, preventing the music itself from working its own power. No one has a right to place himself between music and people—least of all the music educator.[43]

All this is what "objective" means in my use of the word—the describable events in music, the entire purpose of which is to foster subjective interactions. I say in this book and elsewhere, over and over, in as many ways as my strained imagination allows me to, the very same thing—get to subjectivity; *that* is the point of it all. Do not settle for learnings unconnected to feelingful engagements.

Here is how Maxine Greene puts this same idea:

> Mere exposure to a work of art is not sufficient to occasion an aesthetic experience. There must be conscious participation in a work, a going out of energy, an ability to notice what is there to be noticed in the play, the poem, the quartet. "Knowing about," even in the most formal academic manner, is entirely different from creating an unreal world imaginatively and entering it perceptually, affectively, and cognitively. To introduce people to such engagement is to strike a delicate balance between helping learners to pay heed—to

attend to shapes, patterns, sounds, rhythms, figures of speech, contours, lines, and so on—and freeing them to perceive particular works as meaningful.[44]

Yet, with all this being as clearly (or at least as frequently) explained as anything I've labored to explain, Koza represents my view as "valuing objectivity over subjectivity,"[45] thus demonstrating her inability (or unwillingness) to recognize the idea behind the word, so offensive is the word itself.

Another example of a feminist reaction to "objectivity" as a codeword rather than an idea is provided by Roberta Lamb, who portrays my explanation of how we must seek the subjectivity of music in its expressive sounds, as follows:

> Reimer's definition of aesthetic/music education focuses on "arouse[ing] aesthetic reaction" through the expressive "qualities of sound" which are the "objective data" to be illuminated systematically by the music teacher. But who is being aroused? And what can it mean to be aroused by objectivity? Not only does this definition limit music education to the replication of the musical canon, thereby maintaining music as the channelization of noise and celebration of violation, but it also points to the politics of the patriarchal aesthetic. It prevents composition—"a new way of making music," according to Jacques Attali.[46]

How can one respond to such a statement, with its twists and turns and irrelevancies so contradictory to my own positions? "Who is being aroused?" Anyone, I had thought, who cares to be involved with music. "What can it mean to be aroused by objectivity?" We are not "aroused by objectivity": we are aroused by musical gestures, and we can teach in ways that help those expressive gestures be felt. Does this limit us to "replication of the musical canon?" Why would I insist, constantly throughout my writings, that we must go beyond the traditional literature on which we have relied too heavily? Are the canonical works (by which I assume she means the three Bs, etc.) a "channelization of noise and celebration of violation"? Do I "prevent composition"? Has she read my pleas that we include composition as a third essential aspect of music education in addition to general music and performance, as in several places throughout my book and in a great many articles?

How disheartening it is that there seems to be, here, little or no hope for useful communication. How sad that, at least for some, such a state has been reached. How do we deal in positive, healing ways with such a deteriorated (intellectually as well as emotionally) state of affairs?

I am grateful to Koza for quoting Jean Grimshaw, who shines a welcome ray of light on the essential issue: "What a great deal of feminist argument has tried to show is that the devaluation of the feminine has not *only* worked against women, although of course it has done that, but that it has led to a distortion of values, concerns and priorities that is of quite general human concern."[47]

That, I think, reaches to the core of the issue, far beyond the stereotyped binaries, the knee-jerk reactions to code-words, the searching for monsters lurking in shadows, even the aggressiveness of overt distortions intended to serve the larger political cause that marks some of the music education feminist literature we have been offered so far. We do, indeed, need to mourn what has occurred negatively to females as a result of their being devalued in ways that have harmed both them and the males and females who have been party to such mechanisms.

As with all the other negatives so endemic to human social relations—racism, ageism, bigotry in every imaginable guise—all of us both participate in and suffer from these weaknesses of human character, and all of us need to face the consequences of our weaknesses, in their diminution of our own lives and the lives of others. I will not be so presumptuous as to offer some sort of solution for this human dilemma, for, alas, I have none. But I do want to raise some questions for all of us in music education, feminists in particular, to ponder (if not answer, which may not be possible given the complexity of the situation).

Grimshaw pinpoints the toughest issue, in saying we have devalued "the feminine." At one level we understand immediately what that means. For example, women in many if not most cultures have been the nurturers of children, having been considered to be "inside" or "family" oriented rather than "outside" or "political arena" oriented, and have often therefore not been given the vote or other political power or responsibility. "The feminine," here refers to a characteristic attributed to females that has clearly delimited their political influence and also at the same time caused political influence to be grossly unequally distributed and has caused politics to be one-sided in manifesting the attributed "male characteristic" of lesser concern for nurturing, home, and family. All people have suffered as a result; females by being deprived of what males (and many if not most females) assumed was "male" by nature, males by being deprived of what females (and many if not most males) assumed was "female" by nature.

Now we have deeply questioned the validity of such an unshaded binary assumption, equally harmful to both genders. But to question that assumption is to raise the ante on the complexities of the issue. Once rejecting any one of such previously unquestioned binaries (strong-weak, active-passive, mind-body, and so forth) all the rest of them would logically be candidates for rejection as well, all of them being just as suspect and all of them capable of being just as injurious to both genders in limiting both to that narrow band on the spectrum of human possibilities defined by simplistic gender stereotypes. A major goal of the feminist movement has been to repudiate such stereotypes, thus opening the entire spectrum to females, with the attendant result, less noticed, that the entire spectrum is then opened to males as well.

Because females have borne the brunt of life-limiting and ego-diminishing suppressions caused by the higher value attributed to the assumed "male" characteristics, claiming full access to all such values is then experienced by females, reasonably and obviously, as "liberation."

The secondary result is the "liberation" of males from the very same restrictions. This is not so often regarded as liberation for males, however, because, on the one hand, sharing those highly regarded values with females can be experienced as diluting both the values and males' privileged status, and, on the other hand, those other options gained by males have for so long and in so many cultures been regarded as "lesser." Hence the struggle between males and females over this issue: the effects of women's liberation are seen by some or many males to be disadvantageous.

At this level, then, several difficult questions arise amid a welter of confusions. The gender-defined characteristics to which Grimshaw alludes are, on the one hand, seemingly accepted by her as valid. The objection she raises is not to the attribution of such characteristics to males and females but that the female characteristics are regarded as having lesser value. This is a position often taken in feminist literature, as exemplified in Koza's and Lamb's writings (and in the writings Knight criticizes). Apparently it is acceptable to demarcate males and females according to the binary stereotypes: the goal is to elevate or equalize the status of the female side. But how can this be accomplished if equal access is also demanded to the other side of the binary? If the stereotypes are themselves rejected as being invalid would it not seem counterproductive, if not illogical, to demand higher status for just one of the polarities?

The questions deepen. Are gender stereotypes, or gendered characteristics, simply fabrications with no basis in any reality beyond power-seeking social constructions? That is, in the paradox of the universal, the group, and the individual, is gender grouping to be regarded as essentially nonexistent, all humans (and perhaps all other gendered organisms) being universally the same in all ways except the obviously physical?

Koza hints at this possibility in an article on college choral methods texts, when she says in her discussion of the "missing males" problem in choral groups and the deleterious effects on females of undue attention to it, "Faced with an issue clearly related to dominant constructions of gender, a socialist feminist might suggest that the most equitable and lasting solutions to the missing males problem are based on changes in traditional construction of gender or on the abolition of gender altogether."[48]

Here we have a clearly universalist stance being (at least tentatively) proposed: if we were to simply eliminate or abolish gender altogether we would then have reached an "equitable and lasting" solution to the male-female issue. But in other places (and fiercely in the article on which I have concentrated in this paper) the existence of gender characteristics is both accepted and seemingly defended by Koza. Can we or should we hope for a "universalist" answer to the dilemmas gender poses? Would the elimination of gender differences be desirable for human affairs? Would that be possible given that gender associations have always existed in human history? Or is it a matter, not of either/or, with gender either fully determining our destinies on the one hand or, on the other, having no influence on them whatsoever, but of "to some degree" and "in certain respects," as the paradox suggests?

That is how I understand the issue: that gender does, in fact, to some degree and in certain ways play essential or important roles in our lives, roles we would do well to cherish or at least respect. That is the second dimension of the paradox, which is as determining of the human condition as the first.

But how do we avoid all the abuses of gender differences, from which both females and males have suffered in so many aspects of human life including, indubitably, music education? Surely it is universally the case that humans, regardless of gender, enjoy music, find music meaningful, deserve opportunities to learn music. Surely, I would argue, there are attributes of musical experience universally shared by both males and females: that both engage in music with that unity of mind, body, and feeling music depends on for its power; that both are creative in musical thinking, doing, and feeling; that musical creativity and responsiveness can be enhanced for both by education; that both are capable of sharing a broad diversity of musics, and on and on with all the "universals" that Koza (confusedly, I believe) denounces.

Can we recognize the universality of musicality in males and females yet at the same time recognize gender differences that may influence how those universals are played out in the lived experience of each? Can we do this in ways that are not prejudicial, limiting, or disrespectful of whatever gender differences may be both real and valuable? What might such differences be? Can we be educated to better understand if there are differences that are valid and life enhancing and differences that are invalid and life diminishing? How desperately we need guidance toward better understandings of these matters. How difficult they are to address, in their endless complexities and convolutions.

Those difficulties stem to a large extent from the third dimension of the paradox, that despite universally shared qualities beyond gender, and despite gender-associated qualities that may be equally real and important, each person manifests the universal and the partial in an individual way, these individualities ranging across the entire continuum available to both females and males and therefore contradicting, in instance after instance, the realities of any existing gender associations.

For example, it seems reasonable to believe that the propensity to perform music is not limited to either females or males—it is a universally shared trait. Yet a great deal of evidence exists that choice of performance medium is gender associated, not just in modern American culture but in many, perhaps all, cultures and periods of history. Is it too facile to explain these medium preferences as being only societal prejudices or as a male plot to guard power (although no doubt both these explanations are applicable in some instances)? What if there may really be a gendered quality validly attributed to various musical instruments? Would it be harmful to believe that that is possible or even acceptable?

Well, we are likely to argue, not if individuals were then prevented or discouraged from choosing what appealed to them *despite* gender associations. *That* is where the associations become restrictive, and, if applied strictly, injurious to individual need (not to mention injurious to musical culture in that we would not have, for example, the great male flutist Jean-Pierre Rampal or the great female percussionist Evelyn Glennie)! When individual choices contradict group characteristics conventionally accepted, tension, or at least awkwardness, arises. This would seem to be a problem eminently manageable by sensitive people, who can encourage diversity and reward it in face of established expectations (however valid or invalid such expectations might be). But how can we best encourage the individual freedom to choose while also not discouraging or disparaging those who make the more stereotypical choices willingly and genuinely?

These questions and problems represent only a tiny subset of all those arising from the complexities of gender as they interact with music education. All of us need as much help with them as we can get. I freely admit a good deal of bewilderment in face of these complexities: I feel humble, indeed, even in trying to articulate them let alone suggesting solutions. I recognize that my attempts to do both must be inadequate to their magnitude.

I seek, from those who have thought deeply about these issues, guidance as to how I and all other people devoted to the ideal of equality in our personal and professional lives can better understand and cope with these seemingly intractable issues. I have energized on them personally and strenuously throughout my adult years, in large part through my relationships with the significant females in my life, including my two daughters, all of whom have struggled with the often distasteful and sometimes injurious effects of being restricted in a plethora of ways by virtue of their gender. I am fully convinced of the wisdom of Grimshaw's comment that sexism has distorted values, concerns, and priorities of "quite general human concern," in my growing awareness of how males' lives have often been impoverished by the mechanisms of sexist prejudice, just as females' lives have been. I am often aggrieved when I realize how many choices in my life were not and could not have been freely made but were imposed on me by unexamined beliefs about which I only later became conscious, too late to rectify the past.

I do not blame or begrudge the anger in much of the feminist literature, therefore, having shared some of it myself, vicariously through females' and other males' experiences and directly through my own. I do regret the thoughtlessness such anger can cause, however, because that can hurt all of us rather than help, as by attributing evil motives where they do not exist.

For me, when beginning my career, the major attraction of the new (to me) ideas being explored under the name "aesthetic education" was their inclusiveness and their musicality. I was terrifically excited about a point of view giving validity and respect to all musics rather than only the "classics" I had studied in my training to be a musician. I felt uplifted by the populism inherent in the ideas I was encountering—that music is not just for the socially elite or the musically gifted or the culturally privileged: music (and by extension all the arts) is the property of all people, and they do not have to be in the favored class "musicians" to be worthy of musical education.

Education, these views were suggesting, need not be watered down to suit the supposed limitations of those not devoted to becoming musicians: it could be as rigorous, as musically powerful, as challenging to them as it needed to be for those few who chose to become more fully engaged in some aspect of it such as performing. Musical learning could empower *all* our students to know and experience the affective power of compelling music of all types, styles, and cultures. Away with the elitist and restrictive assumptions that only some music, and only some people, are worthy of our professional ministrations, and that only some musical activities are worthy of our time! For me, the old slogan "music for every child and every child for music" took on new and urgent meaning as I began to glimpse new perspectives on inclusion and empowerment that seeming cliché could imply under the liberating ideas to which I was being introduced.

I have not lost my faith in the ideal that all music can be relevant to the experience of all people, or my excitement about the inclusiveness and empowerment that ideal implies. Certainly its subtleties and complexities have become more apparent to me as I have tried to articulate both the underlying principles of aesthetic education and its practical applications. I regret that my articulations have been a good deal less than perfect, reflecting both my imperfect understandings and abilities to communicate. I do not believe, however, that "exclusion and oppression," of females or anyone else, characterizes what I and the many others who have been guided by these ideals have attempted. I trust that music educators still motivated by inclusion and empowerment will continue to pursue these ideals, recognizing as allies in that endeavor, rather than as enemies, all individuals, of all group identities, universally devoted to sharing musical experience more widely and more effectively.

NOTES

1. Judith K. Delzell, "Variables Affecting the Gender-Role Stereotyping of High School Band Teaching Positions," *The Quarterly Journal of Music Teaching and Learning* 4, no. 4; 5, no. 1 (Winter 1993/Spring 1994): 77–84.

2. Molly A. Weaver, "A Survey of Big Ten Institutions: Gender Distinctions Regarding Faculty Ranks and Salaries in Schools, Divisions, and Departments," Ibid., 91–99.

3. Laree M. Trollinger, "Sex/Gender Research in Music Education: A Review," Ibid., 22–39.

4. Vicki L. Eaklor, "The Gendered Origins of the American Musician," Ibid., 40–246.

5. Julia Koza, "Aesthetic Music Education Revisited: Discourses of Exclusion and Oppression," *Philosophy of Music Education Review* 2, no. 2 (Fall 1994): 75–91.

6. Bennett Reimer, *A Philosophy of Music Education*, 2nd ed. (Englewood Cliffs, NJ: Prentice Hall, 1989).

7. Julia E. Koza, "Getting a Word in Edgewise: A Feminist Critique of Choral Methods Texts," *The Quarterly Journal of Music Teaching and Learning* 5, no. 3 (Fall 1994): 68.

8. Koza, "Aesthetic Music Education Revisited," 76.

9. Ibid., 75.

10. Samuel Hope, "Art, Power, and Arts Education," *Arts Education Policy Review* 95, no. 6 (July/August 1994): 2–3.

11. Ibid., 10.

12. Koza, "Aesthetic Music Education Revisited," 76–77.

13. Ibid., 77.

14. Ibid., 76, quoted from Reimer, *A Philosophy*, 145.

15. For many examples from the ethnomusicological literature, see the discussions in part II of my "Can We Understand Music of Foreign Cultures?" in Heath Lees, ed., "Musical Connections: Tradition and Change," *International Society for Music Education*, 1994; in my "Selfness and Otherness in Experiencing Music of Foreign Cultures," *The Quarterly Journal of Music Teaching and Learning* 2, no. 3 (Fall 1991); and in my "Music Education in Our Multimusical Culture," *Music Educators Journal* (March 1993).

16. Koza, "Aesthetic Music Education Revisited," 77.

17. Reimer, *A Philosophy*, 2–3.

18. Koza, "Aesthetic Music Education Revisited," 79–80.

19. Ibid., 79.

20. Quoted in Urs Ramseyer, *The Art and Culture of Bali* (New York: Oxford University Press, 1977), 13.

21. Ibid., 193.

22. Ibid., 16.

23. Ibid., 16.

24. Michael Tenzer, *Balinese Music* (Berkeley: Periplus Editions, 1991), 109.

25. Ibid., 80–81.

26. Reimer, *A Philosophy*, 130.

27. Ibid., 67.

28. Koza, "Aesthetic Music Education Revisited," 81.

29. Reimer, *A Philosophy*, 126.

30. Koza, "Aesthetic Music Education Revisited," 88.

31. Reimer, *A Philosophy*, 126.

32. Ibid., 128.

33. Ibid.

34. Ibid., 127.

35. For an excellent discussion of the relations of thinking and feeling in musical experience, see Ann Stokes, "Thinking and Feeling in Music," *The Quarterly Journal of Music Teaching and Learning* 5, no. 3 (Fall 1994): 37–48.

36. Koza, "Aesthetic Music Education Revisited," 86.

37. Ibid., 88.

38. Ibid., 87.

39. Ibid., 86.

40. Ibid., 89.

41. Hilde Hein and Carolyn Korsmeyer, eds., *Aesthetics in Feminist Perspective* (Bloomington: Indiana University Press, 1993), reviewed by Deborah Knight, *Journal of Aesthetics and Art Criticism* 53, no. 1 (Winter 1995): 95–96.

42. Reimer, *A Philosophy*, 54.

43. Ibid.

44. Maxine Green, "Art and Imagination," *Phi Delta Kappan* 76, no. 5 (January 1995): 379–80.

45. Koza, "Aesthetic Music Education Revisited," 87.

46. Roberta Lamb, "Aria Senza Accompagnamento: A Woman Behind the Theory," *The Quarterly Journal of Music Teaching and Learning* 4, no. 4; 5, no. 1 (Winter 1993/Spring 1994): 12.

47. Jean Grimshaw, *Philosophy and Feminist Thinking* (Minneapolis: University of Minnesota Press, 1986), 74, quoted in Koza, "Aesthetic Music Education Revisited," 89.

48. Koza, "Big Boys Don't Cry (or Sing): Gender, Misogyny, and Homophobia in College Choral Methods Texts," *The Quarterly Journal of Music Teaching and Learning* 4, no. 4; 5, no. 1 (Winter 1993/Spring 1994): 59.

Note: I am grateful to the members of the Center for the Study of Education and the Musical Experience, the Ph.D. student and faculty research group at Northwestern University, for their insights about the topic of this paper, and especially to Donald Casey, Marian Dura, and Jody Kerchner for their helpful comments on a first draft.

8

RESEARCH AND JUSTIFICATION
IN ARTS EDUCATION: AN
ILL-FATED ROMANCE

As the twentieth century draws to a close, the arts in education find themselves in the midst of a major movement to justify their existence on the basis of their imputed contributions to learnings of every imaginable sort other than those related to aesthetic/artistic development. Research attempting to "prove" this transfer capacity of the arts is burgeoning, causing giant rifts in the professional arts education community as to whether such efforts are positive or negative for us.

Early in 2000 a letter arrives from the Getty Trust inviting me to a conference at their famed art museum in Los Angeles. An invitation-only gathering of some three dozen influential arts educators and researchers, the conference focuses on the monumental three-year study by Ellen Winner and Lois Hetland of all this research (published as a special issue of *The Journal of Aesthetic Education*, 2000). Ten of the invitees are asked to respond to particular sections of the study. My assignment is to do so with the two chapters on music and spatial reasoning, no doubt in part because my article on that topic, "Facing the Risks of the Mozart Effect" (1999), has been widely published.

I am reliving, at that time, my discomfort with all this self-serving and largely unproductive advocacy fervor that I had expressed in the first article in this book from a half-century before. To keep my spirits up I decide to approach my remarks with a slightly irreverent attitude, comparing this latest spasm of "sell the arts by any means possible" to the hazards of romantic entanglements. Our research has become so embedded (an apt term here) in the idea of promoting the arts for their possible effects on other learnings as to make our love of art seem tawdry.

Can we—should we—focus our advocacy arguments toward the allegation that they have beneficial effects on learning other subjects, taking us far beyond our core values? For some, anything we claim, no matter how far-fetched, is fair game if it gets us support. For others, our virtue is violated when we dilute the core in any way. Still others are comfortable with compromise. At bottom, I suggest, we are faced—past, present, and no doubt in the future—with a moral dilemma each of us must confront.

The following essay was originally published in Ellen Winter and Lois Hetland, eds., *Beyond the Soundbite: Arts Education and Academic Outcomes* (Los Angeles: The Getty Center, 2000). Used by permission.

When I'm asked to offer remarks about some topic or issue I usually try to give my reflections a title. That helps me concentrate my mind: it gives me direction and focus.

The title I've chosen for this response to the two papers I was assigned allows me to deal with what interests me most about the studies we're considering here; their use as a basis for justifying the arts in education. My interest in research in the field of the arts has mostly to do with whether such research can help us do a more effective job of enhancing people's satisfactions from the arts, and if it can, how we can best take advantage of what research suggests so as to improve our educational practices. Given that orientation, that is, a devotion to what has often been called aesthetic education, and my hopes that research can be a powerful guide for providing it effectively, I find myself dealing in this assignment and in a good deal of research on the arts over the past several years, with a focus opposite to that which I cherish and to which I have devoted my career.

In this I am quite unexceptional. Many, perhaps most arts educators (I'm tempted to say practically all arts educators) believe that the arts (and, of course, their particular art above all) are so valuable to humans for their distinctive characteristics as to warrant their inclusion as a basic component of education. In this cause an ocean of blood has been shed during the course of well over a hundred and fifty years.

So it's a bit ironic, amusing in a kind of twisted way, that we are going through a period in which research, which has only fairly recently been embraced by the arts education fields as possibly being relevant to their desires, has seemed to have turned those desires on their head. Massively, pervasively, and at an astonishingly popular level, research in the arts has given the impression that it has flip-flopped in its purpose, focusing on how the arts can enhance just about everything one can imagine *other than* aesthetic satisfactions.

Never mind that most research in arts education has nothing to do with the effects of arts study on academic achievement. All that research is completely unknown to the public. In the popular perception, and trickling down alarmingly into the arts education fields themselves and to some efforts in those fields to justify their existence, recent research has seemed to establish, conclusively, that the arts are valuable because they contribute, significantly and causally, to learnings having nothing whatsoever to do with the quality of aesthetic/artistic interactions. Those contributions to academic learnings, it is hoped by some and perhaps many, will finally provide the arts with the justification they need in order to be accepted as necessary subjects in the school curriculum. Our romance with research has seemed to have left us embracing a lover whose mind is clearly not concentrated on the aesthetic/artistic benefits of the arts to which our hearts have for so long been devoted. O jilted love!

Disappointed lovers, not always in a clear state of mind, can rationalize their situation to make it seem to be what they had hoped for. Of course! It's all for the best! Our lover's eyes may not be on us, but in gazing into another's eyes they may find there our own true value, thereby returning to us what we crave. If the arts can enhance SAT scores, creative thinking abilities outside the arts, spatial-temporal reasoning, mathematics skills, reading ability, verbal skills, cognitive functioning in a host of non-arts subjects, all these will finally provide us with the esteem, the respect, the affection if not love we have yearned for all these years, and we will be redeemed in our self-estimation.

Pathos, indeed. I envision a "personals" ad in the newspaper: *Arts education, sensitive, fun-loving, creative, heart in its right place, seeks love (will settle for respect) from anyone willing to accept it for what it is. Committed relationship desired. One-nighters considered.*

While my heart dwells primarily on the arts as unique domains for creating and sharing human meanings, my mind, and some of my heart, is and always has been enamored with quantitative research—with the realities, the factualities, it attempts to deal with. So when I examine the research on music's effects on spatial-temporal reasoning part of me is able to put aside my concern for the aesthetic/artistic functions of the arts—the basis for their existence, after all—and to immerse myself with great interest in the methodologies and findings having to do with brain function; in this case interactions between music listening and spatial-temporal (S-T) reasoning and music performance and S-T reasoning. These are topics compelling in and of themselves, quite apart from matters of aesthetics, of education, and of justification. Whatever we can learn about how our brains work is worth learning; in fact is terribly important for us to learn. If we take the admonition "know thyself" seriously we must learn as much as we can about the mechanisms allowing us to know ourselves. So let me, for a moment, focus on the research I was asked to review—the two chapters by Lois Hetland on music and spatial reasoning—as strictly research intended to explore an interesting, even intriguing aspect of brain function.

I admire a great deal about the studies Hetland reviews so thoroughly and painstakingly. They exhibit a high degree of imagination in their clever attempts to pin down several very elusive sets of human capacities and to get a handle on how they might or might not interrelate. But we must remember that listening to music and performing music are each, in and of themselves, among the most complex, most multifaceted, most culturally saturated, and most individually determined endeavors in which humans engage. They each involve mindfulness at its highest levels, which includes and subsumes, by necessity, the feelings and the body as integral components. "Music-think," in any of its manifestations—composing, performing composed music, improvising, listening, conducting, and so forth—depends on a unity of mind, body, and feeling in the cause of creating and sharing meaning as only sounds organized for that purpose are capable of doing. That endeavor takes place at three interactive levels: the universal level reflecting the inherent capacity of all humans to be musical, the cultural level in which that generic capacity is given particularity in the socially constructed regulatory system each culture has devised, and at the individual level, in which all humans both adopt and adapt their musical culture to serve their singular, personal proclivities and capacities.

We are presented, in music, with an activity as rich and dense and complicated as anything humans attempt to do. This activity is a function of mind: not simply of brain. That distinction is crucial. Mind is dependent on brain function, of course, but far surpasses it in both breadth and depth. Here is how Antonio Damasio puts it, in his 1994 book *Descartes' Error: Emotion, Reason, and the Human Brain.*

> There may be some Cartesian disembodiment behind the thinking of neuroscientists who insist that the mind can be fully explained solely in terms of brain events, leaving by the wayside the rest of the organism and the surrounding physical and social environment—and also leaving out the fact that

part of the environment is itself a product of the organism's preceding actions. I resist the restriction not because the mind is not directly related to brain activity, since it obviously is, but rather because the restrictive formulation is unnecessarily incomplete, and humanly unsatisfactory. To say that mind comes from brain is indisputable, but I prefer to qualify the statement and consider the reasons why the brain's neurons behave in such a thoughtful manner. For the latter is, as far as I can see, the critical issue.[1]

When dealing with the arts, human functioning at the level of the thoughtful is indeed the critical issue. Research at the level of brain function must, because of its focus, deal with particles of mind, perhaps eventually being able to be aggregated to approach the level of the mindful but realistically limited to what neurological research is interested in—human functioning at the brain activity level. Even at that level, no research modality, no research technique, no research tool, is capable of embracing and accounting for the totality of a phenomenon as complicated as the brain.

So selections must be made. From the whole, a part, or a few parts, must be chosen for examination. And from all the many possible ways to examine those chosen aspects, only one or a few examinations can be made; those which are feasible given our limited research knowledge, our restricted choices of subjects, limited amounts of time and money, and the severe restrictions in the ways available to us to measure—to specify with exactitude—what is actually going on in even a modest set of behaviors and what effects are actually being produced by them.

What I am suggesting here is that brain research on a high-order human cognitive capacity such as musical experience, itself presenting complexities of such magnitude as to force us to atomize our focus, compounded by seeking relationships between that capacity and others perhaps equally complex, leaves us in a position of great vulnerability as to any expectations of attaining much more than modest insights, if that, into selected, highly restricted, probably isolated aspects of the phenomena to which our research efforts are directed.

These, as we all know, are the realities of brain research—the tough conditions every brain-function researcher must face. That requires us to appreciate such research, to appreciate the courage it takes, the skills and the cunning it calls upon, and the modesty it requires, given that it attempts to open windows onto the most complex phenomenon in nature of which we are aware—the workings of the human brain. We must be grateful to those who devote themselves to such difficult work, and who present us with findings they have been intelligent enough and lucky enough to have hit upon, however insecure, partial, puzzling, and, yes, even inconsequential they may be. It is easy to criticize researchers for not presenting us with significant, flawless, and guaranteed results. I am suggesting that we must temper our expectations to what is achievable, and be generous in our respect for what is, after all, a daunting task.

In that spirit of appreciation I would like to offer a few suggestions for further conduct of research such as I was asked to review, that might lead it in the direction of mind—in the direction of what Damasio calls "the critical issue."

In regard to the so-called Mozart Effect caused by listening to his (and perhaps others') music, it is important to recognize that listening to music, in addition to being complex as I have already mentioned, requires an act of meaning-construction on the part of the listener. To portray music listening as essentially passive, as is often done, seriously misconstrues what it entails. Music listening indeed can be passive, meaning inattentive and perfunctory, as can looking at visual art, watching a dance or a play, or reading a novel or poem. The same is true of "making" music, which, in many people's minds mistakenly means only performing, forgetting that every musical involvement requires music to be "made." Performing can also be inattentive and perfunctory, as every performance teacher knows full well. The same applies, of course, to "making" in all the arts.

The simple admonition "pay attention to the music," given by Rauscher and Rideout to their subjects, seemed to produce in them higher effect sizes than found in other studies where music was played without that reminder. That's very interesting. Just imagine what might happen if genuine instruction in listening, such as music educators are supposed to be able to provide, which activates perceptual, contextual, affective, and kinetic dimensions of creativity in the listening act, were supplied in abundance to subjects, or at least to the levels supplied in the performing instruction studies. Would serious music education devoted to enhancing musical intelligence as it is particularly manifested in the music listening role, affect S-T measures more positively than when no instruction is given, or equally positively, or less positively, or perhaps negatively? And what dimensions of *active* listening are most salient to S-T responses?

Apply the same ideas beyond the performance of composed music, to improvising and to composing. We would then begin to better understand how genuine musical experience, such as music education attempts to cultivate, might be implicated in other brain functions compatible with and affected by musical experience when such experience is at its higher rather than lower levels. We would get closer to understanding how learning affects brain function both within and outside musical experience itself. We would get closer to understanding the implications of brain function for mind.

But a serious effort must be made to reduce the level of triviality of the measures used to ascertain effects in this research. The most common measure of "S-T reasoning" has been the Paper Folding and Cutting subtest from the Stanford-Binet IQ test. The concept of intelligence embodied in that test and others like it represents a now discredited or at least severely questioned construct of what intelligence is, how it works, and how it might be measured. To call by the term "reasoning" a task such as, for example, identifying what pattern is made in a folded paper napkin with holes cut in it and then unfolded, is to stretch to unacceptable limits any concept of reasoning that might be meaningful outside a behaviorist laboratory. Unreal in its construal of what musical experience entails (in these cases listening and performing), unreal in its approach to measurement, in which an atomistic instrumentation substitutes for the role-based making of meaning that reasoning requires, we are left with a few shards, a few glimmers, of possible relationships, at the sub-meaning level, between two artificially represented phenomena of mind.

I believe we can do better than this if we elevate our concept of measurement to include aspects of thoughtfulness; aspects of mind. I believe that is doable if we can relax, to some reasonable extent, the statistical/experimental mind-set governing present brain research. We can indeed admire the pioneering research that has taken us this far, and we can hope that more holistic approaches, added to the more traditional experimental paradigm so far employed, will provide a much-needed dimensionality to research on this topic.

To return to the issue of justification, we cannot ignore the reality that, in the world of education policy-making, the research we are reviewing has caused a mountain to be made of a mole-hill. I do not fault the researchers for this, although a bit more evident modesty on their part might have forestalled the painful and embarrassing exaggerations and misconceptions that have occurred. Hetland ends her chapter on Music and Spatial Reasoning by saying that my concern, expressed in my article "Facing the Risks of the Mozart Effect,"[2] that "music educators might be held accountable for their students' having learned spatial skills, which could corrupt the quality of programs in developing musical understanding, can be laid to rest for now."

She must excuse me for continuing to not rest easily. Her very next sentence explains why. "However," she says, "music educators and policy

makers will need to be vigilant to ensure that music programs are designed
to teach music, and music educators are held accountable for musical,
rather than spatial, understanding."[3] Indeed. Vigilance *is* called for, rather
than rest.

Throughout the entire Winner-Hetland report we are wisely reminded,
time and again, that the arts cannot be and should not be justified on the
basis of any possible and as yet only poorly and partially substantiated
contributions they might make to academic improvement. Fine. But let's
get real. All of us here can produce, at a moment's notice, dozens if not
hundreds of recent examples of claims for the value of the arts in education because of "research-based proof" that they contribute to academic
learnings, to "general intelligence" (as if there is such a thing), and to a
host of other values for which they are a magic bullet, and, on that basis,
that they can be justified as part of schooling. The Winner-Hetland study
demonstrates that in educational policy-making facts play a minor role as
compared with credulity.

This is the case, unfortunately, not only in regard to the arts, but also
in areas as high stakes as teaching verbal literacy. I urge you to read the
paper "The Politics of Literacy Teaching: How 'Research' Shaped Educational Policy," in the November, 1999, *Educational Researcher*. It reports
on how completely misguided representations of supposedly unequivocal
findings about the superiority of a code-emphasis approach to reading led
to adoption of curricula for which no evidence could actually be found in
the research.[4]

So apparently we are not alone in being in a compromised position in regard to research and justification. Nevertheless, we must acknowledge the
moral dilemma with which this romance we have stumbled into confronts
us (as romantic involvements often do). Do we try to take advantage of this
unexpected interest in the arts, despite its shaky foundation, on the argument that anything at all that keeps our foot in the door is worth having,
warranted or not, and we can then surreptitiously go about our aesthetic
business? Or do we stand firm on aesthetic justifications, refusing to have
our virtue (such as it is) sullied by lesser (at least to us) concerns?

If we do take that high road we are then faced with the obligation to
explain in a clear, understandable way, just what it is about the arts that,
on their own terms, is valuable enough to deserve precious educational
time and effort. While philosophers of arts education continue to probe the
complexities of that issue, the profession as a whole is, in fact, able to articulate, quite simply and precisely, explanations that most people are likely
to understand. For example, the Winner-Hetland report says "The arts are

a fundamentally important part of culture, and an education without them is an impoverished education leading to an impoverished society. Studying the arts should not have to be justified in terms of anything else. The arts are as important as the sciences: they are time-honored ways of learning, knowing, and expressing."[5]

For purposes of public advocacy a statement like this, and many others similar to it, seems to me intellectually respectable and quite easily comprehensible. Yet offering such explanations, in a great variety of ways, as arts educators have done for a very long time and continue to do, seems not to be persuasive enough to provide a secure and important place for the arts in education. This is what drives arts educators crazy; that we exist in a culture more enamored with secondary benefits of the arts than with primary ones. It tempts them to abandon or at least weaken their resolve, and to reach out to whatever might improve their sense of self-worth even if their virtue becomes tarnished by doing so.

I have taken the position[6] that it is possible to accommodate both intra- and extra-aesthetic benefits of arts education in advocacy efforts, and even in curriculum, so long as our fealty to aesthetic learnings remains resolute. On the continuum from complete capitulation to unwarranted but popularly effective claims, to complete rejection of any concerns other than aesthetic ones, each of us will have to find our level of moral acceptability. It comes down, I suppose, to what we'll do for love.

NOTES

1. Antonio Damasio, *Descartes' Error: Emotion, Reason, and the Human Brain* (New York: G. P. Putnam's Sons, 1994), 250–51.

2. Bennett Reimer, "Facing the Risks of the 'Mozart Effect,'" Grandmaster Series, *Music Educators Journal* 86, no. 1 (July 1999). Reprinted in *Arts Education Policy Review* 101, no. 2 (November/December 1999). Reprinted in *Phi Delta KAPPAN* 81, no. 4 (December 1999).

3. L. Hetland, "Learning to Make Music Enhances Spatial Reasoning," *The Journal of Aesthetic Education* 34, no. 3/4 (2000): 224

4. Richard L. Allington and Haley Woodside-Jiron, "The Politics of Literacy Teaching: How 'Research' Shaped Educational Policy," *Educational Researcher* 28, no. 8 (November 1999): 4–13.

5. E. Winner and L. Hetland, "The Arts and Academic Achievement: What the Evidence Shows," *Arts Education Policy Review* (executive summary).

6. In, for example, Reimer, "Facing the Risks," note 2 above.

9

ROOTS OF INEQUITY AND INJUSTICE: THE CHALLENGES FOR MUSIC EDUCATION

For a very long time, our profession existed in a state of relative innocence, ignoring or disbelieving that the world's tough political and moral enigmas have anything to do with us. Comforting. Or, perhaps, obtuse.

In recent years a major turn toward interest in issues of equity and justice in music and music education has occurred, including concerns of feminism but going beyond them. Primarily involved at this time are college and university faculty members with advanced skills in scholarship and research who also, in their teacher education function, prepare students to become active participants in and proponents for social justice initiatives. A large, challenging literature has been created, and conferences have been and are scheduled to address such issues. Clearly, our profession is now situated in a much larger context.

As with the feminist movement, I am drawn to the larger issues of social justice and our responsibilities to them. When asked to present at a conference on "Music Education, Equity, and Social Justice" at Teachers College, Columbia University, I take the opportunity to probe the underlying sources of the dark side of human behavior, the foundations of our less than entirely admirable history as a species. I have been engaged in study of such matters for many years, not as a music educator but in my personal work in exploring the human condition at its transpersonal, transcultural level. At that level, inequity and injustice are pervasive in our psyches.

Why? This paper helps me clarify that unfortunate reality and the responsibilities we as music educators bear toward it, recognizing that, important as it is to open ourselves to such matters, we also continue to have an obligation to music and to the teaching and learning of music. Should we—can we—fulfill both imperatives?

The following essay was originally published in *Music Education Research* 9, no. 2 (July 2007). Used by permission from Taylor & Francis Ltd.

ABSTRACT

Equity and justice are human constructs, the inventions of human imagination. They exist nowhere in nature, in which inequality, the root cause of inequity and injustice, is essential for survival. Our history as a race traces back some two million years, when survival had to trump justice, the latter being, historically, a recent conception. Music educators in our times have the same obligation as all other citizens, and all other educators, to support and promote ideals of equity and justice in all we do. But we have the particular obligation to relate those ideals to the field—music—in which we are professionals. Attention to equity and justice need not and should not contradict our responsibility to musical learnings, the two seemingly different concerns being entirely compatible. Enhanced musical experience and enhanced moral behavior are reciprocal contributions we uniquely can make to human welfare.

INTRODUCTION

My topic, inequity and injustice, is not a happy one. It plunges us into dark corners of human experience and the human psyche. I am confronting inequity and injustice in this paper because I believe we cannot understand its counterparts—equity and justice—without a hard look at their shadow sides, sides, as I will explain, that are far more profoundly established than their positive aspects.

In preparation for taking this plunge I reviewed a great many books related to this topic that have been helpful to me over the years (actually the decades) along with some new ones, and I also did something else that I felt would add immediacy to my reflections. I began to clip from the newspapers to which I subscribe (the daily *Chicago Tribune* and the Sunday *New*

York Times), items reporting on and discussing events in the world that clearly illustrate inequitable and unjust situations. My desk was soon piled high with newsprint, in a jumbled and confusing array that I couldn't figure out how to give some organization to and in instances often so horrendous that I could only blink at them with disbelief.

Here is a rough overview of the topics gleaned from only the top layer of the mulch that was forming on my unfortunate desk. The spread of AIDS and starvation in the poorest of poor countries. Religious extremism causing mayhem all over the world, calling into question the belief in multicultural-ism as to its viability and desirability, even its possibility. Sexual predation in every imaginable form. Conflicts involving race, sexual orientation, the treatment of females often amounting to gender apartheid if not worse. Murder, genocide, terrorism unrelenting and savage. An American excep-tionalism that seems to have absolved the United States from the rules and moral expectations it piously demands from everyone else. And, like a basso ostinato underneath all this, corruption, corruption, corruption, in every aspect of human endeavor. Corruption seems to have always been a given in human experience. As Saul Alinsky, the legendary radical politi-cal activist in Chicago in the 1940s and 1950s, a champion of the poor and disenfranchised, put it, "He who fears corruption fears life." All this just a small sample from my disheartening and continually growing collection of news stories.

And yet, despite these daily evidences of moral turpitude I am aware that, while perhaps we are not living in the best of times, we are certainly not living in the worst of times. There is every reason to believe that if there were comparable newspapers at every period of history they would be filled just as much if not more so with tales of human misdeeds.

GETTING TO THE ROOTS

I was led by my saddening preparatory efforts to the conviction that I needed to address these problems at a level below that of the urgency to devise expeditious solutions to them. Of course actions must be taken to cure humanity's ills. But also, we need to comprehend the larger picture in which each instance of them can be understood to be a symptom of under-lying causations. Symptoms should be alleviated. Yet ignoring the broader contexts for them, their roots in foundational propensities of humans, is to forever chase symptoms without curing disease. So I want here to attend to the causative conditions of human malevolence, with a particular slant that seems to me to be productive of useful insights about how we can understand the existence of such conditions and to apply that understanding—that perspective—to what our positions and our actions in music education might be if we are to be responsible professionals in this regard.

First, a necessary look at a concept closely related to my topic, the concept of inequality. If you are unacquainted with New York City, where this conference is taking place (and where I grew up, by the way) and if you wandered the neighborhoods of this remarkable, colorful, imponderably diverse place, you would find yourself drinking in its well-earned reputation as embracing both the best and the worst of human possibilities. You would not escape being struck by the extremes of inequality represented here, most obviously in wealth and the absence thereof, and leaping out from that observation, the profound consequences of that disparity in all that is entailed in the term "quality of life." Those consequences are all on display here, from A to Z and everywhere in between.

Of course extremes of inequality exist not only in this city but throughout the entire world and throughout the entire history of the human race. Inequality is so endemic to the human condition that we should not be surprised that the newly emerging field of econophysics, the use of principles of physics to study economics, tells us that economic inequality follows rules of statistical logic that trump any decisions humans can make and any actions they can take (Shea, 2005).

In the natural world, inequality, defined as disparity or nonuniformity between organisms, or species, in various conditions of life, is inescapable, econophysics aside. Our organic world, of which humans are a part of course, is dependent, fundamentally, on inequality, without which it could not exist. Why? At base because there is a food chain, so that, for living organisms to survive there must be the eaters and the eaten, with all the profound and widespread implications of that fact. At the macro level humans are at the top of that chain, with no predators dependent on us for their dinners, as occurs with all other organisms, animal and vegetable, below the top of the chain. There certainly are creatures on land and in the sea who would enjoy a snack of a human if given the opportunity, but none that depends on us as a staple of its diet.

At the micro level, of course there is, sadly, a different story. There, we are unequal to a host of predators who routinely cause us to sicken and to die that they may live.

Inequality, then, is a natural, not a pathological condition. In that sense the terms equity and justice are irrelevant to, inapplicable to, the natural world including the human species conceived as part of nature.

EQUITY AND JUSTICE AS HUMAN CONSTRUCTS

Those two terms, equity, defined as the quality of fairness or impartiality, and justice, in the sense of moral rightness, what the Byzantine emperor Justinian described as "the firm and continuous desire to render to everyone that which is his due," are terms signifying qualities found nowhere in nature except among humans. They are human inventions, the product of the human imagination. We can apply the conceptions of equity and justice to the rest of nature if we choose to do so (and many argue that we should, even must) but nature itself, outside of humanity, knows nothing of them. They have been added to nature by a property that arose in the human species at a certain time in its evolution—the property of consciousness, which allows us to reflect about and to ponder the consequences of unfairness and unrightfulness, and even, when paired with another human characteristic, conscience, with the desire to do something to alleviate them. However, if we contemplate the uninterrupted, ever-present existence of inequity and injustice, at every level from the bothersome to the monstrous, and in every nook and cranny of human existence around the world, it would seem impossible to regard our history in this regard as something about which to be proud. As psychologist Anthony Storr says in his book *Human Aggression* (1970),

> The somber fact is that we are the cruelest and most ruthless species that has ever walked the earth; and that, although we may recoil in horror when we read in newspaper or history book of the atrocities committed by man on man, we know in our hearts that each one of us harbors within himself those same savage impulses which lead to murder, to torture, and to war.

Storr's insight has been expressed in similar language for a very long time. In his review of a new book on the Iliad, novelist Nick Tosches says of Homer's original that

> this fountainhead of Western literature begins, exquisitely, with the word "wrath," just as the poem itself is one of "dismal death," and "corpse-fire," of "men killing and men killed," of "vile things" and "vile destiny," showing that, like other epic wellsprings, such as the Old Testament, most of which postdates Homer, [the Iliad] is more knowing in its awareness of humanity's most distinguishing trait—inhumanity—than literature of later ages. (Tosches, 2006)

How does one make sense of such a stark, deeply distressing fact of human life?

There are three basic levels at which efforts to understand injustice have been focused. The first is the level of the individual. What is it in particular individuals' lives or character that leads them to carry out instances of harmful or immoral behavior? If we can better plumb the depths of individual psychopathology, this position argues, we can, perhaps, learn how to counteract it, preventing the incalculable harm such humans have caused. To the degree we can cultivate healthy, moral, ethical individuals we will to that degree cultivate a world reflecting those qualities.

This is a venerable and widely held position. I believe it is both valid and necessary.

A second focus has been on the level of the societal, or the cultural. Individuals are always and necessarily products of the cultural surround in which they exist, according to this viewpoint. We must build societies that not only avoid the dangers of inhumane beliefs and policies but instead build conditions for their opposite, for ideals and structures that cultivate equitable, beneficent interactions, and, as a result, individuals who exemplify such values.

This, too, is an enduring and common position. I believe it, as well, is valid and necessary.

ROOTS IN UNIVERSAL HUMAN CHARACTERISTICS

The third focus on issues of human morality has been at the level of the universal. What is it about humans that cause them to act in immoral ways, bringing incalculable misery to themselves and to others? Where does this negative impulse come from, and why have individuals who act this way always existed? Further, every culture contains within it the seeds of corruption, easily fertilized into blooming prolifically. Neither the individual dimension by itself, nor the cultural dimension by itself, nor the two of them together, can fully explain why the human condition is one that is so ripe for, so potentially ridden with, the capacity for moral malignancy. We must search deeper for the roots of inequity and injustice, into the realm of human nature itself.

This conviction is hugely unpopular in much of contemporary philosophy and political theory. Under the postmodern mindset the universal is a concept without foundation. All is contextual, all is conditional, and all is provisional, according to the postmodern view. There are no universals, no essentialities, no stable, defining core of human characteristics separate from the particulars of time and place. This applies also to ideas, or points of view, all of them by necessity having to be localized and transient. So the very notion of a universal level of human beingness must be repudiated, in this way of thinking.

This postmodern viewpoint is one of its fundamental tenets, constituting therefore, an oxymoron; that is, a postmodern universal, which reveals the slippery slope on which much postmodern reasoning teeters. Aside from that, I believe that this conviction is entirely in error. Its doctrinaire narrow-mindedness, exemplifying the very traits it attempts to denounce, severely restricts us from attaining understandings that are more than superficial. The universal is not all. It is, however, along with the other two, necessary for any adequate comprehension of the complexity of human capacities. My focus on the universal, and on what I call the level of "deepest universalism," provides the larger context in which the issue of immorality can be seen in its wholeness. The aridness of much postmodern argumentation, along with its valuable insights across a broad spectrum of issues, can be refreshed when neglected factors are invited to the table of discourse.

The foundational levels of human traits related to moral issues such as equity and social justice are explored with particular salience in two overlapping disciplines—evolutionary psychology and analytical psychology, supported by work in anthropology, ethnology, sociobiology, psycholinguistics, and, strikingly in recent years, neuroscience, among other fields. Both evolutionary psychology and analytical psychology deal with human functions that are so deep-seated in our makeup as to be largely unavailable to our conscious control, or available to consciousness only with special kinds of effort (Lakoff & Johnson, 1999). Both scientific disciplines recognize that, just as humans have inherited from evolutionary developments the same physical structures (heart, liver, lungs, etc.) we have also inherited the same underlying mental structures held in common by all members of our species. This cognitive architecture, comparable to the corporeal architecture of our bodies in its various organs and systems, is called, in evolutionary psychology, "domain-specific functions" (those structures of the brain designed to address particular types of adaptive problems) (Buss, 2003, 2005) and, in analytical psychology, "archetypes" (Edinger, 1972; Mayes, 2005; Stevens, 1993, 2003).

The ability of our species to survive among the many others in nature has been founded on the necessity to adapt itself to the exigencies with which it had to deal if it was to flourish. In that sense our contemporary heads have within them a brain and mind forged in the Stone Age, beginning some two million years ago. That age, the age of hunters/gatherers, occupied the longest developmental period by far in our history as a species, determining to a large extent what we are to this day. Agriculture appeared only some ten thousand years ago—one half of 1 percent of the total time since then— and it is only about five thousand years ago—one quarter of 1 percent of the total—that as many as half of the human population were farmers rather than hunters/gatherers (Stevens, 1993).

All of recorded history is more recent than that. Given how long it takes for evolution to achieve its modulations (nature is in no hurry) we can begin to appreciate how fundamentally unequipped we are mentally to cope with all the moral complexities with which humans are faced in a world so new, so unprecedented, that while we have created it, is nevertheless beyond our capacity to manage it successfully. After all, more progress in how we live and think has occurred in the past five hundred years or so since the advent of the notion of scientific evidence than occurred in the previous two million years. And modern science is barely a hundred years old.

The mental operations and behaviors, that is, brain-specific functions or archetypes, necessary for survival over practically all of human history until extremely recently had to include high levels of fear of a great variety of conditions and situations such as of darkness, of isolation, of paucity of food, water, and habitation, and of strangers—people different from oneself in some way or not known well enough to be trusted. Living in a world of struggle with nature and with other humans competing for nature's sustenance, humans had to be greatly suspicious about, even hostile to, those who were not members of their own family and clan. Aggression was a necessity in securing food, fending off competition for it, establishing dominance over competing individuals, families, and clans, and securing mates so as to propagate the race.

Survival depended on protecting the clan's environment from incursions by those intending to usurp it, and usurping the environments of others when one's own could no longer sustain the clan's needs. Prescribed roles had to be assigned to everyone in the family or clan, including males, females, children, adults, and elders, in order to maximize chances of survival. Also needing to be established were rules and regulations promoting safekeeping behaviors, and punishments for misbehaviors, so as to better achieve security and longevity.

All these and many other requirements for safety and therefore survival are so deeply ingrained in humans as to be active previous to and underneath our conscious awareness of and control over them. They are pre-rational foundations for not only how we as humans *act*, but for how we *think*; how our minds have been structured in order for our species to endure. As Konrad Lorenz, the Austrian ethologist and Nobel Prize winner, argued, innate perceptual mechanisms (such as those I have just delineated) are the necessary preconditions of all cognition. They precede all thought and must do so if thought is to be possible at all. Our cognitive apparatus, he believed, is itself an objective reality that has acquired its present form through evolutionary adaptation to the real world (Stevens, 2003). Evolutionary psychologists and analytical psychologists would agree.

Other adaptations in early humans, of a less immediately protective and aggressive sort, were also factors in the successful maintenance of our species—cooperation, nurturing, education in the sense of instruction in survival skills. These entailed emotional involvement with others so as to build bonding alliances. This was the precondition for something that is notably absent from organisms outside the human community or at best only inferred to be present in rudimentary form in nonhumans; that is, empathy. Without empathy, on which conscience depends, morality as humans construe it could not exist. But empathy, conscience, morality, equity, justice, are constructs so new in human history as to still be very fragile, and certainly not entirely dependable. The more compelling values relating to survival, requiring fear and aggression, often overcome these much more recent additions to the human arsenal of tools for avoiding harm. Many of the behaviors developed to be adaptive to the Stone Age world are, as a result, dangerously maladaptive to the world in which we now live.

ON WAR

One powerful example of the tenacity of ancient, primitive influences on our behaviors and ways of thinking is war, surely at the top or near the top of the list of the most extreme breakdowns in morality we can imagine. A book that I believe is essential background for anyone caught up in the dilemmas we are presently facing as to the issue of war is *The Roots of War and Terror* by Anthony Stevens (2004). Stevens is a British physician, psychiatrist, and analytical psychologist who writes, brilliantly I think, on archetypal dimensions of the mind. He points out that there have been many precipitating causes of war. However, he argues, the underlying predisposition for war resides in the nature of humans themselves, rooted in dominance drives and their relation to the need for one's group to thrive. The injunction "thou shalt not kill" is quickly and easily altered to "thou shalt not kill members of the in-group." All others are fair game when a group sees an opportunity to overthrow a competing group.

How is it possible, even in the contemporary world where morality is widely recognized to be a necessity for human happiness and security, that we are able to so easily and constantly disregard this in favor of the ultimacy of murderous force? It is possible, says Stevens, because of a phylogenetic capacity in men for group violence. (Stevens is convinced, on the basis of a great deal of evidence, that this capacity is largely a male characteristic.) Wars have occurred so frequently and so constantly in human history as to be inveterate. Stevens offers a ten-step description of how the archetypal systems responsible for war have been activated regularly, starting with a perception of threat, whether real or imagined; to an attempt at nego- tiation; to its breakdown; to hostility and pseudospeciation, which is the transformation of the potential enemy into a subhuman species deserving of violent attack—an "axis of evil" for example; to shadow projection; political propagandizing to gather support for the war; to battle; escalation; victory or defeat; and the necessity, finally, for the negotiation phase with varying degrees of compromise and cessation of hostilities.

Does this sound familiar to us today?

Here is another explanation of how ingrained the patterns of war-making are in the human species, quoted by Stevens in his book:

> Why of course the people don't want war. That is understood. But, after all, it is the leaders of the country who determine the policy and it is always a simple matter to drag the people along, whether it is a democracy, or a fascist dictatorship, or a parliament, or a communist dictatorship. Voice or no voice, the people can always be brought to the bidding of the leaders. That is easy. All you have to do is tell them that they are being attacked, and denounce the peacemakers for lack of patriotism and for exposing the country to danger. (2004, p. 137)

Does this also sound familiar?

Of course it does, as it would to people who lived at just about any other time in human history. Those words were pronounced by Herman Göring, the German army field marshal and Nazi party leader at his Nuremburg trial in 1949. They remain as current as today's newspaper and as ancient as war itself. Göring may have been despicable but he wasn't stupid. He knew, very clearly, how people can be made to act in savage ways by appeals to their deepest, most primitive fears.

But what about the peace treaties that often are made as a way out of a war? Don't they demonstrate our capacity for peace as well as for war? Stevens estimates that between 1500 BC and AD 1860 there were more than eight thousand such treaties, all of them intended to remain in force forever. On average they lasted two years (p. 8). That abysmal record lasts to this very day. We live now and have for centuries with one foot in the preconscious age and the other in consciousness, in awareness of morality and of the necessity for equity and justice. Yet we are still driven, still controlled so easily, by the ancient imperatives. Dangerous indeed, in an age of atomic power. As Albert Einstein said to then-president Harry S. Truman in the context of the possible development of the atomic bomb, "I know not with what weapons World War III will be fought, but World War IV will be fought with sticks and stones."

THE CHALLENGES FOR MUSIC EDUCATION

What does all this have to do with music education, a field that in the broad sphere of politics and education is relatively inconsequential, relatively protected from large-scale expectations by people, and not relatively but severely limited in the amount of instructional time granted to it because it has never been able to compete for equal time with the so-called basics?

Let's be real here. The topic of this conference raises issues as venerable and as current, as wide and as deep, as essential yet as perplexing, as any that could possibly be addressed. Are we as a profession in any sort of a reasonable position to tackle these issues with hopes, not of entirely solving them, which would be grotesquely inflated of us, but even of contributing significantly to their solutions, given that all the king's horses and all the king's men have never in history been able to put this particular Humpty Dumpty together again?

One position on this issue is that we have no business whatsoever to be engaged in such matters. For one example, William Thomson, the distinguished music theorist, berates the attempts of "the postmodern, deconstructionist, politically emancipatory hermeneutics in academia over the past three decades" to "apply socio-political criteria to enterprises for which they are not relevant." Such attempts to achieve political aims, he argues, despite their desirability, cannot be served by linking them to musical beliefs and practices intended to serve quite other values, those that relate to the "aesthetic indestructibility" of excellent music compositions (Thomson, 2001). Outside the field of music a strong belief exists among many that education itself has no business mucking about in political matters. George F. Will, the influential American conservative thinker, is a spokesperson for this widely held view. In a recent *Newsweek* opinion piece he vilifies the desire of schools of education to produce teachers whose aims are to "promote social justice, to be change agents, and to recognize individual and institutional racism, sexism, homophobia, and classism." Never, Will charges, is the aim "anything as banal as mere knowledge," never to teach kids to "read, write, and reason." What should schools be doing? Clearly, Will argues, they must "apply rigorous pedagogy . . . practiced by teachers in teacher-centered classrooms where knowledge is regarded as everything." Most education schools, he says in disgust, instead celebrate "child-centered classrooms" that do not "suffocate discourses." Such pursuits are "enemies of rigor," says Will, based on their mistaken espousal of "progressive political beliefs" (Will, 2006).

Thomson and Will represent the tip of an iceberg of public opinion. I suspect that in regard to music in the schools a great many citizens in countries around the world would be at least surprised that a conference such as this is taking place, and that many, perhaps most, would wonder why we are interested in this issue and whether we have any particular expertise in it as a result of our being music educators. However, if a thoughtful lay person inquired as to whether our goal is to correct inequities and injustices in the field in which we are experts, I imagine that a fair amount of sympathy, even approbation, would be given us.

What if that person asks whether our ambitions extend beyond that to wider aims, equity and social justice being the primary ends of our work, music and the teaching of it being a means, an instrumentality to achieving something far beyond music as a domain with its characteristic, identifiable features?

"Ah," we might reply, "music, while it certainly is identifiable as a particular phenomenon with its particular ways to think and act, is also, just as all other domains, inseparably connected to and implicated in political issues. Everything, after all, is political, and therefore intimately embroiled in issues of equity and social justice. So by necessity we must be political first, and musical as subordinate to that primary obligation."

"Well," our remarkably astute lay interrogator might respond, "if music, as everything else, is political, it is also, as everything else, sociological, physiological, anthropological, theological, psychological, philosophical, historical, and economic, each of those domains having many subdivisions also determining the nature of music and music education. Are those also the ends of your educational obligations? And," this persistent person continues, "if you contemplate what all that entails, are you being just a bit, how shall I say it, brazen in your expectations, in what music teachers are likely to be able to teach expertly and insightfully, in a program so circumscribed by minimal time allotments and marginal enrollments as to be barely more than a blip on the educational screen?"

"And one more question, if I may," this now rather annoying inquirer continues. "There are acres of books, old and new, including the sacred texts of the world's religions, that deal with various aspects of morality and immorality (i.e., Dewey, 1960; Fineman, 1991; Held, 1993; Johnson, 1993; Nussbaum, 1999, 2006; Rawls, 1971) and many that provide prescriptions for educational practices (i.e., Bowman, 1998; Durkheim, 1961; Goodlad, Soder & Suotnik, 1990; Goodman & Lesnick, 2001; Jackson, Boostrom & Hansen, 1993; Jorgensen, 2003; Kohlberg, 1981, 1984; Mayes, 2005; Noddings, 1984; Nucci, 2001; Tom, 1984; Woodford, 2005).

"Both the theoretical constructs and their applications are so difficult to implement in schools, requiring such high levels of expertise, sensitivity, and subtlety, not to mention time, that few teachers who have not specialized in these matters to an extremely high degree can be expected to handle their complexities with hopes of avoiding doing more harm than good. Are music teachers willing and able to develop such expertise? Or," our inquirer continues, "is this a matter of politically devoted thinkers in music education communicating their idealizations to others of like mind, leaving aside concerns about how or whether teachers and students in school settings can actually do something instructional with them?"

REFLECTIONS ON THE CHALLENGES

Here is how I would address the challenges raised by what I consider to be a reasonable set of questions, all of which I have asked myself in serious ways and which I have struggled to answer to some degree of satisfaction, although, I readily admit, not to as high a degree as I wish I was capable of achieving.

First, I believe that all music educators, as citizens, have as much right as everyone else, and as much obligation as everyone else, to do all we can to further those benevolent values embedded in cultural beliefs around the world and inherited from the history of our race. Being good citizens, in fact, requires that of us.

Second, I suggest that as educators we are in that same position, equal to all other educators in the obligation to exemplify in our dealings with students, parents, and other professionals we work with, the values of equity and social justice. And we are obligated to promote those values, and to critique opposing values, in all our professional actions. Being good educators, in fact, requires that of us.

In addition, as *music* educators we have special obligations beyond those held by all other citizens and all other educators. The field in which we have professional expertise has characteristics inevitably shared with other fields but also that differentiate it from all others. These special characteristics have to do with the many ways that music is created, and experienced, and reflected about, and with the particular modes of learning associated with each of those ways.

These characteristics are, necessarily, saturated with moral and ethical implications, in one sense as every other human endeavor must be, and in another sense as singularly manifested in this particular endeavor (Reimer, 2003). Here, in the dimension of music's singularity, we can make unique contributions to the common values representing the best of our ideals. I believe that those particular contributions are the most precious ones we can make, not as competitive with the widely shared claims on us but as distinctive benefits that we and we alone can add to the common good.

Should those contributions be the primary goal of our work, or should they be subordinate to more musically focused learnings, that is, learnings having to do with creating and responding to the meaningful and significant sounds that are the basis of music's existence?

Here there is a continuum of choice, some of us putting great emphasis on moral learnings (i.e., Bowman, 1998; Jorgensen, 2003; Woodford, 2005), others, such as William Thomson, on musical learnings. At the extreme ends of the continuum one position holds so much sway as to essentially discredit or negate the position at the other extreme. Somewhere between the two, I suggest, there will be a variety of balances that recognize the validity of what need not be seen to be incompatible positions, and in which both receive their due as necessary components of the multifaceted phenomenon of music. The same can be said about all the many other facets, in addition to the political/moral, that also ground music's reality.

Unfortunately, there is little opportunity to accomplish such balances in music education programs in schools as they have existed in our past and continue to exist to this day. We have concentrated our offerings so monolithically, especially in the United States, on a single way to be musical—to perform it, primarily in large ensembles—as to have unconscionably proscribed the possibilities for issues of morality to be represented with anything like the breadth in which those possibilities exist in the larger musical world. Of course there are such issues connected to ensemble performance and to all other aspects of performance (Reimer, 2007). But that is just one drop in a large bucket. The genre of music most richly and immediately saturated with moral/ethical issues as related to individual, cultural, and universal dimensions of experience, is each culture's popular music, which is represented in music education programs around the world with greatly diverse levels of emphasis. Until all cultures conscientiously include popular music in all its many aspects, our attention to music's social justice dimension can only be meager at best and artificial at worst. And until we broaden our offerings far beyond only that of performing we will remain inequitably and unjustly limiting of our students' opportunities to participate fully in the musical life of their culture, including the many connections to social and political issues inherent in the various musical roles we have historically ignored.

FROM THEORY TO PRACTICE

Do we really care about issues of implementation of our moral/ethical ideals in what teachers teach and what students are given the opportunity to learn? Discussing theoretical backgrounds of this topic is a necessary step toward implementation but by itself is insufficient if we are to have an effect on the lives of young people. Such discussions, including my own, are, with all due respect, easy. Rocket science is easy. Brain surgery is easy. What's *hard* is education. Education in matters of inequity and social injustice is *really* hard, perhaps harder than anything else in education given its deep, problematical roots in the human psyche.

Attempts at implementation, and the garnering of principles arising out of them, are where the rubber of theory meets the road of applicability. There, I would argue, lies the core of our professional obligations. Those who have already undertaken such attempts, or who hope to do so, will have to depend, in the ongoing work this task entails, on two traits of character that are necessary if we are to have an effect beyond scholarly reflections, beyond research projects, and beyond policy developments, necessary as those are.

First and foremost is the need for an attitude of humility, to ground us in the formidable difficulties entailed in this matter. Anthony Storr's lament about the human condition that I quoted earlier, and Homer's, may be one-sided, ignoring the many positive dimensions in our species' character, but it is a side that cannot be minimized. Inequities and injustices are not going to disappear despite our best efforts, even if we actually do achieve some measure of effective implementation. We must content ourselves with modest results, with the recognition that any positive results at all are both welcome and admirable. Progress, no matter how slight, is worth all the efforts we can make.

Also needed is a good deal of courage, to acknowledge the depth of the challenges we face in this arena, such as, for starters, persuading music teachers that they do have obligations of this sort, and equipping them to address such obligations with some small measure of competence, a task of enormous complexity. This is an area, after all, in which those armed with only good intentions are likely to find themselves living in the hell that is paved with them.

It will take particular kinds of expertise, not necessarily possessed by sophisticated thinkers about political morality, or by excellent researchers, or by effective policy makers, or by people who are excellent musicians, to prepare teachers to have the kinds of savvy that will allow them to be effective advocates for and providers of social justice. Anyone who has studied the materials devoted to that end must be painfully aware of the endless perplexities and the formidable demands for both intellectual and emotional maturity entailed in exemplifying and teaching for social justice. While all music teachers can be taken further than they presently are in these regards, some will be needed who achieve sufficient expertise to provide learning opportunities for students in schools who have high interests in this area and who might develop ambitions to pursue those interests as professionals in music education with this specialization.

One more challenge must be mentioned. We will need to continue to preserve and protect the humane values of musical experience itself.

That experience, in the variety of ways it can be attained, has unique and powerful capacities to reveal our collective nature as creatures of great emotive complexity. That sharing with others of our commonly held inner lives of feeling is the very basis of empathy, without which conscience, and therefore potentials for equity and social justice, are not possible. We know, clearly and incontrovertibly, that communal musical undergoings are among the most fulfilling and life enhancing experiences of which humans are capable. That, I would suggest, is a major reason why people love music so much, especially people who are students in schools. Nothing we do as advocates for justice should diminish in any way our role as cultivators of the fulfillments that musical engagements uniquely and abundantly provide, fulfillments that are enhanced by learning more and more within and about music.

The two goals, advancing musical fulfillments and advancing positive social/moral values, are not in opposition. They are mutually reinforcing. There are those of us who have the opportunity, whether in teaching youngsters directly or in preparing teachers to be able to do so, to go beyond political theorizing to its necessary applications, and who reside nevertheless within the circle of music as also being their area of expertise and dedication. They serve as our profession's leaders toward strengthening the reciprocal contributions that enhanced musical experience and enhanced moral behavior can make to human welfare.

REFERENCES

Bowman, W. D. (1998). *Philosophical perspectives on music.* New York: Oxford University Press.

Buss, D. M. (2003). *Evolutionary psychology: The new science of the mind* (2nd ed.). Boston: Allyn & Bacon.

Buss, D. M. (2005). *The handbook of evolutionary psychology.* Hoboken, NJ: John Wiley & Sons.

Dewey, J. (1960). *Theory of the moral life.* New York: Holt, Rinehart, and Winston.

Durkheim, E. (1961). *Moral education.* New York: Free Press.

Edinger, E. F. (1992). *Ego and archetype.* Boston: Shambhala.

Fineman, M. A. (1991). *The illusion of equality.* Chicago: The University of Chicago Press.

Goodlad, J. I., Soder, R., & Suotnik, K. A. (Eds.). (1990). *The moral dimension of teaching.* San Francisco: Jossey-Bass.

Goodman, J. F., & Lesnick, H. (2001). *The moral stake in education.* New York, Longman.

Held, V. (1993). *Justice and care: essential readings in feminist ethics.* Boulder, CO: Westview.

Jackson, P. W., Boostrom, R. E., & Hansen, D. T. (1993). *The moral life of schools.* San Francisco: Jossey-Bass.

Johnson, M. (1993). *Moral imagination.* Chicago: The University of Chicago Press.

Jorgensen, E. R. (2003). *Transforming music education.* Bloomington: Indiana University Press.

Kohlberg, L. (1981). *Essays in moral development* (Vol. 1). *The philosophy of moral development.* New York: Harper and Row.

Kohlberg, L. (1984). *Essays in moral development* (Vol. 2). *The psychology of moral development.* New York: Harper and Row.

Lakoff, G., & Johnson, M. (1999). *Philosophy in the flesh: the embodied mind and its challenge to Western thought.* New York: Basic Books.

Mayes, C. (2005). *Jung and education: elements of an archetypal pedagogy.* Lanham, MD: Rowman & Littlefield.

Noddings, N. (1984). *Caring: a feminine approach to ethics and moral education.* Berkeley: University of California Press.

Nucci, L. P. (2001). *Education in the moral domain.* Cambridge: Cambridge University Press.

Nussbaum, M. C. (1999). *Sex and moral justice.* New York: Oxford University Press.

Nussbaum, M. C. (2006). *Frontiers of justice.* Cambridge, MA: Harvard University Press.

Rawls, J. (1971). *A theory of justice.* Cambridge, MA: Harvard University Press.

Reimer, B. (2003). *A philosophy of music education: advancing the vision* (3rd ed.). Upper Saddle River, NJ: Prentice Hall.

Reimer, B. (2007). Artistic creativity, ethics, and the authentic self. In L. Bresler (Ed.), *International handbook of research in arts education.* Dordrecht, Netherlands: Springer.

Shea, C. (2005, December 11). Econophysics. *New York Times Magazine,* p. 67.

Stevens, A. (1993). *The two million-year-old self.* College Station: Texas A&M Press.

Stevens, A. (2003). *Archetype revisited: an updated natural history of the self.* Toronto: Inner City Books.

Stevens, A. (2004). *The roots of war and terror.* London: Continuum.

Storr, A. (1970). *Human aggression.* New York: Hammondsworth, Pelican.

Thomson, W. (2001). Those strange bedfellows, politics and music. *College Music Symposium, 41,* 126–129.

Tom. A. R. (1984). *Teaching as a moral craft.* New York: Longman.

Tosches, N. (2006). On Barrico's Homer. *New York Times Book Review,* p. 11.

Will, G. F. (2006). Education schools vs. education. *Newsweek,* p. 98.

Woodford, P. G. (2005). *Democracy and music education.* Bloomington: Indiana University Press.

10

ARTISTIC CREATIVITY, ETHICS, AND THE AUTHENTIC SELF

Creativity in the arts gets a mixed press. On one hand is the notion that creative artists are very special people indeed, with an inborn talent that they are compelled to express. That compulsion, it is often believed, makes them a bit unusual, even strange; admirable, usually, but often eccentric, sometimes weird. If their creativity is expressed in acceptable ways, giving pleasure to at least the cognoscenti if not the general public, they can achieve high status as important cultural treasures. If too challenging, too confrontational or defiant, they can be seen as enemies of the culture, requiring management or even suppression.

On the other hand, artistic creativity is often believed to have entirely positive effects and can be and should be cultivated by all people, not just the few who have its special gifts. One of these good effects, it is often assumed, is that nurturing creativity in an art is likely to make the student more creative generally outside art. This assumption is one major reason the arts are supported in education—at least to the extent of being present, if only minimally.

Beyond these popular conceptions is the deeper issue of what the act of artistic creation does to—makes of—those devoted to this endeavor, in their personal selfness, the quality and depth of their psyche. Does creating art make people "better" as human beings? Can "better" mean more authentic and ethical?

In the following "interlude," a short reflection invited by the *International Handbook of Research in Arts Education* editors, I reflect on this possibility, suggesting that the very act of creativity in art entails, at its core, an ethical dimension if the product is to be authentic. Whether or not that makes the person more ethical outside art, creating art entails an inner confrontation with ethical demands, a value uniquely attainable in the act of bringing art into being. This value is intimately connected to and enriching of those at the core of our professional devotion to music education.

The following essay was originally published in Liora Bresler, ed., *International Handbook of Research in Arts Education* (Dordrecht, The Netherlands: Springer, 2007). Used with kind permission of Springer Science and Business Media.

> I do not believe I am sending a message with this movie ["Bad Education"]. But since the nature of movies is to be watched, I try to deliver the strongest version of any scenario. My movies are more sincere than I am in real life. My movies are more honest than I am in real life. My movies are clearer than I am in real life.
>
> —Pedro Almodóvar, filmmaker, 2004

Among many other qualities, being sincere, honest, and clear would seem to be implicated in being an ethical human being. Certainly a person characterized as being insincere, dishonest, and unclear about whether such characteristics are undesirable, is not likely to be regarded as a paragon of ethical virtue. But why would a filmmaker, a creator of scenarios to be viewed in darkened theaters built solely for that purpose, environments carefully arranged to be anything but "real life," assert that the making of his movies allows him to achieve heightened levels of ethical attainment far beyond what his depictions (usually of highly questionable—even outrageous—human interactions) present to our gaze? What alchemical transformation (or is it merely self-deception?) can account for his claim?

Those familiar with Almodóvar's films are aware that they deal largely with behaviors that many or most would regard as being immoral. By that term I mean transgressing the accepted patterns of value and custom of one's society, the operative notion being "mores," defined as "folkways of central importance accepted without question and embodying the fundamental moral views of a group." In some striking way this artist achieves high ethical values, even beyond those attainable in "real life," through his work as a filmmaker, despite the highly suspect nature of his subject matters. And all of us engaged in art, whether as creators of it, partakers of it, teachers of it, researchers in it, are likely to intuit the power and veracity of his self-reflection.

Our intuitions deserve examination, being fertile ground for enhancing our awareness of what we treasure. One thing that educators in the arts are likely to treasure deeply is the presumption, amounting almost to a faith, that creating art, of any sort and of any style, including those instances of it that plunge us deeply into the ethical and moral dilemmas of the lives we all must live, is an endeavor intimately entailing ethical behavior. Such behavior requires, if it is to be successful, the capacity to decide (choose) what is proper, positive, generative, even humane, to do in the creative act. Artistic decisions, we are likely to believe, must be made with a very special sort of sincerity, one in which there is a devotion to genuineness, a rejection of falseness, of the counterfeit. That requires scrupulous honesty, in which we can abide no manipulative moves, no succumbing to the easy when the hard must be pursued. It also requires clarity of purpose to act like a magnet, drawing to itself only what is needed, what is seized upon as the best possible fit for what is occurring, so that what should be done with conviction does not become erratic or indecisive.

"Real life" seldom allows such exquisite interplays of virtues, being, as we all have no doubt noticed, cluttered with systemic ethical noise. Artistic creation, I want to suggest, is the ultimate opportunity for ethical decision making to be accomplished optimally, or, to be reasonable, as optimally as is likely to occur in this vale of tears. No matter how immersed in issues of real life, complexities of real life, constraints, vagaries, and intrusions from every possible unconnected circumstance, artistic creation provides a level of protection, or, perhaps more realistically, a somewhat more sheltered environment from distraction, than most if not all other creative endeavors. That is why artists are so generally and with good reason regarded to be "special," both in what they attempt to do and the freedom they claim for themselves to do it.

"Making special," as artists have always attempted to do, Ellen Dissanayake suggests (1988), pays off for them in many powerful ways, perhaps the most affecting being the psychical reward of the experience of authenticity they may undergo when engaged in the creative act. That, I think, is what Almodóvar refers to in his reflection, his sense that something—some way to engage oneself—is needed to take one to a level of self-achievement beyond the ordinary, beyond the ethical disfunctions and obliquities of real life. Of course we may wince at the suggestion that real life is somehow lesser in ethical demands than the seemingly rarified realm reserved for creative artists, but that seems far from what Almodóvar is suggesting, or from what I am drawing from his suggestion. There is, indeed, a significant difference between the ethical issues with which life constantly confronts us as we live, and the episodes we carve out in which creative decisions must be made within the media with which we choose to work and the intentions we devise for how those media are to be employed. By limiting our purview to a particular set of materials and conditions, at a particular time of our engagement, with a particular set of self-imposed challenges, we *afford ourselves the opportunity* to have some control over who we can be and what we can achieve, precisely because of the necessarily delimited boundaries artistic creation imposes. Does such boundary-setting render artistic creation artificial? "Artifice-ial" more accurately, "a skillful or artful contrivance or expedient." By concentrating our vision, as artistic creation requires us to do, we are enabled to achieve extraordinary depth of clarity, a sense of our self as striving to authentically be who we can be.

How to characterize the authenticity achievable when the creation of art is wholeheartedly pursued? The relation between the authentic and the ethical is key, that relation depending on the existence in humans of conscience, "a structural quality inborn in the psyche, directed to the maintenance of the psychic balance and aiming at its wholeness" (Jacobi, 1965). Conscience, according to Carl G. Jung, has both a collective (moral) and individual (ethical) aspect. Both make demands on us, putting us in a paradoxical position, for the demands of ethical behavior can be and often are in conflict with communal morality, complete resolutions between them seldom being easily attained. In the interface of tensions between them, the rocky path on which conscience exercises its power to sound an inner voice calling us to commit in the face of uncertainty, even danger, our individuation as authentic selves is coaxed to emerge. Without that interface, that confrontation between outside—the communal—and inside—the self—the exercise of conscience would have no reality, leaving us ethically flaccid, weak in autonomy. Precisely when conditions call on us to resolve conflicting or confusing demands with sincerity, honesty, and as much clarity as we can muster, our mettle is put to the fire, our conscience is forged in the heat. In such situations, successfully negotiated, we achieve genuine selfhood—not perfection, which is unattainable, but wholeness, which is. In such moments "a part of the self is actualized as a union between inside and outside. Then a man can repose in himself, because self-fulfilled, and an aura of authenticity emanates from him" (Jaffe, 1986).

The specialness of artistic creation, and of the objects and events it produces, inheres, I suggest, in its capacity to heighten ethical conscience and thereby personal authenticity. Artistic creation is exemplary for its extraordinary ability to afford the tensions of ethical decision-making within the self-imposed constraints of the materiality—the "isness"—the arts provide. The need, the desire, and the capacity to engage in such decision-making episodes are so deeply ingrained in the human psyche, and so satisfying of its needs to "become," that even children, no less than amateurs and professionals, eagerly engage in this special challenge at every opportunity.

Providing that opportunity, in all the diverse ways the arts do, is a foundational obligation of educators in the arts, who are in a position to affect, directly and powerfully, the ethically laden dynamics of choice that creating each mode of art depends upon if it is genuinely pursued. Arranging the conditions for that genuineness is, in a real sense, the central task of arts educators in regard to the artistic creativity dimension of their responsibilities. That is not the only task of education in the arts, however, in that the creativity of aesthetic responsiveness, in all the various ways each of the arts provide for it, is equally important, perhaps more so in the sense that all people respond, with diverse degrees of creativity, to the productions of artists, while comparatively few pursue artistic creation systematically beyond their school experiences of it.

That fact, often ignored by educators in every art, remains one of the major issues unattended to in our profession. But that weakness does not alter the necessity to continue to provide artistic creativity opportunities in every role each art encompasses, beginning with the earliest levels of schooling. Age is no barrier to the requirement of ethical choice-making that creating art imposes, so primally is ethical behavior embedded in human capacities and needs. Sincerity, honesty, clarity, and all the other components of ethical functioning are always matters of degree, from the first encounters with their reality to the furthest reaches attained by the most significant artists each culture in the world has contributed. To affect that degree, to provide the challenges, uncertainties, and complexities of choice that art creating depends on, in ways and at levels appropriate to each learner's capacities, remains a bedrock imperative for education in the arts.

Will creating art authentically make people "more ethical" beyond the confines of the artistic? That question, I must propose, is an empirical one, answerable only by recourse to whatever research evidence throws light on its presumptions. My claim here is that creating art necessarily entails the direct experience of ethical behavior, of encountering choices that call upon qualities entailed in imagining ethical resolutions (Johnson, 1993). People of every age can be engaged in the "knowing within" and "knowing how" that experiences of creating art require in their unique, compelling ways (Reimer, 2003). Perhaps such experiences—such knowings, or undergoings—affect related ones in other aspects of life. Perhaps not. What can be said with confidence is that encounters with artistic creativity, concretizing the qualities of individual authenticity as powerfully and immediately as they do, can be, if any at all are, valued for themselves, uniquely, no strings attached.

REFERENCES

Almodóvar, P. (2004, September 5). *The New York Times Magazine*, 43.
Dissanayake, E. (1988). *What is art for?* Seattle: University of Washington Press.
Jacobi, J. (1965). *The way of individuation*. New York: Harcourt, Brace & World.
Jaffe, A. (1986). *The myth of meaning*. Zurich: Daimon Verlag.
Johnson, M. (1993). *Moral imagination: Implications of cognitive science for ethics*. Chicago: University of Chicago Press.
Reimer, B. (2003). *A Philosophy of music education: Advancing the vision*. Upper Saddle River, NJ: Prentice Hall.

II

ACHIEVING OUR VALUES

IIA

WHAT AND HOW TO TEACH

Our values come to life in what we as professionals choose to do and how well we do it. Our choices and our effectiveness, while tied directly to our values, entail a host of additional issues with which we must come to grips.

From the entire world of musical instances, which will we choose as most fruitful for study, along with the choices our students will make? Are there criteria to guide us in making the most valuable choices? What do we focus our efforts on in teaching if we are to help our students get to the heart of whatever music we select to engage them? What musical examples will best nurture their growth in musical learning? In performing, is skill the major goal, or is understanding *through* skill the value we seek? What about listening—the one thing we can pretty well count on all our students choosing to do with music? Is that something we can or should influence? Can our students be encouraged to be *thoughtful* about music? Are these questions relevant only for us, or are they just as important for all our students to consider, no matter their age, if they are to be musically educated?

These questions are addressed in the following essays, each of which is an attempt to devise a convincing answer as a basis for enlightened practice. Our success depends, of course, on our pursuit of significant values. It depends equally on how well we teach them.

CHOOSING ART FOR EDUCATION: CRITERIA FOR QUALITY

The question of what constitutes quality in the arts is so complex and puzzling that many have argued that there is no useful answer, only individual preference or taste.

That's not good enough for us, I'm afraid. We are professionals, in our case in music and the teaching of music. Surely there are more convincing ways to reflect on quality in music, whether focusing on process or product. Surely we are obligated to help our students, even the youngest ones, exercise some level of reasoned judgment about whether a particular musical product or the musical process of creating it is good, bad, or indifferent. We do this about practically everything else in our lives; we can't escape that reality by saying that music, or any of the arts, are for some unexplainable reason exempt from such judgment.

I struggle over the years to formulate a conception of quality that transcends style or historical period or cultural context, trying to reach a level deep enough to apply to all art of any style or kind at all times and in all places. Yes, too ambitious, I know. Yet even getting close would be worth the effort.

The following article gets pretty close. I am relatively satisfied with it because the four criteria I identify have proven remarkably applicable to a broad range of human endeavors, including the arts and extending far beyond them. Teaching, for example. Building a house or a skyscraper.

Cooking. Raising children. Planting a garden. Investing money. When I am faced with judgments to be made as to better or worse—something all of us face constantly in our lives—I resort to this conceptualization to see if it might help. It does, remarkably consistently.

Applied with care and humility, the conception of quality offered here can be helpful to music educators, all educators in the arts, and all our students as they are guided to apply the criteria in their own artistic lives and in a variety of contexts outside the arts and education. I propose it as a useful tool that helps us get past the "If I like it, it must be good" level of judgment. And it serves as a powerful, accessible explanation, for our students and others, of how and why we choose the music we study in our programs. As professional educators, our explanations deserve to be well crafted, sensitive to the issues being raised, imaginatively enlivening, and authentically grounded. A little experience enables us to demonstrate these qualities readily.

The following essay was originally published in *Design for Arts Education* 85, no. 6 (July/August 1984). Used by permission.

Few issues in arts education are as central—and as vexing—as that having to do with the use of high-quality examples for study and performance. How can we be sure that the works of art we present to our students are exemplary of their particular genre and style and of the arts as a whole? We may sometimes want to use an awful example to make a specific point, but usually we hope to choose works that, because of their excellence, are likely to be deeply experienced in the present and to provide guidelines for quality in the future. Taking into account the age of our particular students and the amount of sheerly technical complexity they are likely to be able to handle, how do we select our examples with confidence that they are good or great or, at least, not bad?

The first principle to consider in this matter is that the goodness of an art work depends on the quality of its form. By form I mean all the forces in a work of art that make it a unified, dynamic phenomenon. Many works have a particular form—rondo, ballad, epic, etc., but my use of the word is broader than that. Form is the process, moment to moment, by which a work is created and experienced. It is the "how" a work of art becomes and is, not the "what" that it is.

The "meaning" of a work of art is always a function of how it is formed, never only of what it depicts or says. A work with trivial subject matter—a painting of sunlight on a pond, or a poem about stopping in the woods for a moment on a wintry night, or a short story about a suburban cocktail party, can, by the power of its expressive form, plunge us profoundly into feeling. On the other hand, a work with the most profound subject matter will, if it is superficial in form, be trivial and meaningless. This is the message of the famous comment by the theologian Paul Tillich that "There is more presence of ultimate reality in an apple by Paul Cezanne than in a picture of Jesus by Heinrich Hoffman."

Now we are confronted by a central question: exactly how does an artwork achieve excellence of form? This is hardly an academic question for those people responsible for decisions about the arts in education, for without a clear answer there are no clear guidelines for our choice of art, the performance of art, or the involvement of our students. Our profession demands that the choices we make be discriminating ones, and the communities we serve assume with some confidence that the art used in their schools will be appropriate for children to experience. These requirements, I would suggest, can be met only by using art of intrinsic aesthetic excellence; that is, excellence of expressive form.

There is a popular assumption that the quality of art cannot be defined—that excellence in the arts is merely a matter of taste, and, as we all know, in a democracy everyone's taste is equal in value to everyone else's. Further, *de gustibus non est disputandum*. It follows, in this view, that what people like us choose for our students and how we present what we choose are strictly a function of our own personal taste, which is no doubt in conflict with that of at least some people in our communities who then regard our taste as faulty if not perverse.

I want to argue that the criteria for excellence in art are in fact well known and can be applied with a high degree of discrimination by people who are trained to do so. Of course subjective judgments are involved and *must* be involved. In that, the arts are no different from a great many other fields in which informed, educated, expert subjective judgments are essential; fields such as medicine, psychology, social work, pastoral work, and on and on. In all these endeavors subjectivity must be applied, but there is a great big difference between ignorant subjectivity and refined subjectivity. In the arts, as in everything else humans do, there is no substitute for knowing one's stuff, and knowing one's stuff includes conscious awareness of the criteria upon which we base our judgments about art and its performance; that is, the criteria upon which our taste has been developed. Further, I believe that our responsibilities in arts education include that we educate our students about those criteria so they can understand what guides us and also so they can use the criteria as guides for their own judgments.

   While the literature on judgments about art, the literature of aesthetic
criticism, is vast and complex, I would suggest that a workable base of operations can be built on just four criteria for establishing the quality of an
art work and, in the case of the performing arts, its performance. These four
are (1) craftsmanship, (2) sensitivity, (3) imagination, and (4) authenticity.
While one can spend a lifetime exploring all their theoretical and practical
implications, I want to try to give enough of a sense of what each means that
they can be used as bases for further thought and action.
   Craftsmanship is the expertness by which the materials of art are molded
into expressiveness. Each art has its own unique material: sound in music,
movement in dance, language in poetry, the various visual media in the visual arts, and so on. These materials, as all materials, resist. That is why art
requires materials: to set up a situation in which resistance must be encountered. The creative act in art consists precisely of a confrontation with resisting material, in which a resolution of the resistances is achieved through
the use of skill, sensitivity, and imagination. The depth of resistance, the
degree of tension in the act of creation and therefore in the resulting work
of art, is one major factor in the greatness of the work. No great work is
achieved without great work. The materiality of art is the battleground, the
field of forces, upon which the creative struggle takes place.
   To struggle successfully, to win through to an expressive form, requires
a high degree of skill in both knowing profoundly about the material and
acting with mastery upon it. This is quite different from skill in the more
everyday sense, which is basically an ability to do things with some degree
of dexterity. Craftsmanship includes that but reaches a level in which the
resisting material is so integrated within the self as to be shaped by a unity
of mind, hand, and heart. I think that is why there is something almost spiritual about craftsmanship, something that so integrates our human powers
that we feel elevated by it. Anyone who has ever achieved real craftsmanship in some aspect of his life knows its tremendous impact, its incredible
satisfactions. So when we labor to refine our craftsmanship, by perfecting
our skills, by deeply identifying with our chosen materials, by feeling out
its expressive potentials, all of which require time and sweat and often frustration, we are not just pursuing dexterity—we are searching for creative
communion with those materials, and to the degree we achieve it we have
achieved craftsmanship.
   Craftsmanship, like just about everything else, exists in degrees. At one
end is virtuosity, and it is no mystery why we regard with awe the chosen
few who display it. But at the other end are those moments we have all
experienced when things come together, when our skill and our insight

reinforce each other and we say about something we or our students have done or are trying to do, "Hey, that's not bad." A song, a drawing, a little dance, a verse of poetry, all can embody the significance that craftsmanship gives when it is present. We must, when choosing art for use in education and when performing art as part of education, be deeply aware of the quiet shining through that shows that craftsmanship has touched the work. Such work touches us.

The absence of craftsmanship is signaled by shoddiness, by disrespect for material, by forcing material to do something rather than trusting it to do something, by skill that is devoid of heart; skill that manipulates rather than serves. Such work demeans us.

Knowing our stuff means having the skill to tell the difference.

The second criterion, sensitivity, has to do with the depth and quality of feeling captured in the dynamic form of a work. The function of art is to give objective existence to feelings, which, by themselves, are private and transitory. In order to transform feelings into something public and enduring a medium is needed—something that will hold on to the fleetingness of subjective experiences and give them outward being. The materials of art do precisely this. Sounds, movements, colors, shapes, the interplay of human forces as in a play or a novel, all of these are the public counterparts of private subjectivities. As artists shape their materials into form they are at one and the same time giving shape to their feelings.

What they are *not* doing is "expressing" those feelings. To express feeling requires no artistic shaping. A baby crying, a child having a temper tantrum, an adult shouting at someone in anger or crying with joy or jumping up and down with excitement, are truly "expressing their feelings." In fact, if we sense that instead of giving vent to the feeling they are having, they are making some conscious decisions about how to do so by assessing the effect they are having and changing their behavior accordingly, we then are immediately suspicious that they are not just expressing—they are being artful. And our response is to wonder what they're up to.

Artists are up to something. Not something manipulative as we might suspect of those who are seemingly expressing their feelings but are not really. What artists are up to is the *exploration* of feeling—the probing of possibilities for feeling to develop, and extend, and repeat, and fade out, and fade back in, and be combined with another, and still another, and then change just a bit in a variation, and then dramatically transform itself into a new feeling, and then reappear as it first existed, and on and on until the journey of feeling brings itself to a close and the creative act is finished.

It is precisely because artists are not giving vent to a feeling they are having but are building up an expressive complex of developed feelings that
we are able to judge the success or failure of the result. We cannot judge
as good or bad or fair a person who is truly expressing his feelings. Would
we say "that baby cries very well," or "only moderately well" or that "lady is
screaming with good craftsmanship," or "she's screaming O.K. but I heard
a lady screaming much better the other day"?

Every time an artist acts on his material he makes a decision. Thousands
of such decisions are made for every painting or poem or film or play. The
decisions are made on the basis of some overall plan: a lyric poem, say, has
certain ways to do what it does; a requiem mass can do certain things but
not other things, and so forth. They are also made on the basis of what just
happened in the unfolding work, what might therefore happen now, what
it might lead to happening a little later. Sensitivity is the "in touchness" an
artist has with the developing, forming feelings, so that he can make ongoing decisions that ring true, that convince, that grasp us by their expressive
power. Some works move us a little—they take us on a pleasant journey of
feeling that we enjoy. Some works plunge us so deeply into complexities
of feeling and intensities of feeling that we emerge from the experience
profoundly changed. All works of art that are sensitively created have the
potential to touch our feelings—to take them on an adventure, small or
large, that deepens our sense of self.

The absence of sensitivity is betrayed by works in which the obvious
overwhelms the subtle; in which the surface of feeling is offered rather than
challenges to feel more deeply. The world is full of art so-called that gives
immediate gratification of feeling, that condescends to our subjectivity
rather than expanding it. Such art cheapens our sense of ourselves.

Knowing our stuff means being sensitive to the difference.

The criterion of imagination deals with the vividness of an art object and
its performance. Most of our lives, moment by moment and day to day, are
lived at a fairly placid emotional level (although there are those days when
all hell seems to break loose and we feel like we're living inside a Wagner
opera). At the everyday level we may, if we're fortunate, feel a general
peace, a sense of ongoing satisfaction and pleasure with ourselves and what
we're doing. That's fine. That's our need for tranquility. But we also need,
from time to time, to make contact with the depths of which human experience is capable.

Art reaches for the depths. It may not try to reach very far. A Strauss
waltz, say, or a Neil Simon comedy, or a light opera, aren't intended to
plunge us into the deepest reaches of feeling. But even when the intent is

modest, as in such works, success requires an out-of-the-ordinary experience. We must, no matter how small or how limited the work of art, be to some extent captured by it, at least for a moment and at least to a degree of feeling that dips us a bit below the surface. Imagination in a work of art is what captures our feelings.

To be captured, something must grab us. When we expect a thing to happen, and it happens, we often move right through the experience without noticing it. It's when we're led to expect something and it does *not* happen, or it happens in a way we did not foresee, or it only happens after several unexpected deviations have occurred—that's when we begin to pay attention. Artists constantly strive to get us to pay that kind of attention. They are experts in setting us up, and then, by making a decision we would not have expected them to make, grasping our feelings and forcing us to respond. It may be the smallest change from the expected: that change is what gets us.

At every moment in the creative act, whether it consists of composing a piece of music or painting a landscape or writing a poem, craftsmanship and sensitivity combine to guide decisions that are also, to some extent, imaginative, that do not follow through in a straight, undeviating line of expectation but reach for the original solution, the unexpected event, the novel twist and turn, the unfolding of events that pull us, as we follow them, to feel more deeply because we cannot entirely predict the outcome. Great works of art present such challenges to our feelings by their richness of imagination—sometimes the audacity of their imagination—as to shake us to our foundations. Every good work of art, no matter how simple, must have enough originality to vivify our feelings, to bring them to more vibrant life. All such works, across the entire spectrum from the modest to the profound, enliven our experience.

When imagination is absent or is insufficient a work of art betrays us. We go to it for vividness. What we get is the docile, the prosaic, the uninspired, the cliché. Many so-called artworks, whether through timidity or literal-mindedness, have the opposite effect on us than art exists to have: they depress our feelings rather than excite them. Such art at best leaves us untouched. At worst it deadens us.

Knowing our stuff means being alive to the difference.

The final criterion for quality in art, authenticity, raises the issue of morality. This is among the most confused topics in the entire realm of aesthetics, and I cannot pretend to be able to unravel it in the context of this article. But I do want to make a few points. The major one is that morality in art, as with meaning in art, has little if anything to do with the nonaesthetic content of art, with the statements art may contain or actions it may depict or events it may tell about or opinions it might offer about the world and its workings. For art all such content is raw material and as such is neither aesthetically moral nor immoral.

It is how the material is treated that makes the difference. A novel or a play, for example, may be filled with lust and violence and war and greed and betrayal and every other problematic behavior of human beings and yet be profoundly moral nevertheless, such as Tolstoy's *War and Peace* or Shakespeare's *Hamlet*. On the other hand a work may be full of sweetness and light yet have the effect of degrading our humanity: I think of some dime-store pictures we've all seen of Jesus in day-glo colors on black velvet.

What then, is morality in art? Simply put, it is the genuineness of the artist's interaction with her materials in which the control by the artist includes a giving way to the demands of the material. As much as an artist shapes her material, her material shapes her. The material of art takes on its own life as it begins to be shaped, making its own requirements which must be felt by the artist. To the degree the artist responds honestly, not forcing his materials to do his will but creatively interacting with the dynamics that have been set in motion, to that degree he is acting morally. It is when an artist ignores the unfolding interplay, or bypasses it in order to achieve something external to the needs of the developing feelings in the creative act, that he has violated his art and thereby corrupted it. As John Dewey says,

> If one examines into the reason why certain works of art offend us, one is likely to find that the cause is that there is no personally felt emotion guiding the selecting and assembling of the material presented. We derive the impression that the artist . . . is trying to regulate by conscious intent the nature of the emotion aroused. We are irritated by a feeling that he is manipulating materials to secure an effect decided upon in advance.[1]

In art that is immoral. What it produces is art so-called that displays sentimentality rather than sensitivity, the surface appearances of feeling rather than its underlying vitality. An honest work takes us wherever it goes—to the unpleasant as well as the pleasant. No matter. It will, by virtue of its fidelity to its inner needs, ennoble our humanity. A dishonest work forces us to a foregone conclusion. We arrive at it with a nasty taste in our mouths. We know we've been used. Our feelings yearn for honesty, not for sentiment. We are honored by the genuine, no matter how tough to take. We are humiliated by the fake, in art as in everything else.

Knowing our stuff means respecting the difference.

An important implication of these ideas has to do with styles of art. Never before in history have so many styles existed simultaneously in each art. There is no "modern music"—there are many "modern musics." There is no "modern poetry"—there are many styles of poetry, each equally viable and with an equal claim to our attention. And so on for all the arts. So as we survey the incredible richness and diversity of artistic styles available from our own times, and all the artistic styles available from past times that are alive and well and continue to be relevant for modern sensibilities, the problem of choice becomes severe.

One aspect of choice is appropriateness for the specific educational objective being planned, and for that aspect it is necessary to deal with particular programs of instruction, which cannot be done here. But since the criterion of appropriateness must always include the prior criterion of intrinsic quality, the characteristics of quality I have suggested can indeed be of assistance. The major point to be made here is that each style in an art must be judged on its own terms. It is fruitless to deem any particular style of music, say, as inherently more or less worthy than any other style. Once deciding that style a or b or c or x is appropriate for a particular educational context, the criteria for quality must be applied to examples within that particular style. Every style, including the ones we are most used to in education, has examples on a continuum from excellent to poor. The obligation here is very clear; to know our stuff so well that we always aim for the best and choose the best no matter the style. Given the complexity of such an obligation our task is not an easy one, but then, no one promised us a rose garden.

The criteria for quality I have proposed for judging art apply in an additional way: they are the bases for judging the work we do as aesthetic educators. What makes us good at what we do? I would suggest that our craftsmanship at our work is a major factor for our success, and that an important part of craftsmanship for us is being aware of and articulate about the criteria we use for judging the quality of the arts we choose. I would also suggest that our sensitivity, both to the expressive values of the arts we deal with and to the expressive potentials of the students we deal with—their abilities to participate actively in artistic expression and to share deeply in aesthetic impression—will be crucial for our impact. Our imagination, our ability to challenge, to vivify, to enliven the experience of art for students, is a factor they depend upon, and depend upon week after week after week. We are the continually flowing fountain of energy that shuns the routine, avoids the easy solution, argues for giving a bit *more* than what everyone expects, so that teaching and learning in the arts will include the delight of freshness. And our authenticity—our devotion to the highest standards of quality, subject to the particular social and educational contexts in which we work—is the bedrock upon which authentic arts education can be fostered.

Put in this way our task is formidable indeed. But it is also a challenge that can provide a lifetime's satisfactions. For underneath the specifics of doing well what we have chosen to do is the knowledge we have that our efforts are connected directly to one of the deepest of all human needs, the need for aesthetic nourishment by the power of good art.

NOTE

1. John Dewey, *Art as Experience* (New York: G. P. Putnam, 1934), 68.

12

WHAT IS PERFORMING WITH UNDERSTANDING?

Music educators who teach performance face a quandary that is as old as music itself. Performance, whether singing or playing, requires a complex set of skills if it is to be more than perfunctory. There's nothing wrong with casual, untrained performance, of course, something people everywhere enjoy doing, often with great pleasure and at every opportunity. We professionals rejoice at that pleasure and in music's power to offer soulful fulfillment in the ways only musical performance can do.

However, music educators are not needed for people to enjoy spontaneous and untutored performance. Nor are teachers of any subject when learnings are accomplished as a natural part of life, requiring no developmental tuition. Education, conceived as the organized effort to provide learnings in pursuit of developing competencies, does indeed require special institutions such as schools and special people—teachers—whose responsibilities are to build on the desire and need for increased competencies to be attained.

For us, nurturing expertise in performing, whether as an aspect of general education in music or as a specialized elective, requires a great deal of attention (actually, an enormous amount of attention) to all the "how to do it" aspects of technique. In fulfilling that responsibility we do a magnificent job, and of that we deserve to be very proud. Yet lurking below that level of success is the old, nagging worry that in pursuit of competency we tend

to neglect the wider contexts of musical understanding on which technical competence must rest to be authentic.

What to do?

First, I suggest, is to more clearly comprehend just what "understanding" consists of—something not as easy as might be assumed. Second is
to apply that comprehension to the particularities of developing it as an
essential dimension of performance education. At these tasks we have
not done very well.

In the first chapter, presented here, of the book resulting from the
first (of four) Northwestern University Music Education Leadership
Seminars, I tackle head-on the issue of precisely defining performing
with understanding. The subsequent chapters of the book, written by the
other attendees, carry these ideas forward in a variety of performance
contexts. The need for a better balance of technique with understanding
in teaching performance remains pressing. That book demonstrates that
it can indeed be accomplished, to the benefit of both

The following essay was originally published in Bennett Reimer, ed., *Performing with Understanding: The Challenge of the National Standards for
Music Education* (Reston, VA: The National Association for Music Education, 2000). Based on a Northwestern University Music Education Leadership Seminar. Used by permission.

BACKGROUND

Throughout its history in the United States the music education profession has
devoted much if not most of its energies to teaching young people to sing and
play instruments. To this day, singing and playing are dominant involvements
with music in most general music classes and are the only music electives offered in most secondary schools. All music education majors in colleges and
universities are required to study performance seriously, and most of them
intend to become teachers of performance in elective school music programs.
The relative few preparing to be general music teachers in elementary schools
spend a good deal of their training learning how to teach singing and playing
appropriate instruments, and those preparing to be general music teachers in
middle or junior high schools also must be proficient in teaching the performance electives, most commonly choral ensembles.

Given the historical and continuing emphasis on performance as the
principal way to involve students with music, the achievements of Ameri-

can music education in this endeavor have been impressive indeed. The community of music educators devoted to performance is active, vital, and well organized. The level of performance of the typical school music groups—bands, orchestras, and choruses—is often remarkably high, especially in that most members of those groups have no intention of pursuing performance study in any serious way after graduation from high school. The number of students in schools electing to become involved with performance, estimated to average somewhere between 9 percent and 15 percent, compares favorably with other school elective offerings and certainly outstrips elective choices and opportunities in the other arts. So in many ways the music education profession deserves to be, and is, justifiably proud of the excellence of its performance endeavors.

THE CONCERNS

But beneath that merited pride has been a long-standing undercurrent of concern about the quality and depth of the musical learnings accruing from school performance activities. The concern is usually not about the level of technical ability students are able to achieve. Music educators are deeply savvy about what is reasonable in that regard and are experts in helping their students develop acceptable if not admirable technical control. The concern has more to do with what students are or are not learning beyond the level of proficient sound production; learnings that cause their singing and playing to be musically authentic, genuinely expressive, fully artistic, and thereby deeply satisfying for themselves and their audiences.

Why should such a concern exist? Two reasons for it have often been expressed, both by performance specialists and others.

First, the performance experience of many students tends to be limited to the correct production of notated sounds as instructed to do so by a teacher who makes every substantive decision about how those sounds should be made. Such students, it is often argued, are not being given the opportunity to develop the individuality and responsibility required to be an artist—in this case a performing musician. Rote instruction, while producing results quickly, leaves students dependent on the teacher, when what is desired is the development of musical independence on the part of students.

The teacher, under pressure to produce public performances with inadequate time to do much more than whip an ensemble into shape, and working with literature at the edges of the students' capabilities so as to make the best impression possible, does not have the luxury to spend time on matters not directly and specifically connected to getting the right sounds made in the right way, "right" meaning as the notation requires and as the teacher interprets.

Students in such very common situations, it has been argued, can become very proficient at being able to do what they are told, but are left with minimal ability to make musical decisions when left to their own devices. They have not been helped to become performers in the genuine sense; that is, people whose excellent craftsmanship is based on their finely developed musical sensitivities, their imaginative ability to make music come alive in personally expressive ways, and their wide and deep perspective on how to accommodate their creative decisions to the demands of particular pieces in particular historical, cultural, and individual musical styles. Performance experiences in schools, it has long been argued, should foster this kind of genuine musicianship to the highest possible level for each student. The concern is that this goal becomes usurped by the pressures of a demanding public performance regimen.

The second concern about the quality of much school music performance experience is an outgrowth of the first. This concern has to do with the future consequences of instruction that has been narrowly conceived and limited in focus. What happens to the students who have undergone such experiences once they graduate from high school?

Solid research on that question is scarce.[1] But a good deal of evidence based on the experience of many professional musicians and music educators allows for several pertinent observations.

For the very small percentage of students who go on to become music majors in colleges and universities, and who therefore are almost always required to continue performance study either as their major or as an important component of their programs, it has been widely expressed that their technique tends to be quite good to remarkably good. Of course, different collegiate institutions have different expectations for what acceptable performance expertise consists of, but even the elite among college, university, and conservatory music programs are generally able to find students fulfilling their high expectations (with, of course, some exceptions for the less common instruments).

The problem with students entering music programs, it is widely observed, is not the level of their technical achievement but the shallowness of their musical understandings and the narrowness of their musical perspectives. There seems to be a disjunction between musicianship in the limited sense of technical facility and the broader sense of solidly grounded artistry. The task for collegiate level education is to bring the two into better balance and to foster the continuing growth of both as being interdependent; that is, to develop mature performing artists.

The cream of the crop of school performers choose to continue in music, and what is left is the vast majority, whose lives will no doubt have been enriched in various ways by their performance experiences but whose continuing involvements with music are likely to change radically from what they were in school, given the exigencies that life will present to them. Some few, who have gained deep satisfactions from having been performers, will be reluctant to just give it all up and will seek continuing involvements as amateurs in a variety of settings depending on what opportunities they find in their communities. Most will seldom if ever pursue performance in any substantial way again. What will they have gained from their brief experience as performers that will inform and enhance their musical experiences throughout their lives, albeit that those experiences are unlikely to come from performance? What will be the residue of musical understanding they have gained from performing, and will it be sufficient for, and relevant to, an enhanced ability to incorporate music into their lives as a precious source of pleasure?

THE LARGER PICTURE

The concerns about the depth, quality, and real-world applicability of performance learnings are part of a much larger movement occurring throughout the education enterprise at this point in history. In every subject matter field in education an intensive self-analysis has taken place to determine whether traditional approaches have been too narrowly conceived to foster what is quickly becoming recognized by education scholars and leaders as the primary goal of education—the development of understanding. The mechanism for that analysis has been the creation of national standards for describing what all students should know and be able to do in each subject area. The effort to produce these standards—to identify the most important knowledge and skills for each field—has had an enormously positive effect on each field's sense of its central values and its central knowledge base. Every field, including music, has had to look itself squarely in the eye and ask itself what really matters about it and what really matters to learn about it.

In doing so, it has become crystal clear that much material previously considered essential was not optimally connected to achieving the ultimate goal of effective education—the deepening of every student's understanding.

Each field, including music but much more broadly than music, has begun to face the challenge of reassessing its previously more limited aspirations and redesigning its curriculum to reflect a concentration on those learnings most relevant to understanding as it is manifested in that field.[2]

The National Standards for Music Education should be read as the attempt, in music education, to precisely define the knowledge and skills required to achieve musical understanding. What leaps out most dramatically from the nine content standards is their identification, as essential learnings, of far more than has traditionally been included. Further, the Standards require that all nine must be represented in all programs within the total music curriculum, including the performance program.

Why these nine? Why should all of them have to be incorporated as essential learnings in Content Standard 1, having to do with singing, and 2, having to do with playing?

The answers to those questions require an explanation of what understanding consists of and, as outgrowths, what musical understanding consists of and what performing with understanding consists of. The following discussions in this chapter will attempt an overview of what a reasonably complete explanation would entail, since a full explanation would require its own book, or, given the complexity of the issue, series of books. (The subsequent chapters of this book are devoted to discussions of and recommendations for achieving the understandings required for artistic performance.)

GENERALITIES ABOUT UNDERSTANDING

Dictionary definitions of understanding are of little help in providing guidelines for cultivating it, offering primarily synonyms, such as "perceiving the meaning or grasping the idea of something, comprehending, being familiar with, apprehending, grasping the significance," and so forth.

What is needed is an explanation of just what it is that such terms actually entail—what mechanism of thinking/doing underlies and operationalizes the achievement of "perceiving the meaning," "grasping the idea," "comprehending," and so forth. Until we are able to identify that mechanism we are not able to be optimally effective in providing educational experiences useful for fostering understanding.

Several recent considerations of this issue have attempted to clarify what this mechanism consists of. Unfortunately, I would suggest, they do not produce the desired result—a clear, elegant, yet powerful identification of the foundational operation of thinking and doing, which underlies what we generally call understanding, comprehending, apprehending, grasping the meaning, and so on. Most discussions remain at too high a level of generality to supply the specificity needed to focus efforts of educators on cultivating understanding. As Howard Gardner puts it in his book dealing with education for understanding, *The Unschooled Mind: How Children Think and How Schools Should Teach*, "generalizations about understanding are elusive, and those that can be made are necessarily expressed at a high level of abstraction."[3] Precisely so. How do we get to a level of detail that can guide educational efforts efficiently?

I do not believe Gardner provides what we need, despite the many excellent insights he offers. In the book mentioned above one searches in vain for a concise definition of understanding that pinpoints its particular nature or character. In a chapter called "What Are the Qualities of Understanding?" written for another book, Gardner, along with Veronica B. Mansilla, offers the following reflection:

> The quality of students' understanding rests on their ability to master and use bodies of knowledge that are valued by their culture. More specifically, it rests on their ability to make productive use of the concepts, theories, narratives, and procedures available in such disparate domains as biology, history, and the arts. Students should be able to understand the humanly constructed nature of this knowledge and to draw on it to solve problems, create products, make decisions, and in the end transform the world around them. Put differently, students should use knowledge to engage in a repertoire of performances valued by the societies in which they live.[4]

Few would disagree with this hope, including me. But it remains at a very "high level of abstraction." What is required for students to be able to "master and use" valued knowledge? How do they develop their ability to "make productive use" of learnings in various fields? What do we learn of the nature of understanding by the assertion that "Students should be able to understand . . ."? What we are searching for is an explanation of what, precisely, that *means*, not only what one uses it for when one has it.

Here is another too-abstract explanation of understanding from the same collection, this one from Vito Perrone. "Teaching for understanding—the view that what students learn needs to be internalized, able to be used in many different circumstances in and out of classrooms, serving as a base for ongoing and extended learning, always alive with possibilities—has long been endorsed as a primary educational goal in the schools."[5]

This calls attention to several useful ideas about understanding. It is something "internalized." It is able to be "used in many different circumstances." It is "a base for ongoing and extended learning." But what, precisely, is it that needs to be internalized so that it can serve these functions? Again, we are left with no guidance beyond generalities.

The chapter by David Perkins, titled "What Is Understanding?" takes us closer to what we are searching for. Perkins identifies three desired goals of education—knowledge, skill, and understanding. Knowledge, he suggests, is "information on tap." Skills are "routine performances on tap." Understanding, however, is more subtle, not being reducible to either or both those two:

> So what is understanding? One answer lies at the heart of this book and this project; it is simple but rich with implications. In a phrase, understanding is the ability to think and act flexibly with what one knows. To put it another way, an understanding of a topic is a "flexible performance capability" with emphasis on the flexibility. In keeping with this, learning for understanding is like learning a flexible performance—more like learning to improvise jazz or hold a good conversation or rock climb than learning the multiplication table or the dates of the presidents or that $F=MA$. Learning facts can be a crucial backdrop to learning for understanding, but learning facts is not learning for understanding.[6]

So now we may regard understanding as an ability to do a specific thing—"to think and act flexibly." Unfortunately, we are again given no explanation about the particulars that would allow thinking and acting to be flexible. We cannot yet identify just what it is that allows knowledge and skill to be "thought with" in a variety of situations; that is, flexibly.

Perkins explains that understanding in the thinking dimension requires a "conceptual model"—a structure in the mind that represents a particular situation, idea, system, and so forth. He labels this "mental model" idea of understanding the "representational view." In this view the model one holds in one's mind is the basis for the actions one takes. The action is not the understanding—it is a signal that the appropriate representation is possessed.

In contrast is the "performance model" of understanding, which argues that the only way we can recognize understanding is through its manifestation in flexible performances—doing things that demonstrate that a person can "operate on or with the model."[7]

Now, there seems to be little difference between the conceptual model and the performance model. Both allow for and depend on mental representations and actions that operate on or with them.[8] The difference turns out to be one of degree. The conceptual model tends to emphasize the structures of knowing, on which actions depend, as being the key factor while the performance model emphasizes the actions one takes as being the key factor, the underlying structures being secondary. As Perkins concludes, "the performance view of understanding yields a brand of constructivism [engaging students in their own efforts to build understanding] that might be called *performance constructivism* because of its emphasis on building learners' repertoire of understanding performances more than on cultivating the construction of representations."[9]

Where does all this leave us? The distinction between thinking and acting is extremely helpful, as is the recognition of their relative interdependence. It would seem that the emphasis teachers put on either mental models or performance models might depend on subject matter. For example, philosophers and psychologists are specialists in articulating the mental models underlying our knowledge, skills, and understandings. Making such models explicit is what they do. The education of philosophers and psychologists (among many others) therefore, would seem to require that students in these subjects be assisted in developing knowledge about the models' underlying actions and in developing skills to explain them conceptually.

On the other hand, musical performers are specialists in making explicit, *through their actions*, the musical thinking underlying the sounds they create. The education of musical performers would seem to require a focus on their actions—their skills of creation of musical sounds—as these are founded upon their musical knowledge and internalized musical models whether explicit or implicit.

The implications of this idea for teachers of performance are clear and profound. Performance teachers must be able to help their students internalize musical models—inner representations of appropriate musical expression—which form the basis for independent artistic decisions carried out in acts of performance. The "mental/musical models" are, for performers, means, not ends. For music theorists, music psychologists, music philosophers, and others, the building of such models is an end, which can then be used by others as means. For performers, the end is realized in their artistic actions. When those actions are based only on their teachers' internalized models rather than on their own, the performers remain dependent on others for artistic decision making. When they are helped to gain and appropriate within themselves the musical models they need to call upon they are enabled to become independent musicians/artists.

Teachers of performance, then, must (a) have internalized valid models relevant to performance in general and to their special area of performance in particular; and (b) be able to make the details of those models explicit, that is, communicable to students in a variety of ways including explaining them, helping students discover them, providing exemplars in actual performance, whether their own or others', providing musical challenges that encourage the application in action of the model aspects being explored, and so forth. Good teaching of performance, this suggests, develops students' mental/musical models as a means to the end of independent, musically grounded, artistic creating.

As useful as the insights of people like Perrone, Gardner, and Perkins can be, they still leave us without a description of what understanding actually consists of, their discussions remaining at too high a level of generality to supply the insights we need in order to do our jobs as teachers optimally. I will attempt a remedy in the next section.

Before doing so, two ideas of great importance, held in common by the three scholars I have been discussing and by many others, need to be brought to attention. They have wide-ranging implications for the topic of this book.

First, understanding exists in degree. There is no single point at which one can say, "Now I have achieved understanding." No matter the level of one's understandings, further understandings are always possible. The responsibility of education, then, is to continually build upon, expand, and deepen students' understandings, recognizing that no hypothetical end point will ever be achieved in potential growth of understanding.

Second, understandings exist in kind—they are specific to the contexts to which they are applicable. There is no such thing as a "general understanding" separate from the specifics of the kinds of understandings called for by particular situations.

The term usually used in the scholarly literature for this contextual embeddedness of understanding is "domain specific." Often the domains in which specific understandings are called into play are considered to be the subjects studied in schools—languages, math, science, arts, history, geography, government, and so forth. Each of these, it is claimed, requires its characteristic ways of understanding. The most influential recent conceptualization of the domains in which understandings are achieved is Howard Gardner's notion of "frames of mind," in which seven categories of mindful functioning (called "intelligences" but applicable to understandings as well) are identified: the linguistic, musical, logical-mathematical, spatial, bodily-kinesthetic, interpersonal, and intrapersonal.[10] (Gardner has more recently considered adding the "naturalist" domain and, possibly, the "spiritual" or "existential.")

Whether domain-specific understandings are conceived to reside in school subjects, in "frames of mind," or in other conceptualizations,[11] it is important to recognize that when we teach musical performance we must focus on developing the specific understandings relevant to that role. We can offer a general definition of understanding applicable to all specific role contexts (I prefer a focus on roles rather than domains) but in actual practice the understandings needing to be developed take their particularity and purpose from the role context in question.

What then, is the answer to the question of what understanding specifically consists of? And what does performing with understanding consist of given that it is a particular way, or role, in which understanding is achieved? Further, how can we best help our students achieve deeper understandings in their role as performers?

THE SPECIFICS OF UNDERSTANDING AND PERFORMING WITH UNDERSTANDING

I want to propose that the specific, underlying operation of thought and action required for understanding is *the forming of relevant connections*. Three concepts are embedded in this proposal: (a) connections, (b) forming, and (c) relevancy.

A. Connections

Connections are interrelations—the ways things have something to do with other things. These ways range broadly over every possible relation that one thing can have with another, from identicality, to similarity, to affinity, association, proximity, pertinence, contrast, dissimilarity, incommensurability, opposition, variation, resemblance, imitation, and on and on with all the myriad operations of the mind in which some level of and sort of connectedness is identified.

The mind's ability to connect disparate things (objects, ideas, experiences, feelings, and so forth) is the basis for human understanding. Without this ability the world we experience would be chaotic—a "booming, buzzing confusion." Meaning, significance, wisdom, knowing, accomplishing; all human endeavors, intentions, and undergoings, are founded on and dependent on our ability to recognize relationships. Recognizing relationships is understanding.

Necessarily, then, as previously explained, understanding exists in degree. Recognizing that one leaf looks like another leaf is a necessary step in understanding leaves. A subsequent step, adding to and broadening that understanding, is the recognition that some leaves differ from others. Identifying, by the connection of dissimilarity, that differences in leaves can be in color, size, shape, texture, thickness, and so forth, is a still further step toward understanding leaves. The understanding of leaves can continue to grow through successive levels of complexity, breadth, depth, and inclusiveness, leading to, perhaps, a worldview of the nature of life itself. At every step toward more comprehensive making of interconnections we may say that understanding has grown.

B. Forming

Forming is the function of the mind actively bringing connections into being. That function requires, consists of, and could not exist without imagination. Here the dictionary is precise: "Imagination is the faculty of forming mental images or concepts of what is not actually present to the senses." Connections among things are not present in factual sensory inputs—they are *constructed* from the sense data we receive. This construction ability is so deeply embedded as a primary function of human minds that it seems to be "given" with the sensory data we receive. It is not. We *attribute* the connections among things, as minds process those things to make experience out of them—to turn them into meanings. The level of our forming—our ability in particular instances to transform data into connected phenomena so that meaning occurs—is the level of our understanding.

Understanding, then, is an accomplishment, something we create at every moment in our conscious lives. Our minds are, inherently, connection-making devices, or, to put it into the context of this discussion, understanding generators. The levels of connections we are able to process about similarities and differences among, say, leaves, from the most limited to the most comprehensive, are levels of imaginative construction. We form the connections—we imaginatively create them—as our experience with leaves, our learning about leaves, our application of those learnings in wider, more inclusive interrelationships, leads us to deeper understandings about leaves and their role in life on earth. Humans are active agents in forming connections—in making understanding. Teachers are active agents in assisting this process.

C. Relevancy

The connections, or interrelations, we form, or imaginatively construct, must be relevant to the task at hand in order to qualify as understanding. In a second-grade classroom studying nature the children are engaged in the role of learners, in this case about leaves. If the teacher were to show several different leaves from different trees and ask the students what they noticed about them that was particularly interesting, answers demonstrating that connections were being made ("They're all green," "They don't look the same—some are bigger than others," "They look like they come from different trees") are, in fact, demonstrating the level of understanding achieved.

If one child's answer was "They all seem to be from deciduous trees, probably from a northern climate, and from trees still in the growth stage of the season," the teacher would have reason to be impressed at that child's unusual level of understanding—of being able to form wider, more completely imagined interconnections than one would expect in that context. Similarly, if another child answered, "My Dad gets really mad when my Mom asks him to rake the leaves," the teacher might register that the child's response was not entirely relevant to the task of learning about leaves as part of nature—that the child didn't understand what relevant connections were being sought in this context.

A useful way to conceive the contexts in which connections are made—contexts that unify and give coherence to the many ways interrelationships among sensory inputs can be constructed—is to focus on the roles we play in our lives. Connections, to be meaningful, must serve some purpose. Our purposes depend on the roles we are pursuing. The teacher in the above scenario was pursuing the development of particular kinds of interconnected recognitions; that is, understandings. He was also, as a teacher, sensitive to clues—connections—signifying additional issues needing attention among his students in relating this lesson with several others. The many connections this teacher was responsible for making in the classroom setting, for his students and for himself as the teacher, constituted his professional role, a role calling on particular, focused, intentional understandings to be exercised.

The students had a different role. They were in school to learn; to build the depth and breadth of their understandings, in this case about one aspect of nature. School is a place that makes sense, that means something, because it delineates to students one of the roles they are expected to play in their lives, a role focused on developing their understandings in a variety of contexts.

Now let us switch the above scenario to that of a music educator who is teaching students to perform. Several things remain the same as in the previous scenario. The teacher in both cases is going to play a particular role calling on a coherent set of understandings related to the role of the teacher. In this case the role of the teacher is that of imparting and developing performance learnings. While still a teacher, the specificity of this particular role influences everything the teacher will do in her professional task of enhancing her students' understandings, specifically in their role as performers.

The performer role requires understandings to be developed—relevant connections to be formed—in a variety of interrelated focuses. One focus for performance understanding, for example, is on the physical actions required to produce the sounds that will serve musical purposes. Breath, vocal cords, throat, mouth, fingers, arms, tongue, lips, diaphragm, hands, wrists, legs, feet, all are involved in various ways depending on the performance medium.

Performers must develop complex, subtle successions of interrelated connections (understandings) regarding such matters, not only as mental constructs but as internalized action patterns. Teachers attempting to help this process occur—teaching for understanding about the physical making of musical sounds—use a variety of devices such as words, gestures, diagrams, modeling, and touching, as means to the end of getting students to so deeply internalize the actions being sought as to render them automatic. Until the actions occur as habituated they have not been "learned" as performers must learn them. So understanding in this context requires the sets of connections about sound producing to become tacit, in the sense of understood with no verbal expression of that understanding as the understanding is being demonstrated. The teacher's ability to make the relevant connections explicit, using a variety of means to bring them to awareness, is part of her arsenal as a professional. The end in view, however, is "awareness in action."

Another focus for performance learnings—for understandings to be developed as required to become a competent performer—is on notation (when, as is dominantly the case in American music education, the music to be performed exists in notated form). I will not attempt here a delineation of all the virtually endless connections that must be formed in order to deeply and widely understand the workings of musical notations, whether standard staff notation or various others. Readers will be able to do that for themselves.

Still another set of understandings are those that must be developed in order for each piece to be performed, in its particulars of pitch, rhythm, dynamics, tempi, articulations, harmony, texture, and form, and on and on with all the specifics comprising "a piece of music." When does one "fully understand" all the musical interconnections existing in even a simple piece, let alone a very complex one? That is, when has a performer become aware of and transformed into automatic bodily behavior patterns all the possible musically meaningful (interconnected) events in a piece being performed? Well, remember, understanding is always a matter of degree.

The three dimensions of performance understanding mentioned above—physical actions, notations, and pieces—are, of course, separable from one another only theoretically. In the actuality of the performance experience all function interdependently. Think, then, of the staggering complexity of the multifaceted understandings required for a performer to (a) be able to physically produce the sounds required for music, (b) be able to translate notated symbols into musically sonic gestures, (c) be able to do both those things as relevant to the particularities of musical meanings contained within the piece being performed, and (d) be able to so coordinate all those facets of understanding that they are unified in the singular act of performing. This challenge, I suggest, is among the most daunting with which humans can be presented.

THE STANDARDS AND MUSICAL UNDERSTANDING

Until the advent of the National Standards for Music Education it was (and of course continues to be) often assumed that if students were able to learn, to an acceptable degree relevant to their age and experience, the three dimensions of performance understandings delineated above—physically producing the needed sounds, being able to interpret notation, and making the pieces they were performing sound "musical" (that is, appropriately expressive)—they were learning all that was necessary to be competent performers. And, as I have pointed out, that in itself has been a formidable task.

The challenge of the standards is the requirement that many other important dimensions of understanding be added to those traditionally assumed to be sufficient.

This challenge signals a sea change in professional expectations of the performance role. It represents the growing awareness that students limited to those three aspects of performance understandings are limited in two important ways; in their musicianship as performers and in their understandings of music outside the performance context. The Standards are conceived and designed to broaden and deepen musical understandings so as to include all major dimensions of music as a human endeavor. Both for those who will continue to perform after high school, whether as professionals in some aspect of music or as amateurs, and for those who will no longer perform, the inclusion of those dimensions of musical learning, it is now believed, will enable all students involved in performance to more fully achieve musical meanings and satisfactions than under the previous, more limited expectation system.

The standards represent the "grand plan" of all the dimensions of understandings achievable in music. Each of the nine content standards constitutes its own vast panoply of possible understandings; of potential relevant interconnections of meanings and actions. But none of the nine stands alone. Each requires and depends upon understandings in all the others to complete it and allow it to serve as a part of a larger whole. Each can serve both as a primary focus to which all the others contribute and as a complement to the others.

The success of music education in the future, I suggest, will depend in large measure on the profession's utilization of the standards to guide the development of a meaningful general education program in music and of meaningful specializations in each of the nine.[12] The purpose of this book is to clarify how the standards can serve as the basis for the development of performing with understanding, understanding as newly conceived, in breadth and specificity, by the standards. My definition of understanding as the forming of relevant connections now comes fully into play.

Standards 1 (singing) and 2 (playing) are those focusing on performance. The connections required to do those things successfully, I have suggested, go beyond the three aspects traditionally associated with performance. Each of these two standards requires that understandings about the other eight—the forming of relevant connections within each of the eight—be incorporated within them. How does that actually play out?

Within Standard 1 is the requirement that, in addition to gaining the craftsmanship necessary for effective production of sung sounds, being able to translate notation into sung sounds, and musically appropriate singing of the piece being performed, understandings about solo and ensemble singing be developed ("alone and with others"). Further, the "varied repertoire of music" clause requires that requisite understandings of the inner workings of pieces in a wide variety of musical expectation systems (styles) be attained. So even before branching out to the other eight the breadth of understandings related to singing has been expanded.

How would Standard 2, having to do with understandings related to performing on instruments, be relevant to singing?

Several aspects of singing are similar if not identical to playing. Both require that vibrations be produced to cause sounds. Both require exquisite physical control over the mechanisms of sound production, sound projection, and sound manipulation. Both are used for the same purpose—to form successions of sounds conceived as musically meaningful in particular cultural/historical/aesthetic contexts. Both require enormous physical/mental/affective energy in order to produce the desired musical results. Both require actions within and according to the parameters of a particular "piece"—a set of composed sound-ideas being brought to sonic reality. On and on with all the shared aspects of performance whether singing or playing. Understanding that these aspects apply equally to singing and to playing enhances the understanding—the aggregate of connections—of students involved with each.

But there are differences between the two, and these are equally as relevant to understanding as are the similarities. Unlike sound production on instruments the vibration mechanism for producing sung sounds is an organ of the body rather than a mechanical device manipulated by the body. The experience of sound producing and manipulating is therefore subtly (or perhaps substantially) different. Instruments are able to produce sounds different from those produced by the voice, and vice versa. Voices are typically combined with other voices according to criteria quite different from those for combining instruments. Vocal music practically always entails words, while instrumental music does not, a significant and far-reaching distinction affecting how voices and instruments are employed to make music. On and on with all the differences between singing and playing. Understanding these differences enhances the understandings of those involved with each mode of performing.

How can teachers go about adding understandings from Standard 2 to Standard 1? Surely the Standards do not require all singers to become players in addition to becoming singers. But supplementing the learnings focused on the development of the skills and understanding required for singing, by referring to, discussing, demonstrating, and even trying to produce the similar and different ways playing relates to singing, broadens the connections singers are able to make. Awareness of how singing and playing are in many ways alike and in many ways not alike adds a significant dimension to the understandings being developed in Standard 1.

Each of the rest of the standards presents rich opportunities for connections to be made with singing, as illustrated by the example of how Standard 2 can do so. As the profession comes to grips with the wealth of learning opportunities—opportunities to develop understandings—in each of the standards, and as the interrelations among them become more obvious, several realizations are likely to occur.

First, we will begin to recognize with more specificity and more clarity how limited our perspective has tended to be on musical learning in general and, since the dominant musical learnings we have pursued have been those connected to performing, how limited our conception has been of what is required to be a broadly educated performer. The vague sense we have had that performance learnings have tended to be restricted in scope and depth, as mentioned at the beginning of this chapter, will take on specificity as we use the standards to delineate the particular understandings that need to be fostered in the ways performance requires; that is, as awarenesses transformed into the actions of performing.

Second, we will learn how to examine the dimensions of musical understanding represented by each of the standards in search of the particular array of connections each affords—the particular sets of interconnected ideas and actions each embodies. As our awareness increases of the particularities of the understandings available in each of the nine dimensions of musical involvement our ability to envision interconnections among all of them will also grow. We will be able to significantly broaden the number of specializations within music study beyond performing, each of them retaining its individuality of focus but also being enriched by learnings from all the others.

And we will also become more clear than we have ever been about the purposes of a general education in music; that is, an education embracing all the dimensions rather than focusing on one particular dimension.

As related to the concern of this book, our ability to provide performers with all that educated performers should understand will grow exponentially. That will achieve two things we need very much to achieve—the fostering of more genuinely artistic performing musicians, and the enhancement of their musical enjoyments beyond performing should they choose not to continue as performers.

Third, we will gain more respect for music performance as a human achievement of monumental proportions. As our understanding of the complexities of performance grows, as a result of our deeper awareness about the breadth of interconnections it takes to perform with understanding, the attitude that performing is simply a pleasant but relatively trivial entertainment will yield to the realization that performance, in its embracing of all dimensions of musical understanding, and in its transformation of them into bodily behavior, is a paradigm of the union of knowing and doing. The unification of mind, body, and feeling required for performing with understanding may well be an example of human cognitive potential at its farthest reaches. Teachers of performance are developers of that potential.

NOTES

1. For a useful review of research on effects of school performance involvements on subsequent listening experience, see James K. Kjelland and Jody L. Kerchner, eds., "The Effects of Music Performance Participation on the Music Listening Experience," *Bulletin of the Council for Research in Music Education* 136 (1998): 1–55.

2. The growing literature on education for understanding is indicated in the notes section of Martha S. Wiske, ed., *Teaching for Understanding: Linking Research with Practice* (San Francisco: Jossey-Bass Publishers, 1998), 351–73.

3. Howard Gardner, *The Unschooled Mind· How Children Think and How Schools Should Teach* (New York: Basic Books, 1991), 118.

4. Wiske, *Teaching for Understanding*, 162.

5. Ibid., 13.

6. Ibid., 40.

7. Ibid., 47.

8. Perkins claims that one can have an enactive (performance) understanding without an explicit mental model. But a model need not be explicit in order to be functional. We have so internalized many of the mental models we hold as to often not be able to make them explicit except with great difficulty: That does not mean we do not have them. We simply do not have them readily available in verbal-conceptual form.

9. Wiske, *Teaching for Understanding*, 57.

10. Howard Gardner, *Frames of Mind: The Theory of Multiple Intelligences* (New York: Basic Books, 1983).

11. See, for example, Philip H. Phenix, *Realms of Meaning* (New York: McGraw-Hill, 1964), and Elliot Eisner, ed., *Learning and Teaching the Ways of Knowing* (Chicago: University of Chicago Press, 1985).

12. An argument can be made that viable music specializations exist in each of the standards except, perhaps, number five, having to do with reading and notating music, which are skills useful or necessary in several of the others but not constituting, by themselves, a field of endeavor as do the others. This argument awaits further elucidation as to its persuasiveness.

13

MERELY LISTENING

How I wish that every essay I write could be as much fun as this one.

When I'm notified that the Canadian Music Educators' Association is planning a book on paradigm change in music education, I immediately get in touch with its editor, Lee Bartel, and ask him, facetiously, whether I can submit six or eight chapters. Having spent most of my career in pursuit of needed changes, I'm delighted that such a book is envisioned, and at least six or eight new topics I would love to tackle spring readily to mind. Not feasible, as I know, so he urges me to choose the one at the top of my list.

That's easy. I have long championed the cause of making the single most practiced role in music, that of the listener, as central to our professional responsibilities as it deserves to be in the face of a long history of resistance to that need. "Teach listening? Why? That's the couch-potato aspect of music." "Listening isn't making. It's a passive response to music, merely letting the sounds come in." "What we're after is active involvement, creative involvement, *doing* music rather than only receiving it. *That's* worth teaching, not encouraging inactivity with music."

On and on with disparagement of what practically everyone in the world chooses to do and deeply cherishes doing: listening to music. The elitism and condescension this widespread attitude embodies repels me, and makes me despair at how out of touch with reality our profession can be, and how misguided about the creative, fulfilling experiences the act of musical listening provides. Not to mention how irrelevant our programs in the schools are to the devoted musical listening engagements of the vast majority of our culture's people, especially those of school age. Our neglect of their needs contributes strongly to the constant threat to our existence as a school subject.

I've got to approach all of this in a positive, engaging way, I decide. It hits me. A satire would do it. One that personalizes the issue, gives it immediacy by setting it in the context of my own experience in music, both real and imagined. To do that, I've got to avoid the usual professional lingo and paraphernalia of scholarship, such as, for example, citations. Go the whole way. And even, heaven forbid, enjoy that freedom.

The following essay was originally published in Lee R. Bartel, ed., *Questioning the Music Education Paradigm* (Waterloo, Ontario: Canadian Music Educators' Association, 2004). Used by permission.

ABSTRACT

In this chapter I relate the sad tale of a sinner in need of salvation. My sin was that I loved too well. Loved to listen to music, that is. Despite attaining the virtue of being a performer I continued my nefarious love affair with listening until enlightened by music educators who, in their wisdom, convinced me of the error of my passive ways. The tale encompasses my sinking into despondence when realizing how pervasive my iniquitous behaviors were. I was in much of my life (this is hard to confess) a consumer. Forgive me. Yet through my vale of tears a beam of possible redemption began to shine. My tale, I hope, has relevance for the music education profession, in its need to rescue itself from its unconscionably high level of irrelevance to the vast majorities of the populations it purports to serve.

I never listen to music. Well, I should say I never *choose* to listen to music. These days it's all around, so sometimes you just can't avoid it. But when I'm somewhere music is playing I try not to pay attention.

I used to listen all the time. My large collection of LPs, cassettes, and CDs are evidence. I spent lots of money on those recordings, and on hi-fi equipment, tickets to concerts and recitals, operas and musicals, cover charges at jazz clubs, all because I wanted to listen. I got a lot of pleasure from it. It was an important part of my life, something I treasured. I read reviews about pieces and performances. I often planned social evenings around musical presentations, talked with family and friends and colleagues about music we enjoyed listening to, planned ahead to get to concerts in cities I was traveling to all over the world, read books about music. So you could say I was a devoted listener, a faithful audience member.

But I gave it all up. I got educated. I read what a lot of music educators had to say about listening and it wasn't a pretty picture. I began to realize what a musical clod I had been. All that energy, time, money, wasted on being a listener. That's not quite accurate. Being *merely* a listener, *passively* a listener, *only* and *just* a listener. Being (I can hardly bring myself to say this) a *consumer*. Kind of like being hooked on drugs. Something you thought was wonderful while you were doing it (listening, I mean) but that was frying your brain. And getting you regarded with contempt by those who know better, who are above all that. Those who are musically active not passive, creative not brain-dead, making music not taking it. Who are not interested in autonomous musical works as I had become. Not caught up in formal elements, auditory designs, sound patterns, in disinterested perception, in rarified and purposeless listening experiences separated from life.

That's what they said about people like me. (You could look it up.) I didn't recognize myself in all this but I knew it had to be me they were talking about because I usually was engrossed in what the sounds were doing when I listened and sometimes I indeed felt like I was in a different world when I was doing so. How could I have gotten so far off track? What possessed me? These people were heavy hitters in music education, who wrote books, articles, gave speeches. If you can't trust music educators in such matters whom can you trust? These people have the musical welfare of everyone at heart, don't they? So if merely listening is *verboten* among these experts surely I had better rethink what I was doing, who I was, what my musical values had been all those years when I loved to listen.

Clearly I was a musical sinner in need of redemption. Who wants to be merely, after all? To be passive, and just and only a consumer rather than a creator? Immersed mindlessly in perceiving sounds and what they're doing, often in works I had regarded as monuments of achievement that I could return to over and over for their challenges and satisfactions. Works, it turned out, that separated me from real life, the life of actively performing them rather than passively only merely just consuming them. I had gone seriously astray.

Of course in the years when I was a performer (on clarinet; bass clarinet; alto, tenor, and baritone sax; oboe and English horn), I was OK. Then I was active. That's because when I listened, not only to myself when I was playing but also to others, I had something to listen for. Listening for is good.

(You could look it up.) It means you should focus on things musicians need to attend to, like all the things performers need to notice in music they're performing. That sure was what I did when I was a performer. I was so intent on being a good player that I listened avidly to music for my instruments so I could learn what other performers were doing and how they did it. I seldom listened to other music, and when I did I waited for the moments when my instruments could be heard so that I'd have something to listen for. The rest of the time I was bored. All the music that didn't use my instruments was a waste of time for me because it gave me nothing to listen for. So I know a lot about listening for.

I had a sneaking suspicion during those years I was a performer that I was missing something when I listened for, but I didn't know what it was. Sometimes I wondered what all the people in the audiences were getting from what we musicians were doing. Some, of course, had played or presently played an instrument, so I figured they were listening the same way I did. Those were the ones who came up after the performance and corralled the performers of their instrument so they could talk about all the listening fors of performance. But lots of others—most others, in fact—were not and had never been performers. They seemed to enjoy what we did also, even though it was clear they couldn't listen for as musicians did. That puzzled me. And my response was to kind of condescend to them. They clearly didn't know what was going on. They just loved it. But who cares? They were, I recognize now that I've become enlightened, the great unwashed, the ones still thinking there was music to be savored, even over and over, musical pleasures to be had unrelated to musicianship, musical experiences so deeply satisfying in their lives that they would go to great lengths to get them. Sad.

And eventually I had become one of them. Sad. I had to give up performing for health reasons. So as the years went by I found myself less caught up in listening for what was once so central to my musical being and more engaged in the sounds than in how they were made. I was gradually losing the musician perspective on music, becoming more a taker than a maker. Never entirely, of course. I still got caught up in listening in the old, correct way, especially when a really fine player on one of my instruments was doing her or his stuff. Then I regressed immediately. Did I say "regressed?" I mean, of course, I returned to really being a listener—to listening for. The rest of the time, more and more as the years passed, I sank into becoming the audience member I once knew enough to disrespect. I gave myself up, shamefully, to just listening, as I described at the beginning of this story. I developed a love for music beyond performing it, taking excellent performance for granted because it was so readily available, appreciating it, of course, but no longer tied to it when I listened. Sad.

I also don't read about music any more. Another thing I learned from the music education experts was that listening and verbal language were like oil and water. It's OK to use language to help learn the processes of music making—musicianship, that is. But when teachers and others use language as a way to enhance what is heard it reduces listening to a slavish memorization of verbal concepts. (You could look it up.)

All the sad years I was a listener I depended a lot on verbal concepts. They pointed out to me all sorts of things going on in the music that I would have missed otherwise. Much of the music I enjoyed listening to challenged me a great deal, from Boulez to Charlie Parker, and I appreciated all the help I could get in hearing what was going on. Each time I heard more there was more to enjoy. And when I read or was told about the backgrounds of the music, issues connected to it, its place in history and culture, I also was affected as a listener, broadening and situating what my ears heard. So I read up about pieces and performers before I went to hear music, studied program notes, even sometimes, when I got really lucky, followed verbal descriptions of what was going on in the music as it was played and sung. That really helped. It was like a guide in a strange city pointing out all sorts of things I'd never notice by myself. Then when I heard that music again on my own, or visited the city again, I felt like it was part of me, not like I was a musical or geographical tourist. I was "in the know" and listened/traveled at an enhanced level of enjoyment.

Sad. I had been deceived again. Words I had depended on to disclose and explain had only led me further astray, making me even more merely only passively just, a musical nonentity. All those teachers, cultural scholars, historians, theorists, commentators, bent on despoiling my listening experience. So I stopped reading about music. An empty gesture, I know, since I no longer listened, but at least symbolic of my newly acquired enlightenment.

I wish everyone was like me, having become educated about the passivity of merely listening. Think of all the time it would save, the money, the effort. Not only for listeners, of course, but for everyone really actively involved in music. Everyone who is a musician, that is. Performers, conductors, improvisers; even, I suppose, composers (are composers musicians?) would no longer have to labor to do what they do. *Because there would be no one to do it for.*

Well, I guess they could do it for themselves, because they are the ones who know enough to listen for what they do. And they could do it for others like them, other performers, conductors, so forth. Not much of an audience, of course. Not enough to sustain all those musicians we now have, all of them trying everything they know how to do to entice lots of people to listen to them, go to their performances, buy their recordings. They are the ones most implicated in promoting mass consumership, persuading people to be passive with music by listening to what they do. That's got to stop. It may cause havoc if we lose the main audience for what musicians provide. It may well end our musical culture or reduce it to the tiniest fraction of what it is now. But at least we'll finally have what we need—a few musicians doing what they do for a few musicians. The enlightened reigning.

Recently I was watching TV in the evening before going to sleep, switching channels looking for something interesting. I came across Leonard Bernstein conducting the New York Philharmonic in the Beethoven Sixth. I immediately clicked to the next channel, of course. A perfect example of what I needed to avoid—passive listening to a work from the canon of dead white males, conducted by another. Whew! Close call.

A little later (I guess this was just not my night) I came across a performance by the Three Mo' Tenors. I confess that I was so riveted by the excitement of their singing that I lingered for a while. I was struck by how much the audience was enjoying it, applauding, laughing, enthralled with these three singers' virtuosity in a great many styles of music and their savvy showmanship in addition to their sensitive musicianship. For a moment I too shared the sheer joy of their performance and of the music they were performing. I let myself go, I'm ashamed to say, fell into the old bad habit of just merely passively only. It lifted my heart. But soon reason prevailed, thank goodness. I clicked on.

Reflecting on that experience the next morning I was struck by a revelation. Not only does listening force one to be passive and uncreative but listening on TV compounds the error. Watching TV is itself the archetypal example of couch potatoship, the depths of merely. It's not just listening to/watching music on TV that exemplifies this vice. It's watching TV in the first place! Few people who watch TV are actors, producers, scriptwriters, camera persons, news anchors, and so forth. Most people don't "do" TV—they just watch. So they can't possibly watch for, as those involved in the TV industry must do. Not being able to watch for they can be only merely etc. Like me. All of us, millions, no, billions of us all over the world, subjecting themselves to subservience, to only taking not making.

I shuddered. How could I have missed this obvious fact literally staring me in the face? How often had I read about the evils of watching the boob tube, never recognizing that I was the boob in question? My enjoyment of some favorite programs, of sports, newscasts, documentaries, yes, even musical presentations, had slipped under my watchful gaze, my now being enlightened.

TV had to go. For some things I had depended on TV for, such as sports events, there was a remedy. I could go to the games in which I was interested. Not often, of course, because I couldn't travel around the world to all the events I would have been able to watch easily on TV. And even where I lived I didn't have the time or money to attend often. Do you know what it costs for tickets to watch successful teams play? (Of course, living in Chicago this is seldom a problem.) And I could go to theater productions instead of watching dramas on the tube, go to the movies instead of watching them on TV, read the newspaper instead of watching the news, go to museums, dance productions, lectures, restaurants instead of watching the food channel. (Oh, dear God, can I please watch the food channel?)

Notice how I was deceiving myself, the depths of my blindness to the fallacy with which my life had become pervaded. Going to a sports event was no better than watching it on TV. Going to a concert or a club was no better than listening on TV or to a recording. Whether in person or once removed one was still a consumer, a taker not a maker. Still a merely.

There was only one way out of the dilemma. I would have to become a football player, a basketball player, and many other athlete types I had so unknowingly enjoyed watching. I would have to become a movie actor or director or something. A theater actor or playwright, a dancer or choreographer, a museum curator, a lecturer, a chef, on and on with all the things I must now *do* instead of only *consume*.

The revelation continued. Read a newspaper? Read fiction, poetry, scholarly books and journals, professional material? Cook food I had not grown or raised myself? Wear clothing I had not made? Drive a car I had not manufactured? Take medications I had not formulated? Where did it all end? Where did my obliviousness to my rabid consumerism reach bottom? I knew I was just scratching the surface. I was staggered by the depth of my unawareness of how dependent I had become on being merely only just a passive consumer.

The nail in the coffin came shortly thereafter. For many years I have been an enthusiastic, no, passionate, collector of contemporary art. I got hooked while a young professor, when I wandered into a student show at the Cleveland Institute of Art and was captivated by a ceramic vase so graceful, so sensitive, so heart-wrenchingly beautiful that I just had to have it. It was twenty dollars, an extravagance I could ill afford. But something inside me made me overcome my frugality and go for it. I still have it, and it continues to shape my inner life. I was changed forever by that purchase, learning that I could surround myself with objects I loved, that challenged and instructed me, that satisfied a deep need for spiritual satisfaction just as music did when I succumbed to being a listener. Over the years I have amassed a large collections of art works in a great variety of media, works reflecting my expanding, deepening tastes as my eye, mind, and body have become more discerning, more widely receptive, more knowledgeable, and more mature. Much of my history as a human being is captured in the works I have acquired, reflecting my journey of inner growth.

All this went through my mind when my awareness of my unfettered consumership had finally surfaced from its unexamined depths. This too, this collection of art, so close to my identity, revealed how contaminated my life had been by passive taking, how thoroughly I had succumbed to the siren call of uncreative merely. I was shaken by this epiphany, this suddenly revealed unworthiness.

I had tried to do the right thing, to make art rather than only take it. I had taken ceramics classes and drawing and painting. Hated it. It was just not me, not only because I was so pathetically bad at it but because it just didn't "feel me." Yet my discernment of what others could do was highly developed, my relationships within the art world very close, and my involvement in the art museum and gallery culture intense. I was, in deep and broad ways, an important player in the world of the visual arts, a world in which I dwelled with great satisfaction, a sense of being at home, and a role to play that I knew was essential. That is, the role of visual art partaker, a partner in the larger enterprise, in fact the end toward which the enterprise aimed—the enlightened, enthusiastic participant in and cocreator of the meanings artists make available. Just as I had become in music when making was no longer possible, and as I had long been in theater, dance, movies, literature, and poetry. I didn't "make" in any of the arts now, yet each of them filled my life with their special joys and challenges to my inner creativity. And, in turn, I and others like me gave those who made them the discriminative audience they depended on to do their best work. So was it possible that I was not entirely merely? That I actually played an active role, a needed role in the world of the arts that my culture provided me?

I felt myself slowly turning a corner, once faced with the enormity of what I would lose if I abandoned my role as a consumer of the arts. I had been headed down a lonely, dark path, in my zeal to follow the prescriptions of those for whom my life represented a fall from the grace of artistry. Those who preached the salvation of making while, perhaps with a sense of guilt but also, perhaps, with unawareness, were takers in much of their lives as all of us are. Had my acquiescence to their argument been unwarranted?

A great weight began slowly lifting from my shoulders, from my spirit. A glimmer of hope that my life, so full with the pleasures the arts had afforded me, my goings out into a world of fascinations, might after all be worth living. Perhaps there was another way to construe what taking meant, what it entailed, how essential it was and how it needed to be nurtured by education. Perhaps, in fact, by the profession of music education, not as an afterthought, not as secondary (if that) to what really mattered, not with disdain, but as a major reason for its being if it truly cared about nurturing universal musicality.

Musicality? Aren't we back to musicianship? Universal? Aren't we back to the notion that everyone, if they are to be involved with music genuinely, must be a musician? And to the widespread belief that the purpose of music education is to see to it that everyone plays that particular role? Further, that even if some (actually most) do not choose to play it, an education devoted to training musicianship is the only valid route for all?

Those, in fact are pervasive beliefs in music education today. For a very long time, when the music in one's life had to be the music one made for oneself, musicianship training was fundamental. But for over a century the world of music, along with all else, has been radically transformed. We may bemoan the loss of a romantic idyll in which people produced all they needed and wanted. But who would choose to return to that condition, which was in fact one of paucity rather than plenty for the vast majority of people? The arts have flourished dramatically during the past century, not just for the few, as before, but for all who choose to become involved. Although opportunities to create art now exist to an extent never before known in history, most either cannot devote themselves to creating art or choose not to do so. Instead, with gratitude and often with great zeal they surround themselves with the arts they prefer, their partaking becoming a precious part of their lives.

As had occurred for me. In music I had the experience of starting with musicianship and then having to continue with listenership. So I too had bought in to the notion that being a musician was the one true path to being musical. That made me vulnerable to the condemnations of those who decried and minimized the partaker role I had come to assume. But I have the advantage of knowing both the benefits and drawbacks of the musician perspective on music and am therefore able to view the role of the consumer with a more discerning eye. It is indeed life-enhancing to create in any of the arts. That is something I deeply know. However, I am able, from experience not from theory alone, to understand the benefits of partaking unfettered by musicianship concerns. There is a purity, an openness, a directness of mind and feeling when one confronts music as, unguardedly, a respondent, free from all the special details and issues to which musicians must attend. Dare I say it? Music has become more spiritual for me, not less, since my change of roles. Gradually, of course, and never entirely because I continue to be a musician in one part of my psyche. But I have tasted what devoted consumers taste, and, I admit, I find it sweet. I suspect that is why the other arts, the visual arts particularly, are so compelling and profoundly satisfying for me, in that my responses to them can be without pretense of professionalism. I can be, for them, wholeheartedly, even guilelessly, an amateur, one who loves an activity or enterprise for the sheer sake of the enjoyment it affords.

But not mindlessly. Not superficially. Not, in fact, passively but with passion and devotion. That is the main point this essay, a mixture of satirical fantasy and reality, leads me to propose. The musicianship roles are active, *but only when those pursuing them are being active when doing so.* That is, *the musicianship role being played can be active or passive depending on qualities supervenient to the role itself.*

That applies equally to the consumership roles, or, if one prefers, the listenership roles. Those roles include listeners in all the multifarious ways and circumstances in which music listening takes place in our real lives, and all the roles supportive of our understandings of musical experience—music theorists, historians, critics, psychologists, philosophers, anthropologists, sociologists, and so forth—all the non-musician roles existent in a culture. Each calls upon a particular way to be intelligent and creative within the domain of music just as the musicianship roles do, and each can be pursued passively or actively depending on qualities of that pursuit, just as with musicianship. *Passive or active are not in themselves determined by the role being played, but on characteristics associated with the way it is being played.*

What are those characteristics? Being active in any musical role requires an investment of energy. All musical engagements are mental/emotional acts, *ipso facto* requiring the body's participation as well. The mind, in all musical experience whether creating, or sharing what has been created, or exploring and explaining what occurs in musical engagements, must be involved as it must for all other experience, in the case of music in the discernment of sounds and their interconnections as meaningful occurrences in the context of the ways various cultures provide for such meanings to come into existence. Musical discernments and interconnections are constructive, imaginative, individual acts of meaning-making, as fully as any-thing else among human endeavors. That is, they are acts of intelligence.

Musical meanings are diverse. They come from the sounds themselves as created and shared. They come from those sounds as situated in particular systems of belief about music. Those systems, being human creations, are saturated with many other beliefs related to musical ones, impinging on, qualifying, and coloring how musical meaning is con-strued. To put it differently, music both reflects and absorbs a host of relevant beliefs, assumptions, values, and practices, transforming them into sound-constructions that both incorporate them and subject them to a metamorphosis—a change in form and substance only sounds re-garded to be musical are capable of accomplishing. All these dimensions of mindful operation are primally implicated in musical experiences. The degree of engagement is the degree of active energy being expended by a person playing a musical role, a degree ranging on a continuum from extreme passivity to extreme activation.

What demarcates the level of passivity or activity, then, is not the overt physicality of the engagement but the quality and fullness of a person's investment of energies in it. Reading a book, surely quiescent physically, can be more active—more fully engaged by one's selfness—than pounding rocks with a sledgehammer. Listening to music with absorption, imagina-tion, discernment, understanding, feeling, and caring, is as active as reading a book when all those characteristics are being manifested energetically. Both can be passive, of course, when none of those qualities are present or are minimally present, as is true of any other activity such as performing. "Hands on," so often invoked as the essential criterion of being active, is in no respect such a criterion, because hands can be engaged with none of the other qualities being evidenced. Whatever the role, requiring actions of the body or not, the degree of the energies of selfness being expended is the degree of activeness attained.

Which brings us to the heart of the dilemma for music education. How do we encourage (unfortunately we cannot insure) optimum levels of active involvement when students are engaged in any musical role? It is unlikely, perhaps even undesirable, for peak activation to occur at all times: few can or should maintain the uppermost reaches of energy expenditure con-stantly. (In fact when some children do, we have to intervene to help them lower the temperature of their inner furnace.) But certainly we want to achieve high levels of activation during the very short periods of time avail-able to us to actually teach, making the most of that precious opportunity in its impact on our students' quality of musical experience.

Perhaps the hardest of all roles in which to succeed in that goal, unfortunately, is in the teaching of listening. Unfortunate because it is the most pursued musical role of all, involving far more people than all the other roles put together. If we want to help all people become more musical, an aim we have embraced in theory but not in practice, we have to get real about how to do so. That is, we cannot go on assuming that everyone must adopt the performer's perspective. That perspective has guided us toward creating the school music program we now have and have had for well over half a century in its present form, and extending back from that to the origins of music education in American history. The good news is that we have been, in my opinion, remarkably successful in that endeavor, a success of which all of us can be very proud. It has been our great achievement.

The bad news is that it has been our only such achievement. In our present world, where performance is an option chosen by relatively few, we have massively neglected all the other ways to be musical in our culture. Which is why it is unfortunate that the teaching of listening, which should be the bedrock of our professional contribution, on which all others are based, is so infernally difficult to do well. Of course all music teaching is challenging, each role presenting its own complexities. But in the case of listening the availability of immediate, reliable, and accurate feedback is scarce or nonexistent. When a student's engagements occur entirely inwardly as they do in listening, with no reliable way to represent them so that teachers can help carry them forward, teaching can only be insecure and uncertain. In education, input without feedback is a recipe for futility.

Exactly how can feedback—demonstrations of what is being heard and with what scope, depth, and investment of energies—be obtained from those who listen? That question has bedeviled every music educator who has attempted to develop those qualities in the act of listening. Many approaches have been tried, including invented notations that indicate what has been heard and how it is being structured in the listener's mind; verbal reports both specifically descriptive (loud, slow, fugue, electric bass, Baroque, early Beatles, raga, etc.) and generally interpretive (sad, happy, like clouds, a storm, winter, "it reminded me of . . . ," etc.); body movements indicating specific or general qualities; iconic, pictorial representations; brain scans of mental activity while listening, and any other attempts teachers and others have made to pin down the otherwise entirely elusive responses of those who listen.

All these attempts to acquire feedback are deeply problematical because of their inadequacy to capture the phenomenological uniqueness and complexity of the listening experience. The hapless teacher of listening operates in a haze of indeterminacy, relying on hunch, hope, and the bits of "data" the various feedback mechanisms might provide. The world of performance could not be more dissimilar, with its ongoing, tangible, exacting demonstrations of what is occurring, able to be addressed directly so as to refine and deepen the qualities of creative expression that performance entails.

I do not mean to overstate the difficulties of teaching listening or to underestimate the complexities of teaching performance. Each, of course, has challenges aplenty, each in its own way as does the teaching of each other musical role. I do want to clarify why listening is peculiarly resistant to security in the teaching act. More so, I would suggest, than even those who teach listening regularly, and feel confident that they are doing it well, imagine. I simply am unconvinced that the distinctive nature of musical listening has allowed us to achieve anything like the expertise—the remarkable skills and insights—we have developed in teaching performance, and I have not seen or heard anything to persuade me differently (although I would be delighted—and amazed—to be proven mistaken).

That reservation applies, I must add, to my own ongoing, dedicated attempts to devise useful and respectful mechanisms to help listeners get more from music than they would likely get on their own. I have long been fascinated by the musical/pedagogical interface of puzzles the teaching of listening presents, and I am far from satisfied that my work in it has been any more than provisional. Given the many determinants of what goes on in the listening act the attempt to be helpful, as teachers are supposed to be, is more than daunting.

Helpful how and for what? Each of the many dimensions of music and of our experiences of it can indeed be "helped" if we conceive that to mean enabling each learner to engage as fully as possible with music in both its contextual and "context made musical" dimensions and with the selfness of creative energies. But that in itself, while one construal (among others) of what "helping" might mean in the listening role, is a generalization. Translating such a generality into the practices called for in the actualities of real teachers dealing with real people in particular settings remains an unfinished, even largely unaddressed, agenda. It is not enough, not *nearly* enough, to posit a general goal and assume that is sufficient to achieve or even improve teaching effectiveness. Until we as a profession take seriously, with the help of coordinated, issue-focused research, our obligation to translate generalities into teaching practices genuinely related to them, we will continue to generate an abundance of "sound and fury signifying nothing."

All this and much more flooded into my mind when I began to see my way out of the despondency to which my acquiescence to the argument of listening as passive had led me. My energies, dampened by my avoidance of beloved activities, began to return, as did my joy in living. I felt the freedom of a liberated attitude—liberated to enjoy, openly and without guilt, the role of partaker to which my life had led me. I began to indulge in all my previous involvements, now with a refreshed perspective on their genuine value.

I even began to read again. I returned to a book I had recently read and found vivifying, Tia DeNora's tightly argued *Music in Everyday Life*.[1] For DeNora the role of the consumer of music is an energetic one in constructing meaning, feeling, and corporeality in musical engagements. "We are now a long way from any conception of music listening as passive," she asserts.[2] (And now my resolve to write an essay with not a single citation has gone down the tubes. Alas, the yoke of academic scholarship binds me tightly.)

Perhaps the actions of listening, as deeply an amalgam of thought, subjectivity, and embodiment as anything in human experience, can, after all, be rescued from the neglect or indifference in which it tends to exist in music education. Perhaps listening can be recognized, finally, as a genuine, precious role in and of itself, not only as a means to other ends. As with every other way to be musical, but more urgently given its primacy in our musical culture, the role of the listener deserves the full devotion of our energies and intelligences, to face its dilemmas, devise useful means to surmount them, and position ourselves thereby to make the fullness of contribution our culture deserves from us.

I plan my activities for the next month. Several musical events to attend, both on campus and in the city. A Saturday at the art galleries and the Art Institute. Two theater productions I'm dying to see. A couple of good movies in town, for a change. My favorite modern dance group in a new production. A novel I've got to finish. A lecture I want to hear on gender and post-postmodern thought. A friend got us tickets to a basketball game. The wine group has a tasting scheduled. Are there some originals of West Wing on TV rather than only reruns? A reservation at that new restaurant that got rave reviews. (Be still my heart.) And, by the way, there's work to be done, as always. Too busy. I've got to get better at scheduling in some time to be passive.

NOTES

1. Tia DeNora, *Music in Everyday Life* (Cambridge: Cambridge University Press, 2000).

2. Tia DeNora, "The Everyday as Extraordinary: Response from Tia DeNora," *Action, Criticism, and Theory for Music Education* 1, no. 2 (December 2002): 6. Available at http://mas.siue.edu/ACT/v1/DeNoraResponse02.pdf.

14

PHILOSOPHY IN THE
SCHOOL MUSIC PROGRAM

Is philosophy only for philosophers?

In preparation for the 2004 MENC national conference, members of the philosophy Special Research Interest Group (SRIG) are asked to suggest a topic for our meeting. I am particularly concerned that so many of our goals and objectives in music education are focused on all the details involved in making and taking music, the endless technicalities related to singing, playing, and notation—what I call "knowing how." We have realized that there is much more to being musically educated than that, largely because the National Standards for Music Education draw our attention to all the other aspects of music that are crying for attention if the technical aspects are to be musically meaningful.

I recommend to those planning the philosophy SRIG meeting that we invite a panel of philosophy-oriented music educators to address the issue of how philosophy can and should be foundational subject matter in every aspect of the music education program at every level. They take my suggestion and ask me to present that argument to kick off the session.

My presentation follows. I make it in full knowledge that (1) the argument, at least at first hearing, is likely to stretch credulity as to whether it even makes sense; (2) even if it is taken seriously, we will be starting from scratch because we have little if any precedents for it in materials, techniques, research, and experience; (3) we will have to enable general music teachers to offer introductory learnings in philosophy of music, adding to their already full plate; (4) we will need to prepare our performance teachers to include such learnings in their work; and (5) we will need to train specialists to offer focused elective courses in it at the secondary level. Finally, adding to the depth of the challenge, as with so many other reforms that are needed if we are to become real in the context of the present musical world, we have few organizational mechanisms to carry plans like this to fruition.

Despite all these obstacles we must think boldly if significant change is ever to occur. That is something I am willing to encourage. We must also be patient and perhaps modest in our hopes as to how quickly and fully such change can be accomplished. Yet, I remain convinced, we must persevere.

The following essay was originally published by Indiana University Press in the *Philosophy of Music Education Review* 13, no. 2 (Fall 2005). Used by permission.

Who is philosophy of music education for? Several groups of people immediately spring to mind. First, it is for those of us in music education who produce it and consume it as a major or important responsibility in our work, people like members of the Philosophy of Music Education Special Research Interest Group of MENC. Second, teachers of music education courses at the undergraduate and graduate levels who deal with it either in a full course or series of courses or seminars devoted to philosophy, or as one part of courses devoted to other topics (as I believe is most often the case). Third, school music teachers, many of whom have taken or are taking such courses (and many who have not) and who are expected to have some level of acquaintance, however rudimentary, with philosophical issues so as to be able to cope with them, as when writing curriculum guides, or explaining to other teachers, administrators, school boards, and parents why music education is valuable and deserves support. If we stretch it, we might include among those who need to be involved with philosophy of music and music education all educational professionals, since all in one way or another exert some sort of influence on the fortunes of music education. But that begins to strain a bit at the edges.

No doubt there are other constituencies that can be identified. But one that has not been conceived as requiring substantive encounters with philosophical issues of music is that of students in schools, K–12. We all assume that philosophy can and should play a major role in determining what is most valuable for students to learn in their study of music. But seldom has it been argued, to my knowledge, that philosophical issues should be addressed in all programs of music education intended to produce people who are, in any convincing sense, musically educated.

My premise is that philosophical reflection relating to music and to the teaching and learning of music should be foundational in school music programs. Further, philosophy needs to be present in our programs in three distinctive ways, reflecting common practices of education in America and all over the world. That is, as integral in the general music education of all students, as a component of all elective offerings, and as one particular, focused offering among the electives available to all students.

My position is that what we call "general music" (which, as we know, goes by a variety of names around the world including just "music") is not complete, in fact is invalid, if it does not provide philosophical challenges of the same level of complexity and the same degree of authenticity as everything else we believe all students should know and be able to do in music. What we call the "music elective program," or the "music specialization program," is incomplete, in fact is invalid, if philosophical matters are not addressed as they relate to the particularities of each elective offered. And, in addition, philosophy needs to be a standard elective offering, taught with the same level of expertise by specialist teachers as we now routinely make available in performance and in the meager smattering of other electives we manage to offer.

What? Philosophical thinking for all children, even in the primary grades, and as electives starting perhaps at the middle school or high school level? Electives taught by music educators whose specialization is the teaching of philosophy of music to youngsters? Am I serious? After all, even those of us who are devoted to it as a major aspect of our professionalism are constantly at the edges of our competence given the deep challenges philosophy presents to our intellect. And I expect children—all children—to be able to deal with it authentically?

Well, we could ask precisely the same questions about, say, mathematics, and science, and history, and social studies, all the ways of thinking that constitute the basic learnings in all grades of our schools. As educators we know better than to conceive the nature of those subjects as being apparent only at the level of professional work in them. We recognize the obvious, that while at their most mature levels they are not directly accessible to youngsters, nevertheless learnings in them can be sequenced so as to both preserve their distinctive ways of knowing and doing and to initiate children into them appropriately for their capacities at every stage of their development.

Philosophy, I want to suggest, is no different in this regard. Maybe it is more difficult to accomplish, but only because few in our specialization have energized on how philosophical ways to think and do can be made available to youngsters in teachable, learnable, developmental involvements. We have no history of fostering philosophical interactions in children as we do the thinking and acting required for musical performance, which is, after all, equally as complex in its own way as philosophical thinking is in its own way. So we start from scratch here, both in the idea that it can and should be done and in all the challenges of building a viable succession of learnings that would lead children toward increasing mastery over time, just as education does in every other school subject including music education as we accomplish so successfully in performance.

But why philosophy, widely regarded as being among the elite of subjects in its limited appeal and its limitless complexity?

That image of philosophy, I would argue, is extremely unfortunate. I suspect that there is as much philosophizing going on in everyday life as there is music going on in everyday life. Perhaps more, come to think about it. Philosophical thinking pervades everyday life, constantly called in to play about values, beliefs, desires, preferences, judgments, politics, ethical behavior, and on and on, matters all people including young people confront as normal aspects of living. In regard to music every one of those matters is an integral component of musical experience and musical understanding and musical enjoyment. Philosophical issues are not disconnected from or incidental to musical experience. They are foundational for musical experience because one's values, beliefs, desires, preferences, and so forth directly affect how one engages with music and what one gets from doing so.

My challenge to the philosophy of music education community, including to myself, is to take seriously our role as educators. Just as we are not only musicians but music educators, a specialization beyond music itself yet intimately tied to music, we are also not only philosophers but need to be philosophy educators, a specialization beyond philosophy itself yet intimately tied to philosophy and also to music.

How do we go about expanding our expertise to become philosophy educators as well as philosophers, thereby fulfilling our special mission as music educators? I wish I had a blueprint we could all just follow. Unfortunately I do not. I am hoping the remarks of our panel will enlighten us about how students at various stages of cognitive development go about being philosophical about music and how we can help them be better at it, leading them in directions of more clarity, more insight, more inclusiveness and thoughtfulness. We need to build a repertoire of understandings and

shared experiences of how children think about music and how that thinking develops. We need research; research which is accumulative, coordinated, and issue-centered, unlike the random, self-interest-centered work
characteristic of our present research endeavor. We need an overhaul of
our teacher education programs so that the number of specializations available to music education majors finally breaks free from the now outworn,
minimally relevant quaternity of band/orchestra/chorus/general music under which we have been straight-jacketed for well over half a century. That
limited vision keeps music education unacceptably artificial; separated from
the realities of musical life as it actually exists in our culture and in those
around the world.

We need some sort of organizational apparatus to keep our efforts in
philosophy education focused and nourished, perhaps a section of the
International Society of Philosophy of Music Education devoted to the
teaching and learning of philosophy in the schools. We need leadership.
We need imagination. We who are devoted to philosophy need to make
a contribution to school music education programs in ways we have never
before conceived of doing. Something, I propose, that would significantly
elevate our own professionalism as both philosophers and music educators,
and also the contribution we are able to make to the health and welfare of
music education.

EDUCATING OUR TEACHERS

Every subject taught in schools requires teachers who are experts in teaching it. Defining what that expertise consists of and how much of it is required has been and continues to be among the most troubling issues in all of education, challenging every society at every time in history.

In the United States, from the singing school masters of the early colonies, self-taught and self-anointed, to the present day with its elaborate state-by-state certification requirements, music teachers have been expected to be proficient both in music, especially the particular kind they must teach, and in teaching. How can we define those expectations, and how can we verify that they have been met sufficiently? Who is qualified to educate those teachers, and according to what criteria? Furthermore, who is entitled to educate those who will be teacher educators, and how are *their* qualifications to be determined and monitored?

No definitive answers to such questions have been generated, the debates about them seeming to have no end. We can only address them with as much wisdom as is available at the time we are working, adapting our ideals to the realities of our opportunities, or lack of them, to achieve what we most desire—as much expertise as possible.

AN AGENDA FOR MUSIC TEACHER
EDUCATION, PARTS I AND II

Music teacher education in the United States, while in one sense almost as old as the country, is also relatively new as an organized national endeavor. The founding of the Society for Music Teacher Education (SMTE) in 1982, and the launch of the *Journal of Music Teacher Education*, first published in 1991, are signals that this aspect of the profession needs and deserves special recognition and a specialized literature devoted to it.

Invited to write for the inaugural issue of the new journal, I ponder which topics to address. While practically my entire career is spent as a music teacher educator, and my writings over the years raise a variety of matters related to that role, the existence of a journal devoted to teacher education allows now for concentrated treatment. Of all the endless concerns that might be addressed, which rise to the top as needing to be included in the initial issue?

In what turns out to be a two-part article, I identify eight areas of music teacher education where we need to be more effective if we are to be as successful as we hope to be. Largely because of the ongoing attention to teacher education now possible because of the SMTE and its journal, we have made important inroads to-ward improvement in many of these areas and others. Yet they all remain in need of further advances. Their complexity is such that it is unlikely that any of them will be "solved" in the sense of being put to rest as issues. This situation exists not only for music education but for education as a whole. Yes, we have made progress. Just as surely, we have considerable work ahead of us to get closer to where we need to be in this core function of our profession, especially if we are to keep up with, and even lead, the many changes occurring in both music and education.

The following essays were originally published in the *Journal of Music Teacher Education* 1, no. 1 (Fall 1991) and the *Journal of Music Teacher Education* 1, no. 2 (Spring 1992) respectively. Used by permission.

PART I

The appearance of a new journal devoted to music teacher education is among the hopeful signs of recent years that the music education profession is attending to the health of its infrastructure. I am honored and delighted to have been invited to contribute an article to this inaugural issue, and I wish for the journal a long, productive, and stimulating life.

"Stimulating" is perhaps too weak—"turbulent" may be more like it. For among all the many aspects of the music education profession none is more important or more complex or more contentious than how we educate our teachers. This is the case, of course, for teacher education outside music, which is at the very center of the present maelstrom over how to improve education in America. Whatever else people might argue about in the heated debate about the state of education, they seldom question the need for significant improvements in—if not a total overhaul of—the way we educate teachers. Few would take the position that teacher education is generally effective or admirable: most would seem to believe quite the opposite. In fact, many argue that at the heart of the failure of our schools is the failure of teacher education, a claim made with absolutely predictable regularity during every education reform effort. So perhaps I should also wish the new journal courage!

But as threatened and vilified as teacher education is in the larger sphere of education few if any participants in school reform have pointed a finger at perceived failures in music teacher education. It would be nice to think that this is because there are none. But of course professionals in music teacher education know better. The reason we have escaped attention so far and are likely to continue to escape it is quite unrelated to the condition of music teacher education. It is a function, very simply, of the fact that music and the arts, with a few notable exceptions such as last year's *Newsweek* story on "Why Jane Can't Draw (or Sing, or Dance . . .)"[1] have been almost totally ignored in the present education reform movement.

That's an old story for us and we have gotten used to both the drawbacks and the benefits of being ignored. On the negative side we are reminded, by our being unnoticed, of how inconspicuous we are in the larger education picture, and we find ourselves, as usual, kicking and screaming to get included more noticeably in that picture. On the positive side, we mercifully escape the opprobrium being heaped on our non-music, non-art teacher education colleagues. So we can go on doing what we have always done, and if we choose, attend to our own self-generated efforts toward improvement largely free from outside pressures or threats.

It is important for us to immerse ourselves as fully as possible in the larger debate about education reform because we have a great deal to learn from it that can help us improve teacher education in music. At the same time we should take advantage of our (perhaps unfortunate) protected situation by attending to issues more central to improvement than the many politically volatile, highly visible ones with which the fields at the center of the storm are forced to cope. We can afford to be more reflective, less pressured, less whipped up by whatever momentary winds happen to be blowing. So it would seem appropriate for the first issues of this new journal to include some agenda setting for future directions and future debates that should fill these pages productively for many years.

I want to offer a projected agenda of eight issues I believe are central to the improvement of music teacher education. They are, I think, responsive both to the larger debate presently going on around us and also to the particular history and needs of our field. They are not in any sense exhaustive: they are intended to be illustrative of the kinds of things about which we need to talk, write, and reach better clarity. I will present no solutions but many suggestions. It is my hope that many people will engage themselves in offering their suggestions about these and other issues and that viable solutions will emerge as a result.

The eight issues are: the balance between general education and teacher education; the balance between professional education and music education; the breadth of musical studies; adding a composition program to the performance and general music programs; broadening the philosophical and critical understanding of music educators; moving from methods to curriculum; managing the status quo effects of field experience; and teachers as researchers.

The Balance between General Education and Teacher Education

Underlying more specific issues about music teacher education is the basic question of how well educated as human beings music teachers need to be. That question has been raised about all teachers and has produced some of the most important changes in teacher education patterns we have ever witnessed. The idea that teachers have been too narrowly educated has led to the notion that the traditional four years of college should be devoted mainly if not exclusively to general education and teacher education should be tacked on during a fifth year. Many universities have moved in that direction: it will take some time to see how many others will do so and what differences doing so will make.

Minimum general education requirements for a degree in music education are set either by states or particular educating institutions. In traditional four-year programs, that minimum tends to become the maximum or very close to it, given the many demands of the teacher education component. Further, the courses chosen to fulfill general education requirements are often of the Chinese menu type—two from this group, three from that—and the criticism has been expressed that they do not add up to a coherent, interrelated whole, especially when choices are often dictated less by excellence of content than by ease of passing or convenience in scheduling. Further still, the lower-division status of many of the general education requirements leads to the practice in many college and universities of staffing them with less-experienced faculty or with teaching assistants, and class sizes tend to be quite large. All these factors lead to the probability that the general education of music education majors is quite weak—certainly weaker, for example, than that of candidates for B.A. degrees in music.

Does this matter? How much do we really care? We can argue that, nice as it is for music teachers to know something about science, social studies, languages, math, humanities, and so on, they don't use that material in their work except in very tangential ways. The more important thing is that they be competent in what they will actually teach.

Many of us do in fact make that argument, either overtly or covertly, by simply acquiescing to the minimum general education requirement as being all we can do. We may feel a little guilty about it but the press of all the music and professional education and music education requirements is real, and overwhelms any twinges of regret we might feel that our students (and we ourselves when we were students) were not able to become deeply immersed in the many learnings outside music and education. "A shame," we are likely to say, and then get on with our work.

We need to address, more directly than we have tended to, the issue of whether we should be satisfied with typical levels of general education for music education majors. As we become more aware of the many musics represented in our multimusical American culture, of the diverse uses of music, of the relations of music with the other arts, of the organic nature of culture, we must consider whether the tendency for music education students to be isolated from other areas of learning is best serving them whether we regard them as individuals or as professionals in training. The problems here are very complex. Are four years enough to do all that needs to be done? Can we simply make five years (or six or seven) the standard? Would more years in training simply turn out to be more years of the existing balance between general education and teacher education? Should general education come first and then teacher education be added, or should the two be integrated from the start (as I strongly prefer)?

We have not had the benefit of focused, lengthy debate about this issue because we have been, understandably, distracted by more specifically professional issues. I believe we must finally give this matter the attention it deserves in any agenda for improving music teacher education because it provides the foundation on which the more specific improvements must be built.

The Balance between Professional Education and Music Education

Just as there is a tendency for us to concentrate on the teacher education aspects of the college curriculum and settle for whatever general education is required, there is the parallel tendency to concentrate heavily on the music education aspects of the teacher education component and settle for or succumb to whatever professional education courses outside music are required. We may even attempt to substitute specific music education courses for professional education courses if we can get away with it. I am well acquainted with many such attempts: sometimes they work and sometimes they don't, depending on the level of awareness of those who monitor the teacher education program. Of course I am forced to generalize about this matter, but it is my distinct impression that attitudes of both music education students and faculty toward required professional education courses outside music education are likely to be negative. This may be because of the widespread assumption that "ed courses" are poorly taught, or have little useful subject matter, or have little relevance to music education, or some combination of such factors.

However valid or invalid such assumptions may be, the effect of them is to produce music educators whose knowledge of the process of education as a phenomenon, of the school as an organism, and of the ways schooling in our culture functions, is likely to be puny. I think it is fair to say that music educators often view schooling through a very narrow lens, having been given by their teacher education programs little breadth of vision about the philosophical, political, sociological, cultural, and historical dimensions of the larger phenomenon we call education and how music might be seen to function within that larger, richer picture.

Of course we must prepare students whose allegiance is to music and whose expertise is relevant to the work they will be doing. But I think we must also be concerned about how well they can operate as responsible citizens of the larger education community of which they are an important but very particular part. Some music educators do, of course, gravitate toward leadership roles in the larger education sphere, often because of their well-developed administrative and interpersonal abilities. But many (I tend to think most) remain enclosed within highly delimited boundaries and step outside those boundaries only when they are forced to by adverse circumstances requiring advocacy efforts or self-protection responses.

It would seem reasonable to assume that music educators broadly grounded in understandings about education in its larger dimensions would be enabled to be more effective, more thoughtful, more influential citizens within their schools and communities. Are we comfortable with the amount of time, interest, and respect we afford to the field of education itself within our music education programs? And if we are not entirely comfortable about it, as I suggest we should not be, what can we do other than throw up our hands and say we simply don't have enough time to do everything? That is certainly true. It just as certainly prevents us from seriously attending to ways we can reconceive our programs to accomplish what we believe they must accomplish. It is time we debate such reconceptions.

The Breadth of Musical Studies

The musicianship training of music education majors is largely if not entirely in the hands of teachers of theory, history, and performance, including ensemble directors. That training tends to gravitate toward the conservative end of the continuum in regard to the literature studied and the skills developed. The history background our majors receive tends to be limited to a survey of common-practice music in the great western concert tradition. The theory training they are given, in ear training, analysis, and music writing tends to be closely tied to the practices of that literature. And the works they study as performers both in private lessons and in ensembles tend also to be highly correlated with that core literature, although perhaps more likely to diverge in this aspect of their training.

This is a literature, in my opinion, that is foundational for our students and for American culture. Those who would take the currently fashionable "politically correct" position argue that western concert music is no more pertinent or important than any other of the world musics represented in the multimusical culture of the United States.

I would disagree. I believe our culture is, in fact, as historically rooted as any other, and that its history is as precious to and determining of its national character as that of any other. It would be damaging to the distinctive history and culture of other countries to instruct them that they must be "multicultural" in the sense of so diminishing their own historical musics that those musics become equal (or lesser) in importance to other musics presently existing within those cultures. It would be just as damaging to do the same for the United States. So the music we have inherited from our Western history must, I believe, remain an important ingredient in the education of those who will be teaching music to new generations.

But it must not be the only ingredient. Our major error in this regard has not been that we emphasize this literature—it is that we tend to do so to the virtual exclusion of other literatures. Such literatures include both the diversity of western musics outside the concert context and the diversity of musics of world cultures, practically all of which are represented in our population. In what history, literature, or theory courses are our music education majors inducted into the musical ways of thinking and acting (performing, improvising, composing, listening) called for by the musics with which so many of our citizens are actively engaged as a natural and important part of their lives? Of course we must make as fully available as possible to all our citizens the western concert literature that constitutes a major aspect of this nation's heritage, both by enabling them to listen to it with understanding and to compose and perform it to some degree depending on each individual's interests in doing so. But to the degree our music educators have been trained to fulfill only that single function they will not be enabled to meet the many other musical needs of the diverse students they will be serving.

Some changes in the direction of interest in and openness to non-concert western musics and world musics are occurring in the history and theory fields, and we should do all we can to encourage them and to adapt our degree programs to include more diverse musical learnings as they become available. This will not happen quickly, of course, because of the inherent conservatism of those fields (and of the performance field also).

Another restraining factor in this regard is that practically all our music education majors are students whose musical backgrounds have been rooted deeply within the center of the western concert music tradition that so dominates present school music education practices. Our college students are mostly those who elected when they were in school to join bands, orchestras, and choruses—the foundations of western concert music ensembles. Their success in those ensembles largely determined their decisions to pursue careers in music or music education by going on to college. Involvement in and identification with other musics, such as rock, jazz, folk, and ethnic musics, are less likely to lead to a decision to go to college to become a music or music education major. So we tend to get a particular kind of student, strong in the dominant musical genre but weaker in those that are poorly represented in our school and college music programs. Here, too, there are changes occurring in the direction of openness to students with alternative involvements. But the system we have had for so long is, naturally, entrenched, and will not easily be stretched into new configurations. What those configurations should be, and how to achieve them, will require a great deal of discussion this journal would do well to encourage.

Adding a Composition Program to the Performance and General Music Programs

Our teacher education programs are dominated by performance training, both for those planning to be ensemble directors and for those planning to be general music teachers. All must take lessons because we feel that, in addition to learning skills from private study that will be transferable to the skills they will be called on to teach, our future teachers' musicianship as a whole requires a serious involvement in actually creating music. And the dominant if not exclusive way we conceive of creating music is by performing it.

There are good historical reasons for this attitude, of course, in that American music education from colonial times to the present has focused largely on teaching performance. And school music needs to continue to do so, I believe, both as one aspect of general music (among many others including, most fundamentally, listening) and as the focus of activity for those who choose to become members of performing groups. It is likely to continue to be the case, at least for the foreseeable future, that performing will be the dominant way people will engage themselves in creating music.

Therefore, many if not most teachers of music will continue to need to be equipped to provide rich opportunities for performance involvements in the schools.

Now a dramatically expanded opportunity to create music by composing has appeared because of advances in computer technologies. For the first time in history we are facing the possibility that many people will be able to compose at high levels of challenge to their musical capacities and will choose to do so as a way of expressing their musical creativity. Already it is common to encounter school kids who own rather sophisticated electronic equipment and have gained a great deal of musical know-how and satisfaction by composing with it. Most school systems have acquired or are planning to acquire such equipment. So we are witnessing a significant movement in a new direction to add composing as a viable option for creative musical activity.

How do we lead rather than follow this movement? We followed, far in the rear, the revolution in available musical experience caused by the invention of sound-recording technologies a century ago. We did not take full advantage of the new opportunities to listen to music those technologies were providing. We still, to this day, do not do as much as I think we should to help all students attain the broad kind of musical literacy our present musical world allows. As a result of our ineffectuality in this regard music education has become, too often, an esoteric field separated from the musical realities existing in the larger culture outside schools.

We should not let this happen in regard to the parallel revolution now occurring as a result of open access to composing through technology. We must move quickly to recruit as music education majors those high school graduates who have demonstrated high musical potentials not through performance (or not alone through performance) but through their involvements with composition. We need to give them a college education focused on developing their capacities to be composers, as we now do with performers, and we need to equip them to establish composition programs in schools as we now do with performance programs. They will be the leaders in building solid composing curricula at all levels of schooling, adding a strong third dimension to music in the schools along with general music and performance programs.

A host of questions are raised by this obligation. Who will be the teacher educators to provide the needed models of composition curricula when such models do not yet exist? How do we begin to formulate, try, and evaluate composition programs to insure that the models we propose will be musically and educationally valid and effective? Who will teach music education composition majors their lessons? We have built an entire college-level system to provide all music majors with lessons in performance: will we have to build a parallel system to provide all or some with composing lessons? Will we find ourselves recruiting composition teachers for college faculty positions as we now recruit specialists in all the instruments and voice? And, if so, what kinds of backgrounds will they need to have—straight composition (comparable to undergraduate and graduate performance majors) or a mixture of composition with music education (as is the case with many performance teachers)? Where will music education composition majors gain clinical experiences and student teach when there is still a paucity of composition programs in the schools?

On and on go the questions—readers will no doubt think of ten others for each I have asked. So we have plenty to occupy us in this important matter, and I look forward to an outpouring of discussion, debate, and helpful guidance toward taking full responsibility for this historic opportunity with which we are now being presented.

These four issues all reflect concerns about the need for greater breadth in our teacher education programs. In the next issue of this journal I will address the remaining four issues of my proposed agenda. Each will raise still further concerns about how we can prepare music teachers for the broadening responsibilities the future is likely to call upon them to fulfill.

Note

1. *Newsweek*, September 1990, special issue on education.

PART II

In the fall issue of the *Journal of Music Teacher Education* I outlined eight issues of importance to music teacher educators. Four of these topics—the balance between general education and teacher education, the balance between professional education and music education, the breadth of musical studies, and adding a composition program to the performance and general music programs—were discussed in that issue, leaving me to comment on the final four: broadening the philosophical and critical understandings of music educators; moving from methods to curriculum; managing the status quo effects of field experience; and teachers as researchers.

Broadening the Philosophical and
Critical Understandings of Music Educators

We are recognizing that the education of music teachers may have to be broader than we had previously thought, as each of my previous four issues suggests. We may be excused for feeling, therefore, that we are splitting at the seams of our present teacher education programs.

Yet still further demands are being made on those programs. One of the demands, heard with increasing frequency as a result of movements toward Discipline Based Art Education programs and the influences they have had on music education, has been that music teachers need to better understand and more fully reflect in their teaching the aesthetic and critical backgrounds surrounding music just as they need to better understand and more actively teach historical and cultural backgrounds of music. We have tended to neglect in our teaching the issues surrounding music as to its nature, its values, its special ways to provide what is generally called aesthetic experience; how claims to knowledge of a particular sort can be made as the result of such experience; how music relates to affect, to creativity, to the mind; and on and on with all the many issues dealt with in the broad realm of philosophy of music or art. In addition, we have paid too little attention to the philosophical sub-domain of criticism, in which relevant criteria for musical judgments are identified and applied.

Surely we want to teach in schools the important ideas surrounding music, because no one can be considered literate about music in any comprehensive sense who has not grappled with those ideas. And we want to do so in ways that do not threaten or substitute for the actuality of musical experience itself. Ideas about music are supposed to enhance the musical experience of listeners, performers, and composers. When they are used judiciously, there is little disagreement that they do. How do we educate our teachers to both understand those ideas and to use them effectively to heighten the musical experiences of their students?

This is an extremely complex issue. I do not believe the field of art education has addressed it effectively (despite its recent concerted efforts to do so in response to the Getty Center's importunings). So we cannot simply assume that answers are out there waiting to be discovered. We are going to have to develop our own answers and it is not going to be easy.

This is due, in large part, to the fact that the field of aesthetics, or the philosophy of art, is composed of controversies. There is not now, and has never been, a single view about music accepted by all as being incontrovertibly correct. To someone who tries to stay current with the debates in aesthetics, as I do, the impression is overwhelming that those debates will keep right on going with little or no hope of convergence on a set of principles or positions sufficiently grounded that significant controversies about them will not immediately arise. This is not a field to which one looks for peace and quiet.

Over the past thirty or so years, however, ideas stemming from the aesthetic education movement have been influential in music education, and many views associated with that movement have been found useful in thinking about the values of music and the criteria by which one might judge music. Having been engaged in propagating such views, I am, naturally, predisposed in their favor. It would seem to me important for teachers in training to become acquainted with the thinking that has permeated our field since the early 1960s, by being introduced to a variety of writings focusing on philosophical ideas and how those ideas have been translated into useful music education practices.

This needs to be done with both a receptive and critical attitude. Receptivity is needed to foster the belief that philosophizing is not just a matter of idle chatter but provides an essential foundation for all the decisions music teachers must make about what to teach and how to teach it. Philosophy, for music educators, is not an end, but a means. It is a means both essential and powerful for determining the directions one takes as a teacher in pursuit of musical values. Such values do not exist in a world separate from human choices. Every musical choice we make reflects a value we hold. To the extent that teachers are aware of the values underlying their choices, and have probed them thoughtfully, their choices can be both consistent and directional. When they have not been helped to think clearly about their values, those values can only be inconsistent and scattershot, and their choices of what and how to teach can only be the same. Music teaching, if it is to be effective, must be based on a solid philosophical grounding. It also must include the explicit teaching of its philosophical values as part and parcel of music instruction.

That is why one's attitude toward philosophy must also be critical. Since philosophy is by nature self-critical, our teachers must understand that philosophy does not deal in objective truth, and that all values are relative to other, sometimes very different, values. So we must not take an attitude of obedient faith about value claims. We must be open to, and encourage our students to be open to, alternatives that seem convincing and useful, and we must be flexible enough to incorporate different views without so abandoning a basic position that we float unanchored. In philosophical matters it is imperative to be consistent without being rigid. It is also imperative to have an open mind without either believing or disbelieving everything. These imperatives are not easy to achieve. But until music teacher educators better incorporate philosophical thinking as an essential aspect of music-teacher education programs, our teachers will continue to be less equipped than they need to be to think deeply about the subject they are teaching. And they will not be able to help their own students understand music as being a product of human values. Good music education cannot take place in absence of such teachings, at either the college or school level.

Moving from Methods to Curriculum

Because of its historical focus on teaching performance and associated skills such as note reading and sight singing as its major if not sole preoccupation, our field has, very naturally, been dominated by the idea that good music teaching consists of the application of good methodologies. Methodologies are sets of rules and regulations for achieving desired outcomes in sequential steps. They apply to learnings for which outcomes can be and should be predetermined, and to learnings that lend themselves to carefully patterned behaviors and responses shaped progressively to move in the predetermined direction. The term generally applied to such learning is "training."

Performance and its associated skills require good training as one essential aspect of effective learning. Methodologies are, indeed, highly relevant for important aspects of performance teaching, and we will need to continue to use and refine the methodologies with which we have had such high levels of success.

But, as the previous discussions have made clear, music teaching is becoming more than performance teaching—it is becoming music education in a far broader sense. This is not in any sense to diminish the importance of teaching the creative, mindful, intelligent, and craftsmanly learnings required for good musical performance. Indeed, musical performance requires among the highest, most complex human capacities for thinking, acting, and feeling. It is just that our field has taken on so many additional functions that good performance teaching is no longer sufficient for good music education.

Those functions are less amenable to methodology than is performance. They require a breadth of learnings, a structure in which those learnings are pursued, and ways of providing for those learnings, signified by the term "curriculum." If music is to become a basic subject in the schools, as we devoutly hope it will some day, we will have to move in the direction of what is required for all basic subjects—a curriculum of studies broad enough to encompass the many learnings each subject entails. We are now better recognizing the breadth of learnings involved in our subject, and we must move toward building curricula compatible with that breadth.

That means that what we now conceive as the core subjects in music teacher education—"methods courses"—must be reconceived to be "curriculum courses." This is not to imply, I must hastily clarify, courses in theoretical foundations of curricula such as are offered as part of graduate foundations programs. I am describing courses at the core of music teacher education that prepare our undergraduate students to build and teach programs in general music, performance, and composition; programs that are both operationally effective and educationally valid. Methodologies play a role in such programs, but no longer a sufficient role. To the degree we continue to think solely of imparting "methods" (methodologies as described above) as the way to teach music, we will continue to produce music training programs in schools and we will continue to be perceived by school professionals as being very different from the basic subjects, all of which, unlike music, require a curriculum.

So our core music education courses will have to become broader in scope than methods courses traditionally have been, including the insights from cognitive science about how to help young people think in terms of the subject they are learning. We are hearing more about the "thinking curriculum" as what schooling should consist of, and we need to begin to conceive of music programs, both required and elective, as "music thinking" curricula. Such thinking has four dimensions in music: "thinking within" musical sounds in our direct experience of them; "thinking how" as we create musical sounds by composing, performing, and improvising; "thinking about" music by all we know of it culturally and historically; and "thinking why" by applying our philosophical and critical understandings to the music we encounter. To encompass all the ways music requires us to think, our teachers will have to present bona fide music curricula in the schools. Their teacher-education programs will have to equip them to be able to do so. We will need a great deal of discussion and clarification as to how music teacher education "curriculum courses" can be developed to prepare our teachers for the breadth of responsibilities they will be facing in today's and tomorrow's schools.

Managing the Status Quo Effects of Field Experience

Pre–student teaching field experiences and student teaching provide a reality base for the learnings in the rest of the teacher education program, and they initiate students into the real world of the schools. In music education we tend to participate in field work enthusiastically and maximally, believing that the payoffs of college study are the actual teaching skills our students acquire. We have every good reason to hold those beliefs.

Unfortunately, there is a negative side to field work that we seldom recognize. A great deal of research on the matter (most of it outside music education) has made it incontrovertibly clear that a major effect of field experience is to reinforce the view that what presently exists in the schools must continue to exist. The more field work college students do, and the earlier it starts, the more it is likely to build an image in their minds that change in the schools is difficult and unlikely, that new ideas are hazardous and unrealistic, and that the training they are receiving in college is out of touch with the hard, unpleasant facts of how schools operate in the real world.[1]

Of course, there is more than a germ of truth in that image. It is true that change is generally slow to come in the schools (with some exceptions, of course, many of which occurred in the 1960s and early 1970s when "innovation" became a byword in education and some schools tried hard to become active agents for change). And it is true that new, untested ideas can cause as much trouble as they can bring about good. It is certainly true that some college teacher educators are, in fact, out of touch with school realities. So there is a convincing basis for the conservative views school teachers and administrators tend to hold about education improvement. But those views can impinge powerfully and negatively on what we are trying to accomplish in teacher education.

The culture of colleges tends to be one in which innovative leadership is highly rewarded. Forward-looking faculty members are often considered the ideal. (Especially when their vision applies to institutions other than colleges!) The culture of schools, on the other hand, tends to be one in which what presently works is cherished and protected. To the extent teacher education programs are innovative in outlook and active in promoting change, they are likely to run into resistance from the schools being urged to change. The most immediate and visible interface between the two competing cultural stances is made up of college students, filled with new ideas, and the school teachers and administrators they encounter in field experiences. The evidence from research is that the new ideas quickly become eroded or even abandoned.

At what strategic point in the complex mechanisms of American education can decisive movement toward change be most evident and effective? I believe it is in teacher education. My pleas for change, and the many others I hope we will read in this journal, are made with the real expectation that something might actually come of them. If we are to be effective as change agents, as I believe we need to be, we must be more aware and in better control of the countervailing forces to which our students will be subjected by their apprenticeship involvements.

I am not suggesting that we should be subversive in the ways we deal with schools: the schools' point of view is real and important. I am suggesting that we provide our students who are engaged in field assignments, including student teaching, with good understandings of the forces at work as they shuttle between campus and school. We need to make explicit to them the reality of the different cultures of college and schools through readings, discussions, and debriefing sessions. We need to provide support for the conflicts they are likely to encounter, so that they can be metacognitively aware that such conflicts are part of the dynamics of our education system. And those students who are experiencing positive reinforcement of the ideas they bring with them from their college courses—and of course that will occur quite often also—need to be encouraged to reassure the others who are not being so reinforced that not everyone out there is negative about making changes. Our conscious attention to and involvement with the political, sociological, and psychological aspects of our students' field work, in addition to the strictly musical-educational aspects, will be necessary if our proposals for improvement are to be nurtured by the graduates of our programs. We need the most cogent thinking we can get about how best to accomplish this.

Teachers as Researchers

No discussion of needed changes in teacher education should neglect mention of an important idea heard more and more frequently in the education research community—that the research structure we have built is probably in need of significant alteration.

Education research is an activity carried on almost completely by faculty members in higher-education institutions, with schools serving as sources of data. Because the dynamics of colleges and universities are fundamentally different from those of the schools—including differences in interests, in concepts of education, in reward and success systems, in ways of solving problems, and in sociological realities—the gap between research and its applications has been and continues to be massive. So long as college faculty members are the (almost) sole producers of research, and school teachers and administrators are expected to be (almost) entirely consumers of research, the gap will remain, and no attempts to persuade or intimidate school people to use research more than they do will be effective. The reluctance of school personnel to use research and their disinterest in it are not, as we have tended to portray it, only because they are unwilling to take the time or make the effort. And our attempts to bridge the gap by popularizing research and making it accessible by softening its language and presenting it in more palatable formats is also not likely to change things significantly.

What could? The argument is being made that the problem is not research itself, it is who owns it. A change in ownership, in which school people assumed responsibility for doing research as a basic and accepted function, would largely eliminate the enormous loss that has always occurred between the efforts put into research and its effects on schooling. When school teachers and administrators are enculturated to regard research as a natural and ongoing function for which they hold major responsibility, and when what gets researched and how research is carried on are determined by the very people who will benefit most from it, research is likely to become the essential source for educational improvement it deserves to be.

This is not to suggest that there will be no role for university researchers. University faculty members, not living their daily lives within the culture of schools, cannot be as close to the intricacies of schooling as school people are. But that very closeness can be a detriment to effective research, just as distance is, because it can cloud the objectivity and perspective needed to search for useful solutions to educational problems. An optimal balance is needed between immersion in those problems and distance from them. The balance has been so one-sided as to have caused research to be far less meaningful than it needs to be.

We must avoid a similar imbalance in the opposite direction. But we must also move significantly toward redressing the present imbalance, and that suggests the assumption by schools of many of the present research activities now almost entirely absent there.

Immediately a host of questions arises. How can new structures be built within school systems so that research can be assimilated as a major function? While all teachers need to be aware of how research can be incorporated into their daily work, will it be useful to have some teachers, with special training, serve in research leadership roles? How can university personnel with special expertise be utilized effectively, and how can truly collaborative school-university projects be mounted? Most important, how can teacher-education programs incorporate appropriate kinds and amounts of research training to enable all prospective teachers to view research as an essential role they will be expected to fulfill, whether as regular teachers or as research leaders?

At present it is almost unheard of for undergraduate music education majors to be given any sustained instruction in methods of research. At the master's level a single course is the rule, and that course is generally designed primarily for consumers rather than producers of research, reflecting the widespread assumption that consumership is the proper role of school teachers. (There are some exceptions, of course.) So we will have to engage in an almost complete reconceptualization of when, how, and what kinds of research training needs to be offered to prepare school teachers to be effective researchers.

This is an issue as relevant to the research community in music education as to the teacher-education community, and it needs to be debated there as well as in teacher education. But the present culture in music education research is marked by an almost total absence of interest in research issues underlying research techniques. No journal of research in music education focuses on, encourages, or commonly presents reflective discussions about the roles, functions, and needs of the research enterprise or how we can go about improving that enterprise. So it may well fall to this journal to do so, and few contributions would be as crucial for the long-term success of our field as this.

It is my fervent hope that these pages will welcome and encourage discussions about research training as an aspect of teacher education, and that such discussions will be offered by thoughtful music educators who are school teachers as well as by university professors. Although the four issues I have identified here—and the four that were discussed in the previous issue of this journal—are important, they only begin to delineate all those that need attention in music education, and every reader will be able to add dozens more. I eagerly look forward to the debates that will appear in these pages, and to the improvements in music education to which they will inevitably lead.

Note

1. This is one of the major points made in John I. Goodlad's important book *Teachers for Our Nation's Schools* (San Francisco: Jossey-Bass, 1990).

16

AVOIDING EXTREMES OF THEORY AND PRACTICE IN MUSIC TEACHER EDUCATION

The theory/practice duality is ubiquitous in human life. It exists in medicine, law, government, religion, business, science, and in practically everything else humans do. It is found in education as well, and certainly in music education. It is implicated directly and powerfully in our field. Theory is half our story, practice, the other half, with the full story relying on their interaction.

This truism applies fully to music teacher education. Without a secure foundation in theories relating to learning music, the practice of teaching it can only be haphazard at best, chaotic at worst. Without a command of the practices of music teaching, theory remains inert—a burden rather than a basis.

In music education as it takes place in the schools, the details of practice have historically tended to overshadow the concerns of theory. That is the case in music teacher education as well, as in our core methods courses, which tend to focus heavily on all the how-to-teach competencies of each particular specialization. We do not need, as an antidote, to reverse the situation, which would leave us, then, as imbalanced as before. We need the wisdom of theory and the wisdom of practice to play collaborative rather than competitive roles.

In this article, I take issue with an argument that music teacher education should concentrate almost entirely on practice. I regard this view as dangerous given our tendency to do that as a matter of course, which is certainly understandable given the endless specificities of music-making skills and the anxiety of teachers in training to get as many of them under control as possible. Keeping a fruitful balance is not easy under that circumstance, but neglecting to do so dishonors and misrepresents the complex realities of the teaching role, reducing it to one of training rather than education. This diminishes our profession, our subject, and the effects we can have on our students. In music teacher education, achieving an equitable symmetry between theory and practice is job one.

The following essay was originally published in the *Journal of Music Teacher Education* 3, no. 1 (Fall 1993). Used by permission.

As discussions of music teacher education increase in both quantity and quality, due in no small measure to the existence of *The Journal of Music Teacher Education*, some basic issues are likely to arise that plead for thoughtful attention. These issues can go unnoticed for long periods of time when few people are bringing them to consciousness. When attention begins to be paid it is important that balanced views be articulated so that the profession is not led into dead ends by extreme positions.

One such issue, largely dormant because it has been simply assumed to be one of those many "givens," has to do with the roles of theory and of practice in music teaching and in music teacher education. By "theory" I simply mean all the "knowings about" and "knowings why" entailed in being a music teacher: knowings about music in all its many aspects and manifestations, knowings about children as people and as learners, knowings about schools and about teaching, knowings related to why music might be worth teaching in schools, and on and on with all that teachers in general and music teachers in particular are commonly assumed to have developed as their basic stock of knowledge.

By "practice" I simply mean the music teacher's ability to bring all he or she knows about, and knows why, to the act of doing what music teachers do—influencing the learnings of their students by "knowing how" to teach music.

So what's the issue here? Few if any people would deny that both theory, or knowledge in the broad sense, and practice, or the ability to apply that knowledge in action, are two sides of the same coin and that both sides are necessary for effective teaching to occur. Is there really much more to say?

Two extreme positions about the relative importance of theory and practice in teaching have cropped up in recent years, bringing to consciousness the dangers lurking beneath what had seemed placid waters. One extreme so emphasizes theory, or background knowledge of the "about" and "why" sort, as to virtually ignore the essentiality of practice—of "knowing how" as a genuine cognitive act—and therefore to seriously unbalance the interrelation of theory and practice required for successful teaching.

The other position goes to the opposite extreme, so overemphasizing practice—knowing how as the be-all and end-all of the teacher's stock in trade—as to throw the balance just as seriously off center, with consequences just as deleterious for both students and for the status of teachers and of teacher education. To serve our students optimally, and to elevate the status of teaching and teacher education beyond what either the theory-centered or the practice-centered positions are capable of accomplishing, requires a better understanding of how teachers must uniquely blend theory and practice in ways that honor and at the same time transcend each element.

IMBALANCE TOWARD THEORY

The position exaggerating the theory side of the coin regards subject matter knowledge as the key if not only ingredient for successful teaching. Teaching is not itself an undertaking or activity or way of knowing requiring more than cursory attention. What *does* require the major attention in the preparation of a teacher is development of expertise in the subject to be taught.

In music this subject matter expertise takes two different forms.

On the one hand, some subject-centered advocates feel that the broadest possible liberal education, including a liberal education about music focusing on music history, literature, theory, and aesthetics, prepares a prospective teacher to best represent music to potential students in that the students can share the humanistic learnings the teacher has gained and benefit from the breadth of knowledge the teacher can offer. This view, conceiving of music as one of the humanities or liberal arts, has a long history in our culture especially apparent in liberal arts colleges and universities (Harvard being a prime historical example) in which to study music is to study it as a humanity and to teach music is to teach it as such. One prepares for such teaching not by learning how to teach, which can be safely left to "instinct" or "intuition" or "experience" or "just plain common sense," but by becoming humanistically educated in music oneself. At most, a little guidance from a mentor or model will suffice for the "how to teach" aspect.

The other form of subject expertise in music is different in every way. It consists of highly developed musicianship, almost always in performance rather than in composition because of the historical focus in Western culture on performance as the way one becomes a musician. Here the *sine qua non* for being a successful music teacher is to be, oneself, the very fine performer one is teaching one's students to be. One's training to be a teacher must therefore consist dominantly if not entirely of training to be a performer. The ability to teach music (to teach performance) can safely be left to the same casual treatment considered sufficient by liberal arts advocates in that teaching itself is not something one can learn to do, or needs to learn to do, or that can be taught to someone. It just happens naturally. At most, one does what one's own teacher or teachers did, which was successful by definition because it led one to being a good performer oneself.

The subject-centered approaches to teaching do have their finger on one important dimension of what teachers must possess in order to be successful—knowledge about and expertise in the subject matter being taught. Surely it would be hard to argue that we don't want and expect every music teacher to be steeped in both broad understandings of music and real expertise as a musician, and we correctly include both as important features of our music teacher education programs. It's not that these, by themselves, are unnecessary. It's just that they are, by themselves, insufficient. For they imply that teaching is itself essentially a trivial endeavor, able to be tacked on to or superimposed over what is to be taught, with no necessary relation to what is to be taught other than simply handing the subject over to learners. The actual practice of teaching—the "knowing how to do"—is looked upon with condescension sometimes bordering on contempt. That is why students and faculty in teacher education programs often find themselves regarded by students and faculty in both the academic and performing aspects of music with precisely those attitudes.

That teaching is itself a knowing how with its own validity, intelligence, thoughtfulness, and craft, intimately related both to the subject to be taught and to the students being taught, goes unrecognized because of the one-sidedness of the theory-centered view. Neither is it recognized that learning how to teach requires systematic, careful cultivation over as long a period of time as either the acquisition of a liberal education or of musicianship.

IMBALANCE TOWARD PRACTICE

The second extreme position in regard to the relative importance of theory and practice focuses on the flip side of the coin from the "teaching as subject-centered" view. It emphasizes the practice aspect of teaching so heavily as to produce the same unfortunate result as does the opposite imbalance—denigrating the complexity of teaching. In this case, the overemphasis on practice diminishes the reality that multiple forms of intelligence are required to be a successful teacher and that teacher education programs must consciously nurture all of them.

Just as there are historical precedents for the view that knowing one's subject is all that really matters, there is a long history both in education and in music education of the contrary view—that knowing how to do is really the key. In music education our typical focus on methodologies—systematic, sequential, prescribed regimens leading to the accomplishment of specified objectives—reflects our historical emphasis on skilled practice as the desideratum for both learners and teachers, not only for the development of performance abilities but also in general music settings. The very name of the courses specifically devoted to preparing music teachers— "methods"—exemplifies where we have tended to put our major interest, which has been strongly driven by the assumption that music is primarily a practice, teaching is primarily a practice, and therefore music teaching *especially* is and must be a practice-dominated endeavor.

The image we tend to portray in the larger domain of education, therefore, is of a technique- and methodology-centered field, ungrounded in and relatively uninterested in larger understandings and issues of education. The very real problem with our practice-dominated history, I would suggest, is not that skilled practice is unnecessary to being a successful music teacher, for surely it *is* necessary, but that it is insufficient for it, just as is the case with the opposite position overly stressing subject knowledge.

In recent years educational research was also dominated by concerns with the practice of teaching. The primary focus of research in the 1970s and early 1980s was on "process-product" studies, "designed to identify those patterns of teacher behavior that accounted for improved academic performance of pupils."[1] This research tended to be based on the assumption that what matters most in successful teaching are the actions teachers perform in educational settings; how they handle presentation of material, explanations, questioning, evaluation, classroom management, direct instruction, time on task, reinforcement, groupings, discipline, timing of feedback, and on and on with all the many "point of interaction" matters entailed in the act of instruction. In music education research as well such studies dominated the literature. This domination was weakened severely by the middle 1980s as it was discovered that both the practical results of such research, and the assumptions it was founded on, were fundamentally flawed.

A major event in that turnaround was the presidential address delivered by Lee S. Shulman to the 1985 annual convention of the American Educational Research Association (AERA), in which he traced the history of extreme positions focusing on either subject matter or practice and argued that a particular kind of unity of the two is essential if teaching is to be successful.[2] The effects of that speech on subsequent research and the assumptions guiding it were far-reaching. As a recent article in the *Educational Researcher* explains,

> In his 1985 AERA presidential address, Lee Shulman tossed off the phrase "pedagogical content knowledge" and sparked a small cottage industry devoted to scholarly elaboration of the construct in a number of different teaching fields and the re-engineering of teacher education programs to include it. In that address, Shulman was proposing a theoretical framework that would reintegrate teachers' knowledge of their subject matter into our view of the knowledge that teachers use in their teaching, teachers' content knowledge having been largely ignored during the years of "process-product" research on teaching and by initial cognitive-science oriented investigations of teachers' planning and instruction. In Shulman's formulation, teachers need pedagogical knowledge, deep knowledge of the subject itself, and knowledge of curricular goals and available materials. In addition, they need a particular form of content knowledge that deals with its teachability, including the most useful forms of representation and an understanding of what makes the learning of specific topics easy or difficult. Tantalizingly ambiguous in its original formulation, and opening new space in the conceptual landscape, pedagogical content knowledge was "that special amalgam of content and pedagogy that is uniquely the province of teachers, their own special form of professional understanding."[3]

I want to explain several of the points Shulman made in his important address because I believe they can help us avoid the hazards of the two extreme positions about what effective teaching requires. Before doing so, however, a recent example of a curiously retrogressive view emphasizing the centrality of practice in music teaching needs to be examined as an example of the dangers of taking reasonable ideas to unreasonable extremes. The persuasiveness of Shulman's arguments about the need to unite knowledge with action will be more apparent for having taken this digression.

TEACHING AS IMPROVISING

In a recent issue of *JMTE* David Elliott argues for a view of music teaching and music teacher education centered on what he calls "educatorship," which "is essentially a matter of *procedural* knowledge"[4] (emphasis his). Procedural knowledge—practical knowledge or "knowledge-how"—consists of the expertise a person possesses at the level of action. That expertise, Elliott concedes, is influenced by "supporting" kinds of knowing—"formal" knowing, such as about educational psychology, philosophy, curriculum theory, and so forth; "informal" knowing, the teacher's ability to make moment-to-moment decisions; "impressionistic" knowing, which is the teacher's feelings as they guide action;[5] and "supervisory" knowing, a kind of disposition or metaknowledge, influencing the other knowings and their employment.

Given this heavy role of knowings that contribute to action (however unwieldy and overcomplex the explanatory model he employs) it would seem that these contributory knowings would have to play a central role both in how teachers teach and in how teachers would be educated to be teachers. But the model proposed focuses so narrowly on the act of teaching itself—the moment of interaction between the teacher and student(s)—that it severely underestimates the backgrounds of knowledge essential for the act of teaching to be more than improvisatory. Dismissed are the very real demands on teachers to demonstrate overtly the knowledge guiding their actions, to students, to parents, to other teachers, and to administrators, by embodying them in what is generally called "a curriculum."

The analogy favored by Elliott is that of the teacher as jazz improviser: "A teacher, like an excellent jazz improviser, is well prepared to deal with moment-to-moment problems and opportunities encountered on the fly . . . in cases of expert music teaching, these problems and opportunities seem to be solved and sorted out spontaneously."[6] But the improvisation analogy, unfortunately, applies to only one part of the much more diverse set of requirements teachers of music must fulfill in educational settings. In fact, while every teaching act is improvisatory at one level, teaching is very far from being improvisatory in many, if not most, of its manifestations, albeit that the "point of contact" level tends to be uppermost in the minds of novice teachers who haven't yet developed the "chops" to be able to handle the moment-to-moment give and take of teaching and therefore, very naturally, focus nervously on that level as their most pressing concern.

Many teacher education programs cater almost exclusively to that concern, forgetting that after a couple of years or so of experience the chops level falls into place (or the teacher unable to develop that sort of expertise falls out of teaching) and what then becomes paramount in the needs of teachers is a philosophical-educational basis for their now in-control actions, a basis neglected by their initial needs to develop basic teaching skills and often neglected as well in their education. The questions driving experienced music teachers returning for graduate work are no longer questions of improvisatory finesse; they are questions of meaning, of structure, of goals more clearly understood, of better means for pursuing those goals, of better understandings of what a music curriculum consists of so they can be more effective in providing one for their students and in explaining what one is to their administrators. This, in turn, is important because some administrators have come to the opinion that music teachers, alone among all the other teachers in the school, *have* no curriculum, but simply do what they do when they do it.

To put it in another way, the analogy of the "teacher as improviser" is not sufficient to cover adequately the other main roles the music teacher must play—the roles of "performer," and "composer." As "performer" the teacher (of every subject, music definitely not excluded) must constantly decide how to bring a planned set of learnings (an educational "score," so to speak) to effective life. At the broadest level the score is a curriculum concept of what is most important to teach, how to organize to best lead students toward useful learning goals, and how to move from one learning to another in an accumulative way.

At one time, during the heyday of behaviorism, attempts were made to stipulate, minutely and concretely, every detail of what needed to be learned and how to progress from one specific learning to the next according to "programmed" materials that followed elaborate behavioristic rules and regulations. That approach to curriculum so underestimated what human thinking and understanding consist of, and so diminished the role of teachers as cultivators of complex thinking/doing learnings, as to pervert education by making it into a restricted kind of training regimen and making teachers into managers and monitors of detailed scripts that students followed assiduously.[7]

We are long past such limited notions of what curriculum planning and curriculum delivery need to consist of if they are to educate students to be independent, critical, creative thinkers and doers. But no curriculum theorist has suggested that appropriate long- and short-term plans need not exist in education.

For example, the present attempt to develop standards for what students need to learn in each of the important subjects, and the degree to which those learnings should occur, is one particular way to provide for long-range planning and a sense of goal directedness while avoiding the extremes to which behaviorism took the planning and goal-setting process. The teacher's role in regard to the standards is one of being an expert "performer." The music teacher is in the position of having to be aware of the standards being proposed by the music education profession, having to decide which if any should be adopted as bases for his or her own program of instruction, having to "interpret," as any good performer must, the most effective ways to translate the score (the written standards documents) so that they are musically and pedagogically valid,[8] having to "perform" the score (provide instruction) with all the teaching craft, sensitivity, and imagination at his or her command, and then to make some relevant judgments about how it all went and how it could go better the next time.

But in addition to assuming the role of performer in much of what the teacher is expected to do, teachers often must also assume the role of "composer" by creating curriculum plans and materials. All of us who teach, at every level from kindergarten to graduate school, must at least add to curriculum materials that are available to help us in our work, or at most entirely create such materials—curriculum plans and ways to achieve those plans. None of us can escape having to originate some, most, or (in extreme cases) all of the instructional goals and materials we depend on to get us through both single teaching episodes and planned sequences of episodes (a curriculum).[9]

Teaching, therefore, requires expertise at three levels—the "composer" level of curriculum creation, the "performer" level of curriculum interpretation, and the "improviser" level of skill in the immediacy of teacher-learner interactions. Nothing less than all three levels working in harmony *begins* to describe the complexity of teaching. (The role of the teacher as "listener," learning about and transforming into personal expertise all the musical and educational knowledge being generated constantly, is worth another whole essay.)

Of all this, the one aspect of overwhelming importance in Elliott's conceptualization is improvisatory skill in the act of teaching; certainly an essential aspect but only one part of a much larger, more complex whole for which all teachers are held responsible. The fact that curriculum plans need to be part of that larger picture; that such curriculum plans, whether made by individual teachers or committees of professionals at local, state, or national levels, are necessarily stated explicitly; that planning for a program of learning requires that some goals be articulated as ends and that the means to reach those ends also be articulated; that the teacher's expertise as a practitioner serves to bring theory (curriculum planning) to fruition; that such expertise requires creativity, intelligence, informed judgment, and deep internalization of both music and the teaching intentions implied in a structured program of music education, are all neglected in Elliott's model because they all go far beyond the improvisatory teaching act.

An improvisatory model of music teacher education can only be of peripheral use to us, unfortunately, because it fails to account for the real world of music teaching as it actually transpires in our schools—a world far more complex than this position can handle and in which teachers must be far broader as professionals than they are envisioned in this model.

It has taken almost two decades for music educators to dig out of the restricted image of teaching and of teacher expertise portrayed by the "curriculum as behavior reinforcement" model, and we still have a long way to go to rid ourselves of the "anyone can teach if they know their subject" model. But real progress is finally being made to both recognize the many demands teachers must fulfill and to prepare them to meet those demands.[10] Elliott's position is a particular, excessive version of a rather benign and healthy view that practice is inherently intelligent—a view generally called "praxialism,"[11] which I find entirely compatible with and a useful extension of other views I have found convincing and useful. We should all be delighted to give all due respect to the intelligence entailed in knowing how, whether that knowing how relates to teaching music or creating music or experiencing music, and we should welcome any clarification of that helpful dimension.[12]

But an exaggerated version of praxialism can de-professionalize teachers rather than enhance the understanding of the many dimensions of their professionalism. That is a direction we can ill afford to take. Lee Shulman's explanation of the need for a unity of theory with practice makes this clear.

THE PROFESSIONAL TEACHER

In Shulman's AERA speech, and in subsequent writings, he criticized educational research for having left out the crucial aspect of subject matter as a factor in successful teaching.[13] "No one asked how subject matter was transformed from the knowledge of the teacher into the content of instruction. Nor did they ask how particular formulations of that content related to what students came to know or misconstrue."[14] Left unanswered about teachers' professional obligations were questions about how content determines much of what they must do. How do college students, filled with knowledge and skill from their education, transform what they know into the forms of representation best suited for school children to learn?

> Our work does not intend to denigrate the importance of pedagogical understanding or skill in the development of a teacher or in enhancing the effectiveness of instruction. Mere content knowledge is likely to be as useless pedagogically as content-free skill. But to blend properly the two aspects of a teacher's capacities requires that we pay as much attention to the content aspects of teaching as we have recently devoted to the elements of the teaching process."[15]

One important factor in presenting subject matter validly is the ability of teachers to use curriculum materials (such as texts, standards, curriculum frameworks, lesson plans, and district or state guidelines) effectively by transforming their own understandings of the materials into instruction that students can comprehend. This transformation is an instance of what Shulman called pedagogical content knowledge—the "ways of representing and formulating the subject that make it comprehensible to others."[16] There is no one way to do this, so teachers must have a great many alternative forms of representation at their command.

To give potential teachers of music a variety of tactics to present basic musical learnings, therefore, is essential in teacher education. This includes the teachers' understanding of "what makes the learning of specific topics [in music this would include skills of performing, composing, improvising, and listening] easy or difficult; [and] the conceptions and preconceptions that students of different ages and backgrounds bring with them to the learning of those most frequently taught topics and lessons."[17]

But in addition to knowing the subject, and knowing how to represent the subject effectively for learners, teachers must also have a highly developed "curricular knowledge."

> If we are regularly remiss in not teaching pedagogical knowledge to our students in teacher education programs, we are even more delinquent with respect to the third category of content knowledge, *curricular knowledge*. The curriculum is represented by the full range of programs designed for the teaching of particular subjects and topics at a given level, the variety of instructional materials available in relation to those programs, and the set of characteristics that serve as both the indications and contraindications for the use of particular curriculum or program materials in particular circumstances.[18]

The tripartite nature of what teachers must know—the subject, the subject as teachable, the subject as a curriculum—is the basis for a teacher's professionalism. That professionalism includes skill in all the direct acts of teaching, obviously, but also requires a great deal of know-how beyond that. Shulman says, "I am not offering herein an argument against the conception of teaching as skill. I am instead arguing for its insufficiency—its incompleteness as an account of teaching ability and performance."[19]

What makes skill insufficient as the organizing, predominant factor in a conception of what professional teachers must know is its inadequacy to cover all the forms of knowledge teachers must possess, and all the many essential obligations entailed in teaching.

> What distinguishes mere craft from profession is the indeterminacy of rules when applied to particular cases. The professional holds knowledge, not only of how—the capacity for skilled performance—but of what and why. The teacher is not only a master of procedure but also of content and rationale, and capable of explaining why something is done. . . . A professional is capable not only of practicing and understanding his or her craft, but of communicating the reasons for professional decisions and actions to others. . . . The vision I hold of teaching and teacher education is a vision of professionals who are capable not only of acting, but of enacting—of acting in a manner that is self-conscious with respect to what their act is a case of or to what their act entails.[20]

The vision of excellent teaching we need to hold in music teacher education is one that is both inclusive and balanced.

We must not disparage any of the many knowings required to be a professional music educator. Each is important, each is necessary, each contributes to the complex reality of what it takes to teach music successfully. The fact that that reality *is* so complex is what makes our profession so admirable and our attempts to prepare teachers so formidable.

Theory and practice are not in competition with each other: it is precisely the ability to interrelate the two that makes a teacher effective. Our primary task in music teacher education is to help potential and experienced teachers develop that ability, avoiding extreme positions in which one dominates the other.

NOTES

1. Lee S. Shulman, "Those Who Understand: Knowledge Growth in Teaching," *Educational Researcher* 15, no. 2 (February 1986): 6.

2. Shulman, "Those Who Understand," 6.

3. Barbara Scott Nelson, review of Pamela S. Grossman, "The Making of a Teacher: Teacher Knowledge and Teacher Education," in *Educational Researcher* 21, no. 9 (December 1992): 32.

4. David J. Elliott, "Rethinking Music Teacher Education," *Journal of Music Teacher Education* 2, no. 1 (Fall 1992): 7.

5. Elliott adopts a view of emotion as being entirely dependent on outside stimuli: "For example, if I feel certain, uncertain, delighted, disappointed, or sad, I feel all these things *about* something. It is *because* I have beliefs and knowledge about situations, people (actions, objects) that I experience emotions" (13) (emphases in original). The oversimplification of this view is clearly explained in Ann W. Stokes, "Intelligence and Feeling" (Ph.D. diss., Department of Music Education, Northwestern University, 1990).

6. Elliott, "Rethinking Music Teacher Education," 12.

7. My opposition to behavioristic approaches to curriculum, and to the "teacher-proof" materials they attempted to develop, stretches back to at least the early 1970s, such as in "Aesthetic Behaviors in Music," in Bennett Reimer, organizing chairman, *Toward an Aesthetic Education* (Washington, D.C.: MENC, 1971). A history of and comparison between behaviorist and present-day cognitivist curriculum principles is given in Bennett Reimer, "Music Education Philosophy and Psychology after Mursell," in Richard Colwell, ed., *Basic Concepts in Music Education II* (Niwot: University Press of Colorado, 1991). For a description of my views of the teacher's role as curriculum provider and a discussion of performance groups as curricular, see *A Philosophy of Music Education* (Englewood Cliffs, NJ: Prentice Hall, 1989), 160–62, 165–72, 196–207.

8. That it is essential for teachers to be able to intelligently interpret curriculum materials and curriculum standards is recognized even by curriculum theorists interested in "the wisdom of teacher practice," as, for example, F. Michael Connelly and D. Jean Clandinin, *Teachers as Curriculum Planners* (New York: Teachers College Press, 1988), in which they discuss how teachers must take curriculum materials and "make of them different things depending on our purposes" (149), and in which they suggest that teachers in training try to make even "mundane" curriculum materials more imaginative so that they can "gather some feel for the idea of the curriculum potential of instructional materials" (151).

9. The need for music teachers to be curriculum designers and providers is explained further in Bennett Reimer, "An Agenda for Music Teacher Education," part II, *Journal of Music Teacher Education* 1, no. 2 (Spring 1992): 7–8.

10. A useful analysis of the variety of roles (intelligences) required for successful teaching is given in Maurice W. Sedlak, "Tomorrow's Teachers: The Essential Arguments of the Holmes Group Report," *Teacher's College Record* 88, no. 3 (Spring 1987): 321–22, which suggests that (at least) five components are involved: the study of teaching and schooling as an academic field; knowledge of the pedagogy of subject matter; skills and understandings implicit in classroom teaching; values,

dispositions, and a sense of ethical responsibility; and pedagogical expertise founded in general principles and theories.

11. For an explanation of the praxialist view and its implications for music education, see Philip Alperson, "What Should One Expect from a Philosophy of Music Education?" *The Journal of Aesthetic Education* 25, no. 3 (Fall 1991): 233–37.

12. Elliott's version of praxialism as it applies to "musicianship" is as excessive, in my opinion, as it is to "educatorship," and as limiting to our understanding of musical experience in its many dimensions. That, however, is a subject for treatment at another time. For several of my own explanations of the nature and necessity of "knowing how" in music and music education, see "What Knowledge Is of Most Worth in the Arts?" in Bennett Reimer and Ralph A. Smith, eds., *The Arts, Education, and Aesthetic Knowing* (Chicago: University of Chicago Press, 1992); "Music Education in Our Multimusical Culture," *Music Educators Journal* 79, no. 7 (March 1993): 21–26; and "Toward a Concept of Curriculum," *Research Perspectives in Music Education* (Fall 1993).

13. Lee S. Shulman, "Knowledge and Teaching: Foundations of the New Reform," *Harvard Educational Review* 57, no. 1 (February 1987): 1–22.

14. Shulman, "Those Who Understand," 6.

15. Shulman, "Those Who Understand," 8.

16. Shulman, "Those Who Understand," 9.

17. Shulman, "Those Who Understand," 9.

18. Shulman, "Those Who Understand," 10.

19. Shulman, "Those Who Understand," 12.

20. Shulman, "Those Who Understand," 13.

17

TOWARD A RESEARCH-BASED FOUNDATION FOR DOCTORAL PROGRAMS IN MUSIC EDUCATION

Of the many aspects of music education, one would assume that the doctoral degree program would be the most thoughtfully grounded, most carefully researched and constructed, and most effectively implemented. After all, it is the highest level of our educational endeavor, the very tip of the music education pyramid in scholarship and leadership for the profession. The faculty members offering these programs and the students selected to them are the most academically accomplished we have. Surely these programs are built on and function according to the strongest possible bases for advanced study.

Too optimistic, I'm afraid. Doctoral programs in the United States and around the world do indeed engage many of our finest minds and are admirably effective in preparing teacher educators, scholars/researchers, and leaders for our common good. Yet the reality is that large gaps and holes exist in the philosophical and operational foundations on which these programs rest.

We need now to look closely and critically at this very specialized yet deeply influential dimension of music education. Improvements at this highest level of study will affect every aspect of our work, not only at the bachelor's and master's degree levels but in what our school programs aim for and the effectiveness with which they achieve their aims. Especially because doctoral degree study is a major influence on those whose responsibility is to educate school music teachers, it must be as carefully conceived and as imaginatively rich as it can be made to be. That is why I include this essay in the section on educating our teachers rather than in the following section on research.

This critique, I hope, will be debated among doctoral faculty members, faculty and students in music education at every college or university level, and by teachers in service. All music educators have a stake in advancing the excellence of doctoral programs, building on their strengths, addressing their weaknesses, and benefiting from their improved influences on our theoretical and practical bases as a profession.

The following essay was originally published in the *Council for Research in Music Education*, Bulletin 173 (Summer 2007). Used by permission

ABSTRACT

We start largely from scratch in the task of building a research-based foundation for doctoral programs in music education. Two dimensions of the task are to address, from a research base, the operational and the philosophical foundations for what our programs have been, now are, and need to become. Little exists to help us do so, either in our research and scholarly literature or in our recognition of the urgency of the need. At the operational level even the most basic questions of why we do what we do are unanswered in any systematic way. And at the philosophical level, having to do with what our goals and values might be, we have no viable mechanism allowing us to work toward a synergistic set of principles that would lead us to provide the profession with its highest-level visionaries, researchers, and leaders. Until we provide for a means to accomplish those ends doctoral degree study will continue to be less influential in forging a more well-grounded, more effective profession than its distinctive mission requires it to be.

THE MISSING FOUNDATION

There is a striking lack, approaching absence, of material discussing what the foundations of doctoral programs in music education might be. Practically no literature, including research literature, can be consulted for guidance as to what foundational ideas, beliefs, and guidelines have existed on which our programs and practices have been or should be based. What I have been able to uncover is extremely spotty and largely tangential.

For example, in the first *Handbook of Research on Music Teaching and Learning* (Colwell, 1992), the only relevant chapter is the one dealing with teacher education, by Ralph Verrastro and Mary Leglar. In it there is no discussion of the role of doctoral programs in preparing teachers of teachers, nor is there any research on this mentioned. In *The New Handbook of Research on Music Teaching and Learning* (Colwell & Richardson, 2002), there is an entire section on teacher education—a major advance. In his introduction to this section, titled "Fuzzy Teacher Education," James Raths says "The complexity of teacher education, its fuzziness, often will not yield to traditional research procedures whether they are qualitative or quantitative. Perhaps dramatic breakthroughs in teacher education await new, non-Aristotelian research procedures to accommodate its fuzziness" (p. 757). By fuzziness he means complexity beyond "data" as we usually construe what these consist of. He may well be correct, but it is difficult to imagine that present research methodologies, no matter their limitations, can tell us nothing at all about what we need to know. That does seem overly pessimistic.

In the chapter "Strengthening the Teaching of Music Educators in Higher Education," by Susan Wilcox and Rena Upitis, there is in fact some discussion of the role of doctoral programs, but practically the entire presentation focuses on teaching in general rather than on the teaching of music or the arts. For example, they state that "a substantial number of Ph.D. graduates start jobs in colleges and universities never having taught before and never having any formal instruction in how to teach" (p. 843). This is practically never the case for college music education teachers, although it is the case that many if not most doctoral students have never taught at the college or university level except, perhaps, as TAs in their doctoral program. Whether that TA experience can be construed as adequate preparation for college teaching is, indeed, an important issue for any foundational basis for exemplary doctoral programs. The chapter authors recognize this, in their recommendations that

1. there needs to be a wider range and deeper intensity of preparation to be a college teacher [although, I would add, many universities are now offering an intensive preparatory program for prospective college teachers];

2. mentoring of TAs by experienced college faculty is essential, along with many opportunities for conversation among faculty and doctoral students about college teaching;

3. use should be made within doctoral programs of a teaching portfolio; and

4. students must be taken beyond performance mastery to mastery of a much broader spectrum of musical learnings. [This is a major piece of unfinished business in our field, I believe, about which we greatly need foundational principles.]

All of these recommendations require a solid research basis on which to base practice, of course, but the authors point out that "We are not aware of any empirical studies of teaching development programs designed specifically for new or junior music faculty" (p. 843).

One more citation before I launch in to my own proposals in regard to needed foundations for doctoral level programs in music education. This is a chapter in the *Handbook of Research on Teacher Education* by Eunice Boardman, on "Music Teacher Education" (Boardman, 1990). She begins by saying "A cohesive body of research directly focused on how best to prepare the new teacher and to implement such recommendations still does not exist" (p. 730). I am confident that this remains the case to the present day. Why? Because a "cohesive body of research" about anything, let alone the complexity of teacher education, does not yet exist, either in music education or in education as a whole.

In regard to graduate study as a factor for influencing improvements in music teaching, Boardman quotes a comment made in 1978 that "Except for broad recommendations by NASM, few standards have been established for curricular structure of graduate programs at either the master's or doctoral level" (p. 730). Again, it is likely that this also remains the case to this day. No other mention is made in the chapter of doctoral study and its central role in teacher education and research. Given that major functions of doctoral programs in our field are to prepare professionals who will teach pre-service teachers how to teach, to assist in-service teachers to teach better, and to contribute to the research literature of the profession, all these being functions crying for a solid foundation upon which effective programs can be built, the skimpy material available leaves us ungrounded in the core responsibilities of doctoral study.

THE NEED TO KNOW OUR HISTORY

I am left by this necessarily cursory review of the literature unencumbered by a wealth of material needing to be digested, relied upon, and critiqued, relating to formulating a set of foundational principles and guidelines for the conduct of doctoral study in our field.

One important factor for successful accomplishment of that task, I want to suggest, is to create a solid historical account of what our explicit and implicit foundations have actually been since doctoral programs came into being, so that we can view a larger picture than any histories of individual programs can provide. Unfortunately, it is likely to be very difficult to ascertain our history of beliefs and practices in regard to doctoral study because little if any serious scholarly work exists to guide us toward creating a comprehensive historical record. We have operated largely independently of each other in our programs; in a real sense secretively. We tend to protect our institutional practices from outside scrutiny except when we go through an obligatory review, either internally by our university or externally by NASM or other accrediting agency. Mostly we preserve a haze of indeterminacy about our programs, as practically all doctoral programs in universities tend to do—the old "mind your own business" attitude in higher education generally.

In that atmosphere we are left bereft of authoritative data on which we can build the story of what we have been and what we now are. We need serious research to first, dig out the data, and second, to construct the story the data tell. That will require cooperative efforts among all the doctoral degree granting institutions, certainly in the United States and perhaps around the world, and a very astute, very insightful researcher who can aggregate the data, or, perhaps, several researchers who focus on particular aspects of the larger story. But such cooperative work is practically unknown both in higher education and in research. The Consortium for Institutional Cooperation, embracing the universities in the Big Ten conference that offer music education doctoral programs (Indiana, Iowa, Illinois, Northwestern, Michigan, Michigan State, Minnesota, Ohio State, and Wisconsin, along with Pennsylvania State) is unique in its ongoing meetings to share information about their graduate programs, but its agenda is far broader than doctoral programs alone, and it has not energized on the systematic, focused, coordinated, long-term research that my call for a substantive history requires. I will mention at the end of this paper our profession's need to establish a mechanism to accomplish that kind of work.

TWO DIMENSIONS OF DOCTORAL PROGRAMS

There are two major aspects of doctoral programs needing attention if we are to construct a solid conceptual, research basis for our work. The first is the operational aspect—the structural dimension of the program. The second is the philosophical aspect, the aspect of the purposes and directions of the program. The two are intimately related to each other, of course, in fact dependent on each other. We cannot have an effective operative program if we are not clear about what its mission is. And it is not sufficient to have a responsible mission without a good operative program that carries it out. For the sake of clarity, however, I will treat each aspect in turn. For each I will offer a variety of proposals and challenges we need to address if we are to create a convincing, defensible, research-based foundation for our work.

I. The Operational Dimension

For each issue entailed in constructing an effective set of operations for our doctoral programs a question must be asked and answers to it sought. Here is a sample of such issues and the questions they raise. The questions are, in fact, rather simple, or obvious. But we have not asked them, we need to ask them, and we need to pursue insights from research with as much rigor as we can muster.

1. Entrance Prerequisites   The pressing question in regard to our expectations of prerequisites for doctoral study is "How do we know what they should be?" For example, if we say "a minimum of x number of years of teaching in the schools," how do we know what the optimal minimum is? Is there an optimal minimum? Is such experience relevant for all potential students? How do we ascertain the quality of the teaching experience we require? Can we really rely on references? What about entrance test results, such as on the GRE, or tests we devise in our own shops, or the old Miller Analogies? (Does anyone still use that test? Why?) Are we certain, based on solid evidence, that these, or others, are valid and reliable tools for separating admissible candidates from those who are not?

Here is the challenge underlying all these questions (and I have only hinted at the many more that can be and need to be asked about prerequisites). How do we educate ourselves about the assumptions underlying our expectations in this regard so that we can operate on more than hunch and hope? Don't we have an obligation to work from a solid foundation of research-centered wisdom about this base-line aspect of our programs?

2. Admission Procedures and Standards   Given that applicants to our programs meet whatever prerequisites exist, how do we choose from among them those who warrant admission, a burdensome decision given all the many obligations of money, time, expectations, and uncertainties entailed in doctoral study? What characteristics guide us to wise choices? Musicianship? What exactly does that term mean, given the historical narrowness of our assumptions about how this characteristic can be manifested? How do we ascertain a potential student's musicianship beyond the cliché of an audition? To what degree is performance musicianship, or any other way people are musicians, relevant to the diverse goals of different students with different ambitions for their careers?

What about personality? Surely we need to attend to this as we weigh each candidate's potentials for success not only as a student but as a leader in the profession. But think of the slippery slope that puts us on. What about the goals of the students when they apply for admission? How do we reconcile their goals for themselves with what we know of our field and where they might fit in to it and also make a substantive contribution? After all, we have an obligation, when we accept a student into our program, to the profession and its betterment, and also to the student as to whether she or he can reasonably be expected to be successful in meeting the demands of our program and is likely to be able to contribute to the field.

The challenge here? Much the same as for the prerequisites issue: how do we make our choices based on the most solid evidence our collective wisdom can produce regarding the kinds of people we should admit and the ways we can best identify those kinds of people? Don't we have the obligation in this matter also to act from a foundation of evidence as to the kinds of people best served by doctoral study and who, in turn, will best serve the needs of the profession? By "evidence" I do not mean, necessarily, quantitative evidence, although that cannot be ignored. I mean carefully, thoughtfully, critically amassed criteria and procedures that we can rely on as being more valid than our own intuitions while also honoring our own intuitions. There are degrees of fuzziness, I'm suggesting, and we need to be as minimally fuzzy as we can make ourselves.

3. Coursework Requirements   Coursework is a central aspect of our programs yet we have little to go by except tradition as to what the optimal design and content should be. What is the most efficacious required set of courses? We have some assumptions but little to back them up. Should there be majors and minors? Electives? If so, should they be open or channeled? Requirements in music history and theory? Performance? Which aspects of music education proper? How do we balance breadth with depth? What are our expectations for the quality of student work in courses? Are grades the best indication of that quality? How do we structure our decisions as to which students should be encouraged to continue, based on their coursework performance, and which students called into question? After all, if all students sail through with all As, so no decisions need to be made about their coursework performance, are we doing our job responsibly?

On and on go the questions about how we operate in regard to coursework. The challenge? Here, too, it is to operate from a foundational set of guidelines, carefully built from our best collective thinking and evidence gathering.

4. Research Requirements   The questions about research requirements and expectations are so complex and far-reaching that a separate paper (at least) needs to be spent on them. A basic question relates to identifying what courses should be required for all and what can safely be elective, a tough question to answer given the dramatically widening scope in the field of research as to what can be regarded as being research in the first place. Another question, perhaps equally complex, is how can we encourage coordination of dissertations so that we can finally break out of the chaos in which research operates both in music education and in education generally? I will not begin to tackle the endlessly complex issues of what we need to do in regard to solidifying our research assumptions and practices and how we can better align ourselves with the debates going on about research in education as a whole. I have expressed myself about many of these matters elsewhere (Reimer, 1985, 1994), as have others (i.e., Stubley, 1992; Elliott, 2002). This is not the place to deal with them because I would soon be enmeshed in their complexities and unable to get to the other issues needing to be addressed. Suffice it to say that we need, perhaps even more crucially here than in all the other matters at the operational level, to get our heads together as to what we do and how we do it and just what it is we intend to accomplish in regard to our expectations for the research requirements in our programs.

Other issues needing to be tackled with the same urgency are exam procedures and contents, monitoring the quality of student work, program advising and dissertation advising practices, criteria for faculty involvement in doctoral programs, provision of teaching opportunities for students during their study and mentoring/supervision of that teaching, dissertation expectations in regard to quality and scope, and many others.

To summarize, we face a host of unresolved questions, immensely complex questions, doubt-raising questions, fuzzy questions, about what we are doing and how well we are doing it. At the same time we can be very proud of what we have accomplished in regard to doctoral study in the relatively short time that work at this level has existed in our field. So we should not be discouraged. We should only recognize that we have a great deal of unfinished business awaiting us if we are to rest our operational structures on the kind of strong research foundations they need if they are to be all we hope they can be. After all, if those who are responsible for the highest academic attainment in our profession do not model the highest academic standards in what they do and how they do it, who else in our profession should be expected to do so?

II. The Philosophical Dimension

The second aspect I will deal with focuses on the philosophical issues connected to doctoral study in music education. I'm taking "philosophy" here in a very broad, very inclusive sense rather than in the stricter sense of what constitutes philosophical research or scholarship as such. I mean by the term philosophy, in this context, the purposes, goals, ideals, and directions we envision for the profession as a whole and for doctoral programs as an important aspect of the larger profession.

As I have mentioned, questions and issues here are intimately related to operational questions and issues because our answers to the philosophical questions provide the basis for what we then do in our operations. If that is not the case, if our operations are carried out absent the guidance of a philosophical foundation; that is, a carefully and thoughtfully built set of beliefs and values about what it is we are trying to accomplish, our operations can then only be ungrounded and incoherent. I leave it to those reading this paper to judge the degree to which our programs are solidly grounded in a shared set of foundational purposes cooperatively created. My own judgment is that no such substantive grounding exists.

The philosophical questions include these: What should we be as a profession? What are our purposes? How can doctoral programs most effectively exercise leadership toward the achievement of the profession's purposes? What are the special dimensions of leadership appropriately addressed through doctoral programs? (There are many aspects of leadership, after all, that are not related to study at the doctoral level.) Such questions assume that there needs to be a direct connection between what the music education profession as a whole needs to be, or can be, and what doctoral study enables. The assumption here is that the profession needs to be clear as to its purposes, and doctoral study needs to both assist in that process of clarification and to serve, in the ways most suitable for study at the doctoral level, the values the profession intends to pursue.

That assumption is itself open to debate, of course. Judging by my acquaintance with many programs over the years I would have to report that there seems to be little connection between some particular programs and the professional realities of music teaching in educational settings. I am not clear as to whether the disconnect between a particular doctoral program and the rest of the life of the profession is the result of a conscious and careful decision that that is the way it needs to be, which then must be regarded as one possible position, or whether, as I suspect is often the case, there is simply an unawareness of, or disinterest in, the value of or need to connect what happens in the doctoral program to the operative life of the profession.

What I am suggesting is that doctoral programs can be so lofty, so academically rarified, that their interface with the needs of school music teaching can be indiscernible or only minimally discernable. I am quite sure that many doctoral students, especially at the beginning stage of their work, have been confronted with an uncomfortable, troubling disconnect between what they are studying and what they have experienced as being the operational life of school music and the needs of school music. At the same time, however, doctoral programs that do not widen the horizons of their students far beyond the workaday matters that school music teachers must confront in their jobs would be derelict in their duty to prepare leaders, even visionaries, for the profession as a whole.

What is the correct posture here? Should doctoral study foster imaginative leadership and scholarship for the profession of which it is one part? Or should it focus on sharpening the teaching effectiveness within existing school music programs? Is some sort of balance between the two aspirations the desideratum? How do we decide, or at least debate this matter? These questions are at the very core of many others needing to be addressed at the philosophical level, because they raise the issue of what doctoral study is supposed to be in the first place—how it might be defined as to its purposes. I do not believe we have reached sufficient clarity about these questions to allow us to be as effective as we need to be.

Clarity about purposes is, inevitably, clarity about values—values of music and the learning and teaching of music. In regard to the issue of the values of music education a history does indeed exist, that history having been told by various music education historical scholars, Michael Mark as one instance (Mark, 1996), and by some philosophers of music education, Estelle Jorgenson for example (Jorgensen, 1994). I will not attempt here to review their work, or that of others, which is readily available. Instead, I want to offer a description of the values that seem to me to be presently in play as being influential in music education and therefore requiring all music educators, at every level and in every aspect of the profession, to be acquainted with them, because they exert enormous influence on what it is that we can be as a profession.

The issue related to this paper is how we can build doctoral programs that prepare leaders for the values music education has come to claim for itself. Remember, the operational level of the program—all the ways I have discussed (and many I have not) where the rubber hits the road in the reality of what doctoral programs actually do and how they do it—depends on the assumptions of what the values of the field of music education ought to be. So this material on current values is not academic: it is foundational. I undertake this explanation with some trepidation because I will have to be very brief, and therefore not terribly subtle, and that is a bit dangerous in matters of philosophical value claims. I accept that danger and hope readers will be forgiving if I am not able to do complete justice to all the extant philosophical positions being taken in our field. (For more extended and somewhat differently addressed discussions see Reimer, 2003.)

THE AESTHETIC EDUCATION BACKGROUND

I start with the most influential set of claims during the time doctoral programs have been in existence; that is, since roughly the 1940s, or the middle of the twentieth century. That set of claims, stemming from the earliest doctoral work, gradually attained the name "aesthetic education." That was the name I was introduced to when I began graduate work with Charles Leonhard, who had been a student in the seminal doctoral program at Teachers College of Columbia University and then went off to the University of Illinois to establish an outpost of the empire, as other graduates of that program did around the country.

There is an entire literature on aesthetic education, of course, not just in music but in all the arts, far too encompassing to attempt to deal with here. But I have tried very hard to summarize the basic beliefs of what I, at any rate, understand as the defining elements of aesthetic education. Others are likely to see it somewhat differently or substantially differently. In philosophy few if any terms attain unanimity about their definition. In fact, philosophy, in one important sense, is largely an ongoing debate about the various possible meanings of terms. Here is my attempt at a definition, or, better, description.

Aesthetic education in music attempts to enhance learnings related to the following propositions:

1. Musical sounds (as various cultures construe what these are) create and share meanings available only from such sounds.

2. Creating musical meanings, and partaking of them, requires an amalgam of mind, body, and feeling.
3. Musical meanings incorporate within them a great variety of universal/cultural/individual meanings (ideas, beliefs, values, associations, etc.) transformed by musical sounds.
4. Gaining its special meanings requires direct experience with musical sounds, deepened and expanded by skills, knowledge, understandings, attitudes, and sensitivities that education can cultivate (Reimer, 2003).

Notice that this set of descriptions, or assumptions, focuses on musical experience as its core value. If you believe that this value system—this set of constructs about what music education ought to be—is valid, you would naturally want to build programs of music teaching and learning in schools that are devoted to the pursuit of that value, and to build doctoral programs that supported and provided leadership for attaining that value. So there would be a consistency of action, in doctoral programs and in their influences, based on a clearly articulated set of philosophically grounded beliefs.

In fact, that was the attempt and the direction of much of the work in schools and in doctoral programs for much of the second half of the twentieth century and continuing to this day. Partly, that was because for a long time there were few if any well argued alternatives. Also, I believe, it was because there was a good match between generally held ideas about music at that time and about the ways music could best be taught. That match also continues to this day.

However (and this is a big however) toward the later years of the twentieth-century philosophical work in music education had progressed to the point where viable alternatives did indeed start to crop up, some of them challenging the notions of aesthetic education or at least expanding and clarifying those notions. Now we are faced with a variety of value stances that need to be attended to as to their convincingness and desirability in addition to, or as substitutes for, the initial set of beliefs and aspirations that had guided much of our work for many years. Here is an overview of what, in my view, are some of the important alternative value orientations in play in contemporary music education philosophy. Remember, please, that this material is not academic. It is foundational background for what our operational programs of doctoral study need to exemplify.

EDUCATION FOR DEMOCRATIC CITIZENSHIP

Given the present conflicted state of the world and perceived threats from a variety of perspectives not in consonance with American construals of democracy, a good deal of attention is being paid to the need for the schools to emphasize values understood by many to be foundational to the nature and success of the American way of life. Here is one typical set of value claims that education should pursue in hopes of maintaining and strengthening democratic citizenship, focusing on the kinds of citizens this nation requires if it is to be viable, and what education should contribute toward fostering a democratic citizenry.

1. The Personally Responsible Citizen: To solve social problems and improve society, citizens must have good character; be honest, responsible, law-abiding; work and pay taxes; volunteer; contribute in a variety of ways and levels to the society's health and functioning.
2. The Participatory Citizen: To solve social problems and improve society, citizens must take leadership positions for social betterment; organize community efforts; apply strategies for accomplishing communal tasks; actively participate in both established and newly formed community structures.
3. The Justice-Oriented Citizen: To solve social problems and improve society, citizens must seek out and address areas of injustice; question, debate, and change unhealthy social patterns; address root causes of inequities; know how to utilize democratic procedures to effect systemic change (Westheimer & Kahne, 2004). Also see, for a theoretical foundation for the obligations of music education in regard to democracy, Woodford, 2005.

This agenda would seem at first glance to be a far cry from that of aesthetic education, with its devotion to the values and influences of musical (and, sometimes, other arts) experiences. If doctoral programs in music education were to pursue democratic citizenship (as construed above) as being their fundamental, primary goal, they would have to change in radical ways, as would music teacher education programs and the school music programs in which such teachers worked. The changes would be nothing short of revolutionary, transforming the history of music education in the United States and around the world in ways few have ever envisioned or desired. I doubt if anyone in education, the authors of the above-mentioned paper included, would argue that such changes are to be expected.

But what might very well be expected is that music teachers, and their supportive structure of graduate study including doctoral study, could and should make reasonable, relevant contributions to those overarching values while attending to those values in the contexts of their specialized and valuable contributions to music education as such. How that might be accomplished without abandoning long-held values for cultivating musical experiences would be an agenda for which doctoral programs might well provide leadership. I suspect that this is a posture with which proponents of education for democratic citizenship would be quite comfortable, and with which many if not most music educators would be more than willing to cooperate, myself among them (Reimer, 2007).

MUSIC EDUCATION AND POSTMODERN VALUES

Under the influences of the postmodern movement in philosophy and in culture generally, much of life has become viewed as being politically grounded and politically motivated. Here are several positions about the obligations of music education in regard to cultivating postmodern values, as have been argued by various music education thinkers.

1. Music teachers must be advocates for social betterment, supporting issues relating to feminism, sexual orientation, and racial, religious, ethnic, economic (etc.) equality.
2. "High" and "low" music is a false, elitist distinction.
3. No canon of musical excellence exists. That notion, that certain musical products or processes are inherently superior to others, is a political power play that must be resisted.
4. There are no valid criteria of goodness in music. The idea that such criteria exist is motivated by those desiring to protect a privileged position, and should be disdained.
5. Musical experience itself is a contested concept, with limited value if it does not recognize the self-serving, narrow constructions embedded within it.
6. Reasoned positions about the nature and value of music, like all such positions about values, are subversive attempts to impose particular elitist views on those with lesser ability to combat them.

7. All musical involvements imply power relations: all must be conceived as opportunities to redress social inequities.

These and many other views based on the premise that "everything is political," have strong implications for what music education, like education in every subject, should attempt to accomplish as its primary mission; that is, a mission that is essentially political. As with the view oriented toward democracy, an adoption of this view would lead music education in a direction it has never before taken. But understood as one dimension of what music educators need to attend to when musical learning raises political issues, as it certainly can and often does, the obligation to view music as intimately related to larger societal issues would seem to be reasonable and desirable. Protecting music from the realities of its societal/political contexts, as if it was somehow too "pure" or "artistic" to associate itself with such matters, can make our contribution seem unreal, as, unfortunately, we have often been seen to be. It may well be possible, and highly valuable, to incorporate within our expertise as educators appropriate attention to the larger political realities in which music dwells, while also, as foundational, sensitizing students to the particular ways that music adds its incomparable meanings to any and all other meanings with which it can deal, including, inevitably, political issues.

I find this synergistic recognition of the relation of music to other realities to be convincing and positive. Surely doctoral level study can incorporate the issue of how the profession can accommodate itself to contemporary concerns with politically driven agendas while also honoring the power of musical experience to incorporate, yet transcend, or transform, those agendas in the ways only music can do. That would, then, influence the ways music teachers in the schools can address such concerns as appropriate to the students they are teaching. I see no loss to musical experience and musical learning in such a posture, and an important gain in the relevance of our work to related issues important to all people.

OTHER (NON-POSTMODERN) OPTIONS

One more set of philosophical value claims for music education needs to be acknowledged; it, too, is important for those of us involved in doctoral programs to incorporate within the dimensions of our operational responsibilities. These are views related to values other than political ones. Here is a sample.

1. Music education for moral betterment: justice, civility, goodness, fidelity, mutuality, humanity, freedom, refinement, dignity, love of wisdom, etc.
2. Music education as either circumscribed in the musical learning opportunities it offers or as comprehensive in offering learning opportunities.
3. Music education as "strong-boundaried" (separated from other studies), or as "weak-boundaried" (integrated with other studies).
4. Music education for utilitarian ends: high test scores, math/science/language learnings, spatial-temporal reasoning, etc.

Each of these options is based on a particular set of value claims for which music education is understood to be responsible.

(1) In the first, music is seen as a means to foster morality, and music teachers are to emphasize that goal, perhaps even make it the primary one. If that was adopted as the basic mission of music education the profession would rightfully be held accountable for achieving its claim of making all students more moral (as defined by the terms listed above). That would necessitate a major reconception of what music instruction validly consists of, and how it would then be carried out. Doctoral study would have to focus on issues of moral education through music and how to prepare school music teachers and programs to pursue such values and to demonstrate that they are being achieved.

If this seems an unlikely—perhaps impossible—prospect, it might be remembered that, as with democracy and politics, music instruction focused on musical experience can and no doubt should include all due attention to values that are as much connected to music as they are to all other subjects in schooling. Some school subjects do in fact focus directly on political, moral, and other such issues—social studies, political science, social psychology, philosophy, and others. Math, the sciences, history, and so forth, like music, have obligations to foster moral values important to the cultures in which schools reside, not by claiming primary responsibility or accountability for them, but by supporting them as related to their particular disciplinary emphases. That, I would argue, is an acceptable and humane position for music education, and I would hope that doctoral programs would clarify for students why that is the case and how they can exert leadership in both teacher education and in research/scholarship that would operationalize that posture in ways respectful both of musical learnings and of various moral issues connected to such learnings.

(2) In the matter of music education programs being limited to, or focused on, a highly proscribed selection of ways to be musical, or as being inclusive of as many was to be musical as possible, strong disagreements exist at present in the profession. On the one hand the appearance of the national content standards for music education signaled in a dramatic way that our long-standing programs of school music need to be reconceived as being responsible for far more inclusive opportunities for musical learning than had ever before been imagined. Each of the nine content areas has its own validity and importance as a foundational dimension of music education, and each must be attended to genuinely in a comprehensive music program. To achieve such a major overhaul toward inclusiveness—toward breaking through the standardized, narrowly constricted offerings that have characterized us throughout our history—calls upon a profession-wide effort for which leadership of a variety of sorts will be necessary. Doctoral programs, in their strategic position to influence teacher education and the research needed to undergird a comprehensive posture, would serve a crucially important role in achieving this new vision.

But on the other hand the centuries-old concentration in American music education on the single dimension of performance as being the sole, or, at least, the principal way to encounter music, continues to hold sway in our offerings with little recognition that there might, in fact, be an alternative way to conceive what music education could and should provide. Given the overwhelming exclusivity of performance as what the American school music program has historically consisted of and continues to consist of, the musical learnings delineated in the content standards can be provided only within performance ensembles and general music approaches that have long pursued other ends, and, therefore, cannot, under present conditions, be addressed comprehensively in any equitable way.

In addition, one recent influential philosophical argument for "praxialism" gives the impression of advocating for the continuation of the status quo of performance as being the obligatory basis for all musical learnings, with other musicianship roles attended to as supplementary, thereby seeming to perpetuate the narrowly delimited conception of music education that has pervaded our history (Elliott, 1995). Other construals of praxialism are strikingly more inclusive, and recent attempts have been made by Elliott to widen the purview of accepted praxial engagements, correcting his initial argument for that position in response to the many severe critiques of it (Elliott, 2005). Under the limited notion of praxial music education, doctoral programs would require little change except to argue more

cogently for music education needing to be, properly, delimited in the ways
it has been historically, and to promote research and scholarship that would
bolster that conviction.

Here, also, I have proposed a synergistic approach to this seemingly but
not necessarily discordant issue, recognizing that performance is one essential learning opportunity among all the others to which the standards call
our attention. In that vision, present opportunities in performance would
in no way be diminished (and, hopefully, can be enhanced), and would, in
fact, provide an excellent model for how one particular way to be musical,
so successfully pursued, could be applied to creating similarly excellent opportunities in each of the other ways that most people in our culture engage
themselves with music. Doctoral programs would need to assist in enhancing both clarity about the issues entailed in this matter and in devising
operational solutions toward maintaining the values of musicianship roles
while expanding beyond them to more equitably represent in our programs
in the schools the values of music for the large majority who do not choose
to engage themselves in those roles.

(3) The soft- versus hard-boundaried issue is an interesting and important one for which doctoral programs need to provide clarity (Detels, 1999).
Music programs in schools and colleges/universities have a long history of
having been given a good deal of leeway to go their own way undisturbed
by interfaces with other subjects/aspects of education, much to the relief of
many music educators. My discussions above of the need for music educators to open up to political, moral, and expanded musical role possibilities
(aesthetic education, if one desires to retain that term, conceived in its holistic identity), may seem somewhat intrusive in the context of our historical
isolation and the comforts that has provided us.

Now an even more severe intrusion has begun to occur, in the expectation
that, in some way so far not clearly understood or implemented, music is
to be "integrated" within education. I will avoid tackling this complex issue
here (see the discussion in Reimer, 2003, pp. 233–237) except to say that
while extremism of isolation has its severe hazards, extremism of integration has them equally. We have often been so separated from the larger life
of the school as to seem irrelevant to its values, and we have often been so
"integrated" as to lose our precious identity. There is a position in which the
two extremes can be moderated sufficiently for music to retain its integrity
as an art and an artful practice, therefore as a cognitive domain, while also
participating in clarifying for students the similarities and differences music bears to all other endeavors. Notice that the national content standard
of relevance to this matter, number eight, is *"Understanding relationships*

between music, the other arts, and disciplines outside the arts" (emphasis added) (*National Standards for Arts Education*, 1994). That language was carefully crafted to avoid any notion that music is to be aggregated with other subjects in ways that dilute or eliminate its unique nature, while also recognizing that relationships with other learnings do indeed exist and are important to understand. At the doctoral level the complexities of this issue can be and very much need to be addressed, so that, in turn, teachers being prepared for school jobs, and the programs they construct, can avoid the difficulties and distortions that extreme boundaried positions, whether isolated or integrated, often cause.

(4) Much the same can be said about the claims for instrumental values to which music can contribute without being held primarily responsible. Every subject in schools, and every school involvement, has implications for and influences on a number of associated values and learnings, music not excepted. When we pursue the learnings related to that which identifies music genuinely, we can accept that many other resulting effects are likely to occur (some beneficial and some, unfortunately, not) and thereby relieve ourselves of taking on responsibilities we cannot and should not be expected to fulfill as our primary contribution. Teacher education programs need to be guided by the wisdom about this matter that well prepared doctoral students can afford. Our programs at the doctoral level cannot be optimally effective when this issue, as the others addressed in this discussion of philosophical value expectations, is left unaddressed.

IMPLICATIONS FOR DOCTORAL PROGRAMS

So what does all this mean for doctoral programs in music education? I believe we have to adapt ourselves to the reality of a new, healthy, exciting, yet more uncertain foundational posture as to the purposes of music education and therefore the purposes of doctoral study in music education. Doctoral-level leadership for the profession, by those who are stewards of doctoral programs and those who are students in them, needs to reflect the philosophical complexity now existing in our profession. We need to both honor those complexities and also build a foundation for our operational work that is sufficiently consistent; that is, grounded in a workably coherent set of values, to keep us from falling into chaos, where, as the poetic image has it, "the center does not hold."

Some would argue that the center does not have to hold; that chaos or at least disarray is inevitable and desirable. I do not believe that this is the case. So I have argued for a philosophical posture in which we both recognize and consider alternatives, and also search for as much overlap, or points of acceptable agreement, or underlying concordances that reach below unnecessary disagreements, to enable us to reach more secure principles under which we can find values that unify us as a profession rather than keep us in constant tension if not belligerence in regard to our values and purposes. I believe this is not only possible but essential if we are to achieve what a genuine profession requires—sufficient unity to provide a basis for sufficient diversity. I believe that is also true for the challenges facing a world in a state of dangerous, possibly catastrophic, discordance, as now is the case, a world hungering for a synergistic rather than an antagonistic value orientation.

If doctoral programs are to cultivate leaders for music education, both for the profession's present status and for its future, our students need to be steeped in the realities of the value issues we face and how these values can strengthen us as a profession rather than weaken us. And they need to then bring their students in undergraduate and graduate programs into the conversation so that as teachers in the schools they can both reflect diverse values and also help build a stronger, more securely founded profession. That is a major responsibility at all levels of music education, with doctoral programs in a key position for the leadership training that will determine our profession's fortunes in the future.

That means that those of us who are engaged in doctoral level work need each other more than ever. We need to share and build on our collective wisdom and experience. We cannot just assume that things will improve, in both the operational and philosophical levels of doctoral programs, if we just wait around for that to happen. We have to *make* it happen. Which means that we need some mechanism to *allow* it to happen, a mechanism that can promote and support the ongoing, cooperative efforts that these kinds of challenges require.

We need, in short, some sort of ongoing association devoted specifically to the many challenges inherent in forging a more secure foundation for doctoral programs in music education. Along with creating a thorough history of our doctoral programs in their operational and philosophical dimensions we need to create a regularized opportunity for debating and planning the future of doctoral study in our field, a task unlikely to be accomplished without a unifying organizational structure.

I urge all of us who are responsible for the highest level of attainment in our field to energize seriously on the accomplishment of these two interrelated projects. The development of a historical overview, cooperatively pursued, can provide a model for a great variety of other such coordinated research endeavors, a model we greatly need if the complexities of our issues are to be dealt with genuinely and sufficiently. And what better way to be able to plan for such endeavors than through an ongoing, structured association focused on doctoral study in all its many dimensions. These are essential and achievable aspirations, not only for the health and viability of doctoral study but for the health and viability of the music education profession as a whole.

REFERENCES

Boardman, E. (1990). Music teacher education. In R. W. Houston (Ed.), *Handbook of research on teacher education* (p. 730). New York: Macmillan Publishing Company.

Colwell, R. (Ed.). (1992). *Handbook of research on music teaching and learning.* New York: Schirmer Books.

Colwell, R., & Richardson, C. (Eds.). (2002). *The new handbook of research on music teaching and learning.* New York: Schirmer Books.

Detels, C. (1999). *Soft boundaries: Re-visioning the arts and aesthetics in American education.* Westport, CT: Bergin and Garvey.

Elliott, D. J. (1995). *Music matters: A new philosophy of music education.* Oxford: Oxford University Press.

Elliott, D. J. (2002). Philosophical perspectives on research. In R. Colwell & C. Richardson (Eds.), *The new handbook of research on music teaching and learning.* New York: Schirmer Books.

Elliott, D. J. (Ed.). (2005). *Praxial music education: Reflections and dialogues.* Oxford: Oxford University Press.

Jorgensen, E. (1994). Justifying music instruction in American public schools: An historical perspective. *Bulletin of the Council for Research in Music Education* (pp. 120, 17–31).

Mark, M. L. (1996). *Contemporary music education.* New York: Schirmer Books.

National standards for arts education: What every young American should know and be able to do in the arts. (1994). Reston, VA: Music Educators National Conference.

Raths, J. (2002). Fuzzy teacher education. In R. Colwell & C. Richardson (Eds.), *The new handbook of research on music teaching and learning* (pp. 757–758). New York: Schirmer Books.

Reimer, B. (1985). Toward a more scientific approach to music education research. *Bulletin of the Council for Research in Music Education* (pp. 83, 1–22).

Reimer, B. (1992). Toward a philosophical foundation for music education research. In R. Colwell (Ed.), *Handbook of research on music teaching and learning.* New

York: Schirmer Books. Revised and republished in Colwell, R. (Ed.). (2006). *Research methodology in music education*. Oxford: Oxford University Press.

Reimer, B. (1994). Thinking globally about a research agenda for general music. *General Music Today* (pp. 10–12).

Reimer, B. (2003). *A philosophy of music education: Advancing the vision*. Upper Saddle River, NJ: Prentice Hall.

Reimer, B. (2007). Roots of inequity and injustice: The challenges for music education. *Music Education Research*, 9(2), 196–204.

Stubley, E. V. (1992). Philosophical Foundations. In R. Colwell (Ed.), *Handbook of research on music teaching and learning*. New York: Schirmer Books.

Westheimer, J., & Kahne, J. (2004). What kind of citizen? The politics of educating for democracy. *American Educational Research Journal*, 41(2), 237–269.

Wilcox, S., & Upitis, R. (2002). Strengthening the teaching of music educators in higher education. In R. Colwell & C. Richardson (Eds.), *The new handbook of research on music teaching and learning*. New York: Schirmer Books.

Woodford, P. (2005). *Democracy and music education*. Bloomington: Indiana University Press.

IIC

THE ROLE OF RESEARCH

"So, what do you do?" a new acquaintance asks me at a party.

I gauge how general or specific my reply should be. "I'm in music," I reply.

"Oh! How nice." Or "Wonderful." Or "I *love* music." Or "Aren't you lucky!" Recently, "That's beautiful."

All of us in music and music education have experienced, time and again, responses like these when we reveal our profession in a general way. And what's not to like about this image of our work? Except, of course, the eerie feeling that, despite being correct as far as it goes, it sure doesn't go very far to explain what our daily realities entail.

I sometimes say, when the question to me warrants more specificity, "I'm in music education, and I mostly do research." I know what to expect in that case. "Research? How can there be research in music?"

I try, then, to give a sense of the things music education researchers do, but I generally observe people's eyes glazing over, being unable to process what I'm saying no matter how clearly I attempt to explain it, or perhaps just finding it enormously boring. "Interesting," they're likely to say. "Um, excuse me. I need to refresh my drink."

Yet music education researchers of all types are among our most devoted, most passionate professionals, secure in the conviction that what they do is foundational for our success. This is a conviction and a devotion I fully share. The following essays consider some of the key issues facing those involved in the field of research in music education, and all who can benefit from their work.

18

TOWARD A MORE SCIENTIFIC APPROACH TO MUSIC EDUCATION RESEARCH

I am committed to research as central to the health of music educa-tion—not, however, to many of the ways we do it.

When invited to address the research community at the 1984 MENC national conference in Chicago, I vow to hit hard at what I see as fun-damental weaknesses in our approaches. Because I am well aware that my criticisms will be difficult for many researchers to take and that counterarguments need to be expressed, I request that when my article is published it be followed by responses from several leaders in research. We have had little opportunity for straightforward debate about research in music education; I feel it is high time to begin. The point of having it is to raise issues that need addressing, to air out important controversies, and to move ahead refreshed by the dialog and more clear about where we need to go.

I am delighted with the directness and thoughtfulness of the responses published along with my speech. (Interested readers will find them in the CRME Bulletin issue cited.) I benefit significantly from the interplay and, I hope, the larger research community does so as well.

Since then, several major changes have indeed been made in what we regard as research, with the rise of qualitative approaches being, perhaps, the most important. Our work as researchers continues to expand in both depth and breadth, and my own perspective has grown also. What our re-search continues to need most, unfortunately, is an organizational structure that will enhance its utility in what our teachers in the schools and colleges/ universities do. We still have a long way to go to achieve that. My proposals in this essay, as well as those made by others, need to be examined, refined, and put into practice. Organizing our research for optimal effect remains a crucial, unfinished task.

The following essay was originally published in the *Council for Research in Music Education*, Bulletin 83 (Summer 1985). Used by permission.

Music education research, like all systematic attempts to understand more about human beings, has as its most fundamental datum that its subjects— people—are paradoxical in essence. The paradox of the human condition is so well known, so obvious, that it usually remains tacit, as a given that needs no mention. Making it explicit will allow me to explore its many implications for the scholarly work we do. The paradox is that every human being is, in certain respects, like all other human beings; like some other human beings; like no other human beings.

In this paper I intend to suggest that modern science, that is, science over the past 400 or so years, has achieved its wonders largely by focusing on the first and second aspects of the paradox—how people are all alike or partially alike. Contemporary science, that is, science over the past 50 or so years, has revolutionized our understanding of the human condition by its discoveries relating to the third aspect of the paradox—how people are unique. This recent development in the human sciences has been paralleled by an equally dramatic revolution in the physical sciences, totally and irrevocably altering the older idea that nature could be understood by reducing its complexities to underlying mechanical principles.

Science in the future will have to embrace all three aspects of the human paradox because all three are true. It will also have to devise new models of how the physical world is organized. The dilemma of our present times stems in large part from this profound shift in world view, because the old retains much of its power, the new cannot be ignored yet is in its formative stages, and the resolution of the issue cannot yet be glimpsed. From the macro level of global politics to the micro level of the meaning of each of our individual lives, the manifestations of this shifting of our ground are being felt, in the uncertainty, the instability, the confusion about our most basic beliefs that characterizes the world we live in, a world in the throes of one of the great turning points in human history.

Our humble work in music education research may seem to be miles away from such grandiose considerations. Not so. We are, or should be, affected by them profoundly, because in several important respects our small world of interest is exemplary of the tensions contemporary science is coping with. First of all, the need for greater recognition of the third aspect of the human paradox—the ways that people are different—is nowhere more basic than in the arts. Second, our approach to scientific work has been dominated by a reliance on assumptions and techniques now being severely criticized for their outdatedness in not adapting to the new realities science has begun to heap on us. When scientific method is backwardly conceived, narrowly applied, and oriented to a declining view of the human subjects it studies, the knowledge it produces is likely to exemplify several curious qualities. It will have a scientific look but only as a thin veneer—as a kind of caricature of science. It will produce individual bits of knowledge, each with a degree of technical polish but with limited or nonexistent utility and implication. The individual bits somehow will not add up: none seems to fit with or build upon another. The technical expertise will seem, to those who know the subject broadly and intuitively, to misrepresent the subject, to obscure rather than illuminate its nature. A mistrust of knowledge is likely to grow among those for whom research is not something to do but something to use. And for the community of research scholars a certain uneasiness is likely to be felt, a certain discomfort, a sense of isolation from its constituency, a lack of larger goals to provide meaning and direction and urgency to its work. The research effort will be at the periphery rather than at the heart of the larger profession.

Needless to say I believe these qualities characterize music education research to an unfortunate degree. I believe they are the product of historical forces, in that music education began its research effort at just that point in history when the old science had started to crumble but the new science was not yet ready—and is only now beginning to be ready—to build upon the old. We therefore did what was natural to do, which was to embrace what science had become and to try with all our characteristic energy and devotion and good intentions to bring ourselves quickly into the scientific mainstream as we understood it. And indeed we did so, achieving remarkable expertise for a field with practically no research history, no structures for the training of researchers, no reward system for those who were drawn to such work, no tradition of reliance on research by practitioners. We can and should be proud of how much was achieved in a very short time. We must, unfortunately, also be chastened by the shortcomings in our efforts and by the new efforts we must be willing to make in light of the fundamental changes we are living through.

Why must we change? How must we change? I wish I were capable of offering complete and authoritative answers to those questions. I am not. What I will try to do, to the best of my limited ability in this area of limitless complexity, is to give some general background about the changes that have occurred recently in scientific thinking about nature and about people[1] and then to pursue some of their implications for music education research at both general and specific levels. I will end by describing a major change in doctoral research procedures that will be inaugurated this year at Northwestern University as a response to the issues I will be raising in this paper and to the suggestions for change I will be offering.

Some 400 years ago, during the 16th century, the Western world began to shift its mental foundations. Before that time, during the medieval age, what people knew and the methods by which they added to knowledge were grounded in religious faith and circumscribed by religious faith. Medieval philosophers (those interested in questions of value) and medieval scientists (those interested in questions of the natural world) shared the same belief system and the same ways for exploring the human and natural realities they lived among. Reason was the major tool of knowing, but reason as an instrument of established belief—belief about God, the human soul, the right conduct, the relation of people to nature, the relation of nature to people. This elaborate mental construct, generally called "Scholasticism," provided the guidelines and tools for scholarship, while the Church, within which Scholasticism operated, provided the social and spiritual guidelines for culture. All aspects of human life transpired within this organic system: political, physical, social, intellectual, psychological, spiritual, artistic.

The medieval world view, like all world views, was a system of truth-making. What was true, what was real, what was factual, was, as it always is, a function of what was believed to be true and real and factual. Their system of beliefs, captured in their dominant metaphors, constituted the foundational myth of their culture, which was the myth of the Christian epic. In that truth-system, God and his magnificent order were locked in a titanic struggle with the Devil, who, unfortunately, seemed to win most of the battles, but who would surely lose the struggle eventually because God and the Church had so ordained it. Human life was ultimately meaningful because no matter how difficult life seemed to be on earth God had higher plans for it. How did one know that? One knew because one had faith. Faith and truth were one and the same.

The term "myth" has taken on the meaning of a fiction—something that is not true but is widely believed to be true. But underneath that meaning is a far deeper one in which a culture's myth is the symbol for what truth can be for that culture in the first place. In that sense, myth and truth are one and the same.

And it is in that profound sense that we must view the oceanic change that occurred 400 years ago, when the older myth was superseded by a new one—one that to a very large extent continues to define the lives we live today.

Our modern myth is based on two revolutionary occurrences in the 16th century. The first was the discovery by Nicolas Copernicus (1473–1543) that the earth revolved around the sun; a discovery so momentous, given the belief system of his time, that he wisely delayed its publication until the year of his death and then presented it only as a tentative hypothesis. Soon after, Galileo Galilee (1564–1642) verified Copernicus's discovery and proclaimed it to the world (an act that did not endear him to the Church).

The second occurrence, even more profound in its revolutionary implications, was the fast-growing conviction that truth-making required a totally different approach from the one then accepted. Truth was to be found, not in human faith, or values, or spiritual yearnings, but in a brand new way to conceive the world and explore the world—a way we now call modern science. Galileo articulated the two basic premises of this new concept of truth. First, the world and the people in it must be understood as objects; that is, objectively. Second, the method used to study the world must be empirical; that is, based on verifiable procedures. In order to follow these two premises Galileo argued that scientists must restrict themselves to studying only those properties of the world that were capable of being measured and quantified. Other aspects, such as colors, sounds, tastes, smells, he regarded as merely subjective projections on to the world and so should be excluded from the realm of science.

Galileo's insights were refined by Francis Bacon (1561–1626) who was the first to conceptualize the inductive procedure of making experiments, drawing conclusions from them, and then testing them in further experiments. These procedures provided a technical methodology for generating truth. They also, as one important side effect, shifted people's relation to nature from one of submission and adaptation to nature to one of control and manipulation of nature. As Bacon put it, nature had to be "hounded in her wanderings," "bound into service," and made our "slave."[2] We are now in the process of reassessing whether our relation to nature is fundamentally askew.

The renaissance of human thought occurring in those years, laying the foundation of the modern world, found its fruition in two magnificent thinkers: Rene Descartes (1596–1650) and Isaac Newton (1642–1727).

From Descartes we inherit a set of presumptions so powerfully internalized that we take them as verities. The first is that anything known must be known with certainty. As Descartes put it, "We reject all knowledge which is merely probable and judge that only those things should be believed which are perfectly known and about which there can be no doubts."[3] The second Cartesian principle was that the nature of nature is, at bottom, mathematical, and therefore totally objective and totally verifiable. The method used to arrive at ultimate objectivity is the method of radical doubt: you must keep doubting until you reach that which can no longer be doubted. And since the one thing that doubt depends upon is the thought of doubt, he arrives at his famous dictum as to what constitutes the fundamental human reality, which is thought. "I think," said Descartes, "therefore I exist." And with this identification of "being" and "thinking," the old mind-body dualism in Western civilization became a cornerstone of modern science and modern culture. We are only now beginning to recognize the limitations of the assumption that mind and matter are totally distinct.

The proper way to use thought to arrive at truth, said Descartes, is analytically. One must continue breaking reality into smaller and smaller pieces, arranging those pieces in logical order. The whole is nothing more than the sum of many parts, and the better you can verify the distinct parts the better you can understand nature and nature's creatures. And from this view arose the metaphor that has so powerfully determined our scientific understanding of the world and of ourselves: the metaphor of the machine. Taking his cue from the wonderful machines being built in his time, especially the clock, which had reached a high degree of sophistication, Descartes had a ready-made metaphor that perfectly suited his assumptions. As he said, "We see clocks, artificial fountains, mills and other similar machines which, though merely man-made, have nonetheless the power to move by themselves in several different ways. . . . I do not recognize any difference between the machines made by craftsmen and the various bodies that nature alone composes."[4]

And with this metaphor, a new system of truth-making—that is, a new myth—was given birth. It has lived to this very day. The specific machines cited as illustrative of reality keep changing, the latest being the computer, but the idea has remained constant. The incredible achievements of modern science have been built on the foundational idea—the myth-making metaphor—that Descartes gave us. That this myth is now breaking down accounts for much of the turmoil in modern intellectual life.

Descartes' revolutionary proposals were carried to fruition by the father of modern science, Isaac Newton, whose mathematical system explaining the mechanistic nature of the world and its creatures was a grand synthesis of the ideas of Copernicus, Galileo, Bacon, and Descartes. Newton's physics, including his invention of a new way to describe the motion of solids (from an apple falling off a tree onto his head to planets revolving around the sun), now called differential calculus, was so stunning an achievement that Albert Einstein called it "perhaps the greatest advance in thought that a single individual was ever privileged to make."[5]

For Newton both space and time were absolute, uninfluenced by anything happening within them. And everything existing within space and time—all matter—was made of the same material substance, reducible to a particle so small that it could no longer be reduced: the atom (meaning "a," without; "tomos," division or cutting). All physical phenomena are accounted for by the motion of these material particles, the motion being a manifestation of fixed mathematical laws. So all of the universe can be understood as a grand mechanical system, completely causal, completely determinate, and capable of being described with complete objectivity without ever mentioning the human observer of the system. Objective description of nature became the ideal of all science including the social sciences. These were so influenced by Newton's achievements in physics that they were regarded by some people to be a new "social physics." The systems of thought built on Newtonian premises spread to most aspects of 18th-century life, an era soon called the "Age of Enlightenment."

The major figure in the application of ideas from science to the realm of philosophy was Newton's contemporary John Locke (1632–1704). Adopting Newton's premises, Locke described society as a system that followed natural laws as determinate as those governing the physical world. The basic building block of society was the individual human being, who, like the identical atoms constituting all other matter, was born completely equal to and identical in potential with all other human beings. In his famous metaphor he declared the human mind at birth to be a *tabula rasa*, and all it was to become would be a function of the sensory experience impinging on it and the systems of behavior it found itself among. People are objects like atoms and their behaviors are a function of objective stimuli applied by society. Arrange conditions properly and individuals as well as their social systems would then behave accordingly. The far-reaching and long-lasting influence of these ideas should be self-evident. (More than one wit has suggested that B. F. Skinner should be "Locked up.")

Newton's system was extended over the next two centuries to include a broader sphere of physical phenomena—the motion of fluids, elastic substances, heat, gases, sounds—and always his basic premises worked. It was confirmed again and again that the truth-system based on the gathering of objective evidence, the myth of reality as determinate, the metaphor of the world as machine, was a complete and sufficient picture of the universe and all within it.

Then, beginning in the second half of the 19th century, Newton's system began to break down. It was discovered that electric and magnetic phenomena involved a new type of force that could not be described by the mechanistic model. Einstein later clarified that electromagnetic fields were entities which could travel through empty space and could not be explained mechanically.

Parallel to this fundamental challenge to the Newtonian view was the birth of a totally different conception of how natural phenomena came into existence: the idea of evolution. Ever since antiquity it had been assumed that there was a chain of nature, but that it was fixed in its hierarchy, starting at the top with God and working down to human beings, lower forms of life, inanimate matter. This view was well suited to the Judeo-Christian outlook and to Newtonian physics. But first with Lamarck (1744–1829), then with Darwin (1809–1882), and later with a great variety of accruing evidence, the universe and everything in it became understood as an ever changing system, a system rife with paradox in that life forms seem to move from simplicity to complexity while the second law of thermodynamics established that physical systems proceed spontaneously in the direction of ever increasing disorder, called entropy.

By the end of the 19th century Newtonian mechanics was full of holes but still believed to be basically correct. Then, as Fritjof Capra points out,

> The first three decades of our century changed this situation radically. Two developments in physics, culminating in relativity theory and in quantum theory, shattered all the principal concepts of the Cartesian world view and Newtonian mechanics. The notion of absolute space and time, the elementary solid particles, the fundamental material substance, the strictly causal nature of physical phenomena, and the objective description of nature—none of these concepts could be extended to the new domains into which physics was now penetrating.[6]

It would take far more knowledge than I possess to explain in any detail the revolution in understandings about reality that modern physics has caused. A few ideas will have to suffice to give a sense of the profundity of the changes that now confront us in trying to grasp what the "real" might be like.

At the level of the building blocks of matter—the level of subatomic structure—experiments early in this century established some startling results. Matter, it turns out, is not made of the solid particles always assumed to exist. Electrons and protons and neutrons and other aspects of matter ("aspects" is the apt word) are sometimes explainable as particles occupying a very small space and sometimes can only be explained as waves spread out over vast regions of space. No subatomic "object" has any intrinsic qualities at all independent of its environment and the means being used to observe it. Matter does not so much "exist" as have "tendencies to exist," and events at that level do not so much "occur" as have "tendencies to occur." The probabilities underlying matter are not probabilities about objects but more like probabilities about interconnections. As Niels Bohr said, "Isolated material particles are abstractions, their properties being definable and observable only through their interaction with other systems."[7]

Another way to put this is that, while classical mechanics assumes that the whole is the sum of its parts, quantum mechanics has demonstrated that the whole determines the behavior of the parts. And what also determines the behavior of "matter-forces" is the question asked of it. Investigate it in one way and it will yield one set of results. Investigate it another way and it will yield a different set. "It" does not exist separate from our idea of it. Apparently, then, our consciousness of the world is inseparable from the existent nature of the world. As Einstein said very early in this revolutionary period, "Physical concepts are free creations of the human mind and are not, however it may seem, uniquely determined by the external world."[8] The myth of objectivity, of verifiability, of truth as something existing out there awaiting our discovery and of science as a value-free and objective description of that truth, is now a myth in tatters.

Parallel to these truth-shaking discoveries about the external world was a comparable set of discoveries about the internal world of human mentality. The most profound of these, comparable in generative potential for a totally new world view to what occurred when it was learned that the earth revolves around the sun, was the revelation by Sigmund Freud (1856–1939) and his followers that human beings have a subconscious. Just as Einstein demonstrated that space and time are not absolute but relative, we now must also come to grips with the fact that consciousness itself is not absolute, but exists in relation to, is in constant interaction with, and perhaps is only one function of a vastly more complex dynamic system that constitutes the human psyche.

I would suggest that consciousness is analogous to a melody in a 19th-century symphony. The unconscious constitutes the rhythm, harmony, counterpoint, texture, tone color, dynamics, and form that surrounds and gives meaning to the melody. It will take centuries, I believe, for the awesome complexity of the human psyche to be understood: we are now only able to take the first few, faltering baby steps in that direction.

Added to this have been more recent understandings about the effects of personality structure on how people process knowledge, such as by Carl G. Jung; the complexity of human intuition and the multileveled nature of knowing, such as by Michael Polanyi; the generative, unpredictable nature of brain function, such as by Karl Pribram; the subjective, self-selecting process by which information from outside is perceived by the senses and organized in our memory systems, such as explained by Thomas Horning;[9] the influence of language and culture and history on what it is possible for human beings to know, such as by Noam Chomsky and Susanne Langer in her last volumes of *Mind: An Essay on Human Feeling* and by Nelson Goodman and a host of others; and we emerge with a picture of the human mind that is as incapable of being grasped by the metaphor of a machine as is the universe incapable of being so understood.

No existing metaphor captures the complexity of what now confronts our understanding of ourselves and our world. Until a new metaphor and a new myth embodying it arise, we must be resigned to making the best of the old while recognizing its limitations, and being open to new, sometimes threatening directions: threatening because unfamiliar. We must resist simplistic regressions to the mechanistic model, such as some recent attempts to explain brain function and human mentality as analogous to computer function. As Gerald Edelman, head of the Laboratory of Molecular and Developmental Biology at Rockefeller University, and scientific chairman of the Neurosciences Research Program, explains,

> The brain, in its workings, is a selective system, more like evolution itself than like computation. Brain function . . . forms a seamless web with our understanding of how life developed on earth. The structure of the nervous system, that is, is not strictly determined by genes. Like the theory of evolution, this . . . puts an enormous emphasis on individual variation. The uniqueness of each human brain proves that our nature is born in freedom and individuality. The brain is *not* a computer. It's more like a garden. Every time the brain does something, it is different.[10]

Edelman's explanation is just one instance of a growing literature, from science as well as philosophy, on the limitations of the old Cartesian mind-body split, a dichotomy now being recognized as untenable outside the confines of the narrow band of phenomena to which Newtonian mechanics might still apply. "Clearly," says the brain scientist Karl Pribram, "we have come to the limit of usefulness of a distinction between the material and the mental."[11] Studies of brain physiology and morphology are helpful—even necessary—but we cannot expect from them an explanation of human history, human culture, human experience, human meaning. *Those* are what define the singular creatures we seem to be.

Within the context of the historical forces I have sketched so briefly, science continues its work. We as researchers—as scientists, if you will—must continue our work. We must, as all scientists must, search for order amid the chaos even as we recognize that chaos may well be inherent in any idea of order. And we must follow some guidelines: we must have some tools of investigation. The old tools developed under Newtonian presuppositions are clearly faulty but cannot simply be abandoned, in that new ones do not yet exist and the old methodologies continue to be valid for some aspects of our reality. We now recognize that those aspects, rather than being fully explanatory of the world, are applicable to only a narrow stratum of our world. So our expectations of what we can learn from the traditional research modes and how we can best use them must reflect our shifted perspective as to their infallibility.

How can we carry on our work with optimal effectiveness given the situation now confronting us? I would like to offer a few proposals, first about each traditional research mode and then about their functions in the unified system.

Philosophical and historical research are the best examples of the confusion from which we suffer as to what constitutes research in the first place. In one sense research is an activity—the basic activity of science. Is philosophy science? Is history science? College and university philosophy and history departments are not included among the science departments in that philosophical and historical scholarship are considered to be essential in the humanities or social studies. Yet there are "Arts and Sciences" divisions that include them, even if, strictly speaking, they are neither art nor science. I have no particular interest in this confusion except that it makes apparent the association of the word "science" with the classical Newtonian assumptions that the universe is completely objective; science therefore is and must be completely objective; and anything not completely objective is, *ipso facto*, not science. Those assumptions, as I have tried to show, are no longer tenable even in the so-called hard sciences.

I would like to suggest that, while it may take several generations for these conceptual dilemmas to be worked out, we can begin to move in the direction of solutions by being more flexible in our definition of science.

We should recognize that if scientific method is strictly conceived as being limited to experiments it is exemplary of the total scientific endeavor only under the narrowest, most regressive point of view. As we shall see the experiment itself has been so thoroughly reassessed that we are no longer sure how to use it. So it would seem reasonable to conceive science as an endeavor, carried out in a great variety of ways, to achieve conceptual clarity about ourselves and our world. That allows for philosophy and history to be part of the endeavor while also honoring the distinctions between science and those fields clearly not science, such as art and religion.

Philosophical research, then, attempts to clarify those concepts underlying the totality of science as broadly conceived. Its major functions are the unification of knowledge as in theories and principles, and the generation of knowledge by providing directionality to scholarship. For contemporary science, philosophy is essential in answering the questions that must be asked before any single further steps can be taken. What do you want to know? Why do you want to know it? What will "knowing it" consist of, given the inherent paradox of the human condition as being always like others and always not like others? I submit that science cannot proceed without the guidance of philosophical research on these questions.[12]

I further submit that much or most music education research is as meaningless as it is because it has proceeded without the guidelines implied by such questions. Science, we know now, is a value-laden, value-directed activity. Philosophy is the means for generating and clarifying values. If our research is not directly connected to that which we value, why should we expect that anyone would value our research? We simply cannot go on doing research study after research study on topics irrelevant to or only remotely related to the central values of our field, because to continue to do so is to continue to violate the most fundamental mission of science—the search for conceptual meaning. And there is, in fact, something we can do to improve the situation.

Historical research is usually associated with philosophical research because their traditional home is in the humanities rather than the sciences and both are inherently nonquantitative. But in many ways historical research is more fruitfully linked with descriptive research, the former attempting to tell us what was and the latter telling us what is.

They are linked as well by their centuries-old domination by the Newtonian assumption that history could give as an objective picture of the past and descriptive studies could give us an objective description of the present. Reflecting the breakdown of that assumption and the rise in the level of recognition that human lives are, in essential respects, unique, a dramatic shift has occurred in what we expect of history and of description. The older approach left us with information so shallow that its impact has been minimal. What can one do, after all, with studies that only scratch the surface of the human condition by limiting themselves to the quantitative and ignoring the only thing that matters about the quantitative, which is its qualitative significance?

In answer to that question an entirely different approach has arisen in recent years to the problem of description, an approach already having an impact on the research in our field. Following the lead of researchers in sociology, cultural anthropology, history, and education, we are beginning to do history which probes for the human dynamic underlying people and events in the past. And we are beginning to do description which takes us far below the surface of head-counting and behavior-counting.

One notable example of the new approach to descriptive research comes from our sister field, art education, in the work of one of its leading scholars, Elliot Eisner. Eisner proposes a research posture based on a concept of research as "educational criticism."[13] The first dimension of educational criticism is the descriptive, which attempts to portray in language the richness of qualitative life as it exists in the experience of children and teachers in schools. Rather than trying to be objective, clinical, quantitative, detached, as language attempted to be under the old science, current descriptive language must be as richly evocative, as deeply subjective, as the phenomena it is trying to capture for our understanding. Reading more like literature than like journalism, such descriptions aim directly to the human condition below the superficialities of how people seem to be all alike, to the level at which children are experiencing themselves and their world as singular individuals. Needless to say, the reality so depicted is radically different from the graphs and tables based on the assumption that to describe is to count.

Eisner's system includes interpretive and evaluative levels beyond the descriptive. Other systems approach the task somewhat differently. All aim for what is being called "deep description" or "thick description." The rationale behind this new approach to educational ethnography is that schools and schooling are among the most complex of human endeavors, and we have barely begun to look closely at their complexities. Older approaches to description have, in fact, obscured the reality they were supposed to clarify.

Description, whether of events from the past or of events in the present, is in its essence a value-laden, value-directed activity; a means for uncovering the fullness of human interactions with their world. If historical and descriptive studies are unconnected to the meaningfulness of occurrences, why should we expect that anyone would find them meaningful? Of course the facts and figures should be known, but these simply establish the outlines of what is being described. Because we have so often settled for the outlines we find ourselves bereft of knowledge about the dynamic interior system that constitutes the human lives we are suppose to understand and influence. And there is, in fact, something we can do to improve the situation.

Experimental research is the paradigm of the application of Newtonian mechanics to human settings. Therefore the contradictions it embodies are the most severe of any research mode. With every step in recent years toward recognition of the limitations of the older science and with every development pointing toward a new concept of the nature of physical and mental reality the experiment has been more severely distrusted both in its basic premises and in its techniques. We are becoming painfully aware of the misrepresentations, the falsifications, the distortions and the irrelevancies of the experiment when it is transported from the extreme point of the continuum where it is most effective—that is, where phenomena are most identical, as in chemicals and seeds and the like, to that extreme point at the other end of the continuum where phenomena are most unique—that is, among human beings. A few instances of these contradictions as they are now being recognized will illustrate the depth of the criticisms being directed toward classical experimental research when applied to the human sciences.

Experiments are convincing to the extent that they are able to control every variable surrounding the treatment. The infinite complexity of human interactions makes this not just difficult to achieve but incapable of being achieved. Every attempt to exercise more control makes the experiment less applicable to the real world in which humans live. This paradox, that the better the experiment the worse its utility, underlies the massive disillusionment with experimental research in education now being experienced.

Experiments depend on the equivalency of the items or factors being studied and the conditions under which they are being studied. Humans are the most extreme instances on earth of nonequivalence, both individually and systemically. Therefore, no experiment with humans can be replicated accurately: replication as such is an inoperable concept in the social sciences. The best we can do is to approximate roughly—not replicate. But without replication all experimental data must remain in a kind of evidential limbo.

Experiments are based on the assumption that there is a direct relationship between a treatment and a result. But in order to be sure of this several factors must obtain that are improbable or impossible in social settings. First, as already mentioned, all impinging variables must be controlled, but we know that uncontrolled variables are overwhelming in importance and complexity as compared to the puny treatments we are able to devise within the constraints of statistical design. The treatment must be sufficiently powerful and sufficiently long-lasting that results might reasonably be attributed to it or at least to some aspects of it, but we seldom if ever have the opportunity or the time to even approach such conditions. The treatment must never be artificial: it must resemble as much as possible the actualities in which we are interested. But to the extent it does it will be full of ambiguities and complexities not amenable to our designs. What we usually do, therefore, is tailor the experiment to some design we are capable of handling, thus insuring artificiality and therefore inapplicability before we even start.

When we look for the results of the treatment we do so in the context of the severe limitations of measurement, with which I shall assume we are all well acquainted. The crudity of our measurements is not just a matter of our inexperience or lack of expertise: it is an accurate reflection of the incompatibility of the concept of measurement when applied to human social settings. This realization has caused dramatic changes in recent approaches to educational evaluation, but the experiment does not use evaluation—it uses measurement. And those measurements, to further compound their inauthenticity, are almost always performed just once, in complete ignorance about the optimal time after a treatment to measure for the outcome, and about the likelihood that results of the treatment, if they exist at all, will not be constant but will rise and fall and blend with other learnings in ways we cannot even begin to comprehend.

Experiments require randomness as an essential component of design. Randomness is impossible in human research: not impossible because Miss Johnson's fifth grade class can't be split up, but impossible in the very essence of the human condition.

Experiments must achieve a minimum sample size in order to generate data. In the most profound sense in which it can be conceived, humans never constitute a sample larger than one.

Experiments require treatment of data. Every such treatment, rather than illuminating human realities, as we are often gulled into believing, subtly weakens veracity. Every single individual response or behavior or datum is, in its essence, already systemic individually and socially. Raw scores are abstractions—meaning subtractions—from reality. Averages are abstractions from reality. Comparisons of means further abstract. Ironies pile up. We depend on statistical significance testing as perhaps the major way to accept or reject our research hypotheses or null hypotheses. In doing so we are blithely ignorant of the scientific perversions we are committing. As Ronald P. Carver points out in his summary of thinking related to the role of significance testing,[14] it is a fantasy to assume that a certain level of significance tells us the probability that chance caused the mean difference between two research groups; it is a fantasy to assume that a certain level of significance tells us the confidence we can have in obtaining the same results if we were to replicate an experiment; it is a fantasy to assume that statistical significance reflects the probability that the research hypothesis is true and that the smaller the p the more true is the hypothesis; it is a fantasy to assume that statistical significance is in any way related to the importance of the size of a difference between two scores.

Carver pleads with researchers to ignore statistical significance testing when designing research, because a study with results that cannot be meaningfully interpreted without looking at statistical significance is a poor study indeed. Bakan, after analyzing the use of significance tests in a wide range of psychological studies, concluded that "the test of statistical significance in psychological research may be taken as an instance of a kind of essential mindlessness in the conduct of such research."[15] After a comparison of several approaches to the use of statistics in psychological research, Clark asserted "The null hypothesis of no difference has been judged to be no longer a sound or fruitful basis for statistical investigation. . . . Significance tests do not provide the information that scientists need, and furthermore, they are not the most effective method for analyzing and summarizing data."[16] Schulman in 1970, argues that "the time has arrived for educational researchers to divest themselves of the yoke of statistical hypothesis testing."[17] In 1975 Lee Cronbach pleaded with researchers to "exorcise the null hypothesis."[18] Morrison and Henkel, in their book of readings on this subject, put it this way:

> What we do without (significance) tests, then, has always in some measure been done in behavioral science and needs only to be done more and better: the application of imagination, common sense, informed judgement, and the appropriate remaining research methods to achieve the scope, form, process, and purpose of scientific inference.[19]

If we were to eliminate from the research literature in music education all the studies using statistical tests of significance according to what
Carver terms "corrupt scientific methodology," what do you think we'd be
left with?

The comments I have made about experimental research pinpoint only a
few of the defects of typical experiments when viewed in light of emerging
conceptions of knowledge and of science. Added to all these shortcomings is our characteristic use of experiments as isolated studies, devoid of
context, of directionality, of linkages which could provide a meaningful
background from which these tiny bits of data might take some measure of
credence. We simply cannot go on doing experiment after isolated experiment, thinking that by doing so we are doing science. What we are in fact
doing is making a mockery of science, a mockery of research, and a mockery
of us, who condone and even propagate an antique methodology based on
a bankrupt myth.

Experiments do indeed have their place within the panoply of social science methodologies. We must learn what that place is and have the courage to adapt experimental designs to our needs. That would take us a long
step toward establishing a veracity of experimental research as an endeavor
related in important and useful ways to the field of music education. There
is, in this area, a great deal we can do to improve the situation.

In order to be more scientific in our approach to music education research we will have to use existing techniques in ways that minimize their
weaknesses and maximize their strengths, and we will also have to be open
to new ways of generating knowledge and to unfamiliar concepts of what
evidence consists of. Several tangible, accomplishable steps can be taken
right away to begin moving our work in helpful directions. The most basic
of these is to begin doing our research in systematic fashion. This entails
several changes.

First, we must cluster our research efforts around significant problems
or topics or issues. Science does not do random studies. Science focuses
on something of value and then works on ways to achieve understanding
about it and expertise with it. An individual research effort should never be
undertaken in isolation: it should attach itself to an issue about which some
knowledge already exists and it should enhance that knowledge by verifying
it or extending it or refining it. Therefore, I propose that at every university
offering a doctorate, a unifying topic be chosen that is both significant for
music education and compatible with the research interests and capacities
of its faculty. Dissertations done at that institution would be related to the

chosen topic, and a major portion of the faculty's own research would be contributions to the developing knowledge on that topic.

Second, our clustering of research topics must entail a period of border-defining. To insure that research will be systematic rather than disorganized the chosen topic must provide fruitful limitations—limitations that compress the knowledge being generated into enough of a critical mass to achieve internal convincingness. The borders within which research is undertaken are likely to shift a bit now and then as new insights are gained and they may widen in time to include a broader range of phenomena, but at every moment they must exist with sufficient clarity to give significant shape to the individual studies within them and to the emerging wholeness of the knowledge being gained. Initial research within the chosen topic is, therefore, likely to be of a border-defining nature, clarifying the topic philosophically, exploring its historical roots, reviewing what now seems to be known about it through existing research, describing present beliefs and practices germane to it. As the border fills in the gaps in our knowledge will become apparent, generating a clear need for a variety of new studies that must then be added.

Third, the studies undertaken to define the topic and to develop the knowledge of it must reflect every existing modality and any modality that might be helpful. Philosophical studies will be necessary not only to define the topic at the beginning but to guide further efforts as knowledge builds. When a student with a flair for philosophy chooses a dissertation topic it will be one with a clear need, a clear function, a clear challenge related to a scholarly reality. That makes philosophy meaningful.

Historical studies will be necessary to provide the human context within which beliefs, practices, attitudes about the topic have grown. Each such insight adds to the dimensionality with which we understand the topic's function in human affairs and therefore to the usefulness of any new direction we might take to add to our understanding of the topic. When a student with a competence in history chooses a dissertation topic it will be one that has a clear relationship to a scholarly problem of significance for the profession. That makes history matter.

Descriptive studies will be necessary to probe how the issue actually exists in the world under a variety of circumstances. Some counting will be useful and students able to handle those kinds of statistics will have many opportunities to choose dissertations that add in vital ways to the unfolding knowledge of the topic—vital because the numbers they generate will help define aspects of the problem needing follow-up studies using other research modes. That makes quantitative description significant. Deep description will also be necessary, including case studies, interviews, observations, of various sorts, all of it serving the dual function of clarifying existing realities and uncovering needed further studies.

Experimental research, when directly related to a growing set of coherent understandings, can be undertaken with the kind of precision that it requires but also with the kind of meaningfulness that can only exist when an experiment is guided by a larger need. The design of an experiment must be determined by what we need to know, rather than having a preexisting design determining what we have to know. An experimental treatment must be chosen and arranged and applied within a rich context of information that indicates a particular gap that calls for a careful probe. The treatment of the data and the interpretation of the data cannot be mathematical exercises: they must be goal directed toward providing significant leads, or clues, that clarify what we have already learned or what we must further explore.

When perceived as a means, when guided by a carefully defined need, when carried out creatively, an experiment can be a powerful exercise of intelligence. And those students who choose to do an experimental dissertation would then be able to regard themselves, in the fullest sense of those words, as scholars and as thinkers.

In addition to studies using the traditional research modes many should be attempted that break the old configurations by combining several modes within a single study and by inventing alternatives and by reaching out to related disciplines for both methodological and conceptual innovations. Imaginative research can be cultivated, and should be cultivated, if only as an antidote to the appalling stultification that now characterizes our research literature. Creativity, in research as in art, requires boundaries, because complete freedom insures complete chaos.

Within the contexts that issue-oriented research centers will provide, creative scholarship is likely to burgeon. We must have the courage to recognize students who are creative thinkers and to encourage them in their creativity, rather than suppressing creativity by forcing our students into preexisting rigid molds, as we now do so often. I suspect that our timidity about research—our conservative or even reactionary posture—reflects our lack of self-confidence. When we start doing genuine science we will build our sense of security and this will allow us to work more freely and comfortably with a much wider spectrum of research methodologies than we are now able to accept.

The fourth change I would propose addresses the need for large-scale, long-term research, which is notable, in music education, by its almost complete absence. Our present fragmented state, in which isolated studies are carried out in isolation, would be replaced under the plan I am suggesting by ongoing centers able to mount concerted research efforts. Scientists cooperate. The image of an individual, alone in a laboratory, working on some new invention or exotic equipment, that no one else could possibly understand, is best left to class B movies. Yet that is the stereotype we impart to our doctoral students, whose dissertation efforts are typically characterized by a sense of quarantine from the world—a pervading detachment so intense as to be remembered throughout life as perhaps the most lonely time the person has spent. This is not science. It is more like some misguided initiation ceremony into a secret order which requires a kind of intellectual celibacy as a condition of membership.

Research can be and should be an intensely humane, cooperative endeavor, in which individuals, while doing their own work, are attached conceptually to a larger issue than their own and socially to a community of like-minded scholars. Such a community, ongoing over a period of years, in which students move in and out and the faculty provides stability, can, as at least one part of the research endeavor, carry out the longitudinal studies we are so sorely in need of. Just as creativity is likely to increase dramatically in unified research centers, cooperative efforts and long-term projects and group-directed studies of a variety impossible to predict are also likely to proliferate. We should welcome such a development joyously, both for its scientific and its human benefits.

Fifth, the systematizing of our research in the ways I have suggested would spill over far beyond the boundaries of individual universities. Natural linkages among universities would occur as a result of complementary work at several or because the particular strengths of one would be needed to bolster the weaknesses of another. Genuine exchanges—of individuals, of facilities, even of groups—could take place, as could cooperative studies embracing several university centers. Single universities or consortiums could sponsor publications that were unified by a scientific focus and therefore were more than the duplication we are now experiencing of journals reporting the same chaotic research studies every other journal is reporting.

At present we have little real research literature—we mostly have endless, disconnected reports of single, unrelated studies—an accurate reflection of our reality, as is painfully evident when we do our sporadic reviews of research on a topic. These publications, far from providing the coherence science constantly seeks, demonstrate how little we know about important issues because of our lack of focus. The mechanism I am suggesting would rectify that situation. It would also provide coherence in research conferences whether among a few institutions allied by overlapping interests, or regionally or nationally. The present SRIG mechanism is a healthy step toward providing coherent groupings of research interests and this mechanism, along with the national MERC leadership, could only be enhanced by adapting to a research base in which coherence existed at the very foundations of the field rather than in attempts to create it organizationally, helpful as those attempts have been.

As a tangible step in the direction of the proposals I have made, doctoral research at Northwestern University will change dramatically beginning next fall. We will, at that time, focus our research efforts toward the study of education and the musical experience. Because of several overlapping research interests among members of other departments, we are exploring a joint School of Music research center in which topics relating to musical learning, musical perception and musical symbol systems will be explored both separately and cooperatively. Doctoral students in music education who have not yet had a dissertation proposal accepted, and all new students next year, and all future students, will be instructed that, in addition to their regular course of studies, an ongoing weekly research seminar will be a requirement in the program, carrying appropriate course credit.

This seminar, which I will direct but which will include all graduate faculty members in music education, will begin the task of border-defining as I have explained, by systematic reviews of existing research relating to the musical experience in the context of educational settings. Students and faculty members will give reports and lead discussions, guest speakers will be invited as needed, students at other universities doing studies related to the topic will be invited to report on their work. We will be interested in exploring a carefully defined set of issues relating to the musical experience and its cultivation, including perceptual aspects of musical experience, affective aspects, the relationship between the two, age differences as they affect musical experience, belief-systems as they affect it, methodologies that seem to influence it, the relation of musical aesthetic experience to the experience of other arts and non-art. All studies will focus on the same phenomenon—the distinctive nature of that human mode of experiencing called "musical," and the influence that the educational process can exert to refine it.

As students in the seminar reach the proposal stage they will present their first drafts for review and discussion and for assistance. At every step from that point on, through the refinement of the proposal and the writing of the actual dissertation, reports will be made periodically to the seminar, and everyone in the seminar will be expected not only to keep informed about the ongoing work but to be influenced in their own developing plans by what is being discovered in the studies on progress. Reports on work being carried out will not just be informational—they will be working sessions in which the total group will be involved at crucial points in the decision-making process. While the individual writing the dissertation, along with his or her major advisor and committee, must take full responsibility for what it contains, the group's assistance will be a major factor in the effectiveness of the individual's efforts.

As the seminar continues new topics relating to musical experience will be suggested by the way nature of the accumulating expertise and new proposals will be direct responses to needs being uncovered. We will be alert to possibilities for multi-student dissertation projects, for innovative individual and group methodologies, for long-term commitments to longitudinal studies that are significant scientifically and feasible for our resources. We will explore linkages to other fields impinging on our topic, such as psychology, philosophy, sociology, anthropology, and the other arts education areas.

When sufficient work has been generated we shall begin to sponsor a variety of professional seminars and conferences for students and faculty at sister institutions whose work can benefit from ours and from whom we can learn. It is likely that some publications will appear along the way, reporting on the accumulating knowledge and raising a variety of research issues and implications that others might want to pursue. We shall actively seek research alliances with institutions that begin to follow this pattern, so that a network of scholars can begin to form, sharing their growing expertise about both their topics and how their research enterprises are being carried out.

A few individual researchers in music education have built their careers on their single-minded devotion to a focused, ongoing scientific endeavor. They are our research monuments. And some institutions have already moved in the direction I am proposing, by their focus on a particular aspect of the field and by their having built a high degree of expertise in it over a period of years. These people and these institutions have been the exceptions, unfortunately. If that pattern becomes the rule, including a more solid structuring of research at the few institutions which do have the beginnings of focus, our scientific knowledge-base should increase exponentially. We would have over 50 research centers, ranging across a variety topics such as (to mention just a few possibilities) musical creativity, measurement and evaluation of musical learnings, learning music in early childhood or adolescence or adulthood, the psychology of musical perception, the musical curriculum, musical performance, the role of attitude in musical learning, the processing of musical symbol systems, music as therapy, learning music of diverse cultures, educating music teachers, and on and on.

Topics such as these, and a great many others we will devise, are focused enough to do well what science does, broad enough to provide years of challenge, and interrelated enough to have many fruitful implications from one to the other. It is difficult to envision all the possible research focus areas that could be both scientifically and professionally viable within music education: a period of a few years would be needed to develop an initial round of them.

I would only caution that we should avoid centers limited to a particular research modality. The multifaceted nature of knowledge requires all possible means of discovery to be brought to bear, and while a particular topic may very naturally require more reliance on one or another research mode, other modes would keep the knowledge being generated from becoming too narrow. Also, students should have the opportunity to become contributing scholars in a mode suitable for their own intellectual strengths. Most if not all of our doctoral students would welcome the existence of an ongoing research community to which they could become attached. But we must be careful to help each student identify the kind of scholarship he or she has the most talent for, and to seek a way for that talent to be developed through a meaningful contribution to a genuinely scientific endeavor. The effects of that kind of research experience on the student's desire to continue to do research after the dissertation should be profound.

Contemporary science has made us aware of such enormous complexities in the universe and ourselves—complexities we are only now beginning to recognize let alone understand—that it is easy to feel overwhelmed and to retreat to the little corners in which we have made ourselves comfortable, pleading our helplessness to do more than our tiny, special part within our tiny, special field. We can sympathize with the plaint so eloquently expressed by the Nobel Prize author Isaac Bashevis Singer, who says:

> There is no answer in this world to the eternal questions. What can we know? It is as if you were to ask a bookworm crawling inside *War and Peace* whether

it is a good novel or a bad one. He is sitting on one little letter trying to get some nourishment. How can he be a critic of Tolstoy?[20]

We can sympathize but we cannot succumb, because scientists must take a different attitude, an attitude articulated by the political commentator George F. Will:

We know next to nothing about virtually everything. It is not necessary to know the origin of the universe; it is necessary to want to know. Civilization depends not on any particular knowledge, but on the disposition to crave knowledge.[21]

Our role as researchers in music education is to crave knowledge. Our obligation is to produce it more scientifically.

NOTES

1. In the following history I have drawn in large part on the views presented in Fritjof Capra, *The Turning Point* (New York: Simon and Schuster, 1982).
2. Ibid., 56.
3. Ibid., 57.
4. Ibid., 61.
5. Ibid., 63.
6. Ibid., 74.
7. Ibid., 80.
8. Quoted in Bennett Reimer and Edward G. Evans, *The Experience of Music* (Englewood Cliffs, N.J.: Prentice-Hall, Inc., 1972), 304.
9. Thomas M. Horning, "The Development of a Model of the Psychological Processes which Translate Musical Stimuli into Affective Experience." Unpublished Ph.D. dissertation, Case Western Reserve University, Cleveland, Ohio, 1982.
10. *New Yorker*, January 10, 1983, 25.
11. Karl H. Pribram, "Transcending the Mind/Brain Problem," *Zygon* 14, no. 2 (June 1979): 105.
12. For a brilliant discussion of the role of philosophy in a period of scientific turmoil see Susanne K. Langer, *Philosophical Sketches* (Baltimore, Md.: Johns Hopkins Press, 1962), chapter 9, "The Growing Center of Knowledge."
13. Elliot W. Eisner, *The Educational Imagination* (New York: Macmillan Publishing Co., Inc., 1979).
14. Ronald P. Carver, "The Case against Statistical Significance Testing," *Harvard Educational Review* 48, no. 3 (August 1978).

15. D. Bakan, "The Test of Significance in Psychological Research," *Psychological Bulletin* 66 (1966): 423–37.

16. C. A. Clark, "Hypothesis Testing in Relation to Statistical Methodology," *Review of Educational Research* 33 (1963): 455–73.

17. L. S. Schulman, "Reconstruction of Educational Research," *Review of Educational Research*, 40 (1970): 371–93.

18. L. J. Cronbach, "Beyond the Two Disciplines of Scientific Psychology," *American Psychologist*, 30 (1975): 116–27.

19. D. E. Morrison and R. E. Henkel, eds., *The Significance Test Controversy— A Reader* (Chicago: Aldine Co., 1970).

20. Interview with Isaac Bashevis Singer, *The London Sunday Times*, September 11, 1983, 13.

21. *Newsweek*, August 3, 1981.

19

QUALITATIVE RESEARCH AND THE POST-POSITIVIST MIND

Over the decade or so after the publication of the previous essay, "Toward a More Scientific Approach to Music Education Research," a great many changes occur in the world of educational research. The awareness of shortcomings of quantitative research, especially in its most characteristic mode, the experiment (or quasi-experiment as must be the case in education), and advances in thinking related to cognitivist conceptions of the human mind take hold in dramatic ways.

An exciting new paradigm for research in education takes shape as an alternative to the traditional reliance on statistical, cause-effect, evidence-as-objective mindset then prevalent. Qualitative research, focusing on the qualities of human experience as it is lived in all its complexities and ambiguities, gradually takes center stage. Research procedures and protocols come to light that are concordant with the view that meanings, in addition to behaviors, need to be examined if education is to be effective. A new world of possibilities for education research appears.

As music education researchers who are open to these emerging ideas work toward adapting them to issues of music learning and teaching, a whole new community of researchers comes into being. Soon there are enough of them, and enough work accomplished, to make a conference specifically devoted to this way of thinking and doing research a logical and compelling need. The University of Illinois takes up the challenge and organizes what turns out to be two such gatherings, in 1994 and 1996.

The CRME Bulletin issue cited here contains conference presentations of great value for all who are interested in the potentials and problems of qualitative research as these are understood at that time. Further work since then has deepened our understanding and skills, of course. My contribution then places this movement in historical/philosophical perspective and pleads for the creation of a music education infrastructure that would enable our work to be issue-focused rather than methodology-focused. Without a structure for coordinative research projects, as I argue in the previous essay from 1985, we cannot achieve the impact on our field that research aims to produce.

Such a structure remains absent to this day. Creating one is among the most pressing needs of our profession.

The following essay was originally published in the *Council for Research in Music Education*, Bulletin 130 (Fall 1996). Used by permission.

I want to reflect about the historical context and epistemological foundation of qualitative research as we now conceive it and to offer some comments about where our research efforts need to go in the future if they are to be as useful for music education as they deserve to be but have never actually been.

Qualitative research is a child of the post-positivist world. It is a clear reflection of the mind-set underlying post-positivist beliefs. The most salient of these beliefs for us as researchers is that there are no pure data. Whether quantitative or qualitative, any data beyond arithmetic (and some would even include arithmetical data) are constructions of the human mind. Although arithmetical facts may be taken at face value (seven children, ranging in age from five to nine, completed the task within three minutes . . .), any construal of them—any attempt to make meaning of them—requires us to recognize that meaning itself is a human construct peculiar to and limited by the particular kind of mental/physical organism humans happen to be. Objective truth—truth having an identity independent of human construals—is taken to be a comforting myth, useful for our narcissistic purposes no doubt, but incapable of being sustained any longer as a viable basis for conceiving the world and our place in it. Knowledge, in the post-positivist belief system in which we now live, is not regarded as conclusive, verifiable, or external to the human psyche, but instead is assumed to be tentative and socially and individually constructed, a matter of human imagination brought to bear on those perceptions humans are capable of having. Knowledge is the basis of meaning. Meaning is a human invention.

In the field of research the positivist and post-positivist positions can be viewed clearly by putting them on a continuum, with dedicated or orthodox positivism at one end and equally dedicated or orthodox post-positivism at the other. Quantitative research historically has dwelled at the dedicated positivism end, whereas qualitative research arose as an alternative when post-positivist thinking began to hold sway.

In the older positivist view language was conceived to be adequate to represent objective reality—the "real" beyond the limitations of human subjectivity. Language, although sufficient to mediate objective truth, is powerfully assisted in that task—the task of research—by numbers, which are capable of even purer approximations of truth-as-such. Numbers get us so close to the "real"—to the objective, the verifiable, the factual, the actual—as to be identical with or at least paradigmatic of truth in essence. In the positivist mind-set, when using language we must push it as far as we can to the objective condition of mathematics, avoiding the sloppiness of subjectivity that can creep in if we are not careful, such as calling ourselves "I" rather than "the researcher," or calling the people we are researching "they" rather than "subjects," and so on.

Positivist beliefs about research are alive and well, of course, in the continuing, underlying conviction so many people in our culture hold (including at least some people at this conference) that until you get to the "proof" of something, to verifiable certainty about something, which usually means mathematical certainty separate from our own constructions of meaning or belief, you still aren't "there" yet. "There" is where the truth lies, and "there" is not "here" inside us, with our dreadfully fallible propensities for error. Research should "prove it." "It" is out there, awaiting proof. Quantitative research, then, is based on a conception of knowledge as *episteme* (the word Plato used). It is propositional, general, provable, and timeless.

Little if any of this is any longer convincing to those favoring post-positivist views. Qualitative research is based on a different conception of knowledge; what Aristotle called *phronesis*, by which he meant practical wisdom. Such knowledge deals with the particular rather than the general. For the particular, the appropriate mode of knowledge is perceptual rather than conceptual. Deeper perception of particularity, called *aisthesis* (the root of the word aesthetic) is what we must gain if we are to be wise about how to deal effectively with singular, complex, ambiguous cases that education almost always presents us with. Any generalities about such cases must always remain secondary if not irrelevant to their uniqueness. Therefore, in a 180-degree reversal of positivism, post-positivism both accepts and revels in the psychological nature of language.

It also is suspicious of statistical treatments as being irrelevant to the individuality of human experience. The individual, always culturally and psychologically situated, constitutes the datum of primal interest, with the logic of the psyche, not of mathematics, as that which guides research in its attempts to explore and understand. So language, rather than being protected from subjectivity by constructions which make it as objective as possible, should instead exploit its deeply subjective, psyche-laden nature.

The usefulness of this analysis of quantitative versus qualitative research in terms of their places at the ends of an epistemological continuum is that it maps out the terrain of research by establishing its borders. Doing so calls attention to the territory in between the borders. What do we do about that territory? Is the best place to be at one of the borders, or at both borders, or at some point between them?

The pendulum effect is a border-seeking phenomenon, a swing from one border to another. It is a reaction phenomenon: in reacting to the suddenly perceived weaknesses of one view we swing mightily to the opposing view. Of course when weaknesses in the second view begin to appear, as they always seem to do, the pendulum swings back. That is the only thing a pendulum *can* do—swing from one border to the other.

The qualitative research movement began as a pendulum swing, not just as an alternative (although it was usually called that) but a *reaction*, an *opposition*. Quite naturally an oppositional psychology appeared. The debate between quantitative and qualitative proponents became heated, derogatory, and conflictual in all sorts of ways. We experienced that in the first qualitative conference here two years ago when quantitative research was seen by some as being the enemy. That sense of opposition has subsided dramatically, as far as I can tell, which may be taken as a sign of the growing acceptance of qualitative research and therefore a growing sense of security among those who do it.

When we are not busy riding the pendulum from one border to another and therefore concentrating on those borders as defining our reality we can step back from the ride and view the entire arc of the pendulum—the continuum between the extremes—and ponder whether or not there are points along that continuum that represent more fruitful positions than either of the extremes. We are able, then, to entertain more than two possibilities. The issue becomes less a matter of choice between opposing alternatives and more of a consideration of the infinite number of alternatives existing between the ends of the continuum.

Now we get to the tough part. How do we accommodate two polar positions that seem to be epistemologically contradictory? Is any movement away from one end of the continuum a validation of the beliefs at the other end? Are we willing to accept the paradox that logically, although both positions cannot be valid in that they are seemingly contradictory, we can nevertheless employ methodologies from each in some supposedly mutually supportive way? Or can we accept the idea that reality itself, at least as we are now able to construe it, seems to be bipolar, as in quantum theory, and therefore requires us to recognize both poles, each relevant to reality in its own way?

In that case what does cooperation mean? Wouldn't we protect our integrity by simply accepting that the two orientations are incompatible and therefore it is better to try to do research of each sort as purely as we can? Is the mix or match solution of eclecticism worthy of the complexities and conundrums these two orientations present to us?

These are the hard, recalcitrant problems continuing to be debated throughout the professional education research community. Read the *Educational Researcher* over the past few years for a sense of the volatility of the debate. I wish I could say I knew the solutions to the problems. Unfortunately, I don't. I do take them seriously, however, and I am not entirely comfortable with the many accommodations and combinations now being made among the two paradigms even though I am reconciled to the need to make them and have for many years encouraged people to make them.

I do have a practical suggestion to make about the situation, not being able to offer a theoretical resolution. It is that we focus less on methodology as the central issue for research, because that focus deflects attention away from the more important questions needing to be asked and answered. Those questions are not methodological but substantive. What problems of music education matter most to us? How can research, of whatever kind, help us achieve more clarity about those problems? What understandings about our important issues, once gained through whatever research helps us gain it, would lead to further gains in our effectiveness to do what our values lead us to want to do? How can we organize our research efforts to develop the understandings we feel are the most important in helping us serve our values?

Simply put, our research needs to be issues-driven rather than methodology-driven. While philosophers of research continue the important debate as to theoretical foundations for research practices we must continue our work as best we can despite the continuing controversy. Our work, I am suggesting, should focus less on methodology as the driving force and more on identified issues as our focus.

There is a very good reason for two conferences to have been held that were driven entirely by methodology rather than by issues. We needed to establish the veracity and importance of a new kind of research methodology in the face of a great deal of resistance to it. These two conferences have played an extremely important role in getting the pendulum out of the stuck position it had been in for too long a time. I believe they have served their purpose very well.

Now I want to suggest that a more important purpose needs to be served by future conferences devoted to research, a purpose now possible to address in large part *because* these two conferences have taken place. It is time, now, I believe, to focus our efforts on the research infrastructure itself, which remains in disarray.

This means, first, that we need to explore how we can go about identifying and perhaps prioritizing the crucial issues about which we need research.

Second, we need to establish mechanisms within the research community (including within that community, by the way, many people who have traditionally have been excluded—teachers, administrators, students, parents, community members) to carry out the large-scale, multi-methodological, longitudinal projects that issues-driven research will require.

Third, we need to build structures to coordinate the work of large-scale projects to maximize their interrelationships in a variety of cooperative ways, including ready access to what each project is doing, how it is doing it, problems being uncovered, results being achieved, and so on. Focusing our efforts on issues, with methodologies conceived for what they are—means to help us achieve our ends—would finally get us going in a direction our research has never been able to take us because we have neglected issues in our fixation on methodologies.

We are ready, now, I think, to move ahead to a new stage in music education research in which our growing expertise with both quantitative and qualitative methodologies, our openness to new, as yet undiscovered methodologies (just wait, folks—they're on their way), and our growing awareness that methodologies are instrumentalities for helping us achieve what we value, now allow us to get our values in order and to use research as one powerful way to achieve them.

To the extent we move in the direction of an issues-oriented research structure, with methodologies conceived as instrumentalities for pursuing all possible meanings necessary for better clarity about our important issues, we can hope that all researchers, of whatever orientation, would support each other in cooperative efforts to pursue meaning. This, in turn, might lead to resolutions of the theoretical research dilemma not yet achievable through theoretical work alone. Cooperative practice may not only yield positive results in our efforts to pursue the issues we most care about but may very well influence theory development positively.

We need, now, in addition to special conferences focused on the improvement of our methodological expertise, to plan conferences organized by issues, in which researchers of various sorts, including philosophers and historians, work together to explore how a particular issue can be pursued in a variety of ways more productive than any single way is likely to be. There are many problems inherent in such cooperation, but I believe the gains would far outweigh the potential snarls. One of those gains might well be the emergence of research paradigms and methodologies transcending the limitations of those presently existing.

Another might be the elevation of research, finally, to the rightful place it deserves at the center of the music education enterprise, because research would finally be addressing in systematic ways the issues of most importance to the profession to which we are all devoted. That would be an outcome much to be desired by all researchers of all methodological persuasions. I believe our work is cut out for us.

NEW BRAIN RESEARCH ON EMOTION AND FEELING: DRAMATIC IMPLICATIONS FOR MUSIC EDUCATION

"We in music education are nurturers of consciousness."

This claim, which I make in the following essay, sounds more than a little grandiose. Brain research is beginning to provide it with a firm foundation.

The burgeoning of brain research in general and in music in particular over the past fifteen years or so has been remarkable—truly a revolution in scientific horizons and potential benefits. Those benefits for music education remain latent at present, with most work exploring the relation of musical experiences to learnings in other subjects—efforts that are interesting, fraught with problems, and, for me, of only moderate importance. Research on the brain and emotion or feeling, on the other hand, has momentous implications for our understanding of the human condition at depths beyond any achieved so far, and is of great significance as well for clarifying music's contributions to human welfare in ways unique to its special characteristics. As that work develops, music education is likely to become strategically positioned in the direction of my assertion above about its role in consciousness, betokening new levels of importance for us in the sphere of education.

When I begin exploring the field of brain research I become fascinated with its perplexities and accomplishments. At first, I am skeptical of its relevance for what we do. Its interests and discoveries seem only tangential to our primary concerns for both music and education. But at a certain point, as in the work of Antonio Damasio discussed in this article, flashes of illumination begin to occur, insights powerfully explanatory of what we in music education value and why we value it—that is, our devotion to musical experience as affective and our intuition that such experience is deeply important. Its importance, the research suggests, relates to what our brains are capable of, what feeling has to do with brain function, and the relation of feeling to consciousness itself. We are in bedrock territory here, discovering new ways to comprehend why music is as crucial to being human as we have always sensed but could not express clearly.

How can we not be excited? We are glimpsing new potentials for understanding what underlies our characteristic dedication to our profession. No definitive answers from brain research yet, or maybe ever. But in matters this deeply complex, any steps toward better comprehension must be celebrated.

The following essay was originally published in the *Arts Education Policy Review* 106, no. 2 (November/December 2004). Used by permission.

> Know then thyself, presume not God to scan;
> The proper study of mankind is man.

These words by the English poet Alexander Pope (1688–1744) reflect a major historical turn in thought about the human condition and how to best understand it. Pope lived during the period that was to become known as the Enlightenment, when the power and potential of reason began to be regarded as the surest source of valid insights about what it means to be human. In a real sense contemporary science in all its many forms is a child of the Enlightenment, its birth signaled by Pope's pronouncement.

If we are to follow the command of the oracle of ancient Delphi, to "know thyself," the words Pope was echoing, we need to know what to study to accomplish this goal. To study ourselves—to look deeply and carefully into the substance of our human being—requires both a mind-set to do so and a system of investigation best suited to the complexities we embody. Science offered both, a way to understand our nature and the instrumentalities to study it. All of us, whatever other beliefs we might hold about the world and our place within it, have been profoundly affected by the scientific revolution Alexander Pope announced.

That revolution, reaching to every corner of human existence including our understandings of the non-human universe, approaches its greatest challenge from its most fundamental premise: We are who we are, we think and act as we do, our reality is what it is, by virtue of the embodied brain that we happen to have. Under this premise all aspects of our lives, physical, mental, emotional, ethical, spiritual—yes, even musical—are functions of brain activity in its embodied environment. The proper study of mankind, finally, Pope might have said, is the brain, the ultimate foundation for all that makes us human.

Here are a few astounding facts about the human brain:

> The brain has an estimated one hundred billion neurons. . . . Each neuron has an average of ten thousand connections that directly link to other neurons. Thus there are thought to be about one million billion of these connections, making it the most complex structure, natural or artificial, on earth. . . . A "synapse" is the connection that functionally links neurons to one another. Because of the spider-web-like interconnections, activation of one neuron can influence an average of ten thousand neurons at the receiving ends. The number of possible "on-off" patterns of neuronal firing is immense, estimated as a staggering ten times ten one million times (ten to the millionth power). The brain is obviously capable of an imponderingly huge variety of activity; the fact that it is often organized and functional is quite an accomplishment! (Siegel, 1999)

When the brain is conceived as a sort of gigantic computer compressed into a very small space we can be forgiven for feeling a bit uneasy about the sense of mechanization this implies. It somehow seems to leave "us," the experiencing beings that we are, out of the equation, as if we were automatons responding blindly to brain impulses. What seems to be ignored by this view is our consciousness, the very condition that allows us to think thoughts such as "to think thoughts." Is consciousness itself entirely a matter of brain function? Is what we feel, moment by moment, hour by hour, day by week by year over the span of our lives, making us the individuals we recognize ourselves to be, reducible to neurons firing within our skulls directing our bodies to act as they do? Are varied states of awareness and our responses merely mechanical functions? Is that what it all comes down to?

CONSCIOUSNESS STUDIES

Such questions are among the great challenges that brain research faces. There have been important strides in recent years toward understanding various brain structures and brain functions; we have no doubt learned more about the brain in the past dozen or so years than in the previous dozen or so centuries. We are still left, however, with a significant gap between such findings and their relation to our experienced lives, our consciousness. That gap is now being addressed, no doubt more thoroughly than ever before in history, by the field of consciousness studies, in which a variety of leads toward an explanation of this fundamental aspect of the human condition are being pursued, one of which I will deal with later on. But we are a long way, I believe, from fully closing the gap between brain research and consciousness research, if in fact that gap can ever be entirely closed.

Why should those of us dedicated to two dimensions of human capacities—music and education—both of which are near the top of the scale of holistic functions of human mentality, care very much about the extremely detailed work going on in present brain research? After all, the natural sciences, including brain science, traditionally have proceeded by processes of reduction and analysis into smaller and smaller parts. Our interest, our professionalism, is very far removed from such work, so far that brain research findings often seem to be either academic for us or even irrelevant. As John Flohr and Don Hodges put it in their excellent overview of music and neuroscience, "Unfortunately, a direct translation from neuroscience research into music education at this time is very problematic" (Flohr and Hodges, 2002).

For example, it may be of passing interest to know which parts of the brain are activated by musical engagements, but in itself this would seem to change nothing and suggest nothing that is useful to us in the actualities of how we go about our work. Is brain research, then, in its focus on operations far below the level of consciousness, too atomistic to be of practical value to us? Could it even be, in a sense, a threat to our values, trivializing them by its reductionism?

Here is how Edward O. Wilson, Pulitzer Prize–winning scientist and author, explains why we should care—in fact why we must care—about all dimensions of brain research.

> Reduction is the traditional instrument of scientific analysis, but it is feared and resented. If human behavior can be reduced and determined to any

considerable degree by the laws of biology, then mankind might appear to be less than unique and to that extent dehumanized. Few social scientists and scholars in the humanities are prepared to enter such a conspiracy, let alone surrender any of their territory. But this perception, which equates the method of reduction with the philosophy of diminution, is entirely in error. . . . Biology is the key to human nature, and social scientists cannot afford to ignore its rapidly tightening principles. But the social sciences are potentially far richer in content. Eventually they will absorb the relevant ideas of biology and go on to beggar them. (Wilson 1978, 14)

I would add to this only one thing: The humanities are just as important as the social sciences. As a person situated within the humanities, I am concerned above all with the quality and breadth of human experience at the levels of meaning, fulfillment, joy, and spirit. I find myself fascinated by brain research because of the inklings it gives us, here and there, of how we are biological organisms for whom those experienced qualities are enabled by the very structure of our physical being, even at its smallest, most elemental levels. Is it possible that knowing what brain research is beginning to suggest to us could help us achieve more deeply what we value in our personal and professional lives and in helping others achieve more of the values music particularly offers? If brain research can be connected to such aims we will have truly begun to beggar that research—to make it seem impoverished—as Wilson claims we should.

Despite the fact that my expertise (such as it is) is as a philosopher and not in any sense as a brain researcher I am, therefore, emboldened to discuss this topic because of Wilson's challenge to the social sciences and humanities. I believe he is correct to suggest that the natural sciences and humanistic scholarship need to be seen as partners, not adversaries, each adding in its own unique way to the validity of the other without in any way merging with or "integrating" with the other. That, by the way, is precisely what he means by "consilience" in his influential book by that name (Wilson 1998). He does *not* mean "integration" as that term is so often used in education. In that spirit I offer my reflections on brain research from my perspective as a philosopher, seeking the human meanings arising from what brain studies suggest.

THE STATE OF BRAIN RESEARCH

I would characterize the bulk of modern-day brain research as a hodge-podge—as provocative, puzzling, astute, clever, courageous, and easily misinterpreted, as we witness so often by popularizations and advocacy attempts that are embarrassing in their unwarranted and misleading claims. My posture in dealing with much of this research is to regard it at the level of "we cannot yet say that . . ." or "it is likely that . . ." rather than "it is now established that. . . ." Nevertheless, and despite its many abuses by those with a stake in using it improperly, I believe we are ready to begin drawing tentative implications from some of its findings that do in fact seem to connect with and even clarify our values. I will begin with a few brain research implications that underlie the major one I want to emphasize, having to do with emotion and feeling.

The first implication is that brain physiology, while displaying an overall structure in which certain locations seem to be central to certain mental and physical functions, nevertheless is surprisingly individual and therefore remarkably diverse. Brain diversity from person to person exists in a variety of ways; for example, in the efficiency of neuronal connection-making; in the numbers of neurons in particular networks; in the amount of energy consumed in the linking of neurons; in the effects of experiential stimuli on neuron activity; in the ease or difficulty of pattern creation among neuronal networks; in the differences in strength and scope of memory storage and retrieval mechanisms; in the developmental aspects of brain maturation not only as a whole but in each particular mode of brain function; in the efficiency and acuity of sensory input to the brain; in the differences of attention patterns that transmit environmental data to the brain; and, by no means least, in the differences in quality of nutrition and in the availability of opportunities to learn. These examples give a sense of the magnitude of brain individuality, which can be compared meaningfully with face individuality. Human faces have shared characteristics, yet amazingly are also always distinctive, even in the case of so-called identical twins, both in faces and brains, apparently.

The major addition to my short list of brain individuality potential is the high degree of likelihood that differing life experiences will cause differing developments to take place in the brain. That applies to *all* life experiences, each getting processed by the brain as particular to the individuality of each person—what life offers to each person and the way and degree that each person attends to the ongoing flow of his or her life experiences. The brain is not separate from the experiencing individual: it is, in fact, the essential intermediary between outside and inside.

MUSIC AND THE BRAIN

In musical experiencing, for example, two fundamental processes underlie all others. The first is the immediate, nonverbal response to musical sounds—the absorption in one's attention of their impact as we create them and respond to them. That "music-think" is what I have termed "knowing within" and "knowing how," or "musical perceptual structuring," and what Bruce Torff and Howard Gardner have termed the "experiential" aspect of engagements with music (1999).

The second process, intimately linked with the first but not identical, is dependent on the contributions of symbol systems such as words, notations, analytical diagrams, and so forth. These are the dimensions I have called "knowing about" and "knowing why," what Torff and Gardner, following my explanations, term the "conceptual aspect of musical processing." Both the experiential and the conceptual dimensions are cognitive. That is, both are processed, each in its own way and with complex interactions among them, by the brain. Both create the conscious, meaningful undergoing we call "musical experience."

Importantly, the diverse emphases among the experiential and conceptual dimensions, required by the diversity of ways music can be encountered, call upon and influence diverse brain developments. For example, we are on fairly firm ground in brain research (albeit not without controversy) in claiming that the brain activates differently for novices and experts. That is the case not only in music but probably in everything else humans do. For example, a study at the Santa Lucia Foundation Neuroresearch Center in Rome found that professional wine experts—sommeliers—have distinctively different brain activation patterns than novice wine drinkers. Although both experts and novices activate the primary and secondary gustatory brain areas, only the experts activate areas involved in memory encoding and emotional responses and the area of the frontal cortex that processes language and recognition ability (Gaffney 2003).

Among musical experts—that is, professionals—brain studies suggest that the conceptual dimension is far more dominant than among novices. This is no surprise because novices, who often enjoy and value music deeply, do not generally bring to their experiences of music the levels of conceptual cognition that professionals must attain, nor do they have the levels of physical mastery required for professional performance.

Of central importance to music education is that all musical engagements, whether at the level of novice or professional—all the way from young children to seasoned veterans—activate both brain hemispheres and involve cerebral cortex activity and memory retrieval mechanisms. There are, however, substantive differences in brain activation patterns stemming from differing emphases in attention and in the strategies employed by the differing ways each musical role is learned. Each role is likely to entail widely distributed brain activity, but not identically with the others. This is true for singing, playing, improvising, composing, arranging, listening, analyzing, describing, evaluating, understanding relationships of music to other subjects and to its historical and cultural dimensions (these being the role identifications in the U.S. National Content Standards for music education).

The individuality of one musical role from another probably stems from two aspects of brain function. First, each role requires a different set of brain involvements because each requires its own particular set of discriminations to be made by the combined brain/body entity. Second, the brain must make the particular connections among those discriminations that are related to the particularities of each role. As Don Hodges explains (2000), musical processing is distributed throughout the brain in neural modules that perform particular functions, the modules being engaged according to the demands that various tasks make on the brain. The brain's responses to the demands of particular tasks—what I have called role requirements—are learned rather than inherent. The particular role that one plays—the "outside," so to speak—programs the brain to serve its needs, with the "inside" responding to the demands made by each role and also to the instructional processes each role requires.

Apparently, then, there is not a singular brain/body set of activations for a singular phenomenon called "music." Instead, there are as many sets of activations as there are viable ways to interact with music, each demanding the brain's support and instructing it as to how to provide that support. Those modes of musical interaction (or musical roles) include, the research suggests, whether or not each role is pursued professionally. To further complicate the picture, all individuals, as mentioned previously, inevitably develop their unique pattern of brain/body activation within each role and within their particular level of interest in that role.

What all this adds up to—let me emphasize again—is that it is simplistic to think in terms of a generalized brain involvement in a generalization termed "music." This, I would point out, is what Howard Gardner's theory of multiple intelligences tends to do, neglecting the substantive distinctions among the many different musical roles that cultures provide and the diversity of brain/body involvements of individuals playing each role.

That oversimplification of musical experience diversity, I am afraid, also pervades music education in our beliefs, program offerings, practices of teaching, assessments, and research. Because of our growing understandings of brain dissimilarity as related to musical role dissimilarity, we are faced with scientific evidence of our need to rethink much of what we do and how we do it. This adds to and complements recent philosophical arguments that we have not yet recognized how non-diverse and uniform our approach to music education has been. We have thereby restricted the opportunities we offer our students, who, taken as a whole, represent the entire spectrum of brain development potentials, interests in, and values for music. This is a striking convergence, or consilience, of humanities and science, each strengthening the other in leading us to a more securely based vision of what music education might be.

THE BRAIN AND EMOTION

That vision has recently been clarified by still another brain-function/value-orientation complementarity that is perhaps even more important in its implications than what I have discussed so far. I refer to the work of Antonio Damasio in his three recent books, *Descartes' Error: Emotion, Reason, and the Human Brain* (1994); *The Feeling of What Happens: Body and Emotion in the Making of Consciousness* (1999); and *Looking for Spinoza: Joy, Sorrow, and the Feeling Brain* (2003). His work, or the work of any other single researcher, is by no means sufficient for any inclusive treatment of recent advances in brain research on the relation of emotion and feeling to human consciousness and cognition. I make no claim that this particular scientist's contribution is the only valid or interesting or helpful one; not at all. It is far too early for any one of the many attempts being made to unravel the mysteries of the brain/emotion interplay to have become dominant, nor can we yet aggregate all the attempts into an authoritative explanation. So we must be modest here, giving provocative work its due but not leaping too fast to an assumption that this issue is resolved.

Nevertheless, I want to call attention to this particular explanation because it so strikingly fits with, and adds empirical verification for, longstanding philosophical work that has had important influence on music education. Science is now verifying beliefs that until now could be verified only intuitively. The consilience between science and philosophy, when it appears out of the blue and so powerfully confirms one's beliefs and practices, is indeed dramatic. It deserves our attention and, if not our unquestioning endorsement, at least our careful, even hopeful, examination.

That examination entails one of the most difficult issues in all of brain research: the brain's involvement in emotion. This is because unlike much other brain function and physiology research, which yields evidence related to sense experience or definable intellectual operations, emotion is the paradigm case of what is called an "essentially contested concept," one that has defied consensual definition over all of recorded history. That the brain is the seat of emotions has been recognized for a very long time. Hippocrates (460–377 B.C.E.) said "From the brain and the brain alone arise our pleasures, joys, laughter and jest, as well as our sorrows, pains, and griefs."

No scientist today would dispute that ancient intuition. Yet, as emotion theorists Paul Ekman and Richard Davidson point out, "Although everyone agrees that more [research] data are needed, they disagree about how much reliable data are now available, and what kind of data will be most useful in furthering our understanding of the emotions" (1994, 47). Damasio's data and their implications do in fact further our understanding, I believe, in ways directly relevant to the values of music. I can give here only a brief overview of his work and what it suggests for our professional beliefs and actions. Readers interested in delving into his writings will find his books remarkably accessible, even charming, and pervaded with a humane spirit.

For Damasio, the historical tendency to overvalue reason and rationality at the expense of emotion and its intimate connection to the body has given us a false picture of the human mind and has negatively affected human values. Furthermore, Damasio explains, emotion is the root of and the basis for feeling, which carries emotion to another level. It is not emotion as such that accounts for our human condition; many animals are likely to experience emotion. The feelings that arise out of emotion are what cause and allow us to be the unique creatures we seem to be.

Feeling carries emotion to the level of conscious awareness of what we are undergoing. Although emotion activates the brain as a collection of changes in the state of the body, feeling those changes—being aware that we are undergoing a set of related, complex brain/body events—requires the juxtaposition of what is happening in the brain and its body with an image of something to which those happenings are related. Damasio suggests that such an image could be "the visual image of a face or the auditory image of a melody" (1994, 145). When this junction of inside and outside, brain/body activation with environmental occurrence, reaches the level of awareness that they are interconnected, we call it consciousness, Damasio explains. To be conscious is to be aware, through a coming together of brain, body, and environing conditions, that we are experiencing, that we are undergoing something, and that we know that we are doing so. Feeling is the connecting mechanism that allows this transition to happen—the transition from a person undergoing something both internally and externally to having the recognition that she or he is doing so. In this case, the person is a "self," feeling what that self is undergoing. As Damasio puts it, "feelings are poised at the very threshold that separates being from knowing, and thus have a privileged connection to consciousness" (1999, 43).

Despite the richness and depth of his explanations throughout his writings, especially in the book *The Feeling of What Happens* (if you can read only one of his books, this is the one to read), Damasio struggles in his attempts to explain how consciousness occurs and the central role that feeling plays in that occurrence. That struggle is attributable, to a large extent, to the fact that we do not have language available to conceptualize the specificities of this phenomenon, and perhaps we may never have it, given the shortcomings of language to express what is above and beyond language. Not everything in our experience, after all, can be represented accurately by language, something music educators, and educators in the other arts, know full well. We certainly experience feeling and consciousness, just as we certainly experience music. Putting those experiences into the representations language is capable of mediating can be very frustrating and unsatisfying because of the disparities between language and felt, aware experience.

Nevertheless, several insights that Damasio offers from his brain studies clarify how music works and how we might be more effective in teaching it. One in particular is both clear and explainable: the notion of "the emotionally competent object."

One aspect of feeling, he explains, is its location within the body. Whether a stimulus to the brain/body entity is received from inside (for example, sensing hunger or pain) or from the outside (for example, listening to a piece of music), the brain/body reacts, in musculature, heartbeat, respiration, blood chemistry, electrical impulses, and so on. The brain maps all this and, at a certain "critical pitch" of the nervous system (Damasio borrows the term "critical pitch" from Susanne K. Langer) the process reaches the level of feeling; that is, awareness or consciousness of what we are undergoing. That capacity—that critical pitch producing consciousness (in our case consciousness of having the experience we call "musical") is built into the human brain/body complex as an inherited mechanism. Even infants exhibit responses to and awareness of the feeling content of music.

Here's the important part for us. Feelings are perceptions, like visual, aural, tactile, or gustatory perceptions. When something is perceived from outside the body, feeling combines that which comes from that object or event with brain/body responses inside the body. Thus, although feelings are internal, they are intimately linked to something that caused them. That outside influence is the emotionally competent object. Damasio puts it this way: *"The sight of a spectacular seascape is an emotionally competent object"* (2003, 91; emphasis in original). The object causes all sorts of brain/body responses which are experienced consciously as feelings. The object need not be a seascape, of course; I would mention as another example the sound of a stirring piece of music.

Furthermore, we respond to the object—to events in the outer world—in a dynamic, interactive way.

> The brain can act directly on the very object it is perceiving. . . . In the case of feeling, the object itself can be changed radically. . . . [F]eelings are not a passive perception or a flash in time. . . . [T]here is a dynamic engagement of the body . . . and a subsequent dynamic variation of the perception. We experience a series of transitions. We sense an interplay, a give and take [between outside and inside]. (2003, 91–92)

That "give and take" changes both the brain's functioning and how we perceive the object or event with which it is interacting. The brain changes by adapting to, say, a musical listening experience one is having. That adaptation is imprinted in brain physiology and function. Even from a recording, the sounds of which remain identical from one listening to the next, what we perceive in the music changes from one hearing to the next because the brain is no longer what it was on each previous hearing. Our brain is changed so we are changed so our experience is changed.

The lesson for us as music educators is that every musical experience we offer our students affects their brains, bodies, and feelings. In short, it changes their minds, permanently. If we are conscientious, it does so progressively.

We call such a process "learning." That capacity to learn, to grow and develop, occurs with everything else that we humans experience in our lives, of course, because of the brain's plasticity—its enormous power to change itself in response to whatever our life's experiences present to it. The function of music education is, precisely, to foster musical learning—the changes that occur in brain, body, and feeling as musical experience becomes more deeply discriminative and more widely situated; that is, more musically intelligent.

Where in music do we find its capacity to offer the experiences of meaningful feeling it so uniquely makes available? Such experiences, after all, have been treasured by humans throughout history and are considered by many, myself included, to be the foundational value of music, the basis for all its many other values.

An extremely simple, elegant way to express where in music one finds its root value—that is, its unparalleled capacity to engage us in significant affective experience—is found in the title of Damasio's second book, *The Feeling of What Happens*. This simple phrase captures within it and finally brings clarification to decades, perhaps centuries, of philosophical debate on the relation of music and affect and why music seems to cause affect as powerfully as it does. It pinpoints what underlies all the missteps that philosophers of music have made over the centuries by trying to explain musical affect at the level of emotion rather than the level of feeling. Acres of trees have lost their lives to the paper required for arguments about why and how some music is "sad" and why we would willingly subject ourselves to such music, no one particularly wanting to feel sad. A whole literature exists on this issue, a literature that, if not sad, is certainly depressing. Damasio's phrase allows us to escape this musical/philosophical black hole.

Sadness is an emotion. Music can certainly indicate sadness or other easily identifiable emotions—what Peter Kivy calls "the garden variety emotions" (1984, passim). Similarly, music can indicate various images, stories, or events. Music is very poor at this kind of delineation but it does so nevertheless. That is not its primary function, however. All such delineations can be accomplished as well, if not much better, in a great variety of other ways. What music does, as nothing else can, is to *make something musical* out of any and all delineations.

How does it do this? By making things happen that only sounds configured to do so can accomplish. *Valse Triste* can validly be called "sad," just as *Jingle Bells* can be called "happy." What makes them *music* is what happens to their sounds as they unfold. The feeling of what happens then includes sadness or happiness; or a description of a march to the gallows, or of the seasons, or of *An Appalachian Spring*, or social/political/moral/religious statements, all of them framed in the animated energies that music brings to awareness. The intricacies, specificities, and exactitudes of what happens to musical sounds as composers, performers of compositions, conductors, improvisers, and arrangers choose to make the sounds happen, is what our brains and bodies process as feeling at the level of consciousness.

We cannot adequately label with words the feelings we undergo as the sounds happen during the course of musical experience because our conscious undergoing of them can not be captured in the delineative manner in which language functions. As Martha Nussbaum puts it in her monumental book on emotion *Upheavals of Thought* (2001), it is an "important recognition that musical structures are not translatable into linguistic structures" (258–59).

That is, what happens in music at the level of our undergoing of it is not translatable into language. We willingly listen to sad music not to feel sad, but to go beyond sadness to where music takes us. It takes us to the feelings of what happens which both contain sadness and transform it into musical experience—into musical meaning. Nussbaum goes on to say that music, in "its very indefiniteness from the point of view of the propositional use of language, gives it, frequently, a superior definiteness in dealing with our insides" (269). I would argue that this happens not just frequently but always. As Damasio comments, "How intriguing that feelings bear witness to the state of life deep within" (2003, 140).

This definiteness, this preciseness, is what we feel and treasure as we experience "the feeling of what happens" in music. In his wide-ranging book *Consciousness* (2002), Adam Zeman states the same idea by quoting Langer, who said, "What is felt is always action in an organism." Creating and responding to art, Zeman explains, are "active processes, consuming time and energy . . . part and parcel of an attentive exploration of the world." That exploration is a process "of seeking and interpreting significant detail" (190–91).

Artists deal, precisely, in significant detail; detail, that is, that grasps our awareness and our feelings by its actions: "what happens" to them in their becoming. Feelings unfold as the music unfolds. That unfolding, created for conscious undergoing perhaps more powerfully and precisely by music than any other of life's opportunities, takes us deeply within the conscious condition achieved by the human brain and body. Experience of that sort, music likely its paradigm, enables us to "know thyself" deeply, reaching to the core of our condition as conscious organisms. At bottom, I suggest, that is what is so satisfying, so spiritual, if you will, about musical experience in all its manifestations.

We in music education are nurturers of consciousness. The experiences and learnings we offer are directly related to the nature of consciousness itself as the feeling of what happens. Being human includes sadness, happiness, and all of the emotional, cultural, political, and ethical dimensions of human life. Music encompasses all of it and takes all of it further, to the feelings of what happens to all of it when it is transformed into the dynamics of musical sound as each particular music in the world creates that dynamic. That is what makes music so special, I propose, its endless capacity to expand the intricacies, depths, breadths, and diversities of conscious awareness, made available to our minds and bodies through felt, sonic experience.

Every musical experience that we have changes who we are. Although musical experience occurs in the present during which we are engaged in it, it also endures within us, in our brains and bodies. As brain research suggests, we are changed by each of our experiences: our selfness accumulates as our experiences accumulate. Why else would we bother to learn anything, except that doing so transforms us beyond the immediacy of a particular learning experience? The brain's plasticity sees to that, allowing us not only to know within a particular experience of music (and of everything else in our lives) but also to develop, to become, to evolve in our personhood, each of our experiences stamping itself indelibly with its contribution.

THE EDUCATION OF FEELING

We are back to learning and to the primary mechanism for it—education. In a more profound way than I have ever before been able to grasp, brain research has deepened the meaning of a phrase I encountered early in my career and have used all my adult professional life: music education is the education of feeling. In light of all I have said here, that well known phrase can be viewed with renewed power. The education of feeling, as music uniquely accomplishes by its employment of the significant unfolding of sounds, is, as directly and abundantly as humanly available, an expansion of our humanity. That sounds dramatic and far from the technicalities of brain research. I am suggesting that there may very well be a defensible consilience of our biology and our devotion to music education.

REFERENCES

Damasio, A. 1994. *Descartes' error: Emotion, reason, and the human brain*. New York: Gosset/Putnam.
———. 1999. *The feeling of what happens: Body and emotion in the making of consciousness*. New York: Harcourt Brace.
———. 2003. *Looking for Spinoza: Joy, sorrow, and the feeling brain*. Orlando: Harcourt.
Ekman, P., and R. J. Davidson. 1994. *The nature of emotions: Fundamental questions*. New York: Oxford University Press.

Flohr, J., and D. A. Hodges. 2002. Music and neuroscience. In *The new handbook of research in music teaching and learning*, ed. R. Colwell. New York: Oxford University Press.

Gaffney, J. 2003. Are superior wine-tasting abilities all in the mind? *Wine Spectator*, September 15, p. 13.

Hodges, D. A. 2000. Implications of music and brain research. *Music Educators Journal* 87 (2): 12–22.

Kivy, P. 1984. *Sound and semblance: Reflections on musical representation*. Princeton, NJ: Princeton University Press.

Nussbaum, M. C. 2001. *Upheavals of thought: The intelligence of emotions*. Cambridge: Cambridge University Press.

Siegel, D. 1999. *The developing mind: How relationships and the brain interact to shape who we are*. New York: Guilford Press.

Torff, B., and H. Gardner. 1999. Conceptual and experiential cognition in music. *Journal of Aesthetic Education* 33 (4): 93–106.

Wilson, E. O. 1978. *On human nature*. New York: Bantam Books.

———. 1998. *Consilience: The unity of knowledge*. New York: Knopf.

Zeman, A. 2002. *Consciousness: A user's guide*. New Haven, CT: Yale University Press.

PRESERVING AND ENHANCING OUR VIABILITY

OUR VALUES IN
SERVICE OF OUR FUTURE

Why trouble ourselves about a future in which we will not be here to engage ourselves? After all, our responsibility is to do the best we can while we can. The future will have to take care of itself.

Makes sense.

It also makes sense to care very much about what our profession will become after the time when we make our contributions to it. First, since those who follow us will inevitably carry our influences with them, just as we do with those who preceded us, we have an obligation to make those influences as beneficial as we can.

Second, looking forward to what we might become allows us to assess, with broad perspective, what we now are. What are we doing that deserves, even demands, perpetuation? Answering that question from the perspective of the future forces us to look closely and honestly at our beliefs and actions. Yes, we treasure them now, but which are worthy of being sustained? Which pass the test of ongoing significance, at least potentially? And which, from that perspective, seem less important, or even superfluous?

Looking back from an imagined future gives us a remarkably clear vision of ourselves—one that makes us want to clear out some of the weeds, straighten up some of the disorder. The view from tomorrow provides us with powerful incentive to clean up our act today.

In the following essays I project into the future as well as my imagination allows, as a means to make our present as viable as we are able and as forward-looking as the future summons us to be. Risky business, given all the uncertainties of future-think—but, I am confident, well worth it for all of us now, and possibly then.

21

IS MUSICAL PERFORMANCE
WORTH SAVING?

What a question! Who would even think of asking it, and why?

Well, several people, including myself, and for very good reasons. Our almost exclusive concentration on performance, both in general music and electives, and our many unconvincing justifications for its predominance, have put us in an extremely tenuous position as to whether we are perpetuating what some have come to regard as an unnecessary, outmoded way to be musical, thereby insuring that we will be viewed similarly.

A compelling argument has been made that we do not need performance any more because of readily available and remarkably effective electronic technologies for creating and sharing music without the arduous labor that performance beyond rudimentary levels entails. These technologies ensure the robust continuation of music because they allow music to be composed by all who desire to do so, and they make it possible for all that composed music to be immediately available to people without the complex paraphernalia and high costs required when performers must be the interface between compositions and audiences. So who needs performance anymore? Let it go, this view asserts, with good riddance to all the time, toil, and trouble it has cost people over the centuries.

Perhaps the demise of performance will not materialize in the near future because changing the entire history of music to a new paradigm would take a fair amount of time. But it deserves our serious attention if we want to avoid or at least forestall what it would do to the world's musical cultures and to music education, especially in the United States, to the degree it does take place—as seems more and more likely to occur.

In this essay, I confront the issue by reviewing several arguments for preserving performance in the face of its potential decline or disappearance. Finding them inadequate, I propose that there is a value unique to performance so compelling that losing it would deprive humanity of a precious, irreplaceable way to be intelligent, a loss of major proportions. We as music educators have the responsibility to acknowledge the issue and to begin creating solutions now so that the future of performance might be one of enduring importance rather than insignificance.

The following essay was originally published in the *Arts Education Policy Review* 95, no. 3 (January–February 1994). Used by permission.

For the very first time in human history the question posed as the title of this article can be—and, I believe, must be—asked. We who are alive today are the first to be confronted with the very real possibility that musical performance, without which music heretofore could not have existed, is in danger of becoming obsolete in or at least tangential to the art of music. Those of us who are devoted to music and to music education cannot escape pondering the possible consequences of this historically unprecedented development and what our obligations might be in face of it.

The threats to the necessity of performance as part of music, and to its hegemony in the musical world in general and in music education in particular, stem from two technological developments, each of which profoundly affects the role of performance as an aspect of musical experience. The first development was the invention about a century ago of sound recording and playback equipment and its rapid refinement to the point at which people, not only in the West where it was developed but all over the world, could afford to take advantage of it.

This technology changed the face of music dramatically. Suddenly, all people were able to experience music of a diversity and complexity far beyond their own limited abilities to produce music themselves, whether by their efforts to perform or to improvise or, in cultures where composing had become a specialized function, to compose. Before the advent of audio equipment people had access only to music that they were able to make for themselves, either alone or with others, or were able to hear by being within physical earshot of other performers. In societies in which professional musicians existed, in the West and elsewhere, amateur music making provided many people with a good deal of musical satisfaction, just as it does today. But only a tiny percentage of the population in such societies had access to anything more than music made by amateurs, since more complex music composed, performed, or improvised by accomplished musicians was available only to those of great privilege in society. And only a very few people could ever experience music of other cultural groups outside their own community.

There is a tendency to romanticize and idealize the days before audio equipment by fantasizing both about the satisfactions people gained by making music for themselves and about the wonderful collective spirit engendered by the communal necessity for people to make the music they had to have. These values were and remain genuine, just as were the values of the self-dependent growing, harvesting, hunting, and cooking of one's own food; the self-dependent education of one's children; the self-dependent building of one's own dwelling; and on and on with all the societal functions that have long since become other-dependent in most places in the world. In the case of music, as with most other communal activities, its sudden availability infinitely beyond self-production was seized upon voraciously, gratefully, and joyously all over the world.

There remain on earth some pockets of self-dependent societies that cling to the values of self-determination and self-fulfillment of many or most needs, and we tend to regard them with the nostalgia and admiration that we project on simpler times. But few would choose to return to the severe limitations inherent in such times and such societies even if it were possible to do so.[1] In music, audio equipment democratized musical experience by making the musics of practically all cultures and periods of history, from the most popular and folk-based to the most professional and esoteric, easily available to anyone who wanted any of it, just as modern supermarkets made easily available to us foods that are produced and prepared with a diversity and level of expertise unimaginable in self-dependent societies. The economy of musical experience changed radically from one of scarcity and circumscription to one of abundance and boundless variety for, effectively, all people. That plenitude of accessible musical experience through recordings and other media is the major characteristic of present-day musical culture and music education in the West and practically everywhere else on earth where the technologies are available.

That abundance had a price. Performing became an activity of choice rather than of necessity. Many people who would have naturally become involved in some sort of performance experience as participants in supplying the music needed by a community, and who would have enjoyed performing even if at a quite modest level of proficiency, no longer had to make the effort. Their musical needs could be met easily and in many ways more adequately by listening, and recordings came to be used in place of live performances in many social situations.

In addition, the limitations of mediocre performance ability became clearer because audio technology professionalized performance. Standards of performance were inevitably pushed ever higher as performers competed with one another to supply music to a music-hungry audience. It would have been impossible for the general public and even for the best musicians in earlier centuries even to conceive of the levels of performance expertise we now accept as normal, both live and on recordings. Most people today, fully aware of a standard they can never hope to achieve, willingly accept the easily available expertise of professionals (not just in music, of course, but in practically every other aspect of life) and therefore need not devote their time and energies to an activity they do not value over others that compete for their attention and cultivation.

Some do value performing, of course, and become part of a still-thriving amateur musical culture. Some 15 percent of the students in U.S. schools choose to engage in performing activities of a fairly serious nature requiring sizable expenditures of time, effort, and to a lesser degree money, although most of them have no intention of pursuing music as professionals.[2] That rate of elective involvement is unprecedented in school systems elsewhere in the world as part of school-offered opportunities taught by full-time certified specialists, and it is one of the great success stories of U.S. music education that we have managed, in the face of often severe odds, to build the size and quality of the performance program to the impressive levels we have attained. Nevertheless, in the musical culture of the United States and in most of the world today performance has become very much a dispensable option as a way to have musical experience.

Now the plot thickens. Until recently performing remained a necessary component of music even though it became unnecessary for most people to engage in it to enjoy music as an important aspect of their lives. In musical cultures that depend on aural transmission of music; that is, cultures in which the functions of composers and performers are not separate, performance has been and will remain the essential musical creative act because every performer is also a composer (or improviser, to be more descriptive).

In cultures such as those in the West and in many others around the world the functions of composers and performers became largely separate, composers becoming dependent on performers to transform their musical ideas into the actuality of perceptible sounds and performers becoming dependent on composers to supply them with music to perform. That interdependence has long been a salient characteristic of Western music other than for improvisatory genres, now most notably jazz.

Now a second technological development has caused nothing less than a revolution in the well-established dependence of composers on performers. With the advent of musical synthesizers and computer technologies performance has become unnecessary in accomplishing the previously essential function of bridging the gap between composers' musical thinking and the sharing of that thinking with listeners through performers' interpretations of it. Composers can now produce every imaginable sound, including those of traditional instruments if they so choose and many sounds heretofore unimaginable, on electronic devices; they can record those sounds electronically; they can manipulate and develop and extend and alter those sounds to their musical heart's content (which is what composing is all about); and they can produce a record of those sounds faithfully captured electronically and immediately available for listeners to experience.

The performer as essential middleperson between composer and audience has become obsolete. Of course some or many composers can and no doubt will continue to compose music that requires performers or that combines electronics with performers, at least at present. The major point—the troubling, even dismaying point for those devoted to performance—is that composers no longer need to do so. And when a societal role such as musical performance becomes unnecessary there is the real risk, perhaps the inevitability, that it will decline or even disappear.

There are signs everywhere that performance is already being seriously affected by technological substitutes. In all aspects of contemporary musical culture, from popular to concert and everywhere in between, previously performer-dependent tasks are being taken over by synthesizers, computers, drum machines, and the like, as substitutes for the many musicians formerly needed to produce the variety of sounds now producible by one or a few players. An American Music Conference survey in 1989 revealed that the most frequently played instruments among teenagers (aged twelve to nineteen) were portable keyboards, synthesizers, and electric pianos (34 percent),[3] all of which significantly alter the traditional performer role by giving their players compositional opportunities that do not require further actions by performers. Further,

> while only a relatively small number of respondents have used a computer
> to make music, more than 80% of [teenagers] are aware of the computer's

music-making capabilities. And, the majority of respondents . . . show at least moderate interest in learning to use a computer for this purpose. Not surprisingly, current players show the strongest interest, but substantial minorities of past and non-players are interested as well.[4]

Interest in computer composition is spreading rapidly. Today no important university in the United States is without an electronic studio or laboratory in which young musicians are being trained to compose using this technology. It is no longer unusual for high schools to have such equipment—sometimes magnificent equipment—and, as the costs become more manageable even larger majorities of youngsters and other people will no doubt take advantage of the composer-performer unification this equipment makes possible.

I believe we are facing a watershed event in the history of music that is at least comparable in magnitude to the invention of the phonograph a century ago. This time the role of performance will be changed even more than it was by the phonograph. That change may well be in the direction of extinction.

Here is how the matter is put by Stan Godlovitch in a recent issue of the *Journal of Aesthetic Education*:

> Here's a wayward question: Are performers necessary to music? Put it another way: Is the performer-interpreter, the specialist musician, the instrumentalist, merely a contingent component in the art form music? Is it merely a contingent fact that music is a performing art, at least as has been understood for some 1,000-plus years? Is it just an accident of technology that for some centuries certain manually skilled specialists were needed to intervene, as it were, between inventors and their audience? . . . No one denies that we enjoy and revere performers. But are they eternal parts of the team? Suppose we argue that the emphasis upon vocal and instrumental training has less to do with anything intrinsically *musical* than with something extrinsically *pragmatic* or, worse, *decorative*. Crudely, musicians are trained as they are in instrumental technique *just because* we've not yet figured out a more efficient way to avoid the trouble and cost incurred in getting the musical invention to the ear or, worse, *just because* enough listeners savor the *visual* spectacle to keep players on the payroll. But once such means are available, instrumental music, familiar as special skilled dexterity, will become as quaintly old-fashioned as boiling water on a wood fire rather than using a microwave, tying shoelaces rather than using velcro, using a hand plane rather than a thickness planer, and so on.[5] (Emphases in original)

Godlovitch proceeds to analyze the issues relating to the status of musical performance as contingent rather than as essential in music, and as assumed to require a sort of "special agency." He concludes as follows:

Once one accepts that the so-called special agency of musicians, traditionally conceived, need no longer play a dominant role in music making, you start to suspect that whatever is *was* that players contributed to music making becomes less and less the exclusive province of the "special agents" of music. That is, whatever specialized music makers were called upon to contribute by way of realizing a work in sound need no longer depend on their services. Once the matter of sound realization is broadened out to encompass any sound making means that achieves the desired end, the tradition of highly skilled physical maneuvers on some special physical resonator becomes nothing more than a tradition—an entrenched yet passing way of doing things. . . . Just consider Glenn Gould's famous recording studio sessions in which the saved renditions were composites of preferred and spliced segments of takes. Even so, all the "bits" required the technical genius of a Gould *at the piano*. But even that is now a mere vestige of tradition, for now someone with great musical insight and maybe *that alone* (i.e., one lacking all instrumental savvy) may conceivably leave behind "piano performances" of matching genius without ever having had any "familiarity" with the piano. Such a "performer" achieves the ultimate relief—the musician liberated from all instruments. Here we reach the final contingency of performance, the final removal of the middleman between inventor and consumer, and the end of another tragic millennium of hard manual labor.[6] (Emphases in original)

What are we to make of the matter so starkly put here? Should we regard the end of performance, or the beginning of the eventual end of performance, as a happy event? Why should we regret losing the "hard manual labor" performing requires? We certainly don't regret losing other forms of manual labor that machines have displaced. We recognize that technological progress causes hardships to people who have been replaced by machines but we nevertheless have to get on with it if the vastly greater benefits are to be realized.

Is this also the case with musical performance? After all, the loss of performance as a separate function in music will be replaced with something never possible before the invention of computer technologies—the ability of all people to *compose* music more easily and readily than ever before in history.

Previously, composing required such an enormously daunting facility with technical prerequisites such as musical notation that only the tiniest percentage of people in Western culture could ever achieve more than very limited results as composers. Now computer technology has democratized composition as recording technology previously democratized listening, and people all over the world are beginning to take advantage of this unprecedented opportunity. Isn't the loss of performing a small price or, anyway, an inevitable price to pay?

Many if not most of us, myself emphatically included, would claim that such a price would be exceedingly high. The prospect Godlovitch presents seems exaggerated, unrealistic, even in a way perverse. He himself is disturbed by the thoughts he has expressed: his last sentence, following the quote above, is "Somehow, I can't yet read this as a happy ending, but I don't know why."[7]

Surely we would agree that the loss of performance as an important or even central role in music would be a decidedly unhappy ending. But that ending is no longer inconceivable, and unhappy as that thought might make us we had better not settle for not knowing why. We had better, if we want to preserve and protect performance, be able to explain just what we would lose if it disappeared or dwindled to a historical remnant of pre-technological civilizations. Just why *do* we value musical performance? Is there anything we can do to forestall or avoid its demise?

Such questions, of course, cannot be answered quickly or easily. We will have to explore possible answers assiduously and from a variety of perspectives ranging from the philosophical to the sociological to the psychological. We will have to be clearer than we have tended to be about what our goals are for involving students in performing, what performing offers that is unique to it, and how best to realize whatever values we embrace through ways of teaching that focus on the enhancement of those values. We will have to be convinced that all the "hard manual labor" performance entails is worth it, and we will increasingly have to convince a public less devoted than we are to such efforts and less and less dependent on them for musical experiences that it should support such efforts through public education. Surely our work is cut out for us.

I want to reflect here about some possible do's and don'ts for our work based on several recent writings dealing with values of performance. I will then offer some suggestions for what seems to me a particularly fruitful line of inquiry about what might be the deepest value, or among the deepest values, of doing the hard work of performing, and why this value should be preserved.

What we need to avoid, I would suggest, are arguments that take us to two extremes.

The first extreme is to base our defense of performance on claims so far-reaching and general that many other activities could equally well fulfill them. We have a long history of doing this. Involvement in performing, we have argued, will develop just about any desirable individual and social goal one might think of, whether discipline, sociality, good citizenship, teamwork, better grades in the academic subjects, divergent thinking, and on and on with a host of virtues circling around but not centering on the unique nature and challenge of musical performance.

Such arguments tend to distract from and distort, and therefore weaken, an explanation of that which is available from performing but cannot be gained equally well from other activities, thereby obligating us to continue to cultivate performance experiences and even expand them in face of a dwindling necessity to do so.

An example of a well-meaning, thoughtful, yet ultimately troubling argument for nonmusical values of performing is Jane W. O'Dea's attempt to link performance training with moral development and the cultivation of virtue.[8] Musical performance, O'Dea points out, requires practice in using a score as a guide to a set of possible decisions, in applying what one knows about performance traditions to that set of decisions, and in taking all such guidelines and applying them to the particular decisions required to bring the music to expressive life in a way original to the performer yet faithful to the internal, musical needs of the composition. All this takes place through a process in which the performer explores possibilities, discovers potential solutions, critically assesses them, and makes decisions accordingly. This process continues indefinitely, "the composition ultimately being realized through a kind of ongoing critical yet creative exploration, where each successive sounding leads to a progressive selection and refinement of interpretive possibilities."[9]

I find this description accurate and convincing. I fully endorse its analysis of the creative process as being, in large part, a series of explorations, discoveries, and the attendant critical and reflective making of decisions. I also agree with O'Dea's claim that this requires a "moral" commitment to adapt one's own needs to those of the music one is serving.[10]

It is less easy to support the claim O'Dea makes that engaging in such activity will develop certain attitudes and dispositions—courage, truthfulness, patience, tenacity, honesty, generosity, modesty, empathy, and "reasoning"[11]—not just in the act of performing music but as traits generalized to the lives of those who perform:

> In summary, music in performance "is" a species of moral education. It fosters the acquisition and exercise of morally relevant and desirable character traits and dispositions, Moreover, it accomplishes this through being itself a form of moral conduct, one where one learns through doing and thereafter comes to love and to be capable of "practical wisdom."[12]

It is not easy to endorse such propositions because there is an unsupportably large leap from the narrow claim that certain traits and dispositions are required in a particular activity to the broad claim that those traits and dispositions will be manifested generally in a person's life beyond that activity as a direct result of engaging in that activity. We can no longer subscribe to "faculty psychology," which did make such claims,[13] and we cannot naively assume "automatic transfer" now that we have become painfully aware of the complexities, difficulties, and uncertainties of transfer.[14]

If such transfer was the point of performance and performance instruction it would have to be taught for directly, persistently, and assiduously. Those who taught it would not only have to spend inordinate amounts of instruction time doing so (perhaps *all* the time available, given the complexities of such matters) but would also have to manifest clearly and strongly that their own lives were models of such traits as a direct result of their being performers. They would also have to demonstrate that they are expert in educating for virtue as a major if not *the* major goal of their instruction.

One may be excused for raising one's eyebrows a bit at the assumptions embedded in such a scenario, not only from the students' perspective of whether performance teachers are to be regarded as particularly appropriate purveyors of virtue, but from the teachers' perspective of being responsible (and no doubt accountable) for the degree to which they inculcate virtue in their students.

Further, and particularly germane to the issues of how we can best explain the values of performance and most effectively teach for those values, the claims O'Dea makes can be at least as well made for many other activities, not just in the artistic realm where the similarities among various creative roles are obvious, but also in a great many other creative endeavors in practically all aspects of education and life. The stumbling blocks of overgeneralization about the effects of performing are strewn in our path when we extrapolate all sorts of factors from the performance context to life in general. We would be well advised, I think, to steer clear of as many of those stumbling blocks as we can as we seek a better understanding of the fundamental values of performing.

The issue of whether musical performance produces nonmusical results is also raised by V. A. Howard's suggestion that, since musical performance requires a particular kind of judgment making in which musical imagination plays a crucial role, the person who has engaged in that activity will be influenced to have better taste.[15] Howard is very cautious about jumping too far from music to other aspects of life, mentioning the now discredited ideas of faculty psychology and more recent attempts to leap from particular learnings to widespread applications:

> Hence, learn "synectics" or "lateral thinking" and ye shall be creative! Learn logic, or some variation thereof, and ye shall be a critical thinker! Nobody of course subscribes to these views as just stated, but they lurk in the background as a hidden agendum, as yet another instance of the wistful wish to achieve high ends by fixed means.[16]

Yet for all his caution Howard cannot resist flirting with this wistful wish, as in "Even when [musical] technical capacities are safely locked away in physical memory, the elements of judgment and choice remain—in the form of decisions of taste and style."[17]

In his excellent explanation of the mindfulness and imagination called for in productive drill (as opposed to thoughtless drill), he suggests that "through drill we not only learn by example and instruction, but become examples of the very things we learn. One might even think of this as the existential predicament of practicing anything at all: you are what you learn to do routinely."[18]

Taken modestly and within the context of musical experience Howard's claims seem reasonable, even self-evident. Within the circle of musical experience and what it does to us it is entirely defensible to believe that, for example, musical engagements "educate feeling."[19] What I am questioning here is not that musical performance (or any other musical involvement) profoundly affects our lives, which of course it does, but whether specific aspects of musical involvement can be claimed to transfer automatically to nonmusical settings. That particular claim should be made only when strong evidence can be given that it is correct, and I do not believe such evidence exists.

Another example of a potential stumbling block that arises when nonmusical value is attributed to performance appears in an analysis of performance as being an instance of play in the sense explored by Johan Huizinga in his important work on this subject.[20] Eleanor Stubley provides a detailed and careful exposition of how performance can be regarded as play, in which the performers establish a "feeling of being apart together" through their immersion in the "rules of play."[21] In the self-created world of regulations in which play exists the participants enter the world of the music, separate themselves from activities in the ordinary world, and obtain a sense of spiritual elevation as they mold decisions about how to best represent the musical thought in a composition or tradition.

Concepts from play theory are both useful and provocative in explaining the phenomenological subtleties of musical performance, I believe, and we gain some excellent insights from analyses such as Stubley's. Again, the problem is not that such insights as Stubley's (or O'Dea's or Howard's) are misguided or irrelevant; they are decidedly not. But in attempting to justify musical performance on the basis of such characteristics we inevitably run into the fundamental question of whether we need performance if we are to attain the claimed values. The values of play in human life may be attained in a great number of ways, many if not most of which do not require the demands, sacrifices, and talents entailed in reaching levels of expertise in which the "play" of musical performance creation is achieved; ways in which far more people are likely to participate. We can and should incorporate the insights that such perspectives add to our understanding of the many values inherent in performance (Stubley's advice about how to make group performance more productive of shared knowing is particularly pertinent) while continuing to search for values yielded by performance that are not readily available elsewhere.

At the other extreme from the one that claims values too broad to be sustained uniquely by the activity of musical performance is a position that so exaggerates the role of performance as an aspect of musical experience, and so elevates the performer as the be-all and end-all of music, that it gives the impression that no other musical involvements are worthy or valid. In this view there is only one way to be genuinely engaged with music: to make music as performers do, understand music as performers do, respond to music as performers do, and value music primarily or entirely because it can be performed.

This argument is what Jacques Barzun characterized as "the professional's fallacy."[22] In this outlook the world is seen properly only through the eyes of the professional, any other view being incomplete, myopic, and naive. To really know something, according to this view, is to know the details known to the professional. Education therefore consists of inducting the uninitiated into the perspectives and skills of professionals. "The universal formula is: 'you cannot understand or appreciate my art (science) (trade) unless you yourself practice it.'"[23]

This view, as Barzun explains, not only disenfranchises all but the expert from any genuine pleasure and insight,[24] but gives the public every right to dismiss such claims as being the specialized, narrowly focused bias one would expect from those whose reality is entirely determined by what professionals must know and do. In this case, ironically, the perspective is that of the particular class of professional musicians, performers, now themselves in danger of extinction, whose special pleadings can and will be understood to be self-serving.

We will have to be wise enough to explain the unique values of musical performance without alienating all those who will not and need not acquiesce to the claims that the entire musical world is encompassed by the performer's perspective on music and that the music education enterprise should consist largely of training students to become performers. We will need to explain what is precious about performing music without denigrating other valid musical involvements and without so emphasizing the teaching of performance that we endanger the larger enterprise of music education in which performance plays an important but not exclusive role. As Estelle Jorgensen points out, defining musical participation exclusively in terms of performance participation rules out the major way most people in our culture actually participate in music—by listening, creating a dichotomy of those who "truly" participate and all the rest, who are merely "passive." Audience members, she argues, can be and should be regarded as active (and essential) participants in musical experience.

> If the broader notion of the musical event is admitted, and participation is construed to indicate the degree of involvement in or commitment to some sort of musical activity—be it composition, performance, or listening—it would not seem necessary to restrict the meaning of participation to so-called "productive" . . . musical activities. Rather, the particular musical activities such participation is directed toward could be specified, such as *participation in* composition, performance, listening, or the like. Such an approach would avoid the error of defining participation too narrowly.[25]

Intimately connected to the professional's fallacy that performance is the primary if not the only way to be truly involved with music is the argument that performance expertise affords the truly proper lens through which music should be experienced even when one is not performing. Performance training, it is claimed, is the correct way to carry on music education for all children in all aspects of the music curriculum, because while the vast majority will not continue to perform after leaving school they will have been left with musical habits and understandings essential for any and all musical enjoyments. The performer's perspective, then, is the proper perspective—the *genuine* perspective—for all musical experience.

Despite the ubiquity of this belief among music educators (practically all of whom were trained to be performers) there is little evidence that it is correct and much opposition to its fundamental premise—that all musical experience should stem from performance experience.[26] The research on the effects of performance experience on subsequent or parallel nonperformance experience has not been sufficiently analyzed to allow any confident conclusions, except that it seems clear that particular skills of listening are inculcated among those who have received substantial performance training.[27] There seems to be little question that performers do indeed respond to music they hear in ways characterized by their performance perspective. This is also the case with composers and critics,[28] just as it is likely to be with conductors, music teachers, instrument makers, sound engineers, and with any others who take the perspective of their particular expertise when responding to music. It is not possible to take no perspective when listening to music: some mindset must exist or no interaction could occur. According to Francis Sparshott:

> These different understandings of music and approaches to it [of performers, composers, musicologists, etc.] do not sum. They are, beyond a certain point, mutually exclusive. Someone who hears as a violinist is not free to listen as if he were not. Nor, when listening to music in one tradition, can one exclude from one's mind knowledge of alternative traditions that may affect one's evaluations and must affect one's understanding, however conscientiously one may relativize one's judgments to what one knows to be relevant. . . . And composers and performers are aware of what they are doing as related only to what functions as the immediate context of their practice and in the ways that relate it to their practice. Again, there are different degrees of awareness of the variety of available approaches and slants, and each of these degrees has its own advantages and drawbacks. There are, then, different ways of relating to music within musical understanding. None of these are for all purposes better than all the others, and no one purpose has such privilege as to warrant exclusive authority for its viewpoint.[29]

Further, while performers are influenced to respond to music from the viewpoint of their performance training, that viewpoint itself is not guaranteed to include musical understanding, which requires a perspective more inclusive than those that performers necessarily have attained. This point is made by Leonard B. Meyer in a discussion of the insufficiency of perception when unaccompanied by comprehension. It is possible to notice a great many of the details performers are likely to notice without understanding the larger musical meaning in which those details play a role.

> It is important to note that neither memorization nor performance necessarily entail understanding. Just as it is possible to learn to read, to memorize, and to recite (perform) a series of meaningless syllables or a text in a language one

does not know, so it is possible to read, memorize, and perform music that one does not really understand.[30]

Meyer's point is hardly surprising to college-level music educators, who are keenly aware of the common discrepancy between entering students' well-developed technical performance skills and their faulty, partial, and naive understandings of the music they are performing in the wider sense of its musical structure, historical-cultural contexts, and aesthetic-musical implications. It is possible of course for performance teaching to include such musical understandings as integral to performing. I will argue in my conclusion that it must do so if the particular understandings performance can yield are to be gained.

A striking example of a view embodying many of the attitudes connected to the professional's fallacy, and the exaggerated assessment of the performer's perspective within musical experience, is provided by the "praxialist" position recently adopted and propounded by David J. Elliott. Praxialism (from the Greek *praxis*—deed, act, action) focuses on the things people practice in action as the locus for knowledge and meaning in human affairs. It is the polar opposite of formalism, which looks to the inner structure of objects and events, captured and displayed by the interrelated elements of which the objects and events are constituted, as the locus for meaning. Formalism and praxialism represent extremes on a continuum, the one claiming "product" as the be-all and end-all of experience, the other making the same claims for "process."

When applied to music (or to any of the arts) both positions help illuminate the complexities of this multifaceted phenomenon in that each identifies one essential dimension of music without which no music could exist. Clearly music entails a practice (as any human endeavor does)—a doing, or engagement, or involvement in something humans find meaningful to do. But just as clearly that practice is aimed toward producing and sharing *music*, a phenomenon recognizable because it consists of sounds purposively put together (formed) to be sonorously meaningful. Musical *praxis* is always *musical* praxis. Form and practice, product and process, I would suggest, are mutually interdependent in all exemplifications of music everywhere in the world and at any time in human history.

When this interdependence is overlooked or minimized we are confronted with the dangers of extremism. Full-blown formalists, best exemplified by certain art critics and theorists in the early years of this century (who were reacting against what they perceived to be the undue and impure reliance on the referential material characteristic of nineteenth-century romanticism) tended to ignore the artistic meanings gained by involvement in musical processes. They believed that the experience of the autonomous artwork was largely separated from the contextual richness of meaning in which the work resides.[31] Since the meanings of music, they claimed, come exclusively from musical form, and since the great masterpieces of classical Western music are monuments of formal complexity—the very paradigms of what form can achieve—the music worthy of serious study and respect is the music of the great Western concert tradition. Such music represents the counterpart to the "great books," "great plays," and so forth, being a repository of enduring, consummatory human meanings, and so must be valued and studied for those meanings as part of any serious education.

The tenets of formalism are, obviously, alive and well in much contemporary thought. Perhaps that is fortunate, because form is a sine qua non of all art, music most definitely included. But taken too monolithically, formalistic positions neglect other aspects of meaning that need acknowledgment if the full dimensionality of human aesthetic potential is to be achieved.

Elliott's full-blown praxialism displays the same hazards at the other extreme of the continuum because exaggerated attention to process causes as much of an imbalance as does the counterpart attention to product. The very act of performing music becomes so magnified in importance that it leads, inevitably, to a skewed, impoverished view of the multifaceted nature of music and the variety of valid ways people can be engaged with it.[32] All other forms of musical involvement, and all other perspectives on what music consists of, are wiped away in Elliott's pronouncement that "music is something that is manifested first and foremost in the deployment of specific sets of musical know-how. In short, 'music' exists in musicians and is what musicians know how to do."[33]

One would think that this definition of music would be startling to most people in the world who are likely to say that music is something they enjoy. That something is the sounds they hear—the products of a process. People may have little or no "musical know-how" in the sense Elliott intends, and may certainly not consider themselves to be "musicians," but will nevertheless correctly claim that music exists for them as an important, even essential aspect of their lives. This would be true, one would think, for musicians who for some reason could no longer perform. Does "music" no longer exist for them? Or are the possible *perspectives* on what music is, and who owns it, simply more diverse than an extreme praxialist position can allow?

There is a villain in Elliott's scenario—what he terms the "aesthetic" view of music—which apparently consists of a formalism so pure and extreme that even the original formalists would be disconcerted by it. Elliott por-

trays this aesthetic view (and the views of aesthetic education that are pur-
portedly based on it) as having sprung directly from the eighteenth-century
philosophers who founded what we now call the discipline of aesthetics.
These philosophers, as Elliott depicts them, were not at all the contentious,
multifarious, ever-changing thinkers any history of aesthetics tells us about
but instead were uniformly fixated on the position that

> *music* is a matter of aesthetic objects that exist to be contemplated aestheti-
> cally; that is, in abstraction from their contexts of use and production. . . . In
> this view, music equals objects, and the mission of music education is to give
> people access to the insight that those objects, works, or "pieces" contain. . . .[34]
> (Emphasis in original)

This picture of what the originators of aesthetics believed is not only simplistic, it is entirely incorrect in implying that whatever it was they believed
is still the canon in present day aesthetics. As Joseph Margolis points out,
"It is easily demonstrated that the master themes of late twentieth-century
aesthetics (and philosophy of science) are either completely absent from,
or have only barely been glimpsed in, the work of our eighteenth-century
cousins. (How could it be otherwise?)"[35]

According to Elliott, not only does contemporary aesthetics continue
to follow slavishly an outmoded eighteenth-century aesthetic position,
but "aesthetic" music educators adhere to this view slavishly. This view is
villainous, Elliott argues, because it denies or denigrates what *really* is important about music—the actions taken to produce it. Aesthetic educators,
says Elliott, consider those musical actions to be trivial, if not worse, as an
aspect of what performers actually do. The skills performers must have according to the aesthetic education view, says Elliott, are simply mechanical
and mindless bodily movements—a view antithetical to proper praxialist
beliefs. According to him I exemplify this view because for me, he says,
"skill is something associated with 'endless, repetitive, convergent drill of
exercises that are devoid of musicality.'"[36]

That quote would surely seem to be a vindication of Elliott's view that
skill has been dismissed as an aspect of music and musical experience by at
least one aesthetic music educator (me) who instead cares only for "music
as object." But the picture changes radically when one reads the quoted
words in their context, in a chapter of my 1989 edition of *A Philosophy
of Music Education* devoted to the performance program as an essential
aspect of aesthetic education, in a discussion of how beginning instrumen-
talists need to be, from the start, educated to be creative musicians rather
than to be limited to drill on the mechanics of technique.

If a beginning instructional methodology is so skill bound that little if any musical expressive exploration is taking place, little if any individualized problem solving of a creative nature is taking place, little if any diversity of stylistic possibilities is being experienced, little if any leeway is provided for using technique imaginatively rather than in endless, repetitive, convergent drill on exercises that are devoid of musicality, then that methodology is engaged in training in the narrowest, most restrictive sense of that word. Such a methodology produces automatons rather than musicians, dependence rather than independence, a view of music as regimented technique rather than as creative expression. The values of such a regimen are antithetical to aesthetic education in performance, which is devoted to *music making* through skillful performing. *Music making* is the point, and the point must be made from the very start if musical values are to be internalized as being primary rather than as being secondary to technique or even nonexistent.[37] (Emphases in original)

Elliott's misrepresentation of an aesthetic education view of performance demonstrates a praxialism so narrowly defined as to be threatened by the reality that in some beginning methodologies skill is abused by being musically decontextualized. Being discomfited by a more balanced view of skill as proposed in aesthetic education (at least in my own version of it) Elliott is willing to distort that view to give the false impression that aesthetic educators must be contemptuous of skill.

Elliott would seem to understand that *informed* skill is an essential factor in making performance what it is, in that in certain other of his comments he makes a distinction between performing that is musical and performing that is merely mechanical. And he is occasionally forced by his explanations to concede that music can be understood from other perspectives than those that see it as being strictly the practice of musicians. But he can maintain these more balanced positions only sporadically, being so driven by the need to exaggerate "practice" as the only true way to know music and to teach it. Listening to music (especially on recordings!) is a distinctly inferior, even suspect, way to participate in music, in that listening, unlike performing, can only be passive and partial:

> In contrast [to performing], the experience of listening aesthetically to recorded pieces (i.e., music conceived narrowly as a collection of autonomous products) is twice removed from the fundamental experience of musical reality. First, the full extent of procedural musical knowledge is not deployed while listening to recordings. Hence, students do not experience the interaction of generative and evaluative musical strategies that performing requires,

nor does listening engage the whole self (listening, by itself, separates cognition and action).[38]

That listening is itself a mode of musical intelligence, requiring the creation of a coherent experience through problem finding and problem solving in an extended act of musical thinking and feeling, receives no credence in this perspective. And, ultimately, the professional's fallacy prevails for Elliott:

> A key aspect of every form of education, then, is to engage students in the thinking process of the subject at hand by enabling them to think as . . . a chemist, a writer, a musician . . . thinks. To think in this way is to *do* chemistry, literature, music, and so on.[39]

It would seem unfortunate, unnecessary, and self-defeating to focus so intensely on skill-based musical acts as the only valid form of musical experience that other musical involvements are alienated or denigrated, especially at this time in history when musical performance skill has already become largely elective as a prerequisite for musical enjoyment and seems to be increasingly at risk of becoming even more so. We do no favor for musical performance, or our musical culture, or music education, when we give the impression that the skills of performance are all that can possibly count in musical experience, just as we also are doing no one a favor to claim, at the other extreme, that performance is a remedy for all of life's ills or a recipe for all of life's virtues. Claiming too much for performance, whether praxially or extramusically, obscures the unique, fulfilling, life-enhancing values of performing music. We need to explain what those values are in clear, convincing, yet balanced ways so that we can encourage people to avail themselves of them as one dimension of a musically satisfying life.

What might such values be? Only a few brief, tentative reflections can be offered here on what needs to be an ongoing agenda to examine the many rationales that already exist for performance and to add whatever new insights might appear. I want to suggest a particular perspective that I think would be fruitful if developed in that it is inclusive of many values traditionally and more recently claimed for performance (encompassing both praxis and social-personal benefits as valid dimensions) yet possibly generative of some persuasive arguments not yet made optimally. My focus here will be on performance in the context of the threat to it posed by contemporary technology; that is, music composed with the express intention that it will then be performed. (Improvised music, while likely to be affected by composers' dwindling reliance on performers, is less immediately implicated in the situation being discussed here.)

The perspective I offer would claim that there is indeed something special about the "special agency" Godlovitch dismisses when he characterizes performance as being an activity of only "hard manual labor." Far from being an instance of brute muscle exertion, as Godlovitch implies, the specialness of musical performance is that it is one of the relatively few ways humans have to be intelligent.

This notion immediately calls to mind Howard Gardner's theory of multiple intelligences as proposed in his influential book *Frames of Mind*.[40] Gardner achieved a kind of breakthrough in thinking about the nature of intelligence (if only by reviving and giving contemporary credence to an old idea)[41] by arguing that it consists not only of the logical/linguistic capacity traditionally measured by IQ tests but that intelligence is a more diverse phenomenon than it is usually conceived to be. The inclusion of musical intelligence as one of the seven Gardner identified was, naturally, a godsend to those long convinced that music calls on the human capacity for mindfulness rather than only being a matter of emotional catharsis or technical agility or idiosyncratic genius. But only seven domains of mind made Gardner's cut—not seventy or seven hundred.

So while intelligence seems to be more varied in manifestation than in the more commonly held view exemplified by IQ testing, in Gardner's analysis there are still only a relatively few ways to be intelligent. Each of those ways requires, as prerequisites,

> a set of skills of problem solving—enabling the individual *to resolve genuine problems or difficulties* that he or she encounters and, when appropriate, to create an effective product—and must also entail the potential for *finding or creating problems*—thereby laying the groundwork for the acquisition of new knowledge.[42] (Emphases in original)

In his chapter on musical intelligence, Gardner hints that there are several ways in which such musical problem solving (intelligence) can be manifested—through composing, performing, and listening. I believe there are, in fact, real differences as well as obvious overlaps among these "musical intelligences." My focus now is on the particularities of the problem-solving activity involved in performance.

I want to suggest, as the underlying concept for why and how performance can be conceived as an act of intelligence, that in addition to giving sounds meaningful form—a condition shared with composers and listeners—this form-giving, in per-*form*-ance, is dependent on and springs from the skills of the knowing body. It is the involvement of the apprehending body in acts of forming sounds purposively—acts of per-*form*-ing—that sets musical performance apart as a realm of intelligence.[43] Musical performance, I am suggesting, depends on the body as executive, in which *executive* is simultaneously noun and verb.

Notice that form and action, product and process, are inseparable in this conception. Notice too that mind and body, or thinking and doing, are also unified. The musical mind of the performer (per-*form*-er) is manifested in the body's actions, the actions themselves consisting of *thought as act* or *act as thought*. Expressed as a "thinking with," the performer thinks musically (thinks of sounds forming) *with* and *in* the body.

Dancers and actors also think this way: they, too, are per-*form*-ers. Unlike those in musical performance (except when musical performers are also acting or dancing) the bodily actions of the dancer and actor constitute the artistic phenomenon itself: the body's actions are themselves the artistic events.

The bodily actions of musical performers are not in and of themselves the music (although the live observation of bodies engaged in the action of *making* the music is a powerful factor in the intimacy, or "self-engagement," we feel when listening to live performances). The body of the musical performer is the core, or nucleus, in which musical problems are dealt with; in which musical thinking takes place. That "thinking in sounds" is a thinking within the physicality of producing sounds, including as essential components of that physicality the feeling of the music, the feeling of the body in the act of producing the music, and all the knowings about how to do so authentically that are subsumed within the body in its musical actions.

Because of the intimate, inseparable relation within the body between the feeling of the musical sounds being formed and the bodily feeling of the acts of forming those musical sounds, each physical manifestation of performing—each particular instrument (always including the voice)—is likely to feel different because of the different bodily action it calls upon. The body's actions, in musical performance, are so minutely and exquisitely context-bound to the particular physical actions required by the particular instrument being performed that the inner feel—that which the body knows by feeling its actions—is coincident with the particularies of that instrument. As Mikel Dufrenne puts it,

> the violin throbs only if the performer himself does, the instrument being to
> the performer what the throat is to the singer, namely, an extension of his

body. Thus it is still in the human body that the music becomes incarnate, but in a body disciplined by the instrument, obliged to submit to long training in order to become the instrument of an instrument.[44]

Musical instruments provide the most extensive and intensive opportunity available to human beings to know within the body, through the body's activation of the acting, feeling, and thinking processes required to form sounds musically. In becoming "an instrument of an instrument," a person, *of any age and of any level of attainment*, is given the opportunity to think musically in the mode of performance—the mode of musical knowing as physical creativity.

Each particular instrument is a particular "theatre of operations" for such knowing to be encountered and developed: each offers its own set of musical problems to be thought/acted/felt according to the particularities of its physical requirements. So, in one very real sense, what pianists know, or what violinists, or singers, or clarinetists, or guitarists, or koto players know, is peculiar to their particular theatre of physical operations. In the broader sense, all manifest the common knowing of musical performing; the "knowing how" of the body when it is being musically creative.

Craftsmanship, then—the control in and by the body of musical thinking—is an essential element in performance: it is the body's manifestation of creative musical problem solving in which skill, thought, and feeling are unitary. The achievement of such unity is so powerful in human experience, and so rarely available in the ordinary opportunities life affords, that when we do achieve it we feel touched by transcendence:

> That is why there is something almost spiritual about craftsmanship, something that so integrates our human powers that we feel elevated by it. Anyone who has ever achieved real craftsmanship in some aspect of life knows its tremendous impact. When we labor to refine our craftsmanship, by perfecting our technical skills, by identifying deeply with our chosen medium, by endless practice with its expressive potentials, all of which require time and sweat and often frustration, we are not just pursuing dexterity—we are searching for creative communion with those materials, and to the degree we achieve it we have achieved craftsmanship.[45]

Music education, I would suggest, must as one essential element of the general music program continue to provide every student with the opportunity to achieve the unique form of craftsmanship available through musical performance. In addition, we must continue to offer special opportunities in performance to all who care to avail themselves of them through a wide variety of small and large ensemble and solo experiences in a great variety of musical styles and genres.

Whether as one part of general education or as the focus of specialized education our approach to teaching performance needs to be guided by the fundamental principle that we are developing, in musical performance, an inherent human intelligence in which thinking, feeling, and acting are uniquely conjoined in the process of bringing musical ideas to sonic fruition. The optimal development of musical performance intelligence will require that we keep in effective balance all its components—understandings we foster in our students about the structure, contexts, and aesthetic implications of the music they are performing; skills necessary to manifest those understandings as bodily actions; the affective involvement that insures that the musical results will be expressive rather than mechanical; and the generous provision of imaginative musical problem-solving opportunities so that genuine creativity is achieved.

None if this is new. None of it is foreign to our best achievements throughout our history. But now these obligations take on new urgency. Just at the time when musical performance has become threatened by technologies that can make it irrelevant, we are learning, more dramatically and persuasively than ever before, that it can and should be understood as a unique instance of that most precious of human attributes—intelligence. The internalization in the body of the knowings experienced by performers is so valuable in human experience, so fulfilling of the human need for creating meaning and sharing that meaning with others, that the very real risk of its loss from the repertoire of ways humans can experience meaning should concern all people.

We are not dealing here with a manual labor to which we can happily say good riddance. We are dealing with what is in very short supply in human potential—an endlessly challenging and diverse mode of intelligence—of meaning making and meaning sharing. The technologies that threaten it are not in themselves pernicious, not without inherent benefits in new opportunities to create musical meaning, not to be shunned or suppressed and certainly not to be reversed. We have only begun, through these technologies, a musical journey the consequences of which we cannot now envision. If those consequences, however, include the loss of performance as a price of the new musical potentials, the cost, I believe, will have been very great indeed.

NOTES

1. In an article in *Newsweek* (December 14, 1992), William Hargrove, a public-affairs worker who recently discovered the joys of saxophone playing, pleads with us to "forsake your CDs, throw off your headphones, and take back the stage." As we shall see, this call to self-creation of all musical experience grossly oversimplifies the realities of how music is shared in technological societies.

2. A national survey of band participation conducted by Yamaha in 1993 indicated that 22.55 percent of the students in small high schools, 12.99 percent in medium high schools, and 8.75 percent in large high schools were band members (national average 14.99 percent): Yamaha, *New Ways*, Spring 1993. Recent percentages are not available for chorus and orchestra participation, but data indicate that somewhat fewer high schools offer chorus experience than band experience, and far fewer high schools offer orchestral experience than band experience: see Charles Leonhard, *The Status of Arts Education in American Public Schools* (Urbana, Ill.: Council for Research in Music Education, 1991), 108–34.

3. *Music U.S.A. 1989* (American Music Conference), 19.

4. Ibid., 20.

5. Stan Godlovitch, "Music—What to Do about It," *Journal of Aesthetic Education* 26, no. 2 (Summer 1992): 1.

6. Ibid., 12–13. Emphases in original.

7. Ibid., 13.

8. Jane W. O'Dea, "Virtue in Musical Performance," *Journal of Aesthetic Education* 27, no. 1 (Spring 1993): 51–62.

9. Ibid., 57.

10. My own explanation of the exploration-discovery process by which artistic creation proceeds, including a description of performers as creative artists and the moral dimension of artistic creation, is given in Bennett Reimer, *A Philosophy of Music Education* (Englewood Cliffs, N.J.: Prentice Hall, 1989), 56–73 and 138–40. For a penetrating discussion of "obligation" as a factor in performing, see Morris Grossman, "Performance and Obligation," in *What Is Music?* ed. Philip Alperson (New York: Haven Publications, 1987). An excellent explanation of the exploration-discovery process in creating paintings is given by Clifton Olds, "Wollheim's Theory of Artist as Spectator: A Complication," *Journal of Aesthetic Education* 24, no. 2 (Summer 1990): 25–29.

11. O'Dea, "Virtue in Musical Performance," note 8 above, 59–61.

12. Ibid., 61.

13. A useful history of the rise and fall of faculty psychology and its theory of transfer is given in Robert F. Biehler, *Psychology Applied to Teaching* (Boston: Houghton Mifflin, 1971), 265–67.

14. For a clear description of recent thinking on issues of transfer and the difficulties associated with teaching for it, see D. N. Perkins and Gavriel Salomon, "Are Cognitive Skills Context-Bound?" *Educational Researcher* 18, no. 1 (January–February 1989): 16–25.

15. V. A. Howard, *Learning by All Means: Lessons from the Arts* (New York: Peter Lang, 1992), 13.

16. Ibid., 20.

17. Ibid., 13.

18. Ibid., 103.

19. As I claim in *A Philosophy of Music Education*, note 10 above.

20. Johan Huizinga, *Homo Ludens: A Study of the Play Element in Culture* (Boston: Beacon Press, 1950).

21. Eleanor V. Stubley, "Musical Performance, Play, and Constructive Knowledge: Experiences of Self and Culture," *Philosophy of Music Education Review* 1, no. 2 (November 1993).

22. Jacques Barzun, *The House of Intellect* (New York: Harper and Brothers, 1959).

23. Ibid., 11.

24. O'Dea, for example, states that "only someone with the relevant [performance] experience can recognize and appreciate what constitutes an original imaginative yet valid interpretation of a particular composition," note 8 above, 53, a claim that seems exaggerated if not simply mistaken. And Stubley also exaggerates the efficacy or primacy of the performance perspective by quoting from Thomas Carson Mark that "the one who knows something about the relation of the movements of the piano player to the production of the music from the piano will hear something the mere layman does not perceive." Thomas Carson Mark, "Philosophy of Piano Playing: Reflections on the Concept of Performance," *Philosophy and Phenomenological Research* 4 (1981): 299–324. "Proficient performers," Stubley goes on to say, "know what to listen for in a given work, and also what to listen for in a musical performance of that work," a typical ascription of primacy to the performer's perspective. Eleanor V. Stubley, "Philosophical Foundations," in *Handbook of Research in Music Teaching and Learning*, ed. Richard Colwell (New York: Schirmer Books, 1992), 10, 11.

25. Estelle R. Jorgensen, "On Building Social Theories of Music Education," *Bulletin of the Council for Research in MUSIC Education*, Spring 1993, 37.

26. A pointed disavowal of the need to "do" a thing in order to appreciate it as amateurs do (amateurs in the sense of people who love the thing) is given by the dramatist August W. Staub, in "Toys, Adults, Frivolity, Understanding, and the Demise of Serious Art Education," *Design for Arts in Education* 91, no. 4 (March/April 1990): 6.

27. A major review and analysis of the research literature on the effects of performing on subsequent non-performance musical experience is being conducted by the Center for the Study of Education and the Musical Experience, the Ph.D. student and faculty research group at Northwestern University. Results will be made available as soon as the research is completed.

28. A remarkably clear and illuminating picture, through protocol analysis, of the differences in listening perspectives of three highly accomplished musicians—a performer, a composer, and a critic—is given in David S. Zerull, "The Role of

Musical Imagination in the Music Listening Experience" (Ph.D. diss., Northwest-ern University, 1993).

29. Francis Sparshott, "Aesthetics of Music: Limits and Grounds," in *What Is Music?* note 10 above, 86.

30. Leonard B. Meyer, *Music, the Arts, and Ideas* (Chicago: University of Chicago Press, 1967), 291.

31. A brief explanation of the suppositions of Absolute Formalism, and their implications for music education, is given in Bennett Reimer, note 10 above, 22–26.

32. Elliott's magnification of praxial concerns extends to teaching music, in which the major aspect becomes, inevitably, the teacher's improvisatory actions in the process of teaching, David J. Elliott, "Rethinking Music Teacher Education," *Journal of Music Teacher Education* 2, no. 1 (Fall 1992): 6–15. For a critique of this view of teaching and teacher education, see my "Avoiding Extremes of Theory and Practice in Music Teacher Education," *Journal of Music Teacher Education* 3, no. 1 (Fall 1993): 12–22.

33. Ibid., 23.

34. David J. Elliott and Doreen Rao, "Musical Performance and Music Education," *Design for Arts in Education* 91, no. 5 (May/June 1990): 28.

35. Joseph Margolis, "Exorcising the Dreariness of Aesthetics." *Journal of Aesthetics and Art Criticism* 5, no. 2 (Spring 1993): 134.

36. Elliott and Rao, note 33 above, 25. The quoted fragment is from Reimer, note 10 above, 192.

37. Reimer, note 10 above, 192. Emphasis in original. Also see, in this book, the pages surrounding this quote, and the discussion of craftsmanship (135–36) as an essential component of artistry.

38. Elliott and Rao, note 33 above, 31.

39. Ibid., 30. Ellipses and emphasis in original.

40. Howard Gardner, *Frames of Mind: The Theory of Multiple Intelligences* (New York: Basic Books, 1983).

41. Ibid., 7–11.

42. Ibid., 60, 61.

43. I want to reiterate that my insistence that form is an essential component of music does not equate my view with that of formalism, which emphasizes the primacy of form to the exclusion of content/context factors. For an excellent discussion of the characteristics of formalism, and on the contemporary anti-formalist stance that acknowledges the necessary role of form but does not negate extra-formal considerations, see Bohdan Dziemidok, "Artistic Formalism: Its Achievements and Weaknesses," *Journal of Aesthetics and Art Criticism* 5, no. 2 (Spring 1993): 185–93.

44. Mikel Dufrenne, *The Phenomenology of Aesthetic Experience* (Evanston, Ill.: Northwestern University Press, 1973), 22.

45. Reimer, note 10 above, 135.

22

MUSICAL DISENCHANTMENT AND REENCHANTMENT: THE CHALLENGES FOR MUSIC EDUCATION

It's hard to imagine that music can lose its power to enchant. Yet an important philosophical viewpoint in our time, postmodernism, has emphasized, cogently and realistically, the dark side of our art and what our responsibilities to it are as educators. I am fascinated with this turn of thought and with its implications for us in both personal and professional dimensions.

I spend a good deal of time reading postmodern literature and trying to develop sensible positions about it, positions that respond positively to its persuasive power while at the same time being critical of foundational errors in its arguments and troubling connotations for how and why music is valued and taught. Not an unusual perplexity for a philosophically minded thinker to face, of course. Just about every philosophical position, old or new, presents us with a mixture of seemingly valid arguments and also troublesome ones. Working one's way through the maze is what it's all about for those who take such matters seriously.

I am in the midst of such deliberations when beginning work on my reconceived version of *A Philosophy of Music Education: Advancing the Vision* (2003) and am determined to include in it a discussion of the issues postmodernism has raised for us. At that time I receive an invitation to present the keynote address to the 2001 conference of the Australian Society for Music Education, a welcome opportunity, a good chance for me to deal in some detail with this important movement, pointing out our need to be aware of it and to try to both benefit from it and to overcome what I see as its dangers.

Despite the cautions and deprecations of postmodernism, we must reclaim our responsibility to share with our students the deep exhilaration and joyous fulfillment music offers abundantly, and to do so unashamedly and generously. Underneath the hard realities that also must be addressed in our teaching, our great gift is to nurture music's ability to enchant—to captivate us with its delights. To the degree we minimize that dimension, our future will be bleak.

The following essay was originally published in the *Australian Journal of Music Education*, no. 1 (2001). Australian Society for Music Education Incorporated. Used by permission.

> And moved by gentle gales, their murm'ring sound
> The tuneful reeds, soft waving, whisper'd round.
> To wake the hollow reed, hence, man acquired
> The melting art, and all the soul inspired.
> Then sounds he learnt to breathe, like those we hear,
> When the soft pipe salutes th' enchanted ear;
> When to the nimble finger it replies,
> And with the blended voice in sweetness vies;—
> That pipe that now delights the lawns and groves,
> Where'er the solitary shepherd roves,
> And speaks the dulcet language of the Loves.

That poem is by the Roman philosopher and poet Lucretius, who lived from 97–54 BCE.[1] It tells how musical instruments might have come into being, taking advantage of the natural phenomenon of whistling reeds of the field, recognizing the "tunefulness" of the sounds they made, their potential musicality, something already existent as a human capacity and need. By waking the hollow reed with breath and nimble fingers, that is, through the skilled body, giving it human as well as nature's voice, the "melting art," music, was acquired, an art that inspires the soul, enchants the ear, delights the lawns and groves, and speaks the dulcet language, not of love, but of "the Loves." Not a language with a singular tale to tell, but a language that speaks of the many ways humans love.

How romantic was this ancient poet. How long-lived his insights, not only into the romantic 19th century when his poem would have been entirely at home, but even I suggest, now, in the cold light of the new millennium, over 2,000 years after Lucretius, a time when speaking of music, or of love, as being "dulcet"—sweet-sounding, soothing, balm to the ear and the heart—is likely to draw titters or perhaps embarrassment. Yet here is the voice of another poet, the American Robert Wallace, whose life and language are entirely of our own times. In commenting about poetry he says, "A poem, if it's any good, is a machine for loving with. It doesn't matter what—the ungainliest thing: a mutt, ourselves, the world. The love depends on the precision."

Love, apparently, is still around but now captured in the arts by their precision, their exactitude, their meticulousness in plumbing the depths and complexities and energies of our passions and giving them voice so we can experience them honestly, with clarity, with respect for what they tell us about the human condition, now, long into the past and, we can hope, at least as long into the future.

So how do we get from thoughts such as these, about music, poetry, love, to music education and to our hopes for it in the difficult world we live in, a world of politics, of competition for time and resources, of competing methodologies, of objectives, and assessment, and multicultural demands, and research, and social issues of all sorts, and teacher education, and dealing with computers, setting standards, and on and on endlessly with the complex lives we live every day as professionals? Who has time to talk of love?

Well, I do. A plenary address, after all, is a luxury, a kind of "time out" from all the pressing concerns that will be dealt with in all the many sessions that will go on at this conference. What I hope to do in this short time is to connect all those concerns, all those necessary dimensions of our shared professional lives, to the love that drives our work and gives it meaning.

I hasten to reassure you that I do not mean love in a sentimental sense (although there's nothing wrong with that). I mean it in the sense that applies to our devotion to our profession, a devotion based on the depths of our feelings about music, which has transformed our lives, and on our deep desire to make the power of music more readily available to people, particularly young people, so that their lives might also be more lovely as music has helped our lives to be. Speaking of love, then, is speaking about why we care so much about what we do and how we can transform that caring into effective education.

Addressing that topic will require a hard, critical look at two dilemmas impinging on an attempt to explain our caring for music and how we might teach music with caring. The first dilemma is theoretical, the second practical. The theoretical dilemma is that, at this time in history, the notion that music, and all the arts, have anything to do with loving, meaning, joy, soulfulness, delight; in short, with enchantment, has been called seriously into question. The practical dilemma is that in many places around the world our carings about music and our students' carings are alarmingly discrepant; even, perhaps, contrary.

These two dilemmas intersect. The theoretical issues of what is valuable about music and the arts; what they have done, what they are doing now, and what they might do in the future for people, have many practical consequences for education. And the practical issues of whether and why we in music education are often out of touch with the artistic/aesthetic needs of our students, are rooted in theory, or to put it differently, in assumptions we tend to hold about the values of music and the arts.

There is another way these two dilemmas relate to each other. Both stem, I believe, from a strong tendency in the music education profession toward unreality. We have tended to live in a world of our own making, ignoring or simply being unaware of currents of thought swirling around us in the intellectual life of our larger world. That unawareness has tended to extend also to the lives and loves of many or most of our students in regard to music, or perhaps an unwillingness to acknowledge the actualities of their musical lives and enthusiasms. I believe that around the world music educators are becoming more and more cognizant that music and the arts exist on a different plane outside the schools from inside the schools. The disjunction between how we conceive an effective music education and what our students want from it, we are realizing, has become, perhaps has always been, problematic.

Perhaps my characterization of music education in many cultures as suffering from unreality sounds harsh or overly critical. I do not mean it to be. I believe it tends to be a consequence of our love, both for music and for young people.

Love, unfortunately, is often blind, not because of ill-will or thoughtlessness or lack of character, but from wanting so much to do what our hearts desire as to neglect the still, soft voice of reason telling us to open our eyes, not just our hearts, to what is really going on. We need, I think, a strong dose of reality, not to disaffect us from music education (heaven forbid) but to strengthen our conception of what we can do, with eyes wide open, to be more effective for both our art and our students. In the cynical, unsettled, and disenchanted world in which the arts now live (I'll explain that in a moment), music education retains a refreshing albeit somewhat naive devotion to music as humane, as a blessing in our lives. We need to preserve that delightful attitude and to share it with young people, who are deeply in need of enchantment. (One could say the same of older people.) But we must do so in full recognition of the many troubling issues in the world of the arts that tend to depress and weaken their power to charm and to nourish.

So bear with me, please, as I rather briefly explain some recent ideas about life, belief, truth, and music, that would seem to disavow many of the values music educators around the world tend to cherish, myself included, and, I would guess, many if not all of you as well. I will then offer some comments about the reality gap in which we tend to exist. I will end on a hopeful note (believe it or not) with proposals about how we can retain so much that is good and admirable about our values and accomplishments while also giving credence to and adjusting ourselves to the dissonant but persuasive voices of both some theorists and many students.

My own love for music began when, after several years of lessons on the clarinet that consisted entirely of playing exercises of increasing difficulty, I played my first piece of actual music, with piano accompaniment. The power of that experience was immediate. I fell in love, and knew that music in some form or fashion was what I wanted to spend my life with. All of you I am sure, and all our colleagues around the world, can tell the stories of how you and they first became captivated by music.

The wonderful early innocence of our love for music becomes immersed, as our careers advance, in issues and problems of both music and music education. On the musical side are far-reaching questions about what we can believe about music, what the purpose of music is, and what in fact counts as being "musical." On the education side are equally difficult questions about the many assumptions on which we base our practices. Those questions arise as the result of a recent wide-ranging critique of the arts as most of us understand them, and of education and the values on which it has traditionally been based. That critique, the most widespread and influential contemporary view in the intellectual community, is called postmodernism.

Perhaps some of you are deeply informed about this most characteristic belief system of our times. Perhaps some of you have a fair grasp of its arguments and perhaps others have heard of it but are not clear as to what it's all about. Let me give a very brief overview that I hope will be useful no matter the state of your present knowledge about postmodernism. I start with this because the postmodern philosophy is the background for, the basis for, the specifics of musical dilemmas and music education dilemmas now facing us.

One way to conceive what a philosophy is, is as a reasoned, structured set of propositions about an important aspect of human life. Under that definition postmodernism is not a philosophy.

First, postmodernists seriously and severely question the validity of reason; whether it is a primary or even valid basis for dealing with issues. Second, the idea of structure, or coherence, that ideas and arguments need to be related to each other in convincing ways, is also regarded as questionable, even misguided. However, reasoned propositions about life and how we should live it, made with great conviction and explained coherently, remain the basis for postmodern thinking despite that they are made absent a belief in reason or coherence. Whether this renders postmodernism unreasonable and incoherent goes to the core of the debate about its intellectual status.

Also deeply puzzling about postmodernism is the uncertainty about what, exactly, the "modern" is that it claims to be "post" to. This uncertainty about modernism has two aspects; the when and the what. As to the when, a variety of answers are found. In one answer the modern period began with the ancient Greeks (Plato in particular) and their use of reasoned argument as the foundation for how we can understand the world and act responsibly in it. But another answer is that the modern period began with the Renaissance, beginning in 14th-century Europe, with the enormous expansion of learning, literature, the arts, and philosophy that took place at that time.

Still another claim is that the "modern" began with the industrial revolution, starting in England in the late 18th century. But others say it began with the rise of avant-garde, experimental art in the early 20th century, or when that period came to an end in the middle of the 20th century. So with all these different conceptions of when modernism actually existed it is difficult to know what period of history postmodernism seeks to displace.

Similarly for the issue of what ideas characterize modernism that postmodernism calls into question. There is little agreement among postmodern thinkers as to just which ideas were central to modernism and which are no longer valid. So trying to explain postmodernism is a little like trying to herd cats. It's awfully hard to get the ideas moving in a unified direction. Nevertheless, it is possible to identify some generally shared postmodern propositions, or convictions.

The most basic one, perhaps, is that there are no and can be no "essentialisms." Essentialisms are universal, foundational, defining characteristics of objects and ideas; their "inner nature" or true substance. For example, postmodernists are likely to argue that there is no essential human nature that defines who we are. We ourselves and our particular culture define who we are. There are no ultimate "real" truths applicable to all people at all times and in all situations. Therefore there are no conclusive standards of correctness or worth. All our ideas and beliefs and values are local, transient, conditional, and partial. There are no higher truths out there awaiting our discovery if we were only bright enough to grasp them. That whole idea is misguided.

Especially misguided is our hope for progress toward a more just, more secure, more liberated world, guided by growth in knowledge, codified in democratic government structures, and celebrated in the arts. A false hope, as the violent 20th century made abundantly clear and as the 21st seems to be continuing to make clear. Our ideals have proven to be self-serving, as have our governments, our laws, our religions, all based on self interest and questionable motives, all instruments of cultural arrogance and the exertion of power over those not as "superior" as the dominant cultures.

Postmodern views present a picture of extreme diversity, disunity, multiplicity, even chaos as inevitable in human life. Uncertainty prevails and must prevail because order always implies power and therefore loss of freedom. Solutions, by nature, foreclose possibilities; every solution to a problem imposes another set of restrictions. So solutions are not the goal in life. Disruption is desirable. Dismantling beliefs is a positive thing to do, to reveal the injustices and faulty premises under which we have acted. Judgments of "better" and "worse" have no validity. After all, who can say what is better or worse? Why should some values be privileged over others, or some standards over others, or some views of goodness and correctness over others? Why should certainty be valued over uncertainty?

True, we are left by all this with little or nothing to rely on except, perhaps, an ironic attitude. Notice the widespread use of irony as a basic device in contemporary comedy. Listen to our comedians, on TV for example. In a world so absurd, so ungrounded in any reality we can rely upon, irony, a detached, sarcastic laugh at ourselves and our plight, is no doubt a useful response, one that allows us to at least blunder on.

Disenchantment indeed.

Does the picture I have drawn, and I want to assure you I have not overdrawn it, make you smile with delight, give you warm, cuddly feelings of pleasure and contentment? If so are probably a natural-born postmodernist (although, come to think of it, that's probably an oxymoron). If my description has made you squirm with discomfort you are not necessarily an unreconstructed, backward, oblivious modernist, as many postmodernists would gladly characterize you. Perhaps you squirm as I do because you feel that much of what postmodernism claims seems exaggerated, simplistic in a way because so insensitive to shades of gray rather than to just black and white. Postmodernists seem to be unwilling to recognize that there has been a great deal of good in the world along with the bad, a great many compelling ideas that have helped rather than hurt the quality of human life, a great many beliefs that have offered comfort and sustenance, and a great many improvements over time in our freedoms, our health and well being, our security, and yes, our pleasures.

Surely the imperfections postmodernism dwells on have been and are real. But do we have to throw the good away to ameliorate the bad? Can we recognize the failures in human history while at the same time recognize also the achievements, often the stupendous achievements, of this faulty yet often admirable creature we call "human?"

What have been the effects of postmodern thinking on our subject, "the melting art," music? Here are the first sentences of the first chapter of the book *Rethinking Music*:[2]

> Music may be what we think it is; it may not be. Music may be feeling or sensuality, but it may also have nothing to do with emotion or physical sensation. Music may be that to which some dance or pray or make love; but it's not necessarily the case. . . . What music is remains open to question at all times and in all places. This being the case, any metaphysics of music must perforce cordon off the rest of the world from a privileged time and place, a time and place thought to be one's own.

You will recognize this to be a postmodern outlook, given its uncertainties and its hint that any generalizations about music must necessarily be exclusionary. The influence of postmodernism on music and the arts has been profound. Indeed, the arts are probably the field most directly and pervasively affected by postmodern thinking. Here are three matters in which postmodernism has had far-reaching influences on the arts, music most definitely included.

First, the arts have become highly politicized, being regarded by many, primarily or at least significantly, as agents of political activism and social reform. Art should be judged by two criteria: the reformist political stances it takes and how effectively it argues for them. Art is good, music is good, if it takes a good position on a political issue, that is, an issue having to do with power relations, and persuades others to adopt that position.

Second, and closely related to the first, postmodernism seeks to erase false and harmful distinctions between "high" art and "popular" art. That distinction is an elitist one, a way to privilege some people who share particular tastes, serving to reinforce their dominance in their culture. The arts need to be "leveled" because there are many traditions in the arts and none is inherently superior to the others. Pluralism, not a single, "correct" standard of excellence, is the aim.

Third, the image of the artist as a solitary hero bringing new meaning into existence needs to be abandoned. Those who respond to art create it as much as artists do because art does not exist until a respondent makes something of it. There is no "correct" way to respond to a work of art, no higher authority as to what is a better response. Art is what those who respond to it make of it. They are creatively equal to, perhaps superior to, artists themselves.

Recently the heat of the postmodern critique of modernism has cooled down considerably because of the recognition by some of its most staunch advocates that it probably went too far. We are witnessing what has come to be called "a return to the aesthetic." For example, Linda Charnes, a leading postmodernist theorist, gave a speech last August at the convention of that hotbed of postmodernism the American Shakespeare Society, which has for years reviled Shakespeare as being "a slave to the power relations of his moment in history." They have argued for a long time that any artistic values of his work are irrelevant, as is the entire idea of artistic value.

Charnes said, "We all avow we speak for oppressed voices of class, race, gender, nationality . . . but is this all we have to offer? It's time to get beyond the institutionalized debunking of the bourgeois autonomist or essentialist humanist self. The time to make a career of beating that horse has passed. Outside the academy," she reminded her audience, "there still exists some precious attributes—some humor, some poignancy, and some openly avowed love for art."

Astonishing words in that context.

And a special issue of the *Journal of Feminist Philosophy* on Feminist Aesthetics will soon be devoted to "the relevance and implications of the renewed attention to the role of the aesthetic; of good, even beautiful art and the pleasure we find in the beautiful." The demonizing of beauty, of genius, of questions of value, of aesthetic judgments, of art as personally illuminating and humanizing, has seemed to run its course. In an essay titled "The Return of the Beautiful," Alexander Nehamas of Princeton University explains that under postmodernism, "beauty came to seem morally and politically suspect as well as intellectually embarrassing. Now," he says, "as the millennium ends, beauty is suddenly back. It is impossible to keep up with the books that address it. Once again," he says, "we are willing to acknowledge that beauty is worthy of our love."[3]

But make no mistake. This return to the aesthetic, to the love of beauty, suggests a third position beyond the excesses of stereotypical modernism and equally stereotypical postmodernism. As Shakespeare scholar Ron Rosenbaum says, it is not "a quaint return of the past, but something new: the post-postmodern, perhaps."[4]

If that is the case, and I agree with Rosenbaum that it is, we will have benefited in a variety of ways from the agonies of philosophical conflict we have gone through in recent history, albeit that the conflict has largely been ignored in music education. Our enchantment with music, or, for those who had begun to lose it, reenchantment with music, can stand on firmer ground, with a clearer understanding that music along with the other arts has sometimes or often been exclusionary, self-serving, limited to only approved values, an approved canon, a set of assumptions too facile, too unexamined, too easily believed. The critique of aestheticism has almost always been of a particularly rigid kind of aesthetic Formalism that has no doubt deserved the opprobrium heaped on it for its limited vision and illiberal beliefs. But while the critique has itself been limited and illiberal it has also breathed some fresh air onto entrenched thinking.

I want to suggest that the most valuable effect the modern/postmodern debate can have on music education is to democratize our ideas about music, to open them up to a more liberal view than we have tended to have. A more open view, forced upon us by the harsh yet penetrating critiques of postmodernism, encompasses a far broader spectrum of musics as being valuable to study, to experience, to enjoy, than has been acceptable in many music education settings. It encompasses also a wider array of musical/societal functions than we have tended to recognize as being valid. Encompassed as well is a greater variety of ways to be engaged with music beyond the traditionally approved music education practices around the world.

All this allows us to be, at one and the same time, both philosophically more in tune with our times and practically more in tune with our students. For it is precisely our limitations of musical literature, musical uses, and musical engagements, that has tended to make school music a world of its own, foreign to the world of music most students live in outside school. I for one, having grappled with the philosophical issues raised by the postmodern movement have been led to recognize, more clearly than I had in the past, how unreal we in music education have tended to be. The challenge to music education of its unreality, while it has lurked for a long time at the edges of our consciousness, has now, I suggest, come out into the world and cannot any longer be denied or delayed.

So what do we do? Permit me to make a few suggestions. The first is attitudinal. Rather than being an imposition on us, the challenges we now face in music education in the United States, and I suspect to some degree in Australia and around the world, are an opportunity to become reenchanted with music and music education, to revel in the excitement and passion of music and the excitement and passion of young people for music.

But to allow that to happen we must open ourselves to "the Loves," to the many ways music can enchant and the many ways music education can be enchanting.

As one important example, it is unreal of us to assume that the way I was captivated by music, through performance—the way I would guess the vast majority of music educators fell in love with music—is the only way or even the primary way most students will cherish music. That simply does not seem to be the reality. For every one who does, hundreds more are enchanted by sharing the music others make.

There is nothing wrong with those people. They simply do not choose to do what so many of us have devoted ourselves to doing. Of course some or many will choose to be performers, and that should gladden our hearts. It's not a matter or restricting or dishonoring that particular way to be musical. Why in the world would we do such a thing? It is a matter, instead, of recognizing that music, and the world in which it exists, does not depend on that one enthusiasm. We must not go on as if the one way to be musical we tend to favor because of the way we have lived our musical lives must be the sole or major way everyone else must live theirs.

Perhaps in Australia this issue is not as pressing as it is in the United States, although I may be mistaken about that. There, the predominance of performance is so great that we may well have passed the point where anything substantial can be done to achieve more realistic balances. Given the diminishing role of performance as an aspect of music because of technological advances that eventually may make performance a relic of history, a profession frozen in performance as the be-all and end-all may be insuring its own obsolescence.

I believe that threat is entirely real. Computer technologies have taken us far beyond the need for performance in the traditional sense of making sounds by "breath and nimble fingers," as Lucretius put it. Music can now be both created and shared with never a performer being even remotely involved. Or with a severely restricted number of performers being involved. When I went to see Stephen Sondheim's *Sweeney Todd*, in New York, on Broadway, I was shocked to discover that this piece, which I consider one of the great works of musical theater (or, if you prefer, opera) of the 20th century, had an "orchestra" of three keyboard synthesizer players instead of the full pit orchestra one would expect for a show like this. And the music is magnificent. But it signals a sea change in our dependence on performing, as we generally conceive it, as being a requirement to have music.

Are we facing this challenge realistically? We need to clarify for ourselves and others what makes performance so unique and so necessary as to be preserved at all costs. For me it is the incomparable combination performance offers, first, for musical creativity, both in the interpretation of composed music and in improvisation, and second, in the use of the body in an exquisitely refined manner to produce meanings. That combination is so powerful, so significant for humans to experience, as to warrant our dismay that it may be and perhaps inevitably will be lost or significantly diminished in influence. What should we do about this? I don't have a good answer, unfortunately, but I do believe we must have the courage and the realism to begin to develop one.

Ironically, the same technologies that may eventually make performance as we now know it an activity for ancient history enthusiasts is presenting a whole new world of opportunity for musical creativity; that is, composing. I mean composing not just in the traditional sense of creating music for performers to present to audiences, but also composing in ways never before possible; before, that is, computers made sounds and organizations of sounds available that go far beyond what performance is capable of. A new horizon for musical imagination, musical challenge, musical meaning, and satisfaction and enjoyment is opening.

That opportunity for creative musical experience will be taken, I suspect, either with the involvement and guidance and caring nurturance of music educators or it will be taken without us. I would prefer that it happen with us playing a major role rather than with us as irrelevant to or even as an obstructive force for one of the great watershed periods of music's history. Are we preparing ourselves to play a positive role in both preserving the best of our past and building an exciting new musical paradigm, a more satisfying paradigm because of our wise, sensitive leadership?

In this I am quite encouraged by our fast and impressively developing expertise in matters technological and our increasing understandings about how to help students develop compositional musicianship in ways never before possible. I see this as a major area in which we can make important contributions to the health and welfare of the art of music in cultures around the world, and by so doing to the health and welfare of the music education profession.

Another issue about which we need to become more realistic. Both now and no doubt in the future the music we as professionals most tend to treasure and the music our students most tend to treasure will inevitably not be identical, if only because of the difference in our ages. That difference is built in to the very fabric of education, in which the older and presumably wiser are the guides for the younger. The differences in tastes and enthusiasms of different age people is exacerbated by the fact that every professional educator in the schools grows older every year, while his or her students remain the same age, year after year after year. The music of this year's youth, of course, is very different or somewhat different from last year's. What is our responsibility to the music most popular among each emerging group of students and to the musics of each preceding group of students?

In a clever and insightful article by the popular music scholar and teacher Glenn Gass, he relates that in recent years the students in his course on the history of rock music at Indiana University have come to regard early rock as "classical music," music of the Great Tradition. He says, "the giggles at getting course credit for rock and roll, and the delight at 'pulling one over on their parents,' have been replaced by a genuine desire to learn about rock's heritage."

"The reaction of my students' parents has changed even more dramatically," he says. "I used to spend a good deal of time writing notes to parents explaining that 'Rock History' was indeed a real and worthwhile class. These days I spend more time fending off parents' requests for copies of my class listening tapes, and nodding politely as they tell me how happy they are that their sons and daughters are being exposed to good music like the Beatles and Elvis rather than the junk they play on the radio these days. It's getting harder" he says, "for rock to perform its most crucial function (driving parents crazy) now that Dad keeps yelling 'turn it up,' or 'I used to love that song.'"[5]

One answer to the question of what our responsibility is to popular music, the answer most often given in the United States, has been "none at all." Or, sometimes, benign tokenism. Other countries have been more forthcoming, at least in recent years, and have taken the need for significant engagement with the popular musics of school-age youngsters with much more seriousness. I hope you here have solved all the problems of incorporating popular music in music education to the degree of importance its major role in the lives of our students and in our cultures generally, calls for. I hope to learn from you while I'm here, because we in the United States need all the help we can get. We have very few people who can provide professional leadership in this matter and we desperately need thoughtful, realistic leadership. Giving popular music its full due as an essential experience for young people (and their aging parents) and as a literature deserving of as much respect on its own terms as other musics on their own terms, will go a long way toward reestablishing both the relevance of music education and its capacity to delight and enchant.

If, that is (and this is a big if) we are wise enough not to destroy our student's love of their music by our attempts to tame it to fit our sober, conformist musical agenda. We as well as our students can gain much in the way of reenchantment if we learn to respect, enjoy, and even revel in both old and new popular musics for what they are and what they do. No, we can't be adolescents again (thank God). But we can share, perhaps, in some of its exhilarating musical pleasures, and even, if we are very wise, enhance those pleasures for our students.

One more issue relating to the unreality of music education among many others that I will have to leave unaddressed here. I'm going to read the titles of several articles from professional journals. Try to identify which of our music education journals they may have come from:

"Provocation and Censorship in Music Education"
"Powerbrokers of Prejudice in Education, Music, and Culture"
"Music Education and Issues of Pornography"
"The Liberating Relevance of Feminist Music Education Pedagogy"
"Music and Fear: Observations on the Perils of Music Making"
"Diversity and Divisiveness in Music Education"
And my favorite, "If You Want to Get Stroked Talk to Your Mother: Music Education as the Discipline It Deserves to Be"

Which of our journals published these articles? That's right, none of them. All of them come from journals in visual art education. I've changed only the terms art, or art education, or artists, to their musical equivalents.

Why are we so isolated from the many social, psychological, political issues surrounding us in the world we live in? I suspect that to some degree our art shelters us. We simply do not so often have to deal with many of the issues the visual arts and the verbal arts constantly face.

Is that enough of an excuse? Is there a degree of otherworldliness or self-protectiveness or even cowardice in our tendency to use our art to shield ourselves from reality? Music surely can be, legitimately, a retreat from the harshness of our lives and the difficult issues confronting all of us in these times. I am not suggesting that we so politicize music and music education that we become what extreme postmodernism tended to become, to the neglect of, even the denial of the comforts and joys of the beautiful. But do we need to get more real? Can a streak of thoughtful realism be a bracing, energizing, even humanizing force within our profession?

I tend to think so. I believe we can deal intelligently with difficult issues we usually ignore and can do so with a spirit of mutual concern and mutual support rather than of debilitating conflict or disaccord. I think we can be strengthened, as people and as professionals, from a more engaged posture than we have traditionally taken, and I think we can offer to each of our cultures a useful perspective, one not often heard in the debates that surround us. That, in turn, could strengthen our position as contributing citizens to the common welfare.

In one sense that may be perceived as being extra-musical. In another, deeper sense, it may instead be regarded as adding the dimension of musical meaning as an enrichment of concerns we all share as responsible members of our society. Also as a way to enliven and revivify our approach to doing what we exist to do; to expand and deepen the musical experiences of all our students.

Those experiences exist both in the world of music and in the larger world in which music dwells. A more realistically close relation between those two worlds might indeed position music and music education closer to the center of human concerns. We can and I think must recognize and honor the special way music encompasses the world by making music of our experience of the world. For me that is a foundational datum. At the same time we need to acknowledge that music is encompassed in that larger world, which gives us the experiences that make us who we are and from which we then make music.

We need not fear a closer association with the real world in which music exists. We can indeed rededicate ourselves to music as an essential source of enchantment that all humans cherish, while at the same time situating the gift of music more realistically in a world we embrace for what it is rather than for what we romantically project it to be. Becoming more real will enhance our efforts to nurture "the Loves" that music offers so powerfully and uniquely.

NOTES

1. The poem is from Thomas Busby, *A General History of Music* (New York: Da Capo Press, 1968), 3.

2. Philip V. Bohlman, "Ontologies of Music," in *Rethinking Music*, edited by Nicholas Cook and Mark Everist (New York: Oxford University Press, 1999), 17.

3. Alexander Nehamas, "The Return of the Beautiful," *The Journal of Aesthetics and Art Criticism* (Fall 2000).

4. Ron Rosenbaum, *New York Times* Book Review section, August 6, 2000.

5. Glenn Gass, "Why Don't We Do It in the Classroom?" *The South Atlantic Quarterly* 90, no. 4 (Fall 1991).

23

MUSIC EDUCATION FOR CULTURAL EMPOWERMENT

An invitation from MENC arrives. Would I be willing to present an address at the opening session of a two-day special event at the 2004 conference? Issues of policy for the future of music education will be discussed, with selected presentations, discussion sessions, planning meetings, and so forth. I am free to choose whatever remarks I feel are germane to the topic.

Right down my alley. As the years go by I find myself focusing more and more on issues of the future, feeling that unless our profession adopts some major new purposes and processes it will become—in fact has already dangerously become—a marginal field in education. Marginal to the existing realities of the thriving musical culture in which we go our own narrow way; marginal to how music is growing and changing, often dramatically, while we pay only token attention to, and leadership for, these changes; marginal to the musical lives of the students whom we are supposed to enable to find their personal role in that emerging culture.

I promise myself to be as straightforward about my increasing concerns for our future as I want to be and need to be. No punches pulled. Too much is at stake to be polite. I am ready, willing, and able to handle whatever response this might cause.

I work hard on my presentation, paring it severely to fit into the limited time slot assigned. That's the hardest thing for a writer to do, despite the fact that it often improves the product. I edit, edit, edit, edit as I always do, but now more unsparingly.

At the conclusion of my presentation, the audience erupts in long applause. Not what I expected. The open-mike comments and questions are enthusiastic.

Have I underestimated our readiness to look at ourselves clearly and honestly, even courageously? Will our clearer vision of the tasks we are facing lead to substantive action?

How I hope so.

The following essay was originally given as a speech the to International Music Education Policy Symposium, MENC National Biennial Inservice Conference, Minneapolis, April 2004.

This International Music Education Policy Symposium is taking place at an extremely opportune time. Our profession is at an important juncture in its history, one requiring serious reflection about its present status and future prospects. In this paper I will share with you, as directly and forthrightly as I am able, my concern that music education as we know it today, particularly as conceived in the United States but also around the world, is facing a potential crisis of irrelevancy. Few have openly and directly called attention to this elephant in our midst or have provided a vision of how we might turn this impending crisis around to our benefit. I will try to do so as concisely as I can.

The bad news about this crisis is that it has been caused largely by us. Music itself is alive and well, even thriving according to many criteria, in many if not most cultures around the world, certainly in this one. It is music education as we have envisioned it that has become dangerously insecure. As reported in the February 2004 issue of *Teaching Music*, music programs in the United States have experienced significant cuts over the past five years; the National Association of State Boards of Education concluded that the arts and foreign languages "are indeed at risk of becoming the lost curriculum."

The good news is that because we are the professionals largely responsible for this crisis we have the obligation and the power to rectify the situation. If we are to be successful in doing so we will need policies sufficiently bold and imaginative to effect a transformation in our ideals and our practices. We will have to accomplish something very difficult to accomplish— to break out of the tight boundaries of solving only those problems our present categories of thought allow us to address.

There is an irony in our dilemma of irrelevancy. The irony is that in the single most characteristic aspiration of music education in the United States and in other countries around the world, which has been to make available to students the opportunity to become a performer of composed music, we have succeeded magnificently. We deserve to be proud of the excellence we have achieved in fulfilling this worthy ambition. Our dilemma has not been caused by our remarkable ability to accomplish what we have most wanted to accomplish. Far from it. Performance as we conceive it, I would argue, provides us with the very model of how we are capable as a profession of being successful at achieving our desires.

The dilemma is that our vision of success, past and present, is insufficiently broad to satisfy the diverse nature of the musical enthusiasms in many if not most of the world's cultures. By our proscribed ambition we have neglected the musical realities thriving all around us and have thereby cut ourselves off from effective ways to help satisfy the needs of the rich, multimusical cultures existing around the globe. As Nicholas Cook, the British music scholar, puts it, "We have inherited from the past a way of thinking about music that cannot do justice to the diversity of practices and experiences which that small word 'music' signifies in today's world." We are left, in this situation, wondering why everyone has not bought in to our limited vision when we are so good at fulfilling it. We are left, finally, with an unsustainable gap between our professional image of what music ought to be and the way it actually is in musical life outside our ensembles and general music classes.

In the United States our avoidance of that actuality, our limitations in thinking outside the box within which our categories have confined us, is demonstrated by various arguments often made by music educators. One is this: We need to appeal to the broadest possible spectrum of students given how their musical tastes and enthusiasms are usually so divergent from ours. How can we accomplish this? We can work even harder to recruit them into our bands, orchestras, and choruses, and once they have adopted our musical preferences we should encourage the best of them to become music educators.

Unfortunately this so-called solution leads us to continue doing the one thing we have chosen to do and have done for some three quarters of a century with no significant change, but to try ever harder to persuade all students, no matter how diverse they happen to be, to devote themselves to the particular program we offer and some of them to commit themselves to propagating this single musical perspective.

This is not a solution: it is the perpetuation of the problem.

Another argument made is this: many students are zealous, deeply involved listeners who can tell us, in depth, after only a few moments of hearing a popular piece, the backgrounds of the piece and of its performers, why they value it, how it relates to similar and different pieces, the musical qualities it incorporates, and so on. (By the way, the musical expertise being described is seldom if ever acquired in school.) What should we do about students who demonstrate these high levels of musical literacy and comprehension? We must divert them from such interests, undermine their enthusiasm, and make performers out of them, in the ensembles we happen to offer, of course.

Such a plea eliminates from our responsibility the majority of students in American schools, who have no interest in becoming performers in bands, orchestras, or choruses but who are devoted to music passionately and intelligently. We cannot pretend to be relevant to the majority when what we offer is overwhelmingly a program reflective of our own values and our own interests attained because we are the ones who *did* achieve success in what has existed for so long as school music, all other values and interests being therefore, in our view, unworthy or even contemptible.

Is there a vision that would both protect and cherish our admirable success at what we have accomplished and also expand that success to all the opportunities for musical growth we have neglected or renounced, thereby allowing us to be whole?

I propose the notion of cultural empowerment as capable of encompassing an inclusive vision and a comprehensive, balanced, and sequential program of music education, an ideal we have long professed but have not yet seriously thought through let alone acted upon.

Cultural empowerment focuses on enabling every individual to accomplish two things in regard to the particular culture of which she or he is a member. First, to be able to share broadly in all the valued endeavors a culture makes available. That is the point and goal of what is called around the world the general dimension of education. Full citizenry in a culture opens the entire spectrum of its opportunities to all students through a general education that immerses them in the important ways they can partake of the benefits their culture offers.

A general education in music, accordingly, engages all students in all the many musical roles people actually play in their culture, affording a wide experience with and understanding of the diversities of musics and ways to be musical existing for their benefit. Such a general education empowers full cultural accessibility to music in all the ways it actually exists in the culture in question.

The second thing cultural empowerment enables is for students to become a contributor to the culture's endeavors by applying the breadth of their acquaintance with its opportunities to a particular aspect—a particular role—that fulfills their individual interests and capacities. That is the point and goal of what is called, around the world, the elective or specialized dimension of education. Full citizenry in a culture empowers students to find their place as contributors, which requires their discovery of a role they might play and effective initial preparation to play it.

An elective music program, accordingly, makes available to all students who choose to become involved in it the full spectrum of musical roles available in their culture, in opportunities for specialized, focused study as preparation for becoming an amateur or professional.

Crucially, cultural empowerment, in recognizing the twin realities of partaking and contributing as the bases for full cultural participation, requires a focus on individuality—the particularity of each person's needs, desires, and capacities as they interact with the entirety of their culture's possibilities. Conversely, when conformity is the goal, we are subjected to the "No Child Left Behind" mentality, which specifies in great detail, through a relentless testing regimen, exactly what every child is expected to achieve and at what level that achievement must occur.

Cultural empowerment is founded on an opposite premise. Three words express that premise, that goal of education: Each Child Fulfilled. Here, in this value, I propose, we embrace a genuinely humane education that honors diversity as being a foundation for a successful, life-empowering and life-enhancing culture. No Child Left Behind, by contrast, demonstrates that in action, the once often-heard slogan "compassionate conservatism" seems to be an oxymoron.

How would Each Child Fulfilled as a guide for action play out in music education? Would we have to start from scratch in pursuing its ambitious agenda?

Not at all. Luckily, we have available to us a powerful, inclusive set of guidelines for achieving the comprehensiveness and balance that mission requires, along with a practicable principle for building sequential programs of instruction. I refer to the U.S. National Content Standards for Music Education. Here is a ready-made, widely approved articulation of the diverse ways that music functions as an art; an art, it must be said, that like all others is deeply implicated with its cultural history, settings, accomplishments, and deficiencies. In short, its social realities.

The standards enumerate the diverse ways that people can partake of and contribute to music. Each content area of the standards translates into a musical role that must be played if this art is to be represented as it actually exists in the realities of its cultural settings. In American musical culture (and in many around the world) the nine content areas of the original standards translate directly into the roles of the performer of composed music (standards one and two), the improviser (standard three), the composer (four), the arranger (also four), reading and notating (which I propose be understood as being embedded in other roles in various ways rather than being treated as a role in and of itself), the listener (standard six), the theorist (analyzing and describing in six), the critic (standard seven on evaluating), the psychologist, philosopher, neuroscientist, educational theorist, and so forth (standard eight on music's relations with other endeavors), and the historian, ethnomusicologist, anthropologist, sociologist, social critic, and so forth (related to standard nine, understanding music's situatedness in history and culture).

Each role is a way to be musical in the culture of the United States, and each culture around the world can identify the ways to be musical it affords its members. And, of course, new and altered roles emerge in vital musical cultures and then need to be embraced.

Truly comprehensive general music and elective music programs represent, in equitable balance, all the viable roles available to be played in music. Each role, we must understand, requires the particular sequence of learnings characteristic of it. Learning to be a performer of composed music has its appropriate, developmental ways by which one becomes competent. Those ways are not simply transferable to every other role. That is one major reason our present response to the standards is both inadequate and unrealistic. We have changed little if anything about our program offerings to reflect the substantive musical-role diversities the standards identify. Instead, we have attempted to squeeze bits and pieces of all the other roles into our existing ensembles.

This does not and cannot fulfill the requirements of comprehensiveness or of balance or of sequential learning. It is entirely unfair to performance to be expected to be something it is not; to accomplish something it can not. Including the other roles as they relate to performance does indeed enrich and broaden students' conception of what being a musically educated performer entails. That is all to the good, and truth to tell it's about time we attempted to accomplish this in some systematic way as the standards now allow us to do. But that is different from opportunities to pursue all musical roles to which students might become attracted, each in its veracity as a genuine way the art of music is enacted in its culture.

Within the presently existing school music program we have no realistic way to fulfill the mission of cultural empowerment. We must break out of the box into which we have confined ourselves, general music reconceived to achieve genuine balance among all the roles, and performance continuing to be one essential component of a reconstituted elective program, but not, as now, the only role successfully available.

Are we capable of the challenge to become something we have never been, something that can create a growing, thriving future rather than one increasingly out of touch with the realities of our culture and therefore doomed to fade into insignificance? One stellar example of a new program within music education in the United States, providing a model for breaking out of the box, was the growth of jazz as an alternative performance elective and as an alternative literature to experience and learn about in general music. While it was accepted only grudgingly at first, being conceived by many as a lower form of music if music at all, we have now succeeded in overcoming that outworn stereotype and are serving a whole new population of students, offering them musical challenges and pleasures never before available in the schools. A whole new subculture has arisen around jazz education, the best possible evidence of the success of the endeavor.

We are now seeing the first stirrings of other possible subcultures such as composing, especially because of the availability of technologies that enable dramatic advances in compositional creativity. But a cautionary note must be sounded. In jazz, in composing, in the creativities and understandings of popular music still awaiting here the respectful attention it is now given in several other countries, and in all the other unrealized potentials for representing our musical culture honestly and comprehensively, we must learn to avoid "music educationizing" them by bleaching them of their veracities.

Every time we succeed in creating an additional, genuine culture of musical involvement in the schools we expand our relevance, our value, our claim to be a basic subject capable of serving all students rather than only a small minority. A new vista of what it means to be comprehensive, balanced, and sequentially effective opens up when we contemplate the possibilities for music education far beyond our historically limited ambitions. Opening ourselves to these possibilities allows our profession to become all it is capable of becoming, to serve all the students it is capable of serving, to demonstrate by its actions that it is worthy of the full support of its culture rather than trying to coerce that support by endless pleadings for a program attractive to few.

Are we capable of expanding our ambitions to embrace rather than evade the musical diversities our cultures embody, to empower each student to take his or her particular place among those diversities? Doing so will stretch us significantly, taking us deep into unexplored territory where success is not guaranteed and complete success is perhaps unlikely. As with any ideal vision it is not so much its full achievement that validates it but the work done toward achieving it and the self-affirming, community-affirming elevation of life such work affords. A meaningful life, after all, at least in one of its dimensions, is a life spent in pursuit of a worthy ideal, the pursuit and the meaning being inseparable.

I urge all of us to think big, to develop policies that pursue consequential changes in our ideas and actions. We need to expand dramatically our limited conception of the school music program.

We need, equally dramatically, to expand our conceptions of teacher education so as to produce the diversity of specialists a comprehensive program must have, each as expertly prepared in his or her area as we have so successfully accomplished with ensemble directors.

We will need a broad spectrum of research to back up our newly developed programs with solid evidence as to how to best achieve optimal effects.

We will need new ideas about and instrumentalities for assessment of diverse musical learnings and of the programs offering them.

We must be helped by philosophers, sociologists, and psychologists to redefine what "being musical" means in the realities of our diverse musical world.

We require policies supporting a whole new array of books, journals, instructional materials, equipment, technologies; in short a significant expansion of the industry that supports music education, without which the profession cannot implement its desires. And we need to refocus our advocacy efforts, emphasizing all we are doing to serve the musical needs of all our students and hence the quality of their lives, presenting ourselves as being in full service of musical empowerment in all the ways that can occur.

Whatever other policies we can devise to strengthen and nurture our field, those dealing directly with a renewed self-conception will have to be at the core of our efforts, a self-conception that elevates us to centrality in our cultures' musical lives rather than which perpetuates the peripheral position we now occupy.

The first step is to recognize, honestly and courageously, that we must expand our vision of music education. The second is to work together to accomplish that goal, guided by our historical mission to be truly comprehensive, balanced, and sequentially effective, a mission still awaiting optimum implementation.

None of that threatens our achieved success. All of that builds on it, to make of our profession the full member of the educational community we all so yearn to be and so deeply deserve to be.

THE WAY IT WILL BE

"What will arts education be like in 2050 or, at the eve of the twenty-second century, in 2099?"

Arts Education Policy Review Executive Editor Constance Bumgarner Gee raises this question as the topic of a millennium-year two-issue special project on "Arts Education in the 21st Century." She invites 21 "prominent and daring thinkers in the field" to contribute short essays.

I'm pleased (and flattered) to be one of them but determined not to do another straight-ahead think piece. Her own rather irreverent approach to issues of the arts in education, especially in her critiques of the unfortunate involvements of the National Endowment for the Arts in arts education matters for which it has a tin ear, gives me an idea. She asks, "What significant changes in teaching and research will we remember with pride or disappointment while sipping our oxygen-enhanced, fruit and rum protein drinks with (recently) retired colleagues at some chic, low-gravity seniors retreat?"

Okay. I'll respond in like spirit.

I offer two scenarios of planning going on for the Year 2075 celebration to be held in a couple of weeks. One is by a music educator (of course), the other by the administrator of a PreK–14 Coordinated Arts Curriculum. Each offers a glimpse into their thoughts about the event and the curriculum for which they're responsible.

The following essay was originally published in the *Arts Education Policy Review* 102, no. 2 (November/December 2000). Used by permission.

SCENARIO I

Judith Allegrini-Katsuo-Mbabwa, general music teacher for three K–5 schools in an inner ring suburb of Midwest Megalopolis #7, sits in her cramped cubicle/office next to the janitor's supply room on her scheduled 6-minute break before her next 33-minute (once a week) class. She's got to get all her schools ready to sing eight songs at the Year 2075 celebration in two weeks, so her curriculum has gone out the window. (She uses a tattered set of the combined Silver Burdett/Macmillan textbooks, the only ones still published.)

"I wonder how the band and orchestra and chorus teachers are doing with their preparations," she thinks. She's met them but can't remember their names, although she knows that their thriving programs are all award-winners—32 kids in the grades 5–8 band, 16 in the orchestra, 22 in the combined chorus, a remarkable achievement primarily due to the frantic advocacy efforts of the UMI, the Unified Music Industry, representing all 12 music companies. (Their latest campaign—music combats acne.)

At the high school (14,280 kids), the performing groups, the only music offerings, reach the astounding sizes of 49 in band, 27 in orchestra, and 31 in chorus. The after-school rock/pop/jazz/ethnic music performance program, taught by uncertified teachers, has an enrollment of 10,680, but the NAPME (National Association for Proper Music Education) does not recognize it, so it doesn't count.

"The art teacher has it so easy," Judith thinks. "The art education industry supplies her with easy-to-use materials for every possible holiday, this one included. All she has to do is have the kids finish those CIM kits (Creativity-in-a-Minute) and display them on the hallway walls. She seems nice, though. I really should get to know her. And the Parents Club will probably have their most talented offspring do some dance and theater stuff. They always do."

Judith feels a bit discouraged with the way her job is turning out in this third year of teaching. Her sophomore philosophy of music education course had gotten her really excited about teaching general music. "It was so exciting to learn about how music and the other arts are basic to the human condition," she remembers. "But my principal wants me to help improve test scores in what he calls 'the reals,' even though not a single classroom teacher believes I can."

She shakes her head. "I don't really understand the post-post-post-modern philosophy of education I'm supposed to follow," she muses, "even after all the faculty lectures we get. And the research lectures also confuse me. All that stuff about the quantitative/qualitative debate. I don't get it. All I know is that I want to follow the Standards (fourth version) adopted by vote of the NAPME membership—Sing, Play, Teach That Other Stuff Some Day. It's not like I have to do any testing, or those portfolio reviews, or anything. That's for the reals. So why do I feel so unsatisfied with what I'm doing? What's wrong with me?"

Judith gets up, checks out her cart with a set of textbooks, the CD player loaded with the single disk containing 870 songs, 320 Orff accompaniments, 225 Kodaly exercises, and 1,412 Progressive Notation Mastery quizzes. She pushes it down the hall on the way to fourth grade classroom #17. "I don't think I'm an important person around here," she worries.

SCENARIO II

Jimbo@wol(world on line).edu sits in the arts pod conference room in Sunnyvale Middle School Coordinating Center, planning the faculty/associate meeting tomorrow on preparations for the Year 2075 celebration.

"Lots to celebrate," he thinks. The PreK–14 Coordinated Arts Curriculum, required of all students for an hour every day, has been used as a model around the world. Its focus on individual art involvements, including the "venerables," (visual arts, music, dance, theater, literary arts, and film) and the "outgrowths" (the various emergent combinations and technology-enabled forms), along with explorations of similarities and differences among them, has provided students with opportunities to gain both specialized skills and understandings the arts require and broad, inclusive insights into their shared nature as meaning-creation modes of thinking/doing.

Certified mentor faculty members proficient in an art specialization and steeped in theory and practice of arts field issues work with individual students and a great variety of groups, assisted by associates from the arts world who are both practitioners and highly trained enablers. Students in this Coordinating Center, as in all others, spend time there each day but also go out physically to carefully chosen, interlinked community arts sites that expand on their core learnings, and go out virtually to arts sites around the world through the Global Education Network Online which houses the Artsworld Education Network.

"What I particularly want to stress with the planning committee tomorrow," Jimbo thinks, "is that we need to make clear to parents and community members that while we give kids every opportunity to get seriously involved as an art maker we don't expect every kid to take that opportunity given all the others available to them. But we do expect every kid to be able to enjoy and treasure the arts they choose for their lives as intelligent consumers, and those who take that path get as much attention and respect as the ones who want to get into art making professionally or as devoted amateurs.

There's still that holdover from the 20th-century illusion that every child will choose to be an art maker and that only those kids who do are worthy of our concern. We've made good progress toward including all the others, which is why we're now a basic and secure know/do domain in American schools, but the public still needs to be assured that we care about the arts health of *all* kids."

Jimbo sits back and relaxes. "I was fascinated with the unit on the history of arts education policy in my third-year (of seven) teacher education course on Aims of Arts Education," he remembers. "What a struggle it must have been back then at the turn of the century to justify the arts as part of schooling. Those people cared so much about bringing the arts and kids together, but their exclusive, limited, and separatist attitudes kept them at the edges.

"I wish they could see our programs, built on a shared philosophical base, supported by ongoing, coordinated, site-based research, with assessment focused primarily on individuals and their needs, a fair share of time, teachers, and facilities for the arts, a comprehensive, balanced, and sequential program, the highest respect by everyone in our society for the value and necessity of the arts in people's lives, and kids, at every age, enjoying what the arts do for their humanity.

"So much to celebrate. Yes, I wish they could be here to join in the celebration."

♪   ♪   ♪

So, dear reader, which of these two scenarios do you think is closer to the way it will be in 2075?

ABOUT THE AUTHOR

Bennett Reimer is the John W. Beattie Professor of Music Education Emeritus at Northwestern University, Evanston, Illinois, where he was chair of the Department of Music Education and founder and director of the ongoing Center for the Study of Education and the Musical Experience, a research group of music education doctoral students and faculty members. He is the author and editor of two dozen books and over 150 articles and chapters. His most recent book, *A Philosophy of Music Education: Advancing the Vision*, 3rd edition (2003), is a 90 percent reconceptualization as compared to the previous two editions. His fields of specialization include philosophy of music education, curriculum theory, research theory, comprehensive arts curriculum, and intelligence theory.

Reimer has lectured and presented workshops and keynote addresses all over the United States and the world. A special double issue of *The Journal of Aesthetic Education*, "Musings: Essays in Honor of Bennett Reimer," was published in winter 1999. He is the recipient of the Distinguished Service Award, State University of New York College at Fredonia; the Presidential Award, Illinois Music Educators Association; an honorary doctorate from DePaul University, Chicago; the Legends of Teaching Award from the Northwestern University School of Music; the MENC Senior Researcher Award, and is an inductee into the Music Educators Hall of Fame.